RKT AND
IDA SITE

VRIJDAGMARKT AND PORTUS GANDA SITE
pp. 82-91

ZUID AND ST.-PIETERSPLEIN SITE
pp. 92-99

MEETJESLAND
pp. 152-161

WAASLAND
pp. 162-171

SCHELDT COUNTRY
pp. 172-183

LEIESTREEK
pp. 142-151

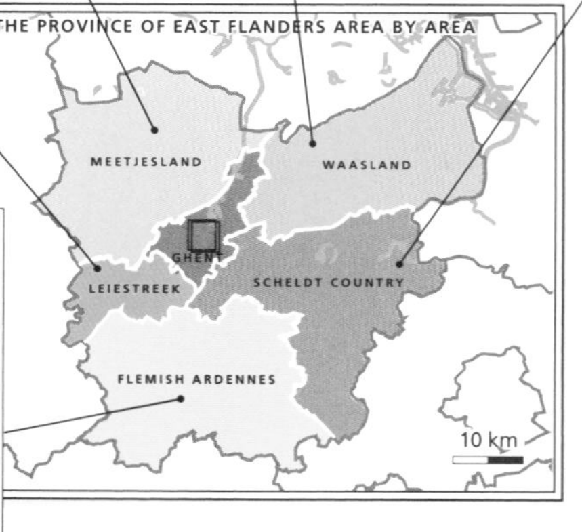

FLEMISH ARDENNES
pp. 184-203

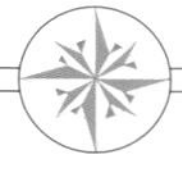

CAPITOOL TRAVEL GUIDES

GHENT
AND EAST FLANDERS

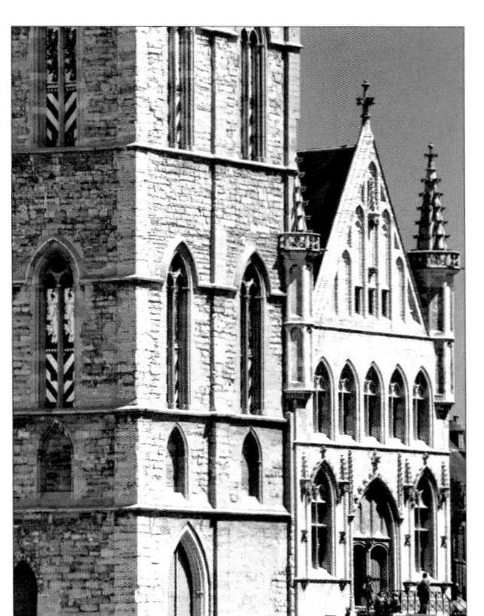

CAPITOOL TRAVEL GUIDES

GHENT
AND EAST FLANDERS

BARTHO HENDRIKSEN

VAN REEMST
UITGEVERIJ UNIEBOEK | HET SPECTRUM BV
HOUTEN-ANTWERPEN

© 2012 Uitgeverij Unieboek I Het Spectrum bv.,
Houten-Antwerpen
www.capitool.nl
www.unieboekspectrum.nl

Van Reemst is affiliated to
Uitgeverij Unieboek | Het Spectrum bv.
P.O. Box 97
3990 DB Houten

Author: Bartho Hendriksen

Design and technique: Teo van Gerwen Design, Waalre in keeping with the artistic concept of the Eyewitness Travel Guides, published by Dorling Kindersley Limited, London

Photography: Rien van der Helm, see photo credits on page 255
Illustrations: Jan Egas, Gieb van Enckevort
Cartography: EMK, Deventer

Every effort has been made to ensure that this book is as up-to-date as possible at the time of going to press. Some details such as telephone numbers, opening hours, prices, exhibitions and travel information are subject to change. It is always advisable to first check the relevant website or the local tourist office. The publisher cannot be held responsible for for any consequences arising from the use of this book.

ISBN 978 90 475 1686 6

This edition has been created in collaboration with: Toerisme Gent en Toerisme Oost-Vlaanderen.

Toerisme Gent

Toerisme Oost-Vlaanderen

CONTENTS

Knight Salomon of Maldegem

◁ The city centre of Ghent with the tower of the former post office on the Korenmarkt (inset) Karel V

The Graventoren in Rupelmonde is built on the ruins of the old castle

The Leie and the Korenlei

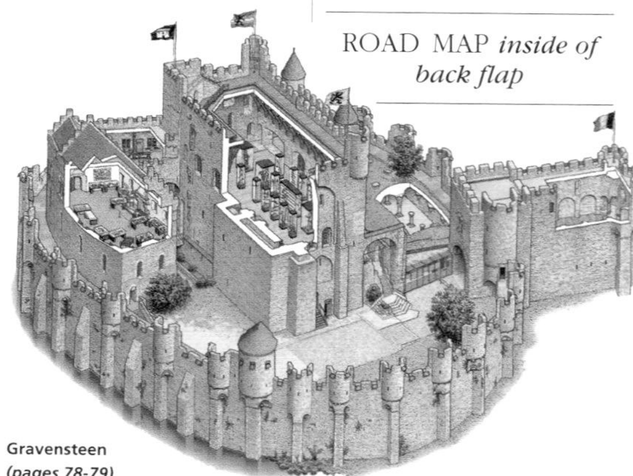

Gravensteen
(pages 78-79)

HOW TO USE THIS GUIDE

This guide will help you to get the most out of your stay in Ghent and East Flanders. *Introducing Ghent and East Flanders* puts the city and the province on the map and places them in the correct historical and cultural context. The chapter on *Ghent* and the chapters on *Leiestreek, Meetjesland, Waasland, Scheldt Country* and *Flemish Ardennes* highlight significant landmarks by means of photographs and illustrations. In *Tips for Travellers* you'll find, along with tips, information about hotels, restaurants, bars and travel information. Buildings described without opening hours or extra information are not open to the public.

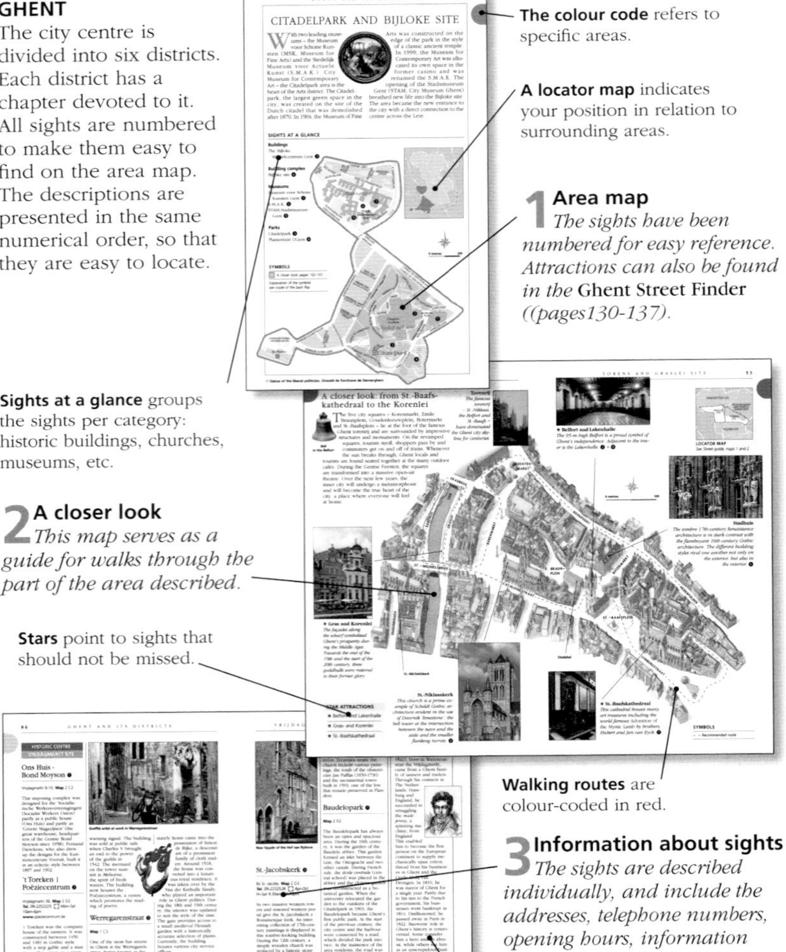

GHENT
The city centre is divided into six districts. Each district has a chapter devoted to it. All sights are numbered to make them easy to find on the area map. The descriptions are presented in the same numerical order, so that they are easy to locate.

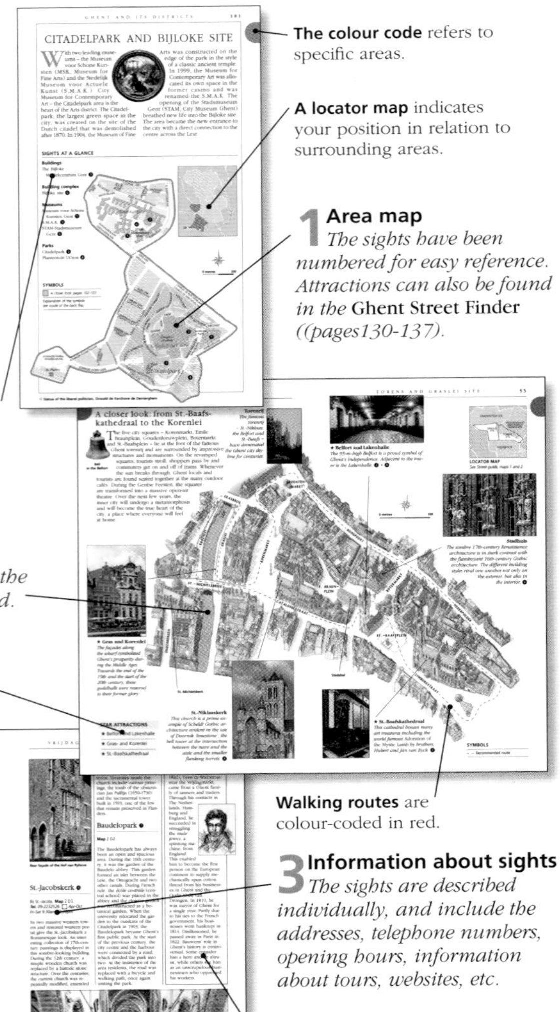

The colour code refers to specific areas.

A locator map indicates your position in relation to surrounding areas.

1 Area map
The sights have been numbered for easy reference. Attractions can also be found in the Ghent Street Finder *((pages130-137).*

Sights at a glance groups the sights per category: historic buildings, churches, museums, etc.

2 A closer look
This map serves as a guide for walks through the part of the area described.

Stars point to sights that should not be missed.

Walking routes are colour-coded in red.

3 Information about sights
The sights are described individually, and include the addresses, telephone numbers, opening hours, information about tours, websites, etc.

In the boxes, specific topics are explored.

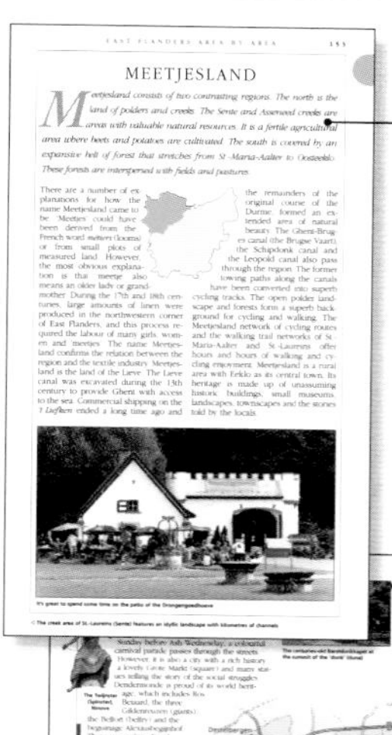

1 Introduction
The scenery, history and character of each district are outlined, showing you how the city or area has changed through the centuries, and what it has to offer today's visitors.

PROVINCE OF EAST FLANDERS AREA BY AREA
In addition to the city of Ghent, the Leiestreek, Meetjesland, Waasland, Scheldeland and Flemish Ardennes have been described, each with a detailed chapter devoted to them. The areas are subdivided into districts. Every district has been numbered, and can be found on the illustrated map. Noteworthy towns and villages are indicated on the illustrated map.

The colour code refers to the city or region *(see inside front flap).*

2 Regional map
This map shows all the important roads and gives a picture of each region. The municipalities have been numbered.

Under **Municipalities** the districts are described per region.

3 Detailed information
All districts are described individually in the same numerical order as on the illustrated map. You will find more detailed information about important buildings and other interesting sights.

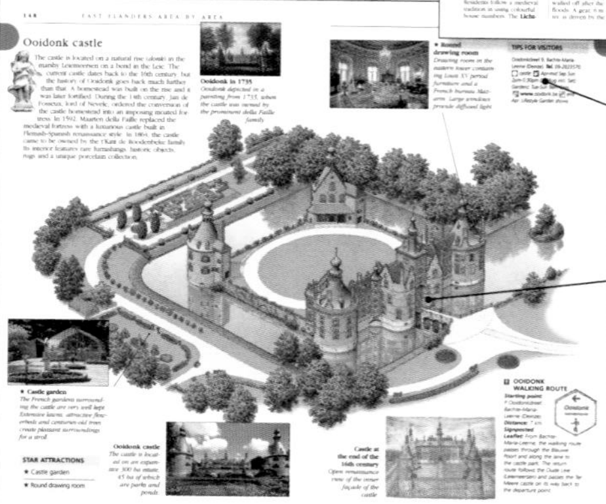

Tips for visitors contains practical information to help you plan your visit.

4 Top Sights
These sights are described on two or more pages. The interior of historical buildings is revealed through cutaway pictures.

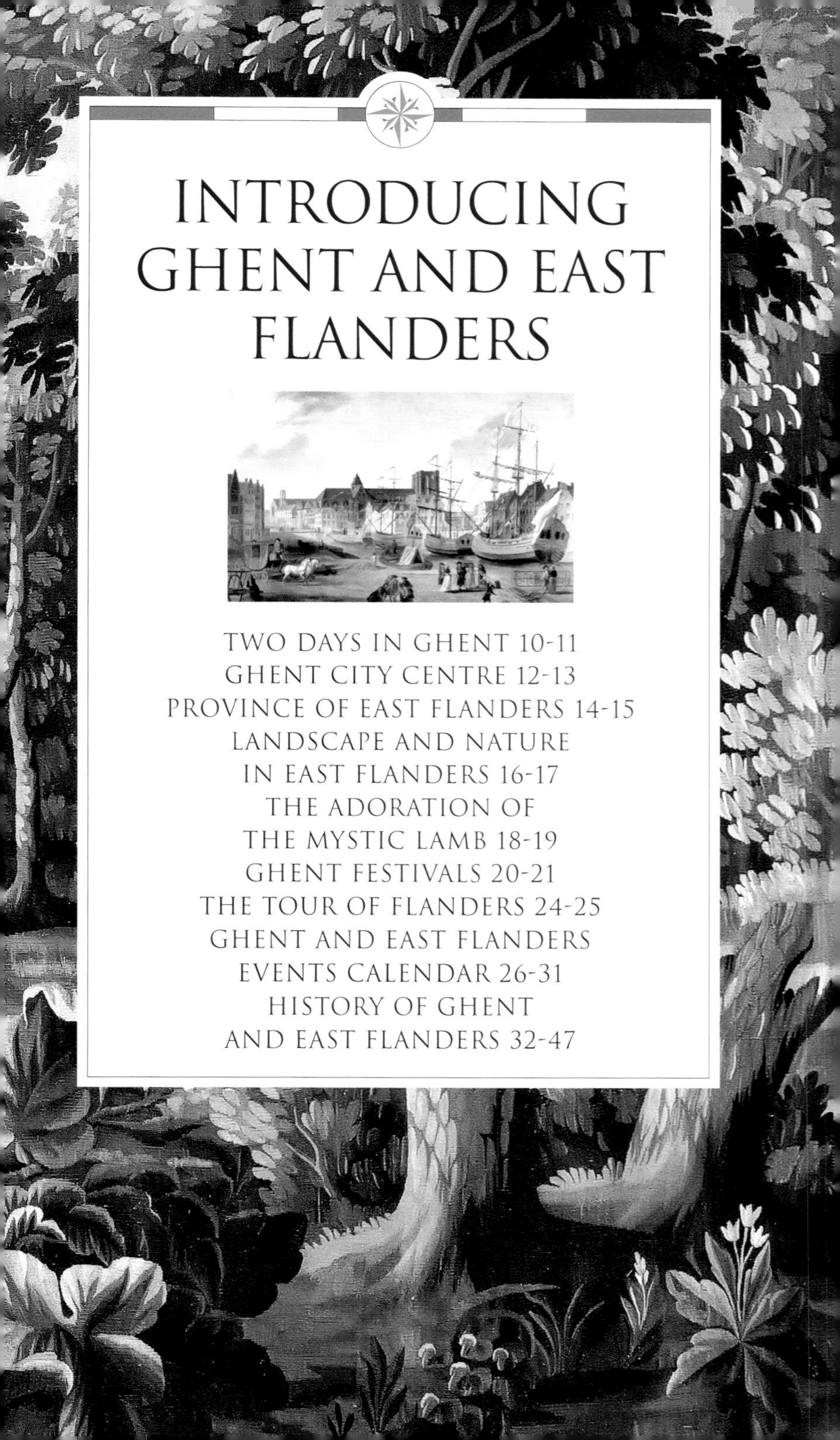

INTRODUCING GHENT AND EAST FLANDERS

TWO DAYS IN GHENT

Ghent is a vibrant city that is rich in impressive monuments, pleasant museums, medieval streets, bustling squares, busy bars and incredible restaurants. But above all, Ghent is the city of the Leie and the Scheldt. These two rivers curve through the city before meeting at the Portus Ganda. Ghent is also a city of festivals. The Gentse Feesten, a ten-day national cultural festival of music and theatre, is well-known outside Belgium. The three squares, Emile Braunplein, the Korenmarkt and St.-Baafsplein, form the heart of the city. The three towers of St.-Niklaas, Belfort and St.-Baafs (also known as the torenrij) dominate the city skyline. Ghent is the perfect destination for a long weekend or a few days. Those who have visited Ghent keep wanting to return to discover more about this Flemish city.

The burial

DAY 1

Historic Centre

- St.-Baafsplein
- Gravensteen and Patershol
- Design Museum

Morning

Start your day at the foot of the **Belfort tower**, the proud symbol of Ghent's independence. Enjoy the spectacular view of the historic city after climbing its 225 steps (although there is a lift). Cross the square and visit **St.-Baafskathedraal**. Descend into the crypt and admire the many works of art in the church. The most significant work of art, the world famous altar piece **The Adoration of the Mystic Lamb** by the brothers Hubert and Jan van Eyck, dates back to 1432 and is displayed in the small side chapel to the left of the entrance. Experience the painting through an audio-visual guide. Those not afraid of some exercise can climb the 444 steps of the tower. They'll be rewarded with a stunning view of Ghent.

Afternoon

After lunch, move on to another part of Ghent. Follow the directions to the **Gravensteen** and, after a short walk, you will come face-to-face with this impressive castle. The interactive movie guide brings the turbulent history of the castle to life. The **Patershol** district at the foot of the castle also breathes history and its bars and restaurants are the place to be. Make sure you visit the exciting exhibitions presented by the **Provinciaal Cultuurcentrum Caermersklooster** (the provincial cultural centre Caermers abbey). Cross the Leie via the Brug der Keizerlijke Geneugten with its four life-size statues, continue on through the **Prinsenhof** and

A street in the Patershol district

Present-day view of the famous historic Ghent torenrij

GHENT MUSEUM PASS

The Ghent museum pass is invaluable when visiting and exploring the city. You can use the card to visit all the major museums and monuments. The pass also includes travel on all De Lijn city buses and trams. The Ghent museum pass can be purchased at participating museums, tourist information points, hotels and Lijn shops.

◁ Part of the ancient wall tapestry from Oudenaarde *De terugkeer van de Markt* (page 195)

stroll through this charming district to the Oud Begijnhof St.-Elisabeth, one of the three beguinages recognized as world heritage sites by UNESCO. The Begijnhof still has a village atmosphere. A perfect end to the afternoon is a visit to the **Design museum Gent**. Inspiring exhibitions can be viewed along with its impressive art nouveau collection.

Evening
Take a short walk through the inner city of Ghent (*pages 126-127*) and marvel at the enchanting way in which the monuments are lit up. End the evening by visiting one of the many outdoor cafés on the city square.

20th-century and contemporary design at the Design museum Ghent

GHENT IN NUMBERS

more than 800,000 hotel stays per year
246,000 residents
65,000 students
650 bars
475 restaurants
56 large and small squares
23 museums (STAM is 23rd)
20 fountains
5 abbeys
3 beguinages (UNESCO world heritage sites)
2 medieval castles (Gravensteen and Geeraard de Duivelsteen)
1 Belfort (UNESCO world heritage site)
1 *The Adoration of the Mystic Lamb* (St.-Baafskathedraal)
1 Nobel Peace Prize winner (Maurice Maeterlinck)
1 largest European street festival (Gentse Feesten)

The Museum voor Schone Kunsten provides an overview of Flemish art

DAY 2

Arts District

- **The new STAM**
- **Traditional and contemporary art**
- **Boat trip and shopping**

In the early morning, the façades of the tranquil **Gras and Korenlei** site are reflected in the Leie. The view from the **St.-Michielsbrug (St Michael's bridge)** is a uniquely Ghent view. Walk along the Leie towards the **STAM** in the Bijloke area. Old and new, past and present meet in this modern city museum. After your museum visit, walk through the Citadelpark and enjoy the sculptures. Choose contemporary art at the **S.M.A.K.** or fine art at the **Museum voor Schone Kunsten** Gent. Whichever museum you choose to visit, you'll be able to enjoy lunch there.

Afternoon
Take tram 1 on the Museumlijn back to the city centre after your museum visit. A visit to Ghent is not complete without a boat trip on the Leie. The rest of the afternoon can be spent taking a leisurely stroll through the city centre, window shopping and making purchases. Veldstraat, Mageleinstraat, the Donkersteeg and the Langemunt are bustling pedestrian shopping streets. The Brabantdam, Koestraat and other small streets also offer a large variety of shops and boutiques. Sample some East Flanders specialities at the **Promotiecentrum voor Oost-Vlaamse streekproducten** in the **Groot Vleeshuis** (market hall).

Evening
There's always something taking place in the *Creative City of Music*. Enjoy a musical or dance show at the theatre, the Handelsbeurs Concertzaal Gent, the Kunstencentrum Vooruit or the Bijloke Muziekcentrum Gent. Or you mightenjoy a performance at a jazz bar.

The new STAM in the Bijloke area is a dynamic city museum

Ghent city centre

Ghent is the capital of the province of East Flanders and has approximately 243,000 residents. The city is divided into two districts – the Historic Centre and the Arts District, both subdivided into sites (areas). Ghent has a unique pedestrian signpost system. Arrows in different colours direct you from one area to the next. Furthermore, stations are indicated on every signpost. The most attractive area of Ghent lies between the St.-Baafskathedraal and the Gravensteen. Here, you'll find splendid historic buildings, city squares and bustling shopping streets. Slightly farther away are the more subdued areas, such as the Kouter, Patershol and Portus Ganda. The Arts District is the heart of the city thanks to its art museums.

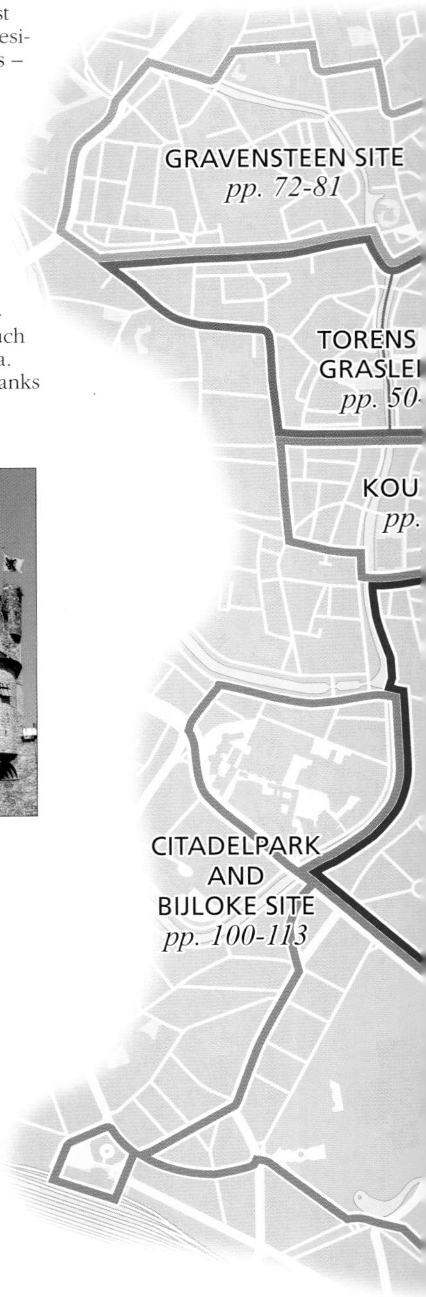

Gravensteen
The residence of the counts of Flanders developed from a small wooden fortress into a fortified medieval castle.

Boat trip on the Leie
Boating along the Ghent inland waterways comes highly recommended; the boats depart from the city centre.

GRAVENSTEEN SITE
pp. 72-81

TORENS
GRASLEI
pp. 50-

KOU
pp.

CITADELPARK
AND
BIJLOKE SITE
pp. 100-113

Portus Ganda
The Portus Ganda marina lies at the centuries-old confluence of the Scheldt and the Leie. In 2003, a section of the previously filled-in Scheldt was re-excavated.

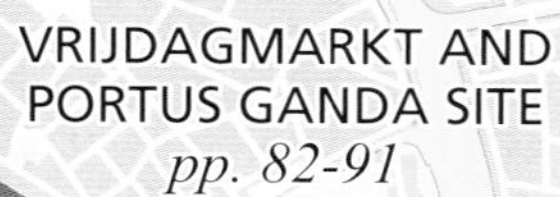

Flea market
On Friday, Saturday and Sunday mornings, the streets around St.-Jacobskerk are transformed into a single massive market square with antiques, curios and second hand goods for sale.

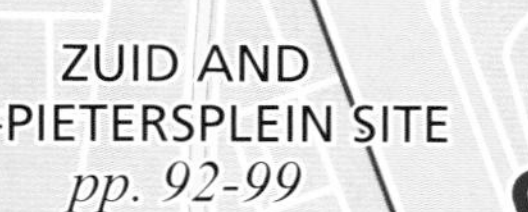

Onze-Lieve-Vrouw St.-Pieterskerk
This imposing baroque church, built on the foundations of a Romanesque abbey church, is found at St.-Pietersplein, the city's major events square.

0 metres 400

HISTORIC CENTRE

ARTS DISTRICT

Province of East Flanders

The Province of East Flanders is centrally located in Flanders, covers a surface of 2982 km² and has approximately 1,143,000 residents. Ghent is the administrative, cultural and industrial capital of the province and, with 243,000 residents, the largest city. Aalst with 80,000 residents, St.-Niklaas with 72,000 residents, Beveren with 46,000 residents and Dendermonde with 43,000 residents are the other large cities. The countryside was highly urbanised due to the textile industry that, over the centuries, spread to numerous smaller towns and villages. The Scheldt, the Dender and numerous other waterways make their way through the province. This guide handles 6 separate regions; Ghent, Leiestreek, Meetjesland, Waasland, Scheldt Country and the Flemish Ardennes.

The Gaver forest at Zwalm in the Flemish Ardennes

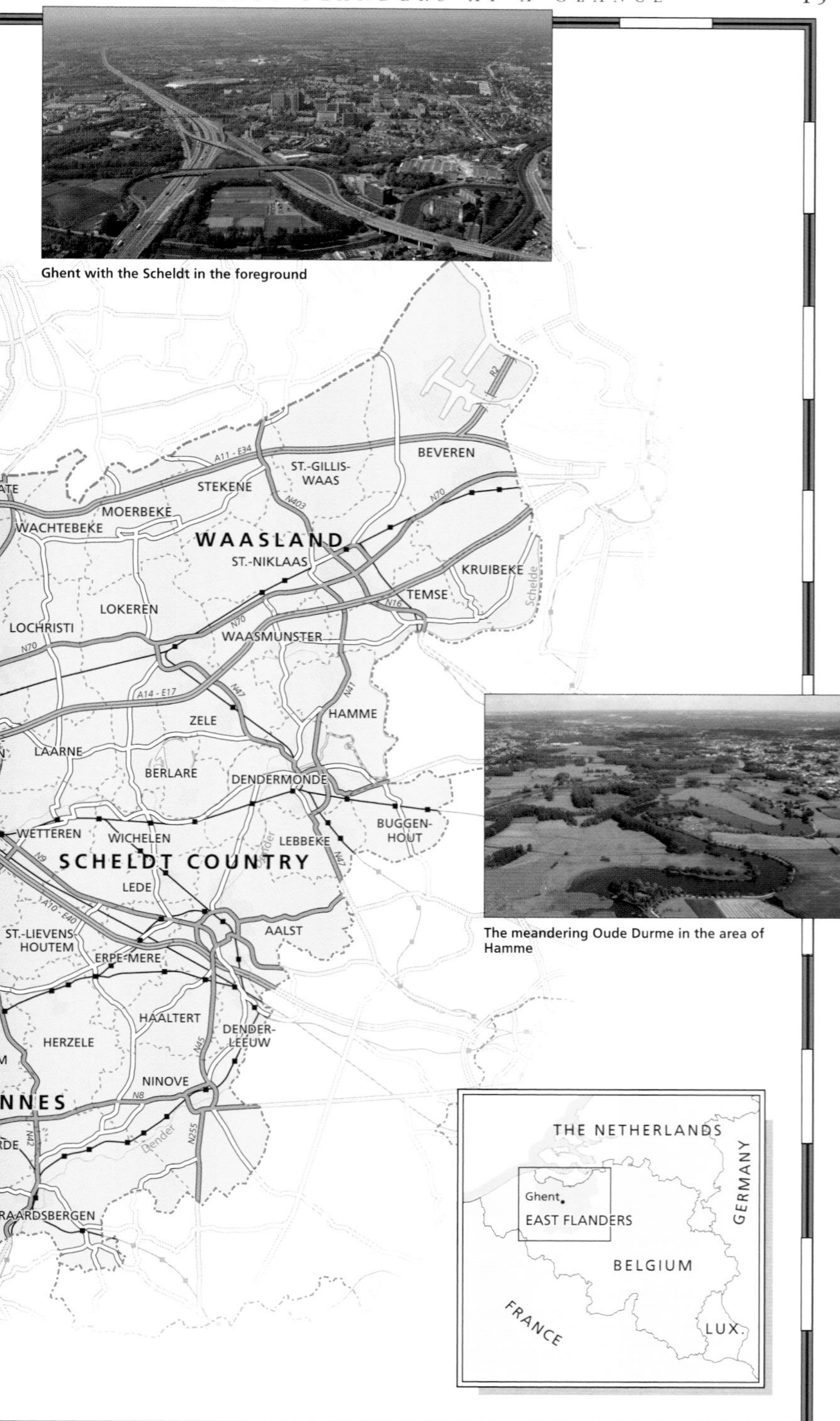

Ghent with the Scheldt in the foreground

The meandering Oude Durme in the area of Hamme

Landscape and nature in East Flanders

BEZOEKERSCENTRUM MOLSBROEK

The Scheldt, Dender, Zwalm, Durme and Leie rivers and numerous canals define the East Flanders landscape. The Northwest is divided into the low-lying polders and creeks of the Krekengebied, and the higher Houtland. The Waasland also consists largely of polders. The Leie and the Scheldt form the transition to the hilly south where the Flemish Ardennes give the predominantly flat Flemish landscape a foreign feel. There are many nature reserves to be found in the southern forests and the northern polder countryside. These are managed by, among others, Natuurpunt, the Nature and Forest Agency, provincial authorities and the municipalities. The regional landscapes are committed to preserving the identity and the well-known natural landscapes of the Meetjesland, Scheldt-Durme and Flemish Ardennes regions.

Kluisbos
The largest forest in the Flemish Ardennes is on the Kluisberg (141 m). This hill is reminiscent of the old plateau landscape that was changed by streams and rivers.

Little owl
The little owl is the smallest of the owl species. This animal grows up to 24 cm tall and lives in tree hollows and old buildings. It prefers secluded areas.

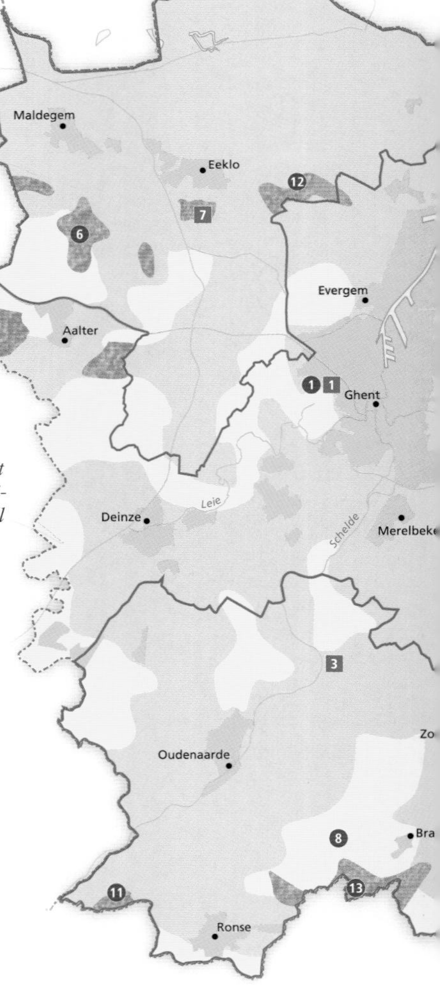

● **Nature reserves**

1 *Bourgoyen-Ossemeersen, Ghent*
2 *Buggenhoutbos, Buggenhout*
3 *De Roomakker, Temse*
4 *Den Bunt, Hamme*
5 *Den Dotter, Erpe-Mere*
6 *Drongengoed, Ursel*
7 *Duivenbos, Herzele*
8 *Het Burreken, Brakel*
9 *Het Molsbroek, Lokeren*
10 *Kalkense Meersen, Kalken*
11 *Kluisbos, Kluisbergen*
12 *Lembeekse Bossen, Lembeke*
13 *Brakelbos, Brakel*
14 *Stropersbos, Stekene-St.-Gillis-Waas*
15 *Vlassenbroek, Dendermonde*

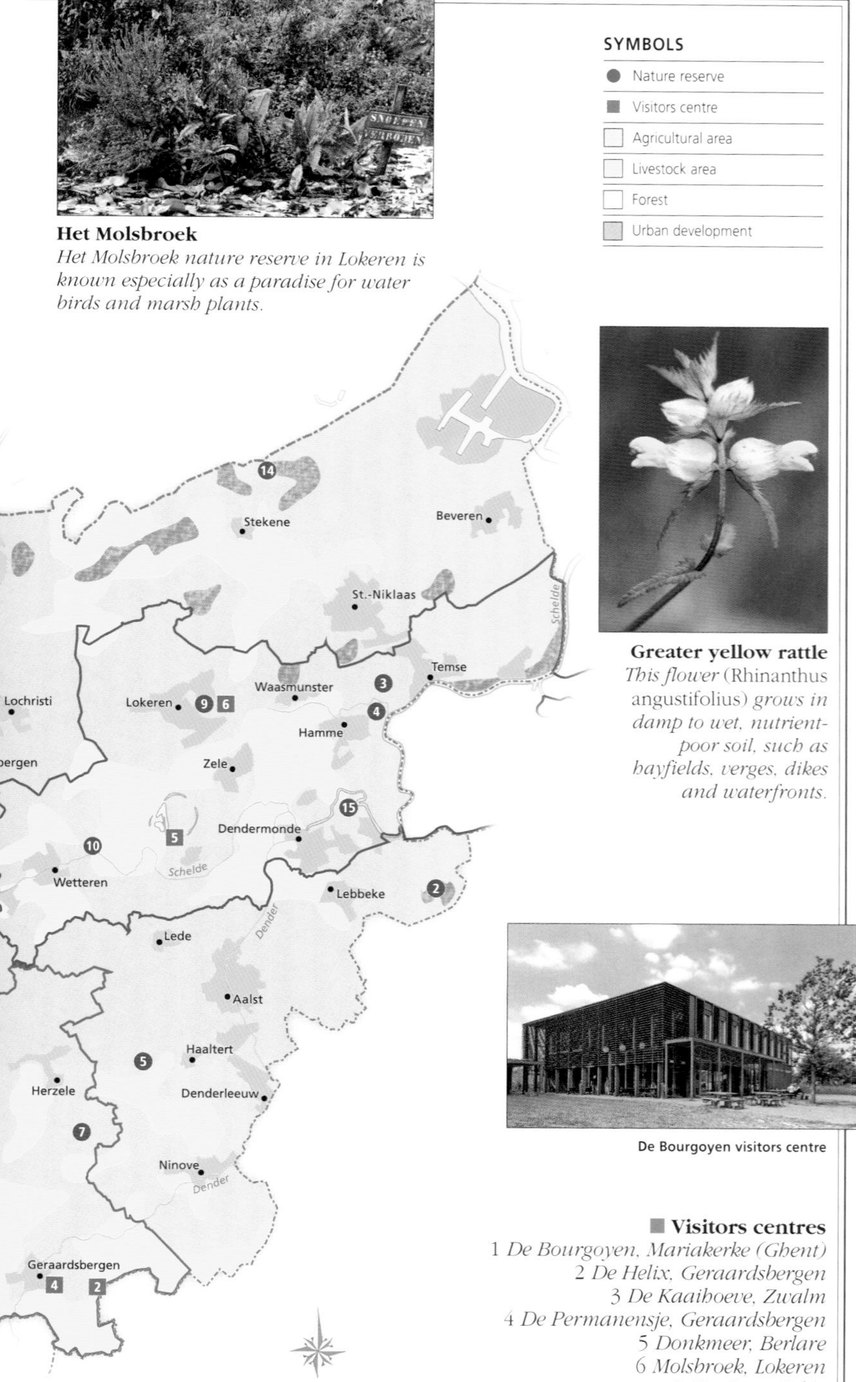

Het Molsbroek
Het Molsbroek nature reserve in Lokeren is known especially as a paradise for water birds and marsh plants.

Greater yellow rattle
This flower (Rhinanthus angustifolius) *grows in damp to wet, nutrient-poor soil, such as hayfields, verges, dikes and waterfronts.*

De Bourgoyen visitors centre

■ Visitors centres
1 *De Bourgoyen, Mariakerke (Ghent)*
2 *De Helix, Geraardsbergen*
3 *De Kaaihoeve, Zwalm*
4 *De Permanensje, Geraardsbergen*
5 *Donkmeer, Berlare*
6 *Molsbroek, Lokeren*
7 *Het Leen, Eeklo*

The Adoration of the Mystic Lamb

The Adoration of the Mystic Lamb is undoubtedly the most famous work of art by the brothers Hubert and Jan van Eyck. The altarpiece can be found in the St.-Baafskathedraal and is named after the middle panel, which depicts a lamb being worshipped by angels, martyrs, prophets and apostles. Judocus Vijdt commissioned Hubert van Eyck to paint the altarpiece. After his death in 1426, his brother Jan continued the work. The altarpiece was erected in the burial chapel of the couple Vijdt-Borluut, and could only be visited on public holidays. On other days, the shutters were closed and only the Annunciation of Maria was visible. The colours on the open altarpiece are much brighter and more festive than those on the closed shutters.

Singing angels
Hubert van Eyck painted heavenly creatures singing and making music to the left and right of the central figures. Although these beings have no wings, they are often called angels.

The clients
Judocus Vijdt, lord of Pamele, was a wealthy and influential citizen (voorschepen) of the city of Ghent. He was married to Lysbette Borluut. In honour of the restoration of an apse in the St.-Baafskathedraal, he and his wife ordered a fine altarpiece. This guaranteed them a daily mass.

The artists
Brothers Hubert and Jan van Eyck came from a well-known Limburg family of artists (presumably) from Maaseik. Hubert accepted the project around 1420 and worked on it up to his death in 1426. His brother Jan (approx. 1385-1441) completed the work between 1430 and 1432. There is no way of knowing which brother did which part of the work.

Mystic Lamb
The lamb's bleeding neck symbolises Jesus sacrificing his life to rid mankind of its sins. There are many spectators, as at the crucifixion.

TIPS FOR VISITORS

St.-Baafskathedraal, St.-Baafsplein. **Map** 2 D3. ***Tel.*** *09-2692045.* The Adoration of the Mystic Lamb *Apr-Oct Mon-Sat 9:30am-5pm, Sun 1pm-5pm; Nov-Mar Mon-Sat 10:30am-5pm, Sun 1pm-4pm.*

Closed altarpiece
The most significant scene on the closed altarpiece is the announcement of the birth of Jesus by Gabriel (left) to Mary (right).

Righteous Judges
The panels featuring the Righteous Judges *and* John the Baptist *were stolen on the night of 10 April 1934. The* John the Baptist *panel was returned more than 6 months later. However, the* Righteous Judges *panel is still missing. It was replaced with a duplicate.*

Festivities in Ghent

During the 19th century, every district held its own Sunday festival. In 1843, city management, at the insistence of the industrialists, decided to incorporate all the festivals to form a 'Communal Fair' with the traditional *bal populaire* as its highlight. After World War II, these festivities called Gentse Feesten could no longer compete with modern influences such as holidays and television. These festivals disappeared from the agenda. A cautious re-launch of the Gentse Feesten was held in 1969. As of 1990, the Gentse Feesten has become the largest cultural outdoor event in Europe, with six spin-offs held over 10 days. These include: 10 days off, MiramirO, the International Puppetbuskersfestival, Boomtown, the Youth circus festival and the Ghent Jazz Festival.

Youth circus festival
The youth circus festival offers performance opportunities to youngsters from circus schools. It also features circus workshops for children aged 4 and older.
www.circuscentrum.be

10 days off
10 days off *is a progressive dance festival featuring local and international DJs and live acts specialising in house, electro, break beats, punk-funk, eighties wave, nu-jazz, broken beats, drum 'n bass and techno.*
www.10daysoff.be

Boomtown
With more than 40 local and international bands, Boomtown has become the most popular pop and rock festival at the Gentse Feesten. The main stage on the Kouter is reserved for well-known (inter) national bands, while the inner stage on the Handelsbeurs is reserved for local and international special genres and niche acts.
www.boomtownlive.be

TIPS FOR VISITORS

Opens: *Saturday before the third Sunday of July.*
Closes: *Monday after the fourth Sunday of July.*
Dates: *2012 14-23 July and 2013 20-29 July*
www.gentsefeesten.be

Ghent Jazz Festival
A prestigious jazz festival that presents jazz in all its forms in the historical gardens of the Bijloke. The festival consists of two four-day sessions. They are 'All that Jazz', where the emphasis lies on mainstream and avant-garde jazz, and 'All that Jazz?', featuring more progressive and danceable jazz.
www.gentjazz.com

International Puppetbuskersfestival
The International puppetbuskersfestival is a puppet theatre festival organised by the Europees Figurentheatercentrum, the European puppet theatre centre. The performances are held in the city centre and at the inner courtyard of the European puppet theatre centre.
www.eftc.be

MIRAMIRO
Due to its open-air productions by professional international companies, The MiramirO street theatre festival is one of the better festivals held in Europe. The festival sets the benchmark for street and open air theatre in Belgium.
www.miramiro.be

Beguinages

The beguine movement in Western Europe started during the 12th and 13th centuries. This was a new religious society, created in response to the wrongs and immoral nature of the church and society. As a result of wars, battles and the Crusades, there were many women left single. Life as a beguine offered these women protection.

The beguines lived a pious and austere life, but with a high degree of autonomy focusing on charity work. They were originally scattered throughout the city, but later withdrew into smaller communities in enclosed areas. Beguinages flourished during the 17th century. New entrants became fewer during the 18th century. After World War II, the entry of new beguines became so low that the beguinages were forced to close.

Beguine home
Two to four beguines were able to occupy a beguine home. Every home had a front garden and a front wall along the street.

Oudenaarde Beguine Gate
This gateway was opened at sunrise and closed at sunset. A statue of St. Begga (patron of the beguines), H. Anna or St. Elisabeth stood in the alcove above the gateway.

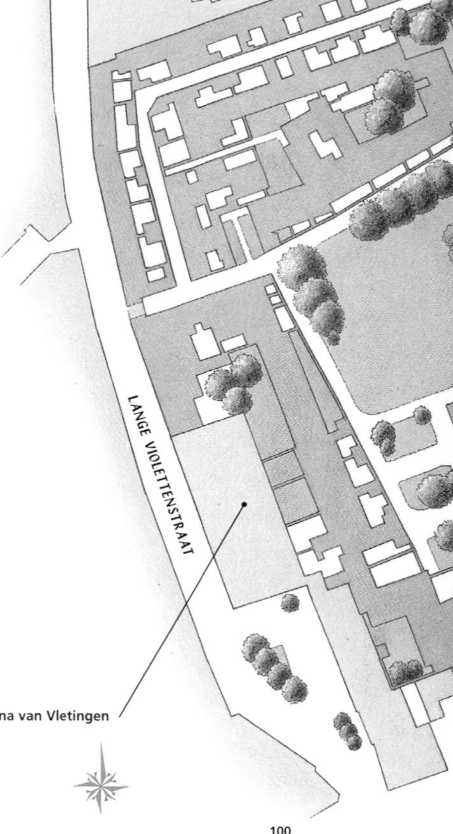

Convents
These community residences for the novices and less influential beguines are typical of every beguinage. Most of the rooms were communal, although every novice or beguine had her own bedroom.

ONZE-LIEVE-VROUW TER HOYEN BEGUINAGE
The 'Klein Begijnhof' is a miniature city that was constructed on what were then the outskirts of the city. A wall with a gateway emphasised the closed nature of the area. In the centre of the beguinage is the church, which was originally surrounded by the graveyard.

Beguinage church
This typical baroque beguinage church was built in two phases (1657-1671 and 1715-1729) to replace a 13th-century church. A statue of Onze-Lieve-Vrouw, the patron of beguinages, with the child Jesus, adorns the door.

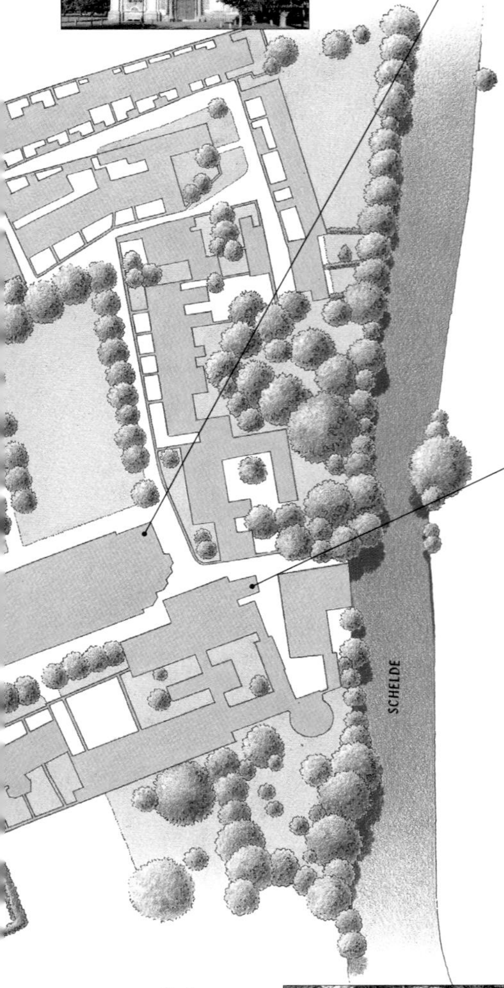

Grootjufferwoning/Groothuis
The Governess, who was annually re-elected or replaced by vote of the nuns, headed the beguinage.

H. Godelievekapel

SCHELDE

Beguinages recognised as world heritage sites
Ghent
Oud Begijnhof St.-Elisabeth (1234)
Groot Begijnhof van St.-Amandsberg (1874)
Klein Begijnhof Onze-Lieve-Vrouw ter Hoyen (1240)
Oudenaarde
Begijnhof (15th-century)
Dendermonde
St.-Alexiusbegijnhof (1270)
Aalst
St.-Katherinen-Op-Den-Zavel (appr. 1261)

Infirmary
The infirmary served as guest accommodation and to house sick and elderly beguines. The adjacent St.-Godelievekapel was a popular haven for people with eye and throat ailments.

Tour of Flanders

On May 25 in 1913, 37 cyclists and five chase cars set off for the first time on Flemish dirt roads. The Tour of Flanders, known as the *Ronde van Vlaanderen* was born. Its founder, Charles Wijnendaele, set out to promote his newspaper Sportwereld (an insert in the daily newspaper *Het Nieuwsblad*) by means of the Tour. During its early years, the Tour was held at the same time as the classic Milan-San Remo. It became more popular after World War II. It is tough and rough and a test of character for riders. It differs from other cycling classics due to its unique atmosphere, the cobblestones, the weather and the dreaded Muur van Geraardsbergen (Wall of Geraardsbergen). Riders like Achiel Buysse, Albéric Schotte, Rik Van Steenbergen, Fiorenzo Magni, Eric Leman, Eddy Merckx, Roger De Vlaeminck, Walter Godefroot and Johan Museeuw, Peter Van Petegem and Tom Boonen have all made history on the Tour.

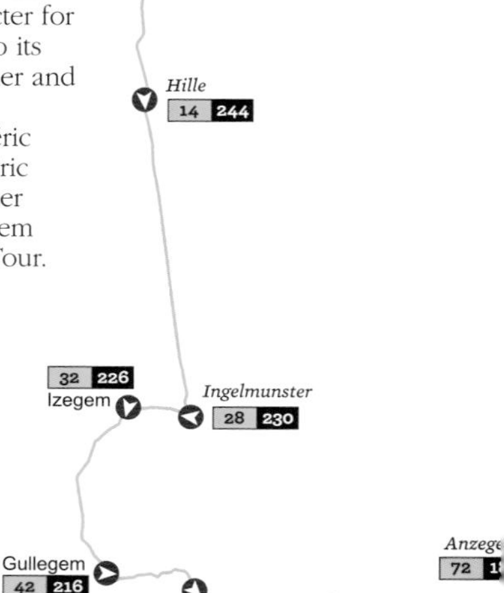

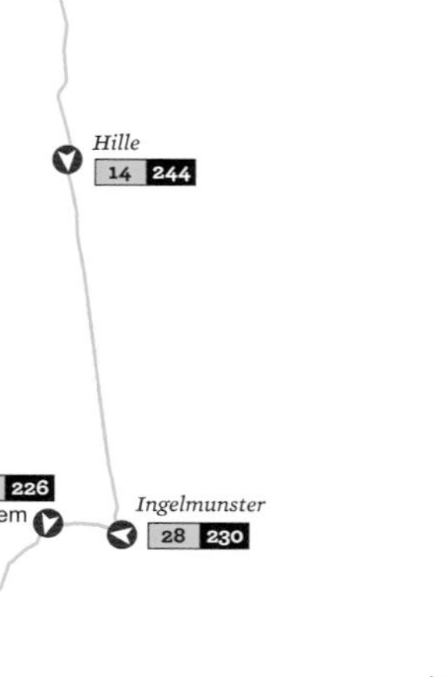

The Koppenberg
The Koppenberg recently made a comeback onto the Tour of Flanders. The 78m 'Bult van Melden' with its 22% gradient is one of the more feared cobblestone climbs.

Tour of Flanders Centre
A visit to the CRVV (Centrum Ronde van Vlaanderen) in Oudenaarde is a one-of-a-kind experience. Visitors experience the Tour of Flanders by means of multimedia (images, sound and computer animation). www.crvv.be. Also see page 194.

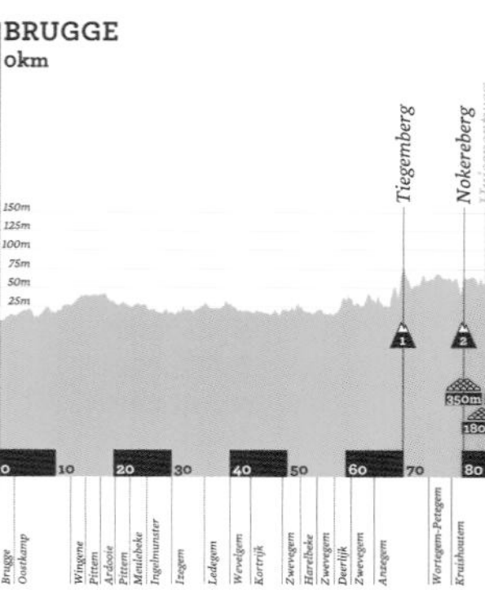

Stijn Devolder

Winners since 2005

2005 Tom Boonen (B)
2006 Tom Boonen (B)
2007 Alessandro Ballan (I)
2008 Stijn Devolder (B)
2009 Stijn Devolder (B)
2010 Fabian Cancellara (CH)
2011 Nick Nuyens (B)

Tour date

14th Sunday of every year

Further information

www.rondevanvlaanderen.be
www.standaard.be/sportwereld
www.sporza.be

The Flandrien

'Flandrien', a nickname that later become an honorary title, was created on the course when a group of Flemish cyclists caused a furore on the cycling tracks of Brussels, Paris and New York. A strong cyclist who sweats and toils 'until he no longer knows what parish he's from' (according to Briek Schotte), is known as a Flandrien.

Briek Schotte

Three-time winners

Achiel Buysse (1940 + 1941 + 1943)
Fiorenzo Magni (1949 + 1950 + 1951)
Eric Leman (1970 + 1972 + 1973)
Johan Museeuw (1993 + 1995 + 1998)

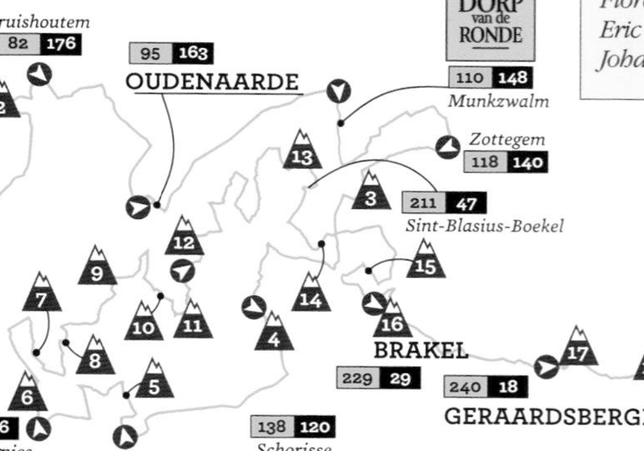

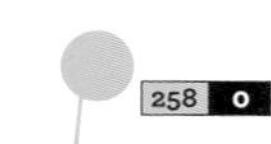

NINOVE
Meerbeke
Aankomst
Arrivée
258 0
253 5
Denderwindeke

Route of the 2011 Tour of Flanders.
The route is changed every year.

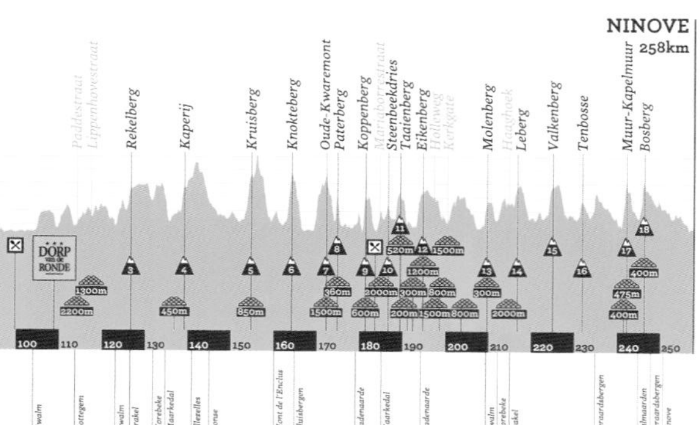

Gaston Rebry (1905-1953)

This famous Belgian rider achieved his greatest success during the 1920s and 1930s. In 1934, he won the double: The Tour of Flanders and Paris-Roubaix.

GHENT AND EAST FLANDERS EVENTS CALENDAR

In July, the Gentse Feesten dominates the city of Ghent. The city bursts at its seams for ten days as it presents street theatre, children's shows, an opening parade and a closing concert that lasts until the early hours of the morning. The Film festival, Ghent Jazz Festival, the Festival of Flanders and the Gentse Zesdaagse also attract thousands of visitors. *Zone09*, the free city magazine, contains an overview of all the festivals and events in Ghent. Numerous other festivities also take place in the province including Carnaval, the Fiertelprocessie, a traditional parade, the Tour of Flanders and krulbollen (national ball sport) championships. Festivals are held almost every month in East Flanders, from major events to specialist markets to traditional celebrations. The website UitmetVlieg is aimed at children and contains information about music, theatre, film, dance and other leisure activities. All events are mentioned on the *Uit in Vlaanderen*, *Uit in Gent* and *Zone09* websites.

UiTmetVlieg

JANUARY

Driekoningencarnaval *(first weekend)*, Zottegem. Large carnival procession on Sunday.
www.zottegem.be

Bommelsfeesten *(weekend after 6 Jan)*, Ronse. Quirky carnival festival with a Bommelstoet (procession derived from 'bonmoss', happy friends), a children's masked ball and the Zotte Maandagbal (Mad Monday ball).
www.ronse.be

FEBRUARY

Geutelingenfeesten *(Sun after 9 Feb)*, Brakel. Parties around the Geutelingenkermis (oven cakes are poured onto hot stones in wooden ovens).
www.geutelingen.be

Carnaval Aalst *(three days prior to Ash Wednesday: 19-21 Feb 2012)*, AalSt.-Largest Flanders carnival, with the highlight being the colourful parade of cars and floats on Sunday afternoon. Tuesday is the day of voil jeanetten: men dressed as woman.
www.aalst.be

Carnaval Dendermonde *(Sun and Mon after Carnaval Aalst)*, Dendermonde. The parade passes through the streets of Dendermonde on Sunday. The carnival closes on Monday with the maandagstoet (Monday parade).
www.dendermonde.be

Carnaval Ninove *(Sun and Mon after Carnaval Aalst)*, Ninove. Zondagstoet (Sunday parade) followed by the Wortelworp (carrot throwing) on Monday. The carnival closes with the traditional burning of the carrot.
www.ninove.be

The Sunday parade of the famous Carnaval Aalst

Krakelingenworp | Tonnekensbrand *(penultimate Sun before the first Mon in Mar)*, Geraardsbergen. Two festivals on one day. Folk parade that ends with pretzels being thrown into the crowd. In the evening a cask is set alight on top of the Oudenberg to drive

Winter is driven away with fire during Tonnekesbrand

MORE INFORMATION

Uit in Vlaanderen, **www**.uitinvlaanderen.be
Uit in Gent, **www**.uitingent.be
Zone 09, **www**.zone09.be
UiTmetVlieg, **www**.uitmetvlieg.be
Meetjesland **www**.uitinhetmeetjesland.be

away the winter and welcome in the spring.
www.geraardsbergen.be
Krokuskriebels *(biennial, during spring half-term around the 7th Mon before Easter)*, Flanders. Museums organise special tours, activities and workshops focussing on families with children between the ages of 4 and 12.

MARCH

Halfvastenfoor *(mid-Mar – early Apr)*, Ghent. More than one hundred fairground attractions.
Carnaval *(Sun after Ash Wednesday)*, Assenede. Carnival parade.
Courtisane *(mid-Mar)*, Ghent. This five-day Courtisane festival showcases a unique blend of film, video, audio-visual performance and equipment in different locations.
www.courtisane.be
Gent-Wevelgem *(last Sun)*, Deinze. One-day cycle race dating back to 1934. Deinze with its rider's village is the start.
www.gent-wevelgem.be

APRIL

Gentse Floraliën *(Apr)*, Ghent. Flower show held every five years (since 1808). Next show scheduled for 2015.
www.floralien.be
Wuitenfeesten *(first Sun)*, Hamme. Three-day carnival during which the legend of 'Hamse Wuiten' is relived.
Opening of Tourist Season *(Easter Weekend)*, Berlare (Donkmeer).
www.berlare.be
Ronde van Vlaanderen *(14th Sun of the year)*, Tour of Flanders ends in Meerbeke (Ninove). Vlaanderens Mooiste, *see pages 24-25.*
www.rvv.be
Gulden Eifeesten *(early Apr)*, Kruishoutem. Festivities surrounding eggs, with the crowning of the egg farmer and egg queen, the parade of giants and numerous other activities.
www.guldeneifeesten.be
Repmond Rock *(late Apr – early May)*, Rupelmonde (Mercator Island). Two-day music festival held on the banks of the Scheldt.
www.repmondrock.be
Bladelinfeesten *(last Sun)*, Middelburg (Maldegem). Medieval celebration in memory of Pieter Bladelin, the founder of Middelburg, featuring a buffet meal and medieval craft market.

Steam engine taking on water at the Stoomfestival Maldegem

MAY

Erfgoeddag *(first Sun after Easter)*, Flanders. Celebration of national heritage.
www.erfgoeddag.be
Stoomfestival Maldegem *(weekend around 1 May)*, Maldegem. Annual steam engine festival.
www.stoomcentrum.be
Tuindagen van Beervelde *(early May and early Oct)*, Beervelde-Dorp (Lochristi) (Park van Beervelde). Garden exhibition with more than two hundred exhibitors. Spring and Autumn editions.
www.parkvanbeervelde.be
Puitenslagersfeesten *(early May)*, Beveren (Pastoor Steenssensstraat). Children's festival with Kids City (kid's activities), arts and crafts market, city fun run and performances by new and established artists.
www.puitenslagers.be
Omloop Kluisbergen *(mid-May)*, Kluisbergen. The ultimate hiking event (8, 15, 25, 50 and 2x50 km) held in the Flemish Ardennes.

The 'Tuindagen van Beervelde' is the greatest outdoor exhibition in Belgium

UNESCO INTANGIBLE CULTURAL HERITAGE

In 2010, UNESCO added the Carnaval Aalst, De Krakelingenworp and Tonnekensbrand in Geraardsbergen and the Houtem Jaarmarkt in St.-Lievens-Houtem to its Representative List of Intangible Cultural Heritage. The historic horse Ros Beiaard and the family of giants, known as the Ommegangsreuzen of Dendermonde (*folklore horse*) were already on this list. Intangible Cultural Heritage (traditions, rituals, song, theatre, dialects or arts) is heritage that lives, is part of daily life and is passed on to future generations.

De Gouden Flandrien *(mid-May)*, Oudenaarde. A 250 km long trip featuring all the well-known and lesser known Tour climbs, including 25 km of cobblestone road.
www.rvv.be

Stoet van Canteclaer *(23 May 2012)*, Deinze. Festivities focussing on chickens, both dead and alive, giant's parade and numerous other activities.
www.stoetvancanteclaer.be

Parktheaterfestival *(end May)*, Lokeren (P.J. Charlottepark). Theatre extravaganza featuring (international) performances, musical highlights and fire-themed evening shows.
www.lokeren.be

Ros Beiaardommegang *(May 2020)*, Dendermonde. This folklore spectacle is held on the streets of Dendermonde every ten years, with the historic Ros Beiaard ridden by four children.
www.rosbeiaard.be

Ambachtenmarkt Velzeke *(end May)*, Velzeke. Flea market with products from the Roman period, including glass, ceramics, jewellery and leather.
www.pam-velzeke.be

JUNE

Fiertelprocessie *(first Sun after Pentecost)*, Ronse (Kleine Markt). Centuries-old procession (32.6km) bearing the shrine of the patron saint of the city, St.-Hermes, along the outskirts of the city.

Openkerkendag *(first Sun)*, East Flanders. Various churches throughout East Flanders present open days.
www.openchurches.be

Open-air performance at the MiramirO festival

Adriaen Brouwer Bierfeesten *(last weekend)*, Oudenaarde (Market and surrounding area). Besides countless types of beer available for tasting, there are street activities, a parade and performances.
http://bierfeesten.dequbus.be

Afsneekermis with boat blessing *(last weekend in Jun)*, Afsnee (Ghent). Funfair held in the smallest district of Ghent.

Popeiland *(last Wed)*, Wachtebeke (Domein Puyenbroeck). Children's festival featuring music and activities.
www.popeiland.be

JULY

Gent Jazz Festival *(early Jul)*, Ghent. A mix of young talent and internationally acclaimed artists. The first part predominantly consists of mainstream and avant-garde jazz, while the second features jazz fusion with different musical influences.
www.gentjazz.com

Walburg- en Pleinconcerten *(every Tue and Thurs, early Jul-mid Aug)*, St.-Niklaasplein. Folk, salsa, rock and cabaret concerts in the park and on the square.
www.sint-niklaas.be

Museumnacht Ename *(second Sat)*, Ename (Oudernaarde). Cultural night festival with the aim of strengthening the bond between the locals and the PAM, Ename (Provincial Archaeological Museum).
www.museumnacht-ename.be

Beeldenstroom *(Jul 2012, 2015)*, Scheldt. Art exhibition held along the Scheldt every three years.
www.beeldenstroom.be

Gentse Feesten *(week of 21 Jul)*, Ghent. Ten-day festival, see pages 20-21. www.gentsefeesten.be

MiramirO *(during the Gentse Feesten)*, Ghent. A stage for all art forms: street and circus acts, onsite theatre, visual arts and dance. From small-scale acts to mass events.
www.miramiro.be

Jazz in het Park *(21 Jul)*, Dendermonde (Stadspark). Jazz on the national public holiday.
www.dendermonde.be

Deinze Feesten *(end Jul, early Aug)*, Deinze. Funfair and festivities along the banks of the Leie.
www.deinze.net

Three days of music during the Adriaen Brouwer Bierfeesten

Lokerse Feestweek *(end Jul, early Aug)*, Lokeren (Grote Kaai). City Music festival. Includes the Lokerse Feesten, the Fonnefeesten and the Polifonics.
www.lokersefeesten.be

M'eire Morough Folkfestival *(end Jul)*, Dendermonde (Olympos swimming pool). Two-day folk festival
www.foldendermonde.be

Meetjeslandse Balloon meet *(last weekend)*, Eeklo. One of the major Belgian hot air balloon events.

Pikkeling in the Faluintjesstreek *(last full weekend)*, Faluintjesstreek. Harvest festival organised by one of the villages in the Faluijntjesstreek.
www.faluintjes-pikkeling.be

AUGUST

Waterfeesten *(first Sun)*, Berlare (Donkmeer). Street theatre, fun fair, spectacular air and water shows and musical fireworks above the Donkmeerlake.
www.berlare.be

Oogststoet Kortenbos-Massemen *(first Sun)*, Geraardsbergen. Annual folklore parade featuring floats and historical performances.
www.oogstfeesten-kortenbos.be

Day of the mattentaart *(first Sun)*, Geraardsbergen. Traditional festival in honour of the culinary pride of Geraardsbergen: the mattentaart (traditional cake).
www.geraardsbergen.be

Schellekesfeesten *(around first Sun)*, Rupelmonde (Oeverstraat). Funfair in Schelleke, parade of giants and giant's ball.

Berlare water festival

Feeste t'Ename *(weekend around St.-Laurentius name day)*, Ename. Street activities, performances and a historical horse market.
www.enameleeft.be

Military History Show *(first weekend)*, Ursel. Original military vehicles and aircraft and a unique open-air swap meet.

Helden in het Park *(every Thurs)*, Eeklo (Heldenpark). Free concerts (world music).

Forest Festival *(mid-Aug)*, Lede. Music festival with four stages featuring different music genres.
www.forestfestival.be

Day of the mattentaart

Volkssportenweek *(weekend of 15 Aug)*, Doornzele. Various traditional games, some competitive and others recreational.
www.krulbol.be

Herbakkersfestival *(weekend around 15 Aug)*, Eeklo. Festival with a 'Zomer van Eeklo' (Summer in Eeklo) theme.

Dancing giant Indian at the Reuzenommegang Katuit

Patersholfeesten *(weekend of 15 Aug)*, Ghent (Patershol). The miniature Gentse Feesten in the oldest district in Ghent. The traditional kaarskensprocessie (religious procession) closes the festival.
www.patershol.org

Antiques and Flea Market *(first sat after 15 Aug)*, Grammene. More than 800 stalls offer antiques.
www.gezinsbondgrammene.be

Begijnhoffeesten *(penultimate weekend)*, Ghent (Beguinages). Performances and a flea markets are the recurring elements of the Begijnhoffeesten.
www.elisabethbegijnhof.be

Boombal Festival *(last weekend)*, Lovendegem (Ghent). Music and dance event for young and old.
www.boombal festival.be

Ajuintjes market and Lights parade *(weekend before fourth Mon)*, Ghent (Ledeberg). The Ajuin market, a funfair, street activities, performances and fair. The highlight is a procession of lights through the streets of Lederberg.
www.ajuinmarkt.be

Buggenhout zomert *(Aug)*, Buggenhout.

Beverse Feesten and street theatre festival *(end Aug)*, Beveren (Grote Markt, Boerenmarkt). Kids and street theatre, music and special days for senior citizens.
www.beversefeesten.be

Temse in de wolken *(end Aug)*, Temse (Wilfordkaai). Annual hot air balloon event, funfair, boat trips and fireworks.
www.temse.be

Reuzenommegang Katuit *(last Thurs)*, Dendermonde. Historical evening parade featuring more than one thousand costumed characters, with the giant Indian, Mars and Goliath as the stars of the show.
www.rosbeiaard.be

Processie van Plaisance *(sun around 24 Aug)*, Geraardsbergen. The relics of St Bartholomew are carried through the city during this amusing procession. The three giants from Geraardsbergen also take part in the procession.

Hot air balloon event during the Vredesfeest at St.-Niklaas

Jazz in 't Park *(last weekend of Aug and first weekend of Sep)*, Ghent (Zuidpark). Contemporary Belgian jazz. Free concerts and jazz films screened at midnight.
Kunst&Zwalm *(biennial, end Aug-early Sep 2011, 2013)*, Zwalm. Contemporary art in the idyllic landscape of the Zwalmstreek.
www.kunst-en-zwalm.be
Openluchtspektakel Festivaria *(biennial, end Aug, early Sep 2011, 2013*, Berlare (Donkmeer). Open-air musical event with the Donkmeer lake as the background.
www.festivaria.eu

SEPTEMBER

Vredefeesten *(first weekend)*, St.-Niklaas (Grote Markt). Hot air balloon celebrations commemorating the liberation of the city in 1944. The Villa Pace festival presents music, markets and workshops.
www.sint-niklaas.be

Bloemencorso *(first Sun)*, St.-Gillis (Dendermonde). Colourful procession featuring floral floats and music.
www.bloemencorsosintgillis.com
Rockabilly *(first weekend)*, Wachtebeke (provinciaal domein Puyenbroeck)
www.rockabillyday.be.
Prinsenhoffeesten *(first weekend)*, Ghent (Prinsenhof). Cultural, creative and relaxing activities at the historical Prinsenhof area.

Internationaal Hooghuysfestival voor draaiorgels *(second Sun)*, Geraardsbergen. Festival of street organs with performances, street shows and a funfair.
www.hooghuysfestival.be
Open Monumentendag *(second Sun)*, East Flanders communities. Various monuments in Flanders are open to the public.
www.openmonumenten.zita.be
Pierlastoet *(second weekend)*, Ursel. Parade of floats that depict the life and adventures of Pierlala (a legendary folk figure).
www.pierlala-ursel.be
Bazel anno 1587 I Bazelse Feesten *(second weekend)*, Bazel (Koningin Astridplein). Annual funfair with a Saturday market and traditional crafts demonstrated by people in period costumes.
OdeGand *(mid-Sep)*, Ghent. Music festival and Festival of Flanders opening party featuring concerts to which people are transported by boat over the canals.
www.festivalgent.be
Versus V tentoonstelling *(biennial, from end Sep, to end Oct, 2011, 2013)*, Oudenaarde. Initiative focusing on modern, contemporary art from in and around Oudenaarde.
www.versus-v.be
Gent Festival of Flanders *(Sep–Oct)*, Ghent. Feest op het Plein (third weekend), Bachte-Maria-Leerne (Kerkplein).
www.feestophetplein.be
Gîrnaertfeesten *(end Sep)*, Boekhoute. Prawn parties with a folklore-style parade.
www.vzwbou8.be
Avantie!-festival *(end Sep)*, Ghent area. Musical bicycle tour through Ghent with

OdeGande, annual Music festival in Ghent

various mini concerts along the route.
www.festivalagent.be

OCTOBER

Tuindagen van Beervelde *(early Oct)*, Beervelde. Autumn edition, see May.
Kaaifeesten *(first weekend)*, Eeklo (Gebr. Van De Woestijneplein). Performances by various artists and Flanders' largest flea market on the Sunday.
www.kaaiken.be
Firtelstoet *(first Sun)*, Zulte. Parade of floats and show wagons through the streets of Zulte.
www.flirtel.be
Dag van het Paard *(mid-Oct)*, Maldegem (St.-Annapark). Day devoted to horses.
www.maldegem.be
Filmfestival Gent *(Oct)*, Ghent. Focus on film music, featuring amongst others the presentation of the World Soundtrack Awards. The festival, along with Almost Cinema, stays abreast of new developments in the film industry, fading the boundaries between film, media art and music.

NOVEMBER

De Week van de Smaak *(mid-Nov)*, Flanders and Brussels. This culinary event (the week of taste) bonds people through taste and dining culture.
www.weekvandesmaak.be
I Love Techno *(mid-Nov)*, Ghent (Flanders Expo). Techno event presenting local and international DJ's. Has developed into one of West Europe's largest entertainment events.
www.ilovetechno.be

The Christmas market in Dendermonde attracts many visitors

Gravensteenfeesten *(Wed around 16 Nov)*, Ghent (Burgstraat). Festive commemoration of the 1949 student uprising against the increase in the price of beer from two to three franks. A large group of students occupied the Gravensteen castle and had to be removed by the police.
www.skghendt.be

Cattle market at the annual Winter market in St.-Lievens-Houtem

Winterjaarmarkt *(mid-Nov)*, St.-Lievens-Houtem. The Historical horse and cattle market has been held since medieval times.
www.sint-lievens-houtem.be

Gentse Zesdaagse *(end Nov)*, Ghent (Het Kuipke). Cycling classic on the climbs of Flanders.
www.z6daagses.be

DECEMBER

Massacantus *(Wed two weeks prior to Christmas holidays)*, Ghent (St.-Pietersplein). Student song festival.
www.massacantus.be
Sinterklaas *(mid-Nov-6 Dec)*, St.-Niklaas. Celebrations focussing on St Nicolas, patron saint of children. On the first weekend after 11 November, he enters the city from which he received his name.
www.sint-niklaas.be
Winterdroom *(early Dec-mid-Jan)*, Ghent (St.-Pietersplein). A unique winter event.
www.uitbureau.be
Kerstmarkt Dendermonde *(3rd Sun of Dec)*, Dendemonde. Christmas market in the centre of Dendermonde (filled-in Dender, Grote Markt, Heldenplein, Oude Vest and Vlamarkt).

The Film Festival in Ghent enthrals the city

OFFICIAL PUBLIC HOLIDAYS

New Year's Day (1 January)
Good Friday and Easter Monday
Labour Day (1 May)
Ascension Day
Whitsun
National public holiday (21 July)
Mary's Ascension (15 August)
All Saint's Day (1 November)
Armistice Day (11 November)
Christmas Day (25 December)

HISTORY OF GHENT AND EAST FLANDERS

The city of Ghent formed at the confluence of the Leie and the Scheldt rivers. The name comes from the Celtic word *ganda* that means 'merging' or 'meeting'. The oldest traces of human occupation date back to the Stone Age, when hunters and gatherers used to roam the area. The first farmers settled in small villages around 3000 BC. During the Roman period, a settlement (Ganda) developed at the confluence of the Leie and the Scheldt. During the 17th century, Amandus founded two missions – Ganda and Blandinum – which later developed into prominent monasteries. In the 10th century, Ghent was a prosperous city thanks to the textile trade. The castle Geerard de Duivelsteen and church St.-Janskerk (later St.-Baafskerk) lay inside the walled city along the Scheldt. The counts of Flanders resided in the Gravensteen. During the 13th century, Ghent was a prospering trade city with hundreds of stone houses. In 1540, Charles V issued the Concessio Carolina in response to revolts by Ghent's citizens. The city lost its privileges and the St.-Baafs abbey had to make way for the Spanish castle. At the end of the 18th century, the economy of Ghent slowly started to recover and, during the 19th and 20th centuries, it became an industrial city, 'the continental Manchester'. In 1816, Ghent became the capital of the Province of East Flanders. The 1913 World's Fair led to a revitalisation of the medieval inner city. Ghent was spared ruin during both World Wars. Ghent remained a centre for the textile and machine industry until well after World War II. Over the past twenty years, large parts of city centre have been redeveloped thereby making it more inhabitable. The early histories of East Flanders and Ghent are closely intertwined with one another.

East Flanders coat of arms

View of Ghent (Gandavum) in 1567 by Willem Blaeu

◁ Panoramic view of Ghent in 1534 with its three central towers

The origins of Ghent

Ghent's first inhabitants settled here 60,000 years ago on the sandy heights at the confluence of the Leie and the Scheldt. They survived mainly by hunting and gathering plants and fruits. The first permanent settlement rose around 3000 BC in the Scheldt region. Its inhabitants made a living through agriculture, livestock farming and trading. At the end of the Iron Age, two Celtic groups – the Menapii to the north and the Nervii to the south of the Scheldt – inhabited the region around Ghent.
The Romans invaded Gaul in 57-56 BC. A century later, several small Roman-influenced settlements arose.
The settlement at the junction of the rivers was named Ganda, the Celtic word for 'merging' or 'meeting'.
The Franks took the reins of power in the 5th century.
The establishment of two abbeys during the 7th century marked the start of a new era in Ghent's history.

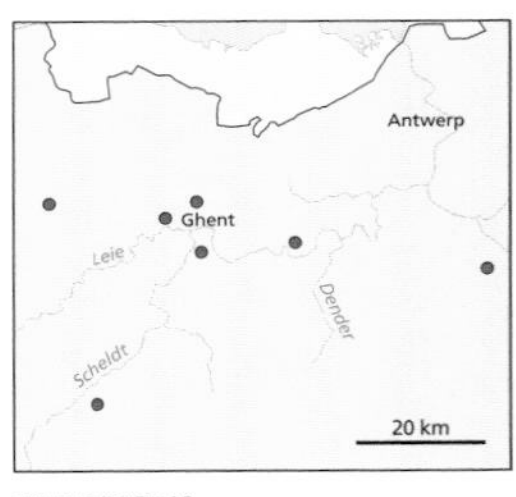

THE ORIGINS

- Paleolithic site
- Current border

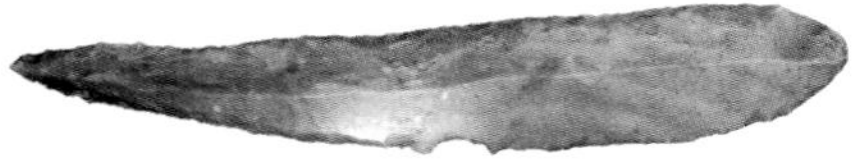

Blade
This blade (dagger) was made from light grey silex (flint or cobblestone). It was discovered at the Goudenleeuwplein, Golden Lion Square, and dates back to the Neolithic Age or early Bronze Age. A blade was made by detaching it from a larger piece of silex or flint.

Amandus of Ghent
According to the Vita Sancti Amandi, an 8th-century biography, Amandus was born in Aquitania (Southwestern France). He was ordained as a missionary bishop in 628. He went to Ghent where he initially had little success until he performed a miracle. He founded several monasteries, including Blandinium and Ganda in Ghent and was ordained the Bishop of Maastricht in 647.

TIMELINE

Flint fragments (9000-5500 BC)

160000-2000 BC Stone Age.

2000-700 BC Bronze Age.

1800 BC First farmers.

2000 BC	1750 BC	1500 BC	1250BC	1000 BC	75

55000-35000 BC Mesolithic period.

60000 BC First inhabitants hunt and gather fruit.

Neanderthal fist-axe (appr. 55000 BC)

700-0 Iron Age.

Bronze Age Mounds
Aerial photographs show mounds (tumuli) dating back to the Mid-Bronze Age (1400-1100 BC). Besides these traces of settlements, mainly bronze axes, swords and spear tips were discovered.

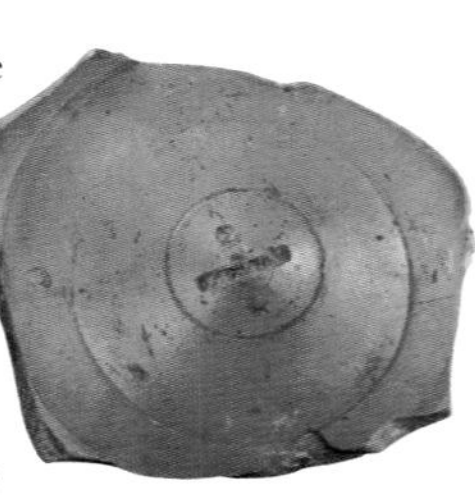

Roman earthenware
Terra Sigillata is the term for a luxurious form of earthenware. The inhabitants of the Roman settlement at the confluence of the Leie and the Scheldt were traders.

BRONZE JEWELLERY
This unique collection of bronze objects (1100-750 BC) was discovered during World War I during excavations at Port Arthur. The jewellery most likely originates from Northern France.

Merovingian age
From the end of the 5th century and the start of the 6th century, German tribes settled permanently in Flanders. The Franks formed the most significant group. The Merovingian civilization exemplifies their influence.

7th century
Amandus arrives in the Ghent area. Founding of Ganda (St.-Baafs) and Blandinium (St.-Pieters) monasteries.

500 BC	250 BC	0	250	500	750

0-400
Roman period.

Paddestraat, Roman road in Velzeke

481-751
Merovingian age.

Medieval trading city

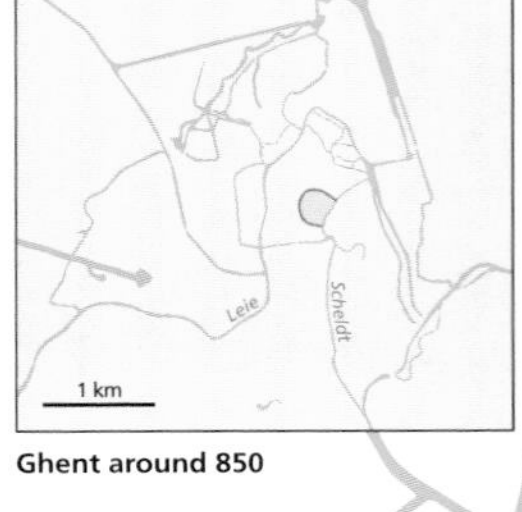

Ghent around 850

The medieval trading city of Ghent came into being during the late 9th century as a walled area. This trading post, or Portus Gandavum, was located along the Scheldt or where the St.-Baafs cathedral is situated today. This area had previously been inhabited for centuries. The founding of two monasteries by the missionary Amandus in the 7th century was a major stimulus for the development of the future trading city. Blandinium, on the Blandijnberg, was the oldest monastery. Ganda, at the confluence of the Scheldt and the Leie, gave its name to the settlement and the trading city that subsequently developed.

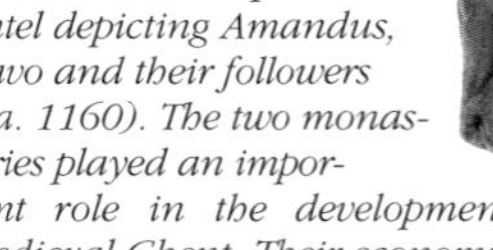

Ganda and Blandinium
Double sided sculpted lintel depicting Amandus, Bavo and their followers (ca. 1160). The two monasteries played an important role in the development of medieval Ghent. Their economic surplus, in combination with the presence of a number of wealthy merchants, formed the basis for the development of an independent trading city.

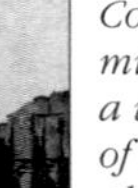

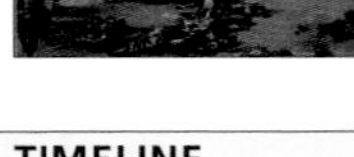

Count's Fortress
Count Arnulf I (889-965) commissioned the first fortification, a wooden building, on the site of the present Gravensteen along the Leie. During the 11th century, a stone castle replaced the wooden buildings.

TIMELINE

after 850
Norman invasion.

851
Normans destroy the Ganda and Blandinium monasteries.

ca. 862
Boudewijn I of Flanders, 'with the iron arm'.

879-880
Normans set up a winter camp at the St.-Baafs abbey.

end of 9th century
Collapse of Frankish Empire. Creation of the county of Flanders.

9th-10th century
Wall around Portus.

942
Consecration of St.-Janskerk (now St.-Baafskathedraal).

800 | 850 | 900 | 950

Geeraard de Duivelsteen
The viscount, the local representative of the count of Flanders, controlled trade on the Scheldt from the castle in Portus Gandavum that was named after Geraard de Duivel.

Normans
In 1851, the Normans invaded the Ghent settlements and, in particular, the monasteries. This was not the last time that this occurred. In 879-880, the Normans set up a winter camp in the Ganda monastery. The monks fled with their priceless art and relics. The monks only returned to Ghent once peace had been restored and slowly repaired the abbey.

Ancient deed, 1178
Trade between Ghent and the Rhineland started at an early stage. This document confirms that the Archbishop of Cologne granted Ghent's merchants safe passage on the Rhine.

MEDIEVAL PORT
Illustration of the ancient port wall, built during the 9th-10th century, nestled between the waterways of ca. 1100. This wall was considered the first city wall in Ghent.

12th century
Second city wall (Leie, Ketelvest, Houtlei and Scheldt).

1180
Count Philip of Alsace (1142-1191) ordered a new fortress built on the foundations of the Gravensteen castle.

1050 | 1100 | 1150 | 1200

late 11th, early 12th century
Construction of St.-Jacobs and St.-Niklaas parish churches.

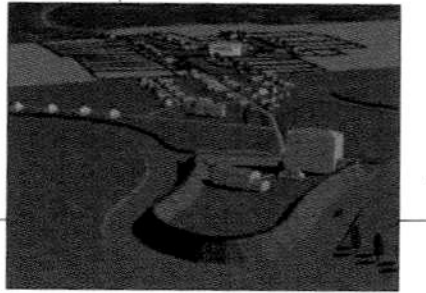

Ename Castle

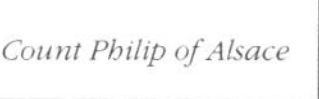

Count Philip of Alsace

Late medieval city

As of the 10th century, Ghent developed into one of the most important cities in Northwestern Europe thanks to the flourishing textile industry and trade. In the 14th century, the city had 66,000 residents, making it the largest and most populous city North of the Alps after Paris. Power in the city was wielded by a small group of wealthy citizens. These aristocrats lived in 'stenen', tall stone houses. In 1302, the guilds broke the might of the aristocrats through strikes and revolts. The weavers and the fullers, the two most important guilds in the city, featured most prominently in public life. As of 1300, a new fortification wall with moats, ramparts, walls and gates was built around the city.

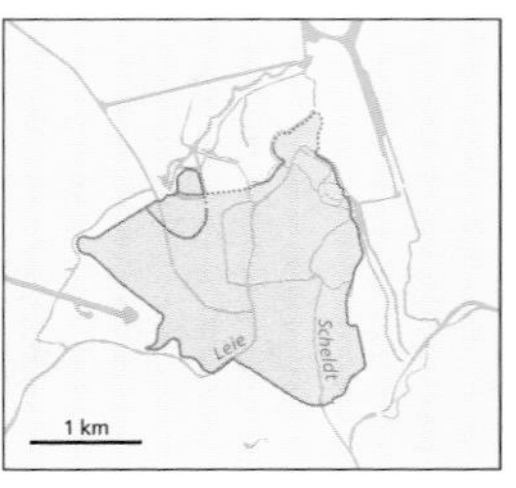

GHENT 1200-1600

Jacob van Artevelde
At the start of the Hundred Years' War between England and France, the Flemish Count Lodewijk van Nevers sided with France. In response, England halted wool exports to Flanders. This devastated the Flemish economy. The Ghent population under the rule of Jacob van Artelvelde (ca. 1290-1345) revolted, and he made a pact with England. When Van Artevelde returned from his negotiations with the English king, he was caught up in a riot between weavers and fullers and killed with an axe.

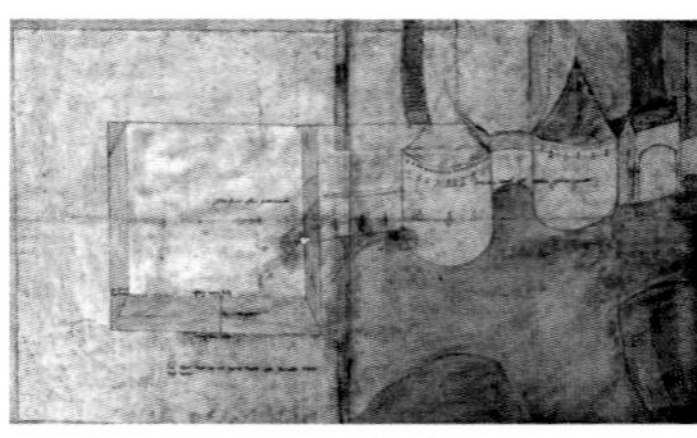

The excavation of the Lieve
In 1251, Countess Margaret of Constantinople granted permission for the excavation of a connection between Ghent and the Zwin-harbour near Aardenburg and, in 1262, the excavation of a tributary to Damme. The existing waterways were to be followed where possible. The canal became Ghent's commercial lifeline.

TIMELINE

1242 First mention of the St Elisabeth beguinage.

1302 Guild revolts. End of autocratic rule by urban elite in city management; craftsmen come into power.

1338 Jacob van Artevelde is elected leader of the revolutionary regime.

1200 | 1250 | 1300 | 1350

Early 14th century Third city wall.

1337-1453 Hundred Years War between England and France.

1345 Murder of Jacob van Artevelde.

1366 Hof ten Walle (Prinsenhof); new count's residence.

St Elisabeth beguinage

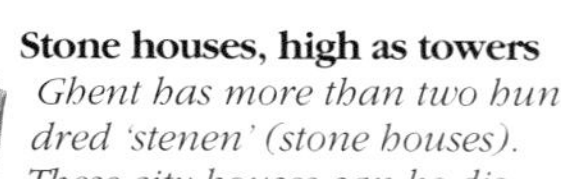

Stone houses, high as towers

Ghent has more than two hundred 'stenen' (stone houses). These city houses can be distinguished from others because of their grey Doornik limestone construction. These stone houses exemplify the economic prosperity experienced between 1150 and 1350. Famous 'stenen' include De Grote Arend, De Kleine Sikkel, the Korenstapelhuis, De Spiegel and the Borluutsteen.

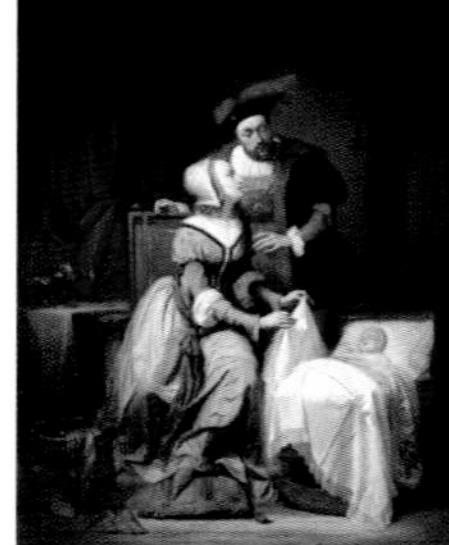

Charles V and Oudenaarde

In 1522, a daughter was born to Charles V and Johanna van der Geenst in Oudenaarde. She was Margaretha of Parma who was governess of The Netherlands from 1559 to 1567.

GHENT AS THE CENTRE OF THE WOOL AND TEXTILE TRADE

During the Middle Ages, Ghent was the core of the wool- and textile trade. The textiles manufactured within a 5 km radius of the city were taken to the Lakenhalle. Here, the material was inspected by three officers and subsequently sold.

CHARLES V AND GHENT

Charles of Austria was born at the Prinsenhof in Ghent on 24 February 1500. He was the first son of Philip the handsome and Joanne of Castille and was christened on 7 March in St.-Janskerk, the present-day St.-Baafskathedraal. At the age of six years, he inherited the rule of the Bourgondic Netherlands. In 1516, he became king of Spain and, three years later, king and later emperor of the German Empire. In 1539, the population of Ghent – his city of birth – revolted in protest against extra taxes used to fund the war against France. The consequences of these revolts were far-reaching for Ghent. Besides a hefty fine and the execution of a number of the instigators, the people of Ghent were publicly humiliated. The city's prominent citizens had to walk barefoot and dressed in black to the Prinsenhof, where they had to beg forgiveness from the emperor and the governess. At the back of the procession were the 'creesers' (instigators), dressed only in their undershirts and with nooses around their necks, symbolising their deserved punishment by hanging. On top of that, a citadel was built on the site of St Baafs abbey. It was first called the Nieuwe Kasteel (New Castle) and later named Spanjaardenkasteel (Spanish Castle). The emperor also issued a new charter for Ghent, the *Concessio Carolina*, restricting the rights of the guilds.

Prinsenhof

1500
24 February: Charles of Luxembourg, the future emperor Charles V, was born at the Prinsenhof.

1539
Ghent revolts against Charles V.

1577
Second iconoclasm.

1566
First iconoclasm.

1577-1584
Calvinist republic. New fortifications with bastions.

)	1450	1500	1550	1600

1432
Jan van Eyck ›mpletes Ghent Altarpiece.

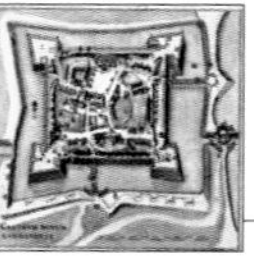

Spanish castle

1540
Concessio Carolina, the charter by Charles V according to which Ghent loses all its privileges. St.-Baafs abbey makes way for the Spanish Castle.

1547
Construction of the Nieuwe Vaart or Sassevaart; connection to the Western Scheldt via the Braakman.

1584
Conquered by Alexander Farnese, duke of Parma.

A peaceful city

During the 17th and 18th centuries, Ghent was a peaceful provincial city. After 1600, public life was dominated by the Catholic revival. Neglected monasteries, churches and beguinages were rebuilt in baroque style. The economy slowly recovered after the construction of the Brugse Vaart (1613-1623) that connected Ghent, Bruges and Ostend. Between 1670 and 1750, the Ghent economy suffered due to its occupation by French and English forces. For the first time since the Middle Ages, Ghent experienced economic prosperity under the rule of Austrian empress Maria Theresa. Ghent became an important transit port and new sugar factories and cotton mills heralded the arrival of a new industrial period.

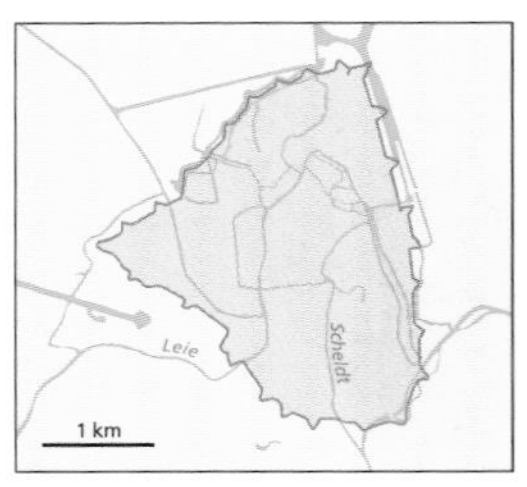

GHENT AROUND 1780

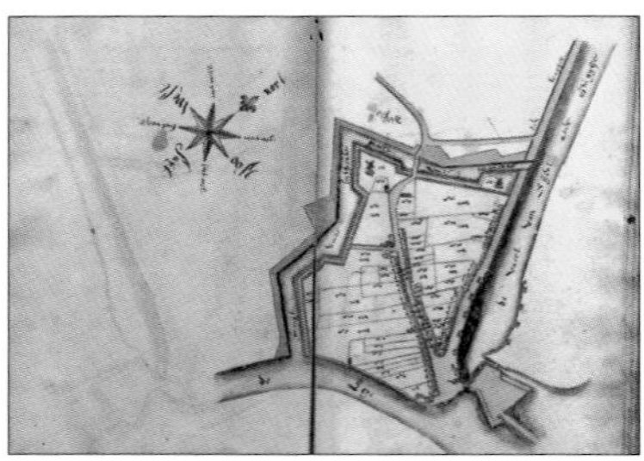

Construction of the Brugse Vaart
In 1613, archduke Albrecht and archduchess Isabella granted permission for the excavation of the Brugse Vaart. This canal connected Ghent and Bruges. The canal ended at the fortifications of both these cities. It opened in 1623.

Coupure
The Coupure (French for shortcut), constructed between 1751 and 1753, connected the Brugse Vaart to the Leie, allowing large ships to sail into the city of Ghent.

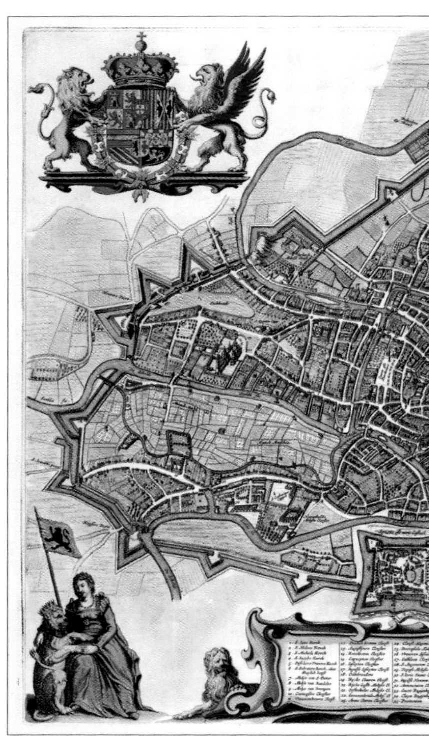

TIMELINE

Brugse Vaart

1613-1623 Construction of Brugse Vaart.

1614 Building of the Schepenhuis van Gedele.

1648 Closing of Western Scheldt by the Dutch. Sasse Vaart falls into disrepair.

1678-1708 Louis XIV occupies Ghent.

1600 | 1625 | 1650 | 1675

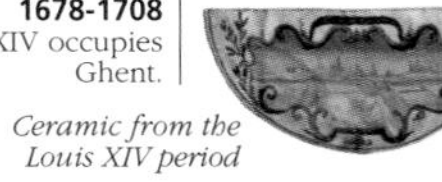

Ceramic from the Louis XIV period

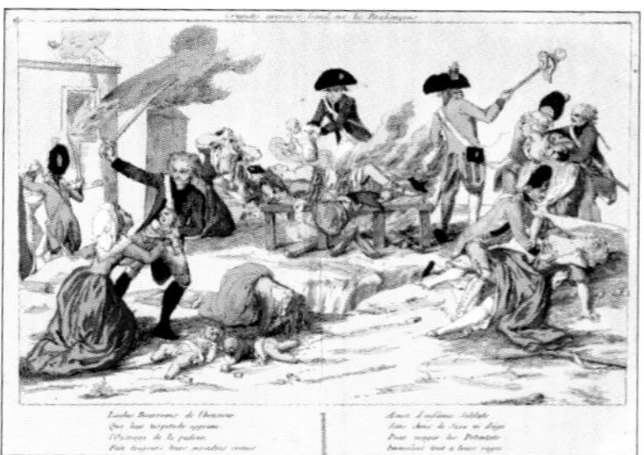

Brabant Revolution

In 1789, the southern Low Countries revolted against the reform policies of much-loathed emperor Joseph II. The revolt started in Brabant, but quickly spread to Flanders. On 13 November, rebel troops took over the city in a surprise attack. In December 1790, Joseph II reclaimed power.

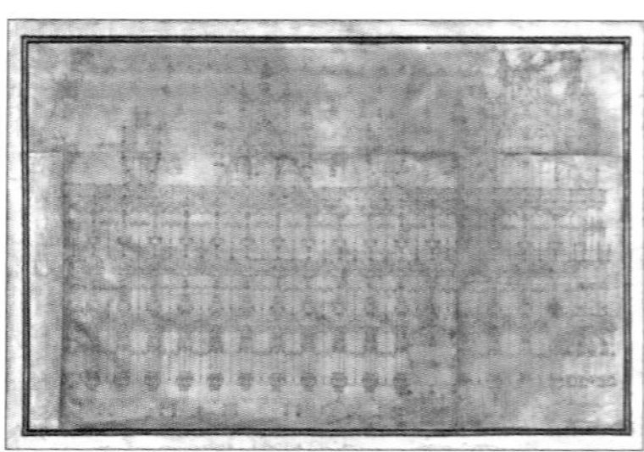

Schepenhuis van Gedele

In 1614, a new phase in the construction of the Schepenhuis van Gedele (Renaissance wing of the city hall) started under the command of architects Lieven and Pieter Plumion. The Tuscan, Ionic and Corinthian columns were inspired by an Italian renaissance palaces.

GHENT 1641

Map compiled by Antonius Sanderus and Hendrik Hondius.

During Calvinist rule, a fortification with bastions (the Geuzenvesting) was constructed around Ghent, consisting of earthen walls with bastions at strategic points. The Nieuw Kasteel (Spanjaardenkasteel) that Charles V commissioned as a citadel was also incorporated into the fortification. This defence system around the city had a triangular shape.

1-1714
ish Succession war.
flict between Austria and n over succession to the ish throne.

1714-1794
Southern Low Countries fall into Austrian hands.

1751-1753
Excavation of the Coupure.

1789-1790
Brabant Revolution.
Revolts by the southern Low Countries against the rule of emperor Joseph II.

1725 **1750** **1775** **1800**

1708-1713
Duke of Marlborough occupies Ghent.

1748-1780
Maria Theresia.

Maria Theresia

1795
French occupation.

Industrial city

During the first half of the 19th century, Ghent developed into the most significant industrial city on the European mainland. The cotton and flax industry stimulated the development of other branches of industry, such as machinery manufacture. The population of Ghent doubled from 55,000 in 1801 to 115,000 in 1866 and increased even more to 166,000 in 1910. As a result of this industrialisation, the city's waterways became open sewers. After 1880, the Reep, the Ottogracht, the Oude Houtlei and other canals were filled in. After patent rights (toll fees for the import and export of goods) were abolished in 1860, the city quickly expanded. Its fortifications were replaced with streets (the present-day inner ring).

GHENT IN 1933

- Urban development in 1933
- Current development
- Current municipal border

Zuidstation
The Zuidstation, train station, was the most important means to access the city of Ghent for 75 years. Trams departed to the city centre and the outlying districts. When St.-Pietersstation opened in 1928, the Zuidstation was demolished and the present-day Zuidpark was built in its place.

Labour movement
Labourers, including women and children, worked long hours for minimal wages. Pieter Daens, a priest, denounced the poor working conditions in the textile-producing city of Aalst. Along with Ghent, Aalst was the birthplace of the socialist and Christian labour movement.

TIMELINE

1792-1814 French rule.

1800 Lieven Bauwens smuggles a mechanical spinning machine, the Mule Jenny, across the English Channel.

1815-1830 Dutch period.

1822 Construction of the Hollandse Citadel.

1827 Opening of canal between Ghent and Terneuzen.

Ghent-Terneuzen canal

1831 Belgian independence under Leopold I.

1837 Opening of Ghent-Mechelen railway line. Zuidstation.

1843 First Gentse Feesten.

1860 Patent rights abolished, fortifications demolished.

1866 Cholera epidemic kills 2,76

1800 | 1825 | 1850

1913 World's Fair
The World's Fair was held on both sides of St.-Pietersstation. It was a great success. Despite a large number of visitors to the Expo, the city was left burdened with enormous debt.

Emile Braun
During liberal politician Emile Braun's term of office (1895-1921), Ghent's image changed radically. New streets such as Belfortstraat were laid, bridges were built and the city was enhanced with the addition of the Nederlandse Schouwburg (Dutch theatre), the Museum voor Schone Kunsten and St.-Pietersstation. The houses around the Belfort, St.-Baafskathedraal and St.-Niklaaskerk were removed, as were the surrounding alleyways. This clean-up operation was meant to give Ghent a modern city image.

FACTORIES

New industries established factories in vacant monasteries, or constructed new buildings. The factories were a great hazard to those living around them.

Beluiken
Many labourers lived in run-down, unhygienic worker's accommodations found in so-called beluiken *– small, dead-end alleyways located in the inner courtyards of the larger city complexes. In 1904, there were 613 beluiken with 7,061 homes housing 24,829 people in Ghent.*

…horse-drawn

1887
De Vigne and Zollikofer plan. Zuidstation linked to the Kuip.

1913
World's Fair.

1914-1918
World War I.

1934
Theft of Righteous Judges.

1940-1944
World War II.

1900 **1925** **1950**

1878
Coöperatieve Vooruit established.

1904
Electric tram. Museum voor Schone Kunsten opens.

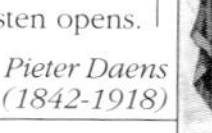

Pieter Daens (1842-1918)

6 september 1944
Liberation of Ghent.

Ghent liberated

After 1950

The Watersportbaan and the high-rise apartment blocks on Jubileumlaan were the first signs of economic recovery following World War II. Steel, petrochemical and automobile assembly industries arose along the widened canal between Ghent and Terneuzen. As of 1960, major infrastructure developments took place. The freeway network around Ghent, the Ringvaart (ring canal), the R4 ring-road and the harbour extension were all constructed. On 1 January 1977, the communities of Afsnee, Drongen, Gentbrugge, Ledeberg, Mariakerke, Oostakker, St.-Amandsberg, St.-Denijs-Westrem, Wondelgem and Zwijnaarde were incorporated into Ghent. However, this has not slowed the relocation of residents from the inner city to suburban communities.

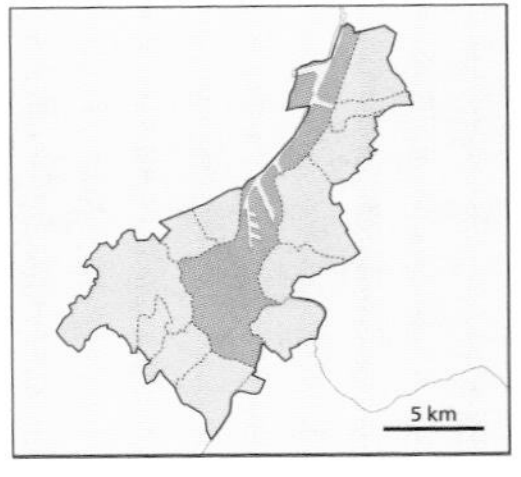

GHENT AFTER 1977

Incorporated communities

Municipal border

Ghent harbour
Ships access the harbour via the Western Scheldt and sail up the canal at Terneuzen. A number of major corporations are represented along the harbour, including Arcelor-Mittal (formerly known as Sidmar) and Volvo Cars.

KoBra Plan
Due to the reconstruction of the Korenmarkt, the Emile Braunplein and Belfortstraat in 2009, and Cataloniëstraat, Goudenleeuwplein and the Botermarkt in 2009-2012, the area around the three towers will become more suitable for walking, shopping and sightseeing. A new Stadshal (city building) will be constructed on Emile Braunplein.

NUMBER OF INHABITANTS

1961: 157,811	1990: 230,543
1970: 148,860	2000: 224,180
1977: 248,667	2010: 246,719

TIJDBALK

- **1955** Watersportbaan opens.
- **1959** Universitair Ziekenhuis (University Hospital) opens.
- **1962** Sidmar steel company established along Ghent-Terneuzen canal.
- **1969** Ringvaart around Ghent opens.
- **1977** Outlying communities incorporated into Ghent.

1950 | 1955 | 1960 | 1965 | 1970 | 1975

GEEN FUSIE MET GENT

Opposition to incorporation into Ghent

Watersportbaan and apartment blocks
The Watersportbaan (water sports circuit) was constructed in the Neermeersen, a marshy area between the tributaries of the Leie. Large apartment blocks were built beside the water.

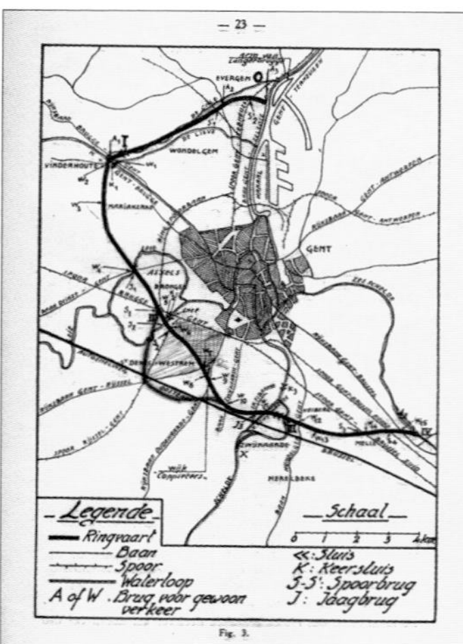

Construction of the Ringvaart (ring canal)
Through the construction of the Ringvaart (1948-1969), which runs around Ghent in a semi-circle and links all the waterways of the city, inland vessels did not have to sail through the city anymore. The canal also limited the risk of flooding in the inner city.

OPENING OF THE STAM – STADSMUSEUM GENT

On 9 October 2010, this new interactive, multimedia museum dealing with the history of the city opened its doors in the Bijloke area.

Reconstruction of the Vrijdagmarkt (1981)
Between 1960 and 1985, large-scale infrastructure plans to make Ghent more accessible were implemented. Underground parking areas were constructed in the inner city. Improved infrastructure around the city went hand-in-hand with the urbanisation of the Ghent region.

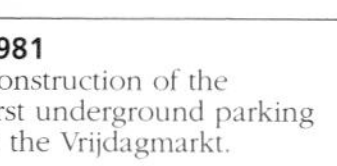

981
:onstruction of the
irst underground parking
t the Vrijdagmarkt.

The end of the road for the Arbed steel company

1999
S.M.A.K. opens.

2009-2012
Reconstruction of the Korenmarkt, Emile Braunplein and Belfortstraat.

1985 | **1990** | **1995** | **2000** | **2005** | **2010**

Veldtstraat before 1987

1987
Cars barred from Veldtstraat

1993
Arbed steel company in Gentbrugge closes.

14 juli 2009
Final trolley bus trip.

2010
STAM – Stadsmuseum Gent – opens.
East Flanders severely affected by flooding of the Scheldt and the Dender.

City of the future

Various major construction projects, set to take place over the coming years, are planned for the city. These projects will drastically change the city's image for Ghent residents and visitors alike. The Waalse Krook with the Library of the Future and the Wintercircus will determine the look of new developments in the Zuid (South) area. As part of the Gent St.-Pieters project, the station area will be modified to meet the demands of the 21st century. It will include a public transport junction (train, bus and tram), new residential developments, work and leisure facilities and a green area between Citadelpark and the Blaarmeersen.

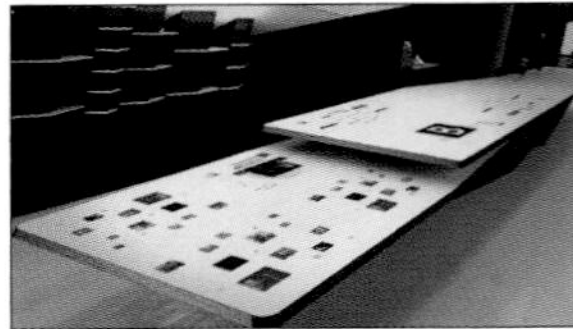

Oude Vismijn

The fully restored Oude Vismijn building will accommodate the new Ghent Tourism information office. An interactive data table produced by Studio Arne Quinze (SAQ) will form its most eye-catching feature.

Stadshal

The Stadshal (city hall), a 40 x 15 m wooden structure will rest on four concrete cornerstones. It will contain a bicycle storage area and a semi-subterranean grand café leading onto a low-lying park (the 'green').

Gent St.-Pieters

The area around the station of Gent St.-Pieters, developed on the eve of the 1913 World's Fair, is to be modified to meet the demands of the 21st century. Apartment blocks and office space will be constructed along Koningin Fabiolalaan. ***www****.projectgentsintpieters.be*

De Krook

This new city district in the Zuid district, with its Library of the Future and Centre for New Media, will become a multimedia centre for science, culture and economy. The Wintercircus, one of the most important theatres in the city between 1895 and 1944, will be given an new purpose containing apartments, offices and restaurants.
***www**.dewaalsekrook.be*

OUDE DOKKEN

150 Years ago, the beating heart of Ghent harbour was the Achterdok, the Handelsdok and the Houtdok (Rear Docks, Trade Docks and Wooden Docks). Over the years, harbour activities have been relocated northwards and the Oude Dokken, Old docks, lost their purpose. The dokken will be revived as a residential area featuring plenty of greenery and water.
***www**.oudedokken.be*

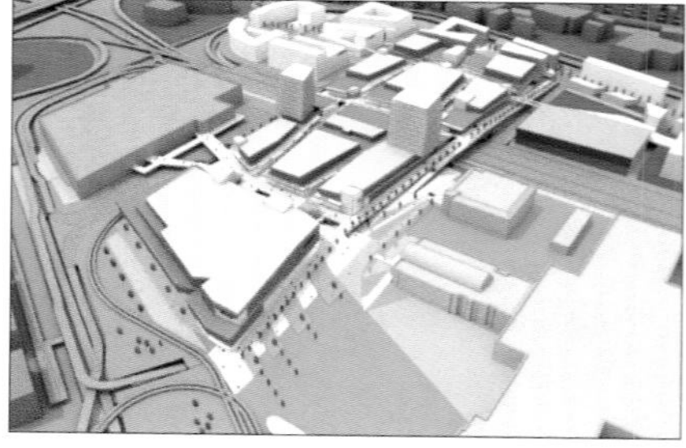

Gent The Loop

Gent The Loop is the name given to a new city district in the south of the city. It will feature a blend of office, shopping, residential and leisure facilities. Archaeological research has uncovered traces of settlements and graves from the Neolithic era up until the Middle Ages. During World War I, an airfield was constructed here. This district is named in honour of French pilot Adolphe Pégoud, the pioneer of the aerial loop.
***www**.theloop.be*

GHENT AND ITS DISTRICTS

TORENS AND GRASLEI SITE

The Torens and Graslei site – the beating heart of Ghent's historic centre – contain the Medieval Gras and Korenlei (streets), the torenrij (three tower steeples in a row) and Jan van Eyck's masterpiece *The Adoration of the Mystic Lamb*. Over the years, the large city squares have undergone a true metamorphosis and now form a single great square with the Stadshal building as the central meeting place.

For centuries, the three steeples of St.-Niklaaskerk (church), Belfort (tower) and St.-Baafskathedraal (cathedral) have dominated the city's skyline. The beautiful façades on the Gras and Korenlei are reflected in the waters of the 'Tusschen Brugghen', the old city harbour. On sunny days, the streets become one large terrace on which Ghent locals and tourists, young and old, enjoy the sun, the city and the water.

SIGHTS AT A GLANCE

Churches
St.-Baafskathedraal pages 56-57 1
St.-Michielskerk 16
St.-Niklaaskerk 8

Buildings
Achtersikkel 12
Belfort 4
Geeraard de Duivelsteen 9
Groot Vleeshuis 21
Koninklijke Nederlandse Schouwburg 2
Lakenhalle 3
Mammelokker 5
Metselaarshuis 7
Pand 17
Postgebouw 14
Stadhuis 6

Museums
Design Museum Ghent 18
School van Toen 19

Streets, squares, bridges
Bisdomplein 10
Groentenmarkt 20
Korenmarkt 13
Reep 11
St.-Michielsbrug 15

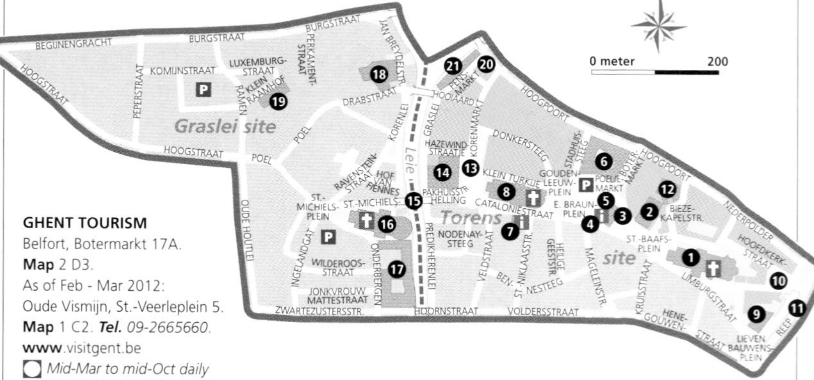

GHENT TOURISM
Belfort, Botermarkt 17A. **Map** 2 D3.
As of Feb - Mar 2012: Oude Vismijn, St.-Veerleplein 5. **Map** 1 C2. ***Tel.*** *09-2665660.* **www**.visitgent.be
Mid-Mar to mid-Oct daily 9:30am-6.30pm; mid-Oct to mid-Mar daily 9:30am-4:30pm.

EAST FLANDERS TOURISM
Metselaarshuis, St.-Niklaasstraat 2. **Map** 1 C3. ***Tel.*** *09-2692600.* **www**.tov.be
Mon-Fri 9am-12pm and 1:15pm-4:45pm.

GETTING THERE
The Ghent city centre (Korenmarkt) is easily accessed by taking tram 1 from Gent-St.-Pieters and bus 3 from Gent-Dampoort. There are a number of parking garages in the city centre.

SYMBOLS
A closer look *pages 52-53*
Explanation of the symbols *see inside of the back flap*

◁ **St.-Michielsbrug with the Belfort and St.-Baafskathedraal in the background**

A closer look: from St.-Baafs-kathedraal to the Korenlei

Bell in the Belfort

The five city squares – Korenmarkt, Emile Braunplein, Goudenleeuwplein, Botermarkt and St.-Baafsplein – lie at the foot of the famous Ghent torenrij and are surrounded by impressive structures and monuments. On the revamped squares, tourists stroll, shoppers pass by and commuters get on and off of trams. Whenever the sun breaks through, Ghent locals and tourists are found seated together at the many outdoor cafés. During the Gentse Feesten, the squares are transformed into a massive open-air theatre. Over the next few years, the inner city will undergo a metamorphosis and will become the true heart of the city, a place where everyone will feel at home.

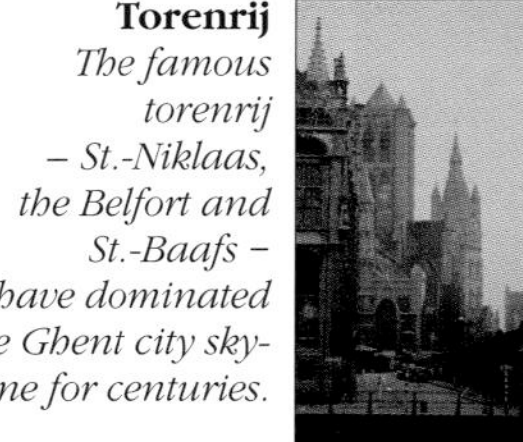

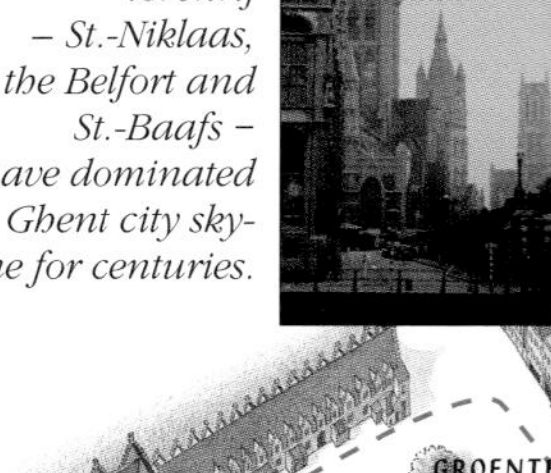

Torenrij
The famous torenrij – St.-Niklaas, the Belfort and St.-Baafs – have dominated the Ghent city skyline for centuries.

★ Gras and Korenlei
The façades along the wharf symbolised Ghent's prosperity during the Middle Ages. Towards the end of the 19th and the start of the 20th century, these guildhalls were restored to their former glory.

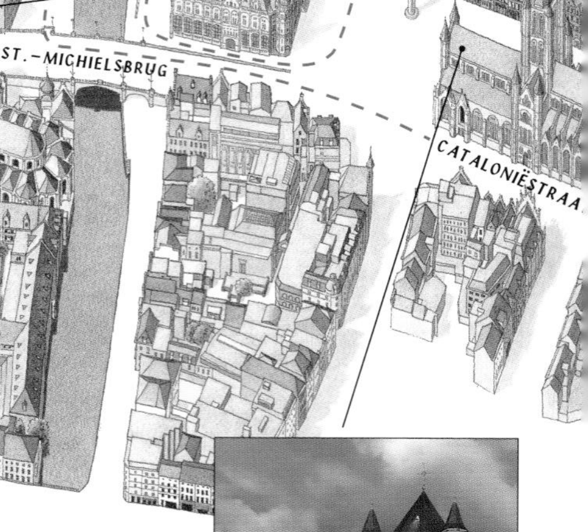

St.-Michielskerk

St.-Niklaaskerk
This church is a prime example of Scheldt Gothic architecture evident in the use of Doornik 'limestone', the bell tower at the intersection between the nave and the aisle and the smaller flanking turrets. ❽

STAR ATTRACTIONS

- ★ Belfort and Lakenhalle
- ★ Gras- and Korenlei
- ★ St.-Baafskathedraal

★ Belfort and Lakenhalle
The 95-m-high Belfort is a proud symbol of Ghent's independence. Adjacent to the tower is the Lakenhalle. ❸ + ❹

LOCATOR MAP
See Street guide, maps 1 and 2

0 metres 100

HOOGPOORT

BOTERMARKT

E. BRAUN-PLEIN

NEDERPOLDER

ST.-BAAFSPLEIN

LIMBURGSTRAAT

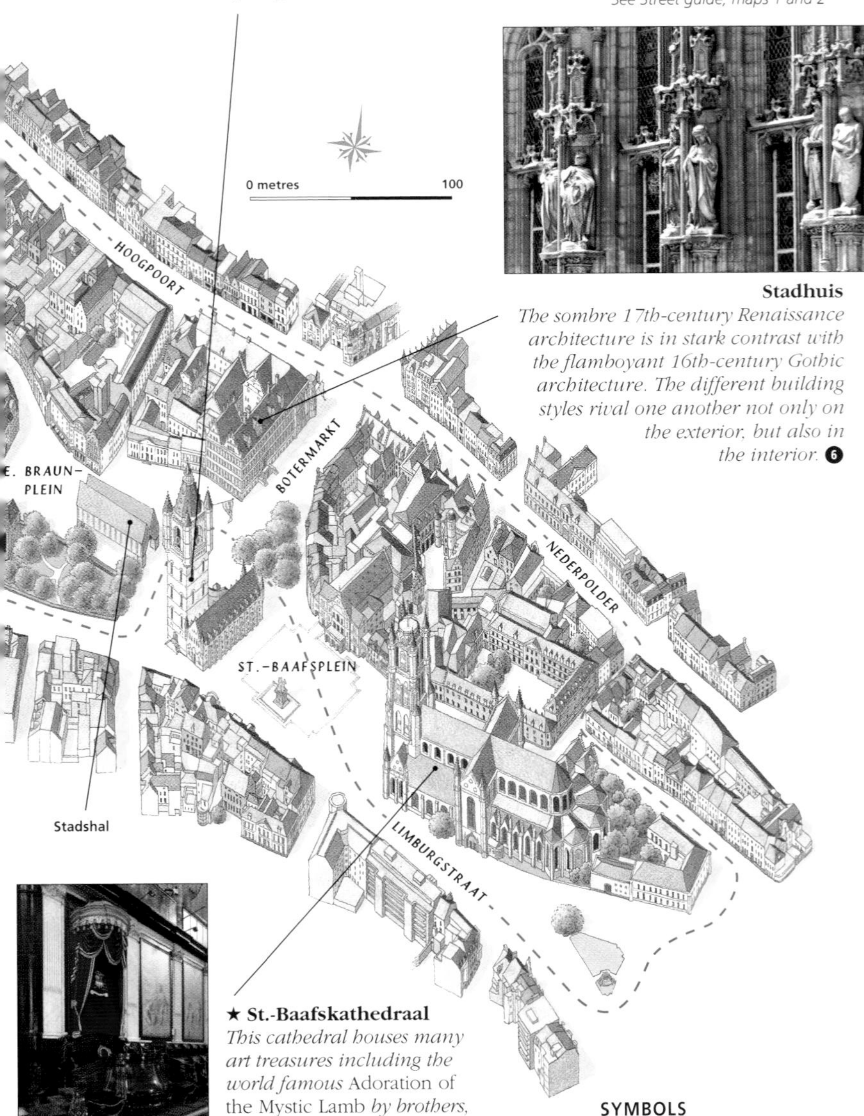

Stadhuis
The sombre 17th-century Renaissance architecture is in stark contrast with the flamboyant 16th-century Gothic architecture. The different building styles rival one another not only on the exterior, but also in the interior. ❻

Stadshal

★ St.-Baafskathedraal
This cathedral houses many art treasures including the world famous Adoration of the Mystic Lamb *by brothers, Hubert and Jan van Eyck.* ❶

SYMBOLS

– – Recommended route

Bells in the Belfort bell room

HISTORIC CENTRE
TORENS SITE

St.-Baafs-kathedraal ❶

Pages 56-57.

Koninklijke Nederlandse Schouwburg ❷

St.-Baafsplein 17. **Map** 2 D3. *For reservations, see page 237.*
www.ntgent.be

The north side of the square is dominated by the Koninklijke Nederlandse Schouwburg (KNS). This theatre dates back to 1899, although Ghent's first company, the Nederlands Toneel Gent (NTG), now known as NTGent, was only established in 1965. **Apollo** and his muses look out over the square from the façade above the entrance. Within the four alcoves are the images of the most significant Ghent drama societies of the 19th century: De Fonteyne, St.-Agnete, St.-Barbara and Mariën Theeren. A monument to Jan Frans Willems (1793-1846), Flemish author and prominent pioneer of the Flemish Movement (the emancipation of the people of Flanders), can be found in front of the theatre.

Lakenhalle ❸

St.-Baafsplein. **Map** 2 D3.
For more, see Belfort.

The wool and cloth merchants used to congregate in the Lakenhalle. The wool and cloth were inspected, measured and sold in the huge hall. Construction of the building started in 1425 but, sixteen years later with just more than half completed, construction came to an end due to a lack of funds. By then, the cloth industry had reached and surpassed its peak. The building was completed between 1889 and 1913.

'Young man and the Maid of Flanders'

Belfort ❹

St.-Baafsplein. **Map** 1 C3.
Tel. *09-2333954 or 09-3753161.*
daily 10am-6pm. 2:30pm and 3:30pm.
www.belfortgent.be

The Belfort symbolises the city's autonomy. The city's charters were kept safe in the 'secreet', a Medieval archive chamber. The tower served as a lookout post for detecting possible enemy attacks and fires. The bells used to warn people during emergencies also hung in the tower. Construction of the tower started at the beginning of the 14th century. Around 1380, the legendary 'Draak van Gent' ('Ghent Dragon'), a weather vane made of gilded copper plate, was placed at its summit. A clock was first added in 1457. Over the course of the centuries, the steeple was repeatedly renovated or repaired. At the start of the 15th century, the Lakenhalle was erected on the east side of the Belfort. A visit to the tower begins in its basement and ends on its balcony, which provides spectacular views of the city. The gatekeeper's chambers in the tower contain, amongst others, ancient gargoyles and scale models of the structure. The Belfort also houses a bell museum and a carillon.

Mammelokker ❺

Botermarkt. **Map** 1 C3, 2 D3.

The former city prison was constructed in 1741 next to Lakenhalle's west wing, replacing the old city prison (Chastelet), which was located

'Appolo and the muses on Parnassus' on the gable of the Schouwburg

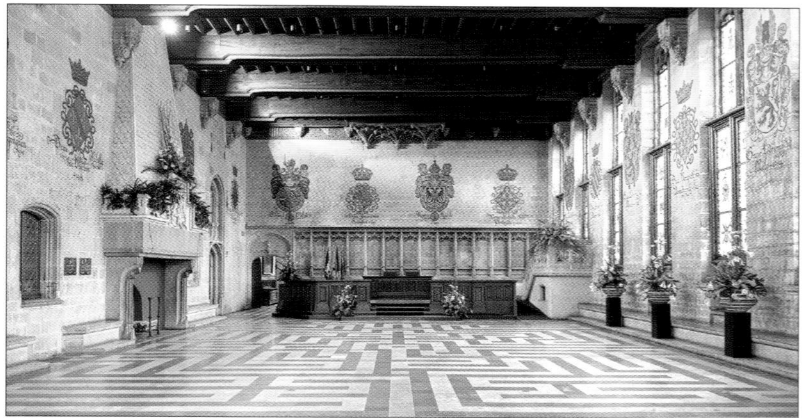

In the Pacificatiezaal, the Habsburg Netherlands decided to drive out Spanish forces in 1576

at the Korenmarkt and demolished in 1718. The relief on the tympanum of the façade represents a Roman myth, Cimon. According to this myth of a young woman saved the life of her father, who was condemned to death by starvation, by breast-feeding him. This is why the citizens of Ghent call the prison the 'Mammelokker'.

Stadhuis ❻

Botermarkt 1. **Map** 2 D3. *May-Oct. Mon-Fri 2:30pm, departing from Ghent Tourist Info office.*

The Stadhuis can be viewed from two distinctly different angles. It has a flamboyant Gothic wing on the corner of the Botermarkt and the Hoogpoort, and an austere Renaissance wing along the Botermarkt. For the construction of the Stadhuis, the city managers called on two famous Brabant master builders, Rombout Keldermans (1460-1531) and Domien de Waghemakere (1460-1542). They designed a resplendent court in late Gothic style with highly decorated façades. Sculptures of the counts of Flanders were to be placed in the alcoves on the façades. However, with just over half of the design complete, work came to an abrupt end due to the Ghent Uprisings of 1540. In 1580, the wing was extended with the addition of the Bollaertskamer built in the Renaissance style. In 1595, the second construction phase started. A number of different architects worked on the design of the complex, which was constructed in the style of an Italian *palazzo*. Visitors are led through the halls by a guide. The **Pacificatiezaal** originally served as the court of justice for the lawmakers. The black and white floor tiles create a maze, symbolising the search for justice and happiness. In 1576, the Pacification of Ghent was signed in this hall. The lawmakers also had the use of their own chapel. A Gothic staircase leads to the first floor. In the Troonzaal, only completed in 1635, the life-sized paintings attract the most attention.

Masons coat of arms

Metselaarshuis with its six dancers

Metselaarshuis ❼

St.-Niklaasstraat 2. **Map** 1 C3.

In 1526, the guild of Masons commissioned the construction of a splendid façade in a style combining late Gothic and early Renaissance architecture. However, in 1852 this façade disappeared behind a thick layer of plaster until, in 1975, it was rediscovered during renovation work. The façade was restored to its former glory and now pleasantly contrasts with the adjacent newly-built steel and glass structure. The six bronze Morisken Dancers on the pinnacles are the work of the sculptor Walter De Buck. The Morisken dance was a popular dance during the 15th and 16th centuries and was performed by six men with bells tied to their legs to provide the rhythm.
There is also a Mason lodge on the Graslei. A replica of the original building, thought to be lost, was built for the 1913 World's Fair based on the original building plans.

St.-Baafskathedraal ❶

942 marks the year when St.-Jan de Doperkerk (church of St John the Baptist), the parish church of the Gentse Portus was consecrated. In the 11th century, a Romanesque church was built in its stead. All evidence of their existence are found in the crypt. From Romanesque to Gothic: beginning with the choir, construction of the current church began in the 14th century. Built in French high Gothic style using blue Doornik limestone, it took two hundred years to complete. The choir was consecrated in 1353; the radiating chapels were completed by the early 15th century. During the second phase of construction, between 1462 and 1538, the 82-m-high steeple was erected in the Brabant Gothic style. The third phase, the building of the nave, began in 1533. Further extensions were later added. In 1541, the church was taken over by the St Baafs chapter, changing the name from St John's Church to St Baafs Church. When the Diocese of Ghent was erected in 1559, it received the name St.-Baafskathedraal. The Cathedral is currently being restored.

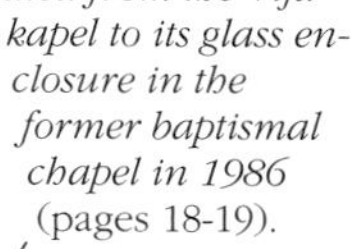

★ Adoration of the Mystic Lamb
The masterpiece by the Van Eyck brothers (inset shown here) was relocated from the Vijdkapel to its glass enclosure in the former baptismal chapel in 1986 (pages 18-19).

Wall art
The frescos on the pillars and arches in the crypt originate from the period between 1480 and 1540.

STAR ATTRACTIONS

- ★ The Mystic Lamb
- ★ Romanesque crypts
- ★ Presbytery

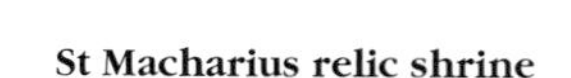

St Macharius relic shrine
This rectangular silver shrine, held up by four recumbent lions and designed by Hugo de la Vigne Montensio (17th century), can be seen in the crypt.

TIPS FOR VISITORS

St.-Baafsplein. **Map** 2 D3.
Tel. *09-2692045.* *cathedral: Apr-Oct. Mon-Sat 8:30am-6pm, Sun 1pm-5pm; Nov-Mar. Mon-Sat 8:30am-5pm, Sun 1pm-5pm. Steeple: during Gentse Feesten (fourth week of July) 11am-6pm.*
www.sintbaafskathedraal-gent.be

Bavo enters the monastery in Ghent
Peter Paul Rubens created this canvas in 1623-1624. Allowin van Haspengouw, the future St. Baaf, also known as St Bavo († 653), repented after the death of his wife. He gave up his riotous existence and became a monk.

Grote Eucharistie Cyclus
Thirteen grisaille artworks in Neoclassical style by Pieter Norbert van Reysschoot (1738-1795), located between the black and white marble of the presbytery, create an optical illusion. Between 2006 and 2010 these artworks were restored.

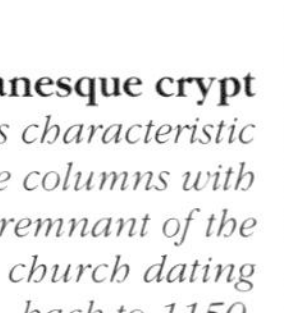

★ Romanesque crypt
The crypt with its characteristic Doornik limestone columns with projecting capitals is a remnant of the Romanesque Christian church dating back to 1150.

★ Presbytery
The restoration of the presbytery was completed in 2010. The complete restoration of the cathedral will still take a number of years.

Interior of the St.-Niklaaskerk

St.-Niklaaskerk ❽

Cataloniëstraat. **Map** 1 C3.
Tel. *09-2342869.* ◯ *Mon 2pm-5pm, Tue-Sun 10am-5pm.* ♿
www.stniklaas.com

By the 11th century, a Romanesque church building already occupied this site. At the start of the 13th century, it was demolished to make way for a new church. Around the year 1200, construction of the new church commenced using Doornik limestone. This church is a prime example of Scheldt Gothic architecture. The bell tower with its round turrets served as a lookout before the Belfort took over this role. During the 14th and 15th centuries, the church was further extended. The St.-Niklaaskerk, devoted to the patron of merchants and seamen, was a church for the wealthy merchants and guildsmen. During the 17th century, the interior of the church was adapted to suit current fashion. After this, it suffered centuries of neglect. Towards the end of the 20th century, the steeple was stabilised and the choir and transept restored. The restoration of the nave was also – for the most part – completed, while a suitable purpose for this area is still being considered.

Geeraard de Duivelsteen ❾

Geraard de Duivelstraat 1.
Map 2 D4.

The first stone castle along the Scheldt was erected before or during the 11th century. This sombre fortress owes its name to Gheeraert Vilain, the second son of count Zeger II. His dark features and black hair earned him the nickname of 'the devil'. He was portrayed as a cruel person in various myths that surrounded him.
Around 1328, the city of Ghent purchased the castle, after which it served many different purposes, ranging from knights' barracks and weapons arsenal to monastery and bishops' seminary. In 1623, it became a mental asylum and orphanage, while part of the building was used as a prison or house of correction.
After drastic restoration towards the end of the 19th century, the fortress housed the National Archives from 1904. In addition to the restoration that took place, a Neo-Gothic wing was added in 1904.

Bisdomplein ❿

Map 2 D4.

The name of the Bisdomplein square was derived from the Bishop's palace that is situated on the west side of the square. It was put into use in 1843. The coat of arms of bishop Delebecque, under whose reign the palace was constructed, is proudly displayed above the doorway. The National Bank of Belgium (1905) can also be found on the Bisdomplein, although the building is now put to use as a branch of the Vlerick Management School. This square leads onto the Wijdenaardbrug, a bridge that spans the Reep, which is still filled in at this point in time.

Reep ⓫

Map 2 F2-3.

Within a few years, the present-day cityscape between Brabantdam and Dampoort will undergo radical, sweeping changes. The waters of the Reep (Nederschelde) will be made to once again flow through this area. This future flow of water will be flanked on both sides by inviting promenades, cycling paths, lower quay walls, pleasant outdoor cafés and squares with plenty of green spaces. In 1959-1960, because of the constant stench, it was decided to fill in the Reep between Bisdomplein and the Nieuwbrugkaai, thus transforming the river into a parking area. The first bridge across the Reep was constructed in 1884.

Geeraard de Duivelsteen, a 13th-century fortress on the banks of the Scheldt

Achtersikkel ⓬

Biezekapelstraat. **Map** 2 D3.

The Achtersikkel House, dating back to the Middle Ages and built by the Van der Sickelen family, is located on a bend in Biezekapelstraat. Its high, natural stone tower and belvedere dominates the courtyard. The Conservatorium of the University College Ghent is housed in the house.

HISTORIC CENTRE
GRASLEI SITE

Korenmarkt ⓭

Map 1 C3.

The Korenmarkt has once again been transformed into a genuine square. The tram stop has been relocated to a nearby street. The square, previously known as the Koornaard, is dominated by the western façades of the St.-Niklaaskerk and the Postgebouw. The new Korenmarkt accommodates major events and outdoor cafés. Grain shipped in via the Graslei was traded at the Korenmarkt. It is one of Ghent's oldest and most historically significant squares. The new Korenmarkt is an inviting city square with many outdoor cafés and is an important link between the southern (Veldstraat) and northern (Langemunt) commercial areas of the city centre.

Along the Reep (Nederschelde) near the Wijdenaardbrug

Postgebouw ⓮

Korenmarkt 16. **Map** 1 C3.

The Postgebouw used to be the central Post Office. It's the only large public building on the 'new' Korenmarkt. Constructed between 1898 and 1908 in an eclectic style that combined mainly Neo-Gothic and Renaissance elements, it replaced a number of beautiful old houses on that site. Its façade is profusely decorated with images and coats of arms. Incorporated into the façade are illustrations representing Belgium, Flanders, Wallonia and the former nine provinces, as well as likenesses of 23 of the European Heads of State at the time. The Belgian monarchs are depicted above the main entrance to the Korenmarkt. In 1998, De Post (Belgium postal service) relocated to new premises outside the centre and the building was sold. It now houses the Post Plaza shopping centre. This site will soon be given a different purpose.

Limestone tower of the Achtersikkel building

The monumental St.-Michielsbrug

St.-Michielsbrug ⓯

St.-Michielsbrug. **Map** 1 B3-C3.

At the start of the 20th century, the Neo-Gothic St.-Michielsbrug (St Michael's Bridge) replaced a small wooden swing bridge that was unable to cope with ever-increasing volumes of traffic. The new bridge offered visitors to the 1913 World's Fair a stunning view of the torenrij – the St.-Niklaaskerk, the Belfort and the St.-Baafskathedraal – as well as of the Tusschen Brugghen, the old Ghent inner harbour with the guildhalls lining the Gras and Korenlei.

St.-Michielskerk ⓰

St.-Michielsplein.
Map 1 B3.
Tel. *09-2342869.*
Apr-Sep 2pm-5pm.

By the year 1105, a small chapel dedicated to St Michael already occupied the site of the present-day church. In 1440, the decision was made to replace the derelict church, which had been razed by fire a number of times, with a new place of worship. Construction took more than two centuries and the church is still not completely finished. In 1566 and 1579, the church was plundered by iconoclasts. The steeple was also never completed and remains at the modest height of 24 m. The church harmoniously blends into its surroundings, a miracle given its long construction period.

St.-Michielskerk

Pand ⓱

Onderbergen 1. **Map** 1 B4.

In the year 1228, the Dominican Friars established their monastery on the banks of the Leie. A long wing with a kitchen, refectory, chapter hall and dormitory was built along the Leie. This was followed by a church that was demolished in 1860. The monastery fell prey to the iconoclasts, who vented their rage on the precious books from the library. For a short time, the monastery housed the Calvinist University. In 1584, the priests returned until they were forced to sell the monastery in 1823. During the second half of the 19th century, the monastery was converted into barracks. The Leie wing was restored for the benefit of the 1913 World's Fair, but the rest of the building fell into disrepair. Ghent University saved the building from being

The gardens of the Pand are surrounded by monastery halls and the library wing

demolished by transforming it into a culture and conference centre after it had been restored.

Design museum Gent ⓲

Jan Breydelstraat 5. **Map** 1 B3. ***Tel.*** *09-2679999.* *Tue-Sun 10am-6pm.*
www.designmuseumgent.be

In 1922, the Museum voor Toegepaste Kunsten (Museum of Applied Art), built in 1903, relocated to the 18th-century Hotel de Coninck. Since 2002, the museum has been called the Design museum Gent. The 17th and 18th century collections have been accommodated in the drawing rooms of the former mansion. These drawing rooms with their authentic parquet floors, panelling and period furniture are reminiscent of life in an 18th-century mansion. The ceiling artwork with its theme of love, the wooden chandelier, the furniture and the dinner service all make the dining room an extraordinary area. In 1992, a transparent newly-built structure arose behind the old building. This houses the modern collection (1880 to present-day). The ground floor and basement are used for temporary exhibits. The museum possesses one of the best Art Nouveau collections in Belgium. Both the exuberant Art Nouveau with its floral motifs and flowing patterns, and the more structural trends are on display. Works by prominent Belgian artists like Henry Van de Velde, Victor Horta, Paul Hankar, Gustave Serrurier-Bovy and Philippe Wolfers can be viewed here along with works by international designers. An overview of post-1970 applied art is presented on the second floor. Here, in addition to many other works, the multicoloured chair, Poltrona di Proust, by Italian designer Mendini, attracts much attention.

Collection of design furniture

School van Toen ⓳

Klein Raamhof 8. **Map** 1 B3. ***Tel.*** *09-2252903.* *Mon-Fri 9am-12pm and 2pm-4pm.*
www.gent.be/schoolvantoen

A small, nostalgia-evoking museum about the history of education in Ghent presented with the aid of photographs, documents, school furniture and school books. The museum is housed in a typical 1901 schoolhouse. In *The Klas van Toen*, visitors can experience the punishment and strict discipline handed out in days gone by.

Wall map of historic Belgium

Groentenmarkt ⓴

Map1 C2-3.

This rectangular square with its leafy chestnuts is located in the middle of the inner city. Streets from this square lead to the Vrijdagmarkt, the Stadhuis, the Korenmarkt and St.-Veerleplein which features the Gravensteen *(pages 78-79)*. The fish market – and the vegetable market since the 18th century – are consecutively held on this square. In 1812, a freestone pump was placed in the middle of the square. The Groot Vleeshuis building is an eye-catching feature of the Groentenmarkt.

Groot Vleeshuis with its tripe stalls

Groot Vleeshuis ㉑

Groentenmarkt 7. **Map** 1 C3. ***Tel.*** *09-2232324.* *Tue-Sun 10am-6pm.*
www.grootvleeshuis.be

The Groot Vleeshuis was constructed between 1407 and 1419 based on a design by city architect Gillis De Suttere. It was a covered marketplace where the freshness and quality of meat was monitored. In 1542-1543, tripe stalls were built along the south-eastern façade of the market hall. For hygienic reasons, offal, visceral fat and other remains from slaughtered animals had to be sold from these separate stalls. The roof structure of main hall is rather extraordinary because its oak trusses look like an upturned boat. By the end of the 19th century, people were allowed to trade in meat from their homes, which many of them did. As a result, the Groot Vleeshuis lost its main purpose and was used as a post office, storage area, exhibition centre and banquet hall. In 2002, the Groot Vleeshuis received a new purpose. Regional East-Flanders products are now sold in the 'glazen kubus' (glass cube).

Gras and Korenlei

Development of the 'Tusschen Brugghen' Lei harbour, the present Gras and Korenlei, began in the 11th century. The harbour gained even more importance when, during the 13th century, the Lieve was dug, connecting Ghent to the North Sea via Damme. Grain, imported from Artesia (Northern France), was unloaded here. Part of every shipload of grain was stored in the lofts of the warehouses around the harbour. In this way, the city always had a reserve stock for use in times of need. Various buildings along the quay are reminiscent of the former trade activities and represent the prosperity of the Ghent guilds. During the 19th century, the Gras and Korenlei lost much of their original character. The historic buildings were drastically restored with the 1913 World's Fair in mind.

Korenstapelhuis
The step-roofed warehouse was built in the Romanesque style during the 13th century. The warehouse was used for grain storage, hence the numerous doorways and windows.

8 Metselaarshuis (De Inghel)

9 Eerste Korenmetershuis

10 Korenstapelhuis (De Spijker)

Korenlei
The Korenlei was a busy commercial quay in the Leiehaven until the harbour and the company houses fell into disrepair during the 18th century. At the start of the 20th century, the buildings were carefully restored according to original building plans.

Graslei, the heart of Ghent
When you ask Ghent locals to choose which city site is the most beautiful, most of them will say that it's the Graslei. Today, the Medieval harbour with its quay walls, outdoor cafés and historic buildings has become a place to meet for young and old and for Ghent locals and tourists alike.

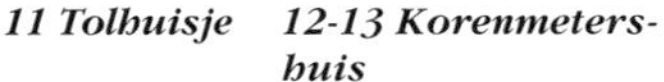

Tolhuisje
The Tolhuisje (Toll House, 1682) accommodated the city's staple masters who were tasked with receiving staple duties or taxes on goods traded in the harbour.

11 Tolhuisje ***12-13 Korenmetershuis*** ***14 Gildehuis der Vrije Schippers***

GRAIN TRADE

Along with the Korenmarkt, the Gras and Korenlei formed the focal point of the Flemish grain trade. After all, the city had staple rights on the grain traded in Flanders. The buildings along the quay are reminiscent of the former harbour activities and reflected the prosperity of Ghent trade and its companies.

Gildehuis der Onvrije Schippers
In 1739, the guild of Onvrije Schippers constructed their company house, with its richly decorated Dutch gable, on the Korenlei diagonally opposite the Vrije Schippers company house.

ROSSINI
SPOG

KOUTER SITE

No other square has retained its 19th-century character like the Kouter. For centuries, the Kouter has been the ideal meeting place for Ghent's citizens. On Sunday mornings, the square is transformed into a colourful flower- and plant market. City locals and tourists alike stroll around the market, enjoy a cup of coffee and round off their visit with a glass of white wine and fresh oysters from the Blauwe Kiosk. From way back, the Kouter been used for all kinds of festivities, as well as for holding public meetings. During the Middle Ages, it was referred to as the 'Peerdecouter'. Horses and weapons were paraded, tournaments were held and the rifle guilds of St George and St Sebastian guilds held their festivals here. During the 19th century, the square was known as the Wapenplaats or 'Place d'Armes'. In 1998, the square was restored and an underground parking area constructed.

SIGHTS AT A GLANCE

Buildings
Aula UGent 5
Handelsbeurs Concertzaal 1
Hotel d'Hane Steenhuyse 7
Hotel Falligan 2
Justitiepaleis 4
Vlaamse Opera 3

Museums
Hotel Clemmen | Museum Arnold Vander Haeghen 8

Street
Veldstraat 6

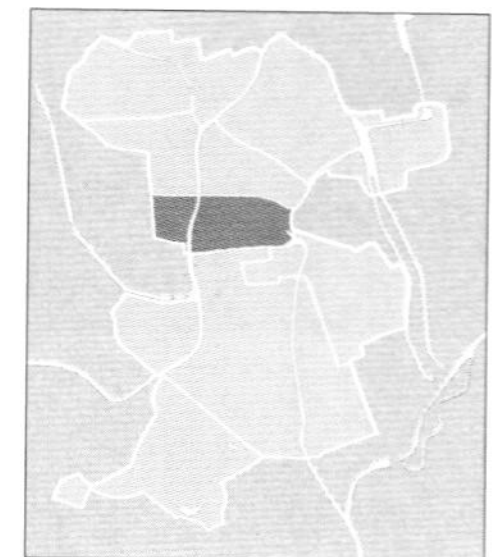

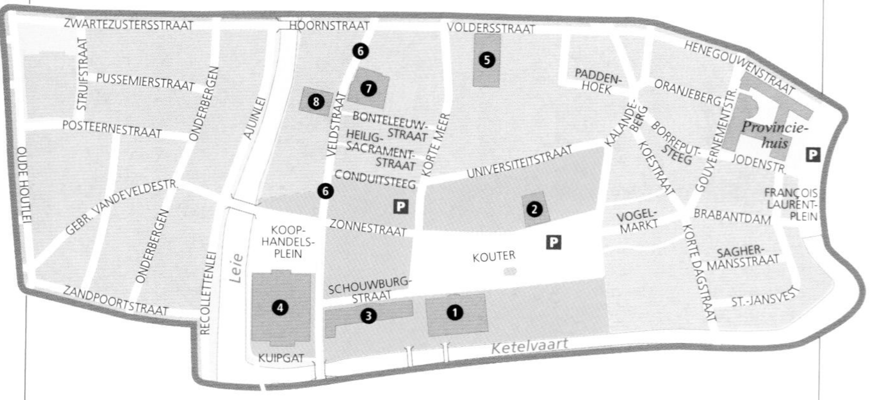

SYMBOLS

A closer look *pages 66-67*

Explanation of the symbols *see inside of the back flap*

◁ **The elegant cast-iron bandstand on the Kouter**

Exploring the Kouter

The 'Kijter' is a large rectangular square. For centuries, it's been the place where people go to be seen, and it quickly received the nickname *Place m'as-tu-vu,* 'Have you seen me' Square. Ghent locals still like to come here on Sunday mornings to stroll around the flower market. In the middle of the square is an elegant bandstand constructed in 1878. The curly leaves on the square are a work by American artist Jessica Diamond titled *Mystic Leaves*. The square is surrounded by stately buildings, including the 18th-century Handelsbeurs (concert hall) and Hotel Falligan. The name Kouter is derived from the Latin word *cultura*, meaning cultivated land.

Vlaamse Opera

This oval-shaped ballroom derived its name from the Société des Redoutes, which hired the hall for parties and balls. Its large windows let in plenty of light. ②

Handelsbeurs Concertzaal

The modern rear façade of the Handelsbeurs Concert hall – constructed of steel, glass and red columns – borders the Ketelvest. ④

Ketelpoort

The Ketelpoort was one of the gates in the old city wall. In 1540, the gate was mostly destroyed. From the Ketelpoort, there's a lovely view of the Leie and the canal Ketelvaart. ③

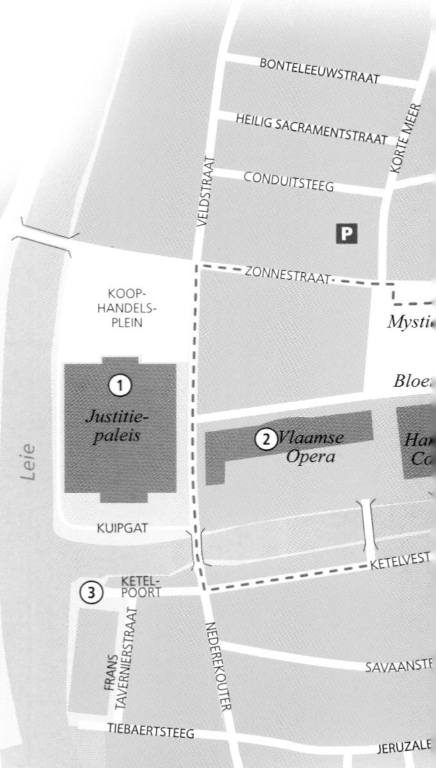

Justitiepaleis

This triangular pediment on the front façade is a depiction of De Gerechtigheid, *(Justice) by Geo Verbanck.* ①

Hotel Falligan
This stately mansion, built in the Rococo style in 1755 on behalf of the successful Hector Gabriël Falligan trading company, is an attractive 'hôtel de maitre'. ⑥

Kiosk
This elegant cast-iron bandstand, constructed in 1878, is located on the square and bears the names of Mozart, Gretry, Rossini and Auber, four esteemed composers. ⑦

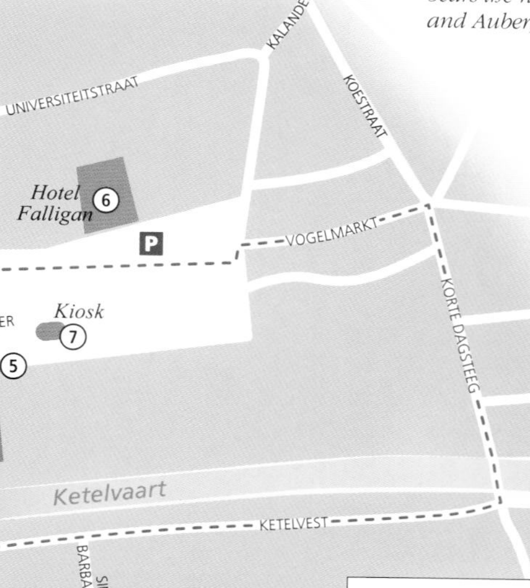

Flower market
On Sunday mornings, the Kouter is transformed into a massive flower market, where flower and plant growers display their colourful wares. ⑤

MYSTIC LEAVES

This artwork by American artist Jessica Diamond (1957) consists of large steel leaves incorporated into the paving of the square. Only one of the eighteen individual leaves is upright. They are made of cast-iron, bronze and brass. The names of the leaves have been added using large, elegant letters, making them difficult to read. The artwork reflects the Kouter as a flower market, but also refers to the varied flora pictured in *The Adoration of the Mystic Lamb* by the Van Eyck brothers.

SYMBOLS

– – Recommended route

HISTORIC CENTRE
KOUTER SITE

Handelsbeurs Concertzaal ❶

Kouter 29. **Map** 1 C4. *See page 237 for information about performances.*

Between 1738 and 1739, David 't Kindt designed the *Corps de Garde*, the main guardhouse of the Austrian imperial army. In 1875 the Hoofdwacht, along with the adjacent horseback postal depot (later the l'Union banquet hall), was turned into the stock exchange. After years of being left vacant, the exchange was converted into a concert hall in the year 2000. The new complex continues all the way to the Ketelvest, where its rear façade, made of mirror glass and steel, emphasises its new function as a concert hall.

Hotel Falligan ❷

Kouter 172. **Map** 1 C4.

This superb city dwelling, a Ghent rococo masterpiece, is the pride of the Kouter. The home was built in 1755 for businessman Hector Falligan and his wife Jeanne Agnes de Pestre, the heir of a wealthy colonial-ware dealer. The Corinthian columns feature decorative images of Apollo, the god of poetry, and Diana, the goddess of the hunt. In 1804, the *Club des Nobles* literary society took occupation of the building.

Vlaamse Opera ❸

Schouwburgstraat 3. **Map** 1 C4. *See page 237 for information about performances.*

During the first half of the 19th century, wealthy Ghent entrepeneurs initiated the construction of a new city theatre to match the look of modern Ghent. On 30 August 1840, the *Grand Theatre* – which could accommodate 1800 to 2000 patrons – was opened. The building consists of two wings: a short, deep wing, perpendicular to another 90 m long wing located on the street front. The first wing houses the horseshoe-shaped **theatre hall**, where the Vlaamse Opera (Flemish Opera) performs. The long wing holds the richly decorated foyer and the Redoute and Lully hall. To ensure smooth supply to the set, a bridge crossing the Ketelvest was built. From a city planning perspective, the opera building creates a remarkable union with the Justitiepaleis.

Justitiepaleis ❹

Koophandelsplein 23-24. **Map** 1 C4.

The Gerechtshof or Justitiepaleis (Palace of Justice) was built at virtually the same time as the Opera. Louis Roelandt, the Ghent architect who also designed the Opera and the Aula (lecture hall) at the University of Ghent, designed an imposing building in neoclassical style. Because of the unstable ground, construction was subject to much delay. The Gerechtshof only opened in 1846, ten years after work started. Corinthian columns support the pediment, which bears a depiction of Lady Justice surrounded by lawyers, the accused and the condemned. Most legal services have been relocated to the New Court of Ghent in Opgeëistenlaan. The Court of Appeal (Gerechtshof) is still housed in the Justitiepaleis.

Theatre hall of the Vlaamse Opera

Aula UGent ❺

Voldersstraat 9. **Map** 1 C4.

In 1817, King Willem I established the Rijksuniversiteit Gent. The new university occupied vacant monasteries and the town hall was used for official events. However, the city of Ghent believed that a special academic reception hall was necessary, an Aula Academica. On 4 August 1819, the cornerstone of this building was laid on behalf of Willem I on the site of the demolished Jesuit church. Louis Roelandt designed the building in the

Eight columns support the triangular pediment of the Gerechtshof

style of a classical temple with eight gigantic Corinthian columns that support an undecorated pediment. The portico leads to a large reception hall, while the grand staircase in the reception hall leads to the half-round doctorate and assembly hall, where academic ceremonies take place.

Veldstraat 6

Map 1 C3-4.

During the 18th and 19th century, the Veldstraat was a prominent street that featured beautiful mansions, city palaces and shops. King Louis XVIII of France briefly stayed in the Hotel d'Hane Steenhuyse, the duke of Wellington resided in Hotel Clemmen and the American delegation, present for the signing of the Treaty of Ghent, was accommodated in Hotel Schamp. At the end of the 19th century, the street was widened and it grew to become the city's most significant shopping street.

The Veldstraat is Ghent's most significant shopping street

Hotel d'Hane Steenhuyse 7

Veldstraat 55. **Map** 1 C4.
information at Ghent Tourism, ***Tel.*** *09-2665660.*

The Hotel d'Hane Steenhuyse reflects the aristocratic lifestyle lived by people during the 18th and 19th century. A small exhibit, depicting the historic events in which the palace played a role, can be viewed in the Koningssalon. Along with Hotel Clemmen, Hotel d'Hane Steenhuyse is set to form the cultural axis of the Veldstraat in the future. It is possible to visit the building as part of a guided tour.

The Aula was designed for receptions

Hotel Clemmen | Museum Arnold Vander Haeghen 8

Veldstraat 82. **Map** 1 C4.
Tel. *09-2698460.* *Mon-Fri 10am-12pm and 2pm-4pm. Ring doorbell to visit.*

In 1746, the famous Ghent city architect David 't Kindt built his own home here. Following his death in 1770, the house fell under the ownership of Joseph Clemmen, Ghent's first textile baron. Unique 18th-century wall hangings have remained preserved in the Chinese drawing room. In the museum, you will find a reconstruction of the library and the office used by the writer Maurice Maeterlinck (1862-1949). It is a replica of his office in the Orlamonde castle in Nice. In 1911, Maeterlinck received the prestigious Noble Prize for Literature. By the time he received the award, his worldwide fame was already an accomplished fact and his literary genius was widely recognized. His works were translated and published in a number of languages. Although Maeterlinck was Flemish and from Ghent, he wrote in French.

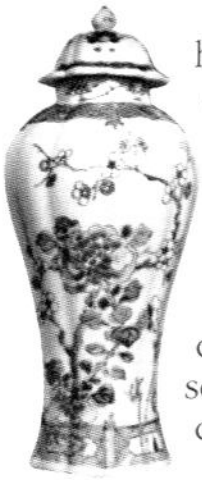

Vander Haeghen

Ghent: Creative City of Music

Ghent is a fascinating, dazzling musical city. This was confirmed in 2009, when Unesco bestowed the title of Creative City of Music on the city. Ghent shares this title with only three other cities, namely Glasgow, Seville and Bologna. Music thrives in the cultural haven that is Ghent. Any style or genre of music can be found performed on the stages of the Handelsbeurs, the Bijloke Muziekcentrum, the Vlaamse Opera, Kunstencentrum Vooruit, Intercultureel Centrum De Centrale, Kinky Star and Logos Tetrahedron. Music is also a focal point of the Ghent Film Festival, the Ghent Festival of Flanders, Ghent Jazz and the Gentse Feesten. Ghent is also home to innovative musical companies, including the Collegium Vocale Gent (chamber choir), Flat Earth Society (bigband) and Les Ballets C de la B (dance), as well as music academies, such as the Conservatorium, the Flanders Opera Studio and the Orpheus Institute. The city also boasts more than six hundred pop and rock bands.

The Bijloke Muziekcentrum
The Bijloke, the Ghent city hospital from 1228 to 1980, was converted into a stunning music centre that forms the axis around which Ghent's musical life revolves.

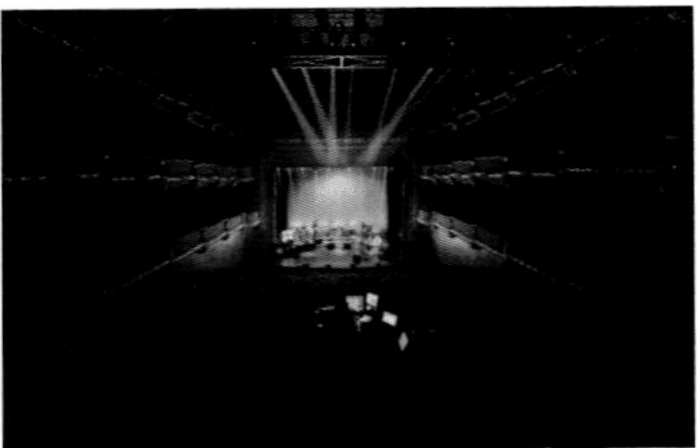

Vooruit
Vooruit, a progressive centre for the arts, schedules many musical performances from Ghent's rich and varied music scene into its programming.

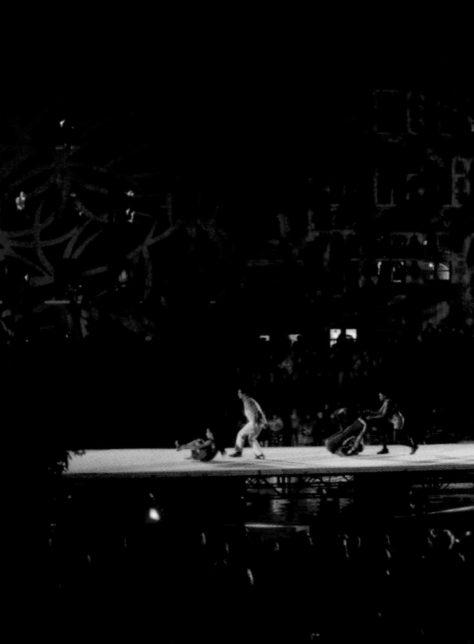

Score
The score from a musical performance in the Conservatorium.

Ghent Jazz Festival
This multi-day festival has, over the past ten years, grown to become a leading jazz event.

Handelsbeurs Concertzaal
The Handelsbeurs (concert hall) is where musicians, companies and cultural organisations are welcome and are invited to showcase their talents, shift boundaries and forge new relationships with audiences and the surroundings.

MORE INFORMATION

Addresses
Pages 236-237.

Pages 236-237.

Music in Ghent
Uit in Gent
www.uitingent.be

Music academies
As a city of music, Ghent is home to many academies of music, an internationally renowned music conservatorium and the Orpheus Institute, the Institute for Advanced Studies and Research in Music. In addition, Ghent also has its own opera academy, the Operastudio.

BOLERO

Ravel's famous opus, performed by Les Ballets C de la B, was the closing act of the Flanders Festival in 2009. Choreographer Lisi Estaras adapted the work, giving it the essence of daily city-life.

St.-Jacobskerk
The 'Scaladecor', (scenery) with its life-size dummies fixed to the wall of the St.-Jacobskerk during the Gentse Feesten.

RESTAURANT
HERTOGSTRAAT
BY DER WYZER EN DER ZOT
RESTAURANT

GRAVENSTEEN SITE

The area between the Leie and the Lieve was part of the jurisdiction of the count of Flanders. The Patershol developed at the foot of the Gravensteen. This was initially a military area, later becoming a district for advocates and lawyers and eventually becoming an industrial area. In the 14th century, the counts of Flanders gave up the uncomfortable Gravensteen for the more luxurious Prinsenhof where, on 24 February 1500, Karel van Habsburg – the future emperor Charles V – was born. The Prinsenhof was approximately 2 ha in size and was fully walled in. Not much remains of the enormous complex. The Rabotwijk area along the Lieve is Ghent's largest industrial district.

The Oudburger, near Patershol

SIGHTS AT A GLANCE

Church
Augustijnenklooster St.-Stefanus ❾

Buildings
Gravensteen ❶
Karmelietenklooster ❹
Oud Begijnhof St.-Elisabeth ❺
Oude Vismijn ❸
Provinciaal Cultuurcentrum Caermersklooster ❿
Rabot ❻

Museum
Huis van Alijn ⓫

Streets and squares
Prinsenhof ❼
St.-Veerleplein ❷

Other
Stroppendrager ❽

GHENT TOURISM
Belfort, Botermarkt 17A.
Map 2 D3.
As of Feb-Mar 2012:
Oude Vismijn, St.-Veerleplein 5.
Map 1 C2. ***Tel.*** *09-2665660.*
www.visitgent.be *Mid-Mar to mid-Oct daily 9am-6:30pm; mid-Oct to mid-Mar daily 9:30am-4:30pm.*

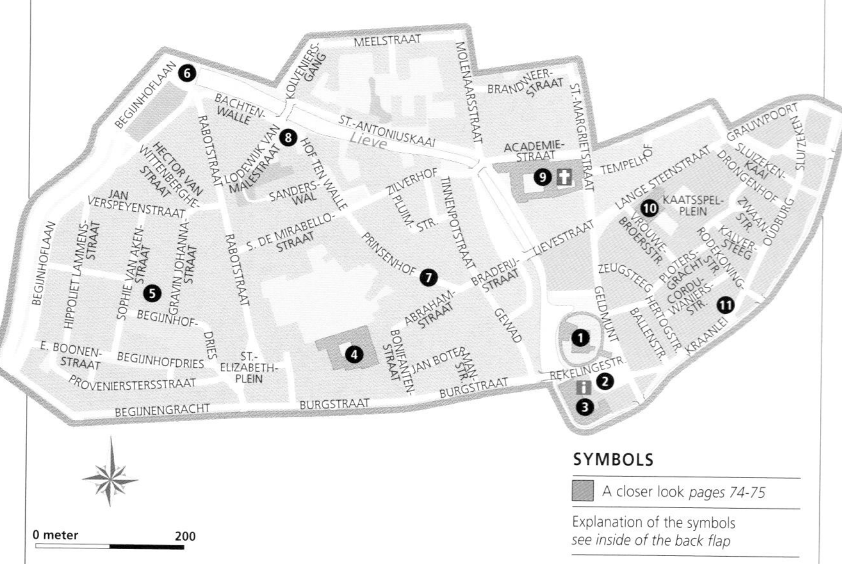

SYMBOLS

A closer look *pages 74-75*

Explanation of the symbols *see inside of the back flap*

◁ **Exploring the Patershol, a medieval district in the shadow of the Gravensteen**

A closer look: Patershol and surroundings

The Patershol is one of the oldest districts in Ghent. Its enclosed medieval street design is still clearly evident. Until the 17th century, this was the *ploter* (tanners') district. During the 17th and 18th centuries, advocates and lawyers involved with the court of the Council of Flanders established themselves in the district. When the Gravensteen was sold and transformed into an industrial area, the magistracy disappeared from the Patershol. The houses in the Patershol were divided into small residences for factory workers. Narrow alleyways closed in any remaining free space. At the start of the 20th century, the Patershol was a poor area that featured taverns, brothels and inns. Starting in 1980, the district was revitalised and now it is an attractive residential district with many restaurants.

Plotersgracht
In 1872, the canal Plotersgracht was filled in. It now forms the main street of the Patershol.

★ Gravensteen
In this fortress, the counts of Flanders lived, the judges of the Council of Flanders held office, suspected criminals were tortured and labourers toiled for their daily bread. ❶

LIEVE

GELDMUNT

REKELINGESTRAAT

ST. VEERLE-PLEIN

LEIE

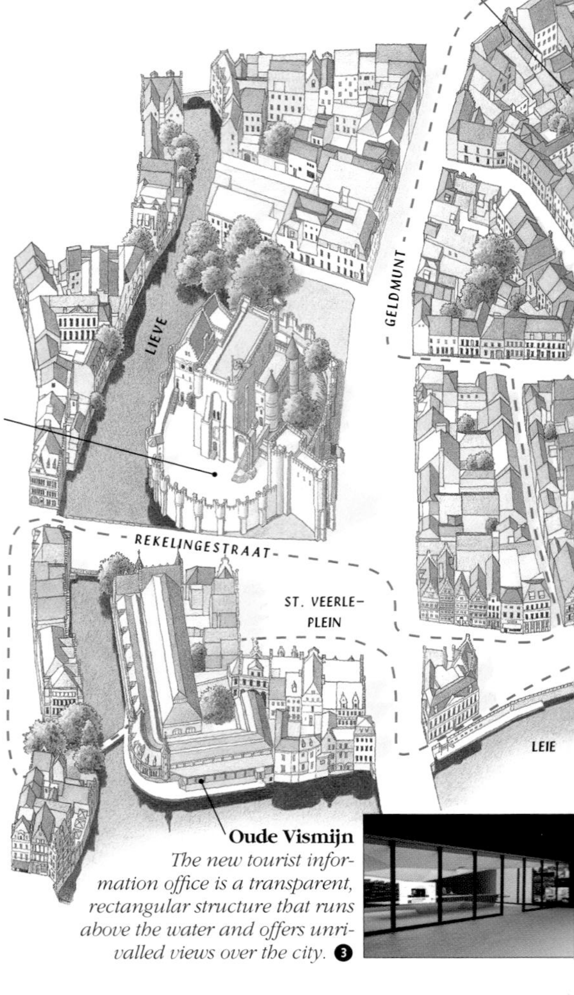

Oude Vismijn
The new tourist information office is a transparent, rectangular structure that runs above the water and offers unrivalled views over the city. ❸

STAR ATTRACTIONS

- ★ Gravensteen
- ★ Provinciaal Cultuurcentrum Caermersklooster
- ★ Huis van Alijn

★ Provinciaal Cultuurcentrum Caermersklooster
This cultural centre, that presents one-of-a-kind exhibits, is located in the former chapel of the monastery of the Calced Carmelites. ❾

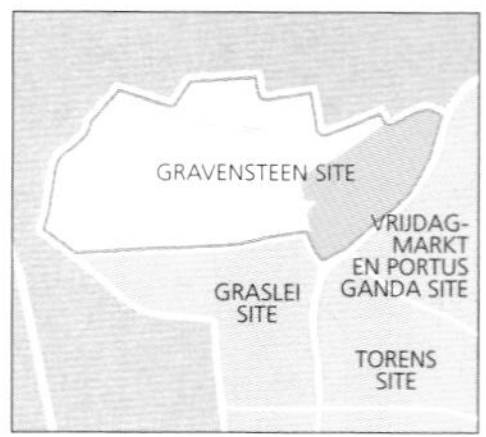

LOCATOR MAP
See Street guide, map 1.

SYMBOLS

– – Recommended route

0 meter 100

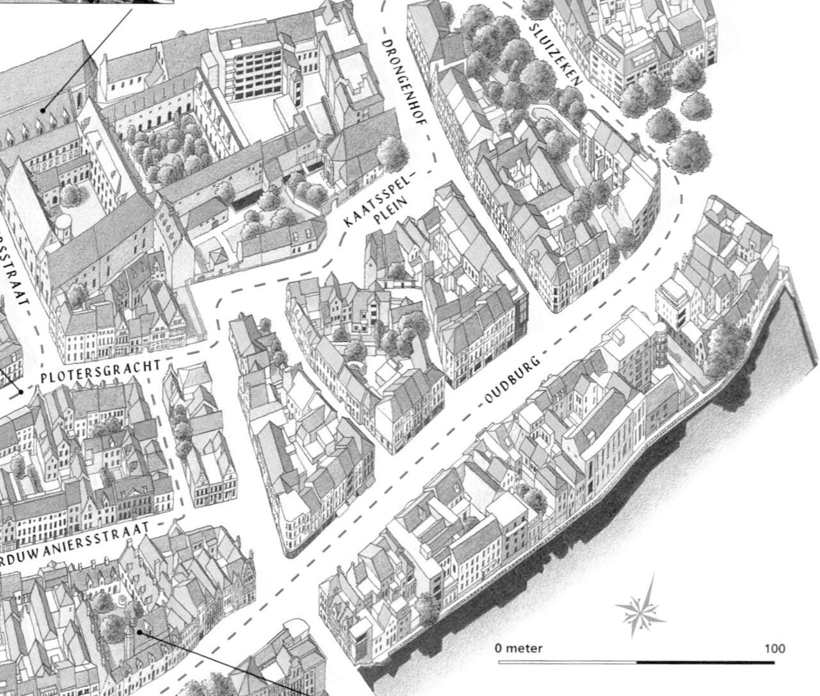

THE NAME PATERSHOL

Patershol

The residents of the district used to draw their water from the Plotersgracht. When the priests from the Caermersklooster extended their monastery across the Plotersgracht, they left open an entrance to a well, where residents could draw water. This was quickly named the 'Hol van de paters', hole of the fathers, or Patershol. Later, this became the name of the entire district.

★ Huis van Alijn
A fascinating museum that uses objects, curios, film and audio to cast light on daily life during the 20th century. ❼

HISTORIC CENTRE
GRAVENSTEEN SITE

Gravensteen ❶

Pages 78-79.

St.-Veerleplein ❷

Map 1 C2.

At the foot of the Gravensteen lies the intimate and beautiful square St.-Veerleplein. This name refers to the St.-Veerlekerk, the royal church of the counts of Flanders, which was constructed in 1212 and demolished in 1581. Until the end of the 18th century, the square was the place of justice for criminals and the only place where forgers were punished. From 1780 to 1900, a market was held here where exotic fruits and vegetables were traded. The square is surrounded by beautiful uniform buildings, originally built between the 16th to the 18th century, and restored with historical accuracy prior to the 1913 World's Fair.

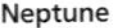

Neptune

Oude Vismijn ❸

St.-Veerleplein 5. **Map** 1 C2-3.

The 17th-century Vismijn or Vismarkt (fish market) is endowed with a monumental baroque-style entrance gate built in 1689. Above the gate, **Neptune** stands with his trident on a chariot drawn by two winged horses. He is flanked on the left by Hercules, representing the Scheldt, while on the right, the graceful young Venus symbolises the Leie. As of Feb-Mar 2012, Ghent's new Tourism information office will be located here.

Karmelietenklooster ❹

Burgstraat 46. **Map** 1 B2.
***Tel.** 09-2255787. Mon-Fri 7am-11:30am and 2:30pm-7pm (Sat-Sun to 6pm).*
www.karmel-gent.be

In 1651, the order of the Calced Carmelites purchased the Leeuwenmeers, part of the former Prinsenhof. Its name is derived from the

Chapel of the Carmelite monastery

lions brought back by emperor Charles V after his victory over the Ottomans at Tunis (1535) and kept here. Their last descendants, *Burgundia* and *Flandria*, lived until around 1650. Behind the austere façade of the **kloosterkerk** (1714) one finds a large church combining baroque and classical styles. The Rustpunt is a centre for spirituality, tranquillity and the deepening of insight.

Oud Begijnhof St.-Elisabeth ❺

Begijnhofdries. **Map** 1 A2.
www.elisabethbegijnhof.be

St.-Veerleplein at the foot if the Gravensteen on a sunny day

Beguine homes in the Oud Begijnhof

In 1234, countess Johanna of Constantinople founded the St.-Elisabeth beguinage in 'Het Broek', a district just beyond the first city wall. This beguinage was intended for impoverished women from the elite and middle class. With its rectangular bulwark, it formed a city within the city and could only be accessed through a single gate. Towards the middle of the 19th century, the beguinage became embroiled in the struggle between the liberal and catholic movements in the city. As a result of this conflict, the beguines were forced to relocate to a new beguinage in St.-Amandsberg (*page 118*) and the St.-Elisabeth beguinage was dismantled. The monumental entrance gate was demolished, new streets were laid and old streets were widened. Existing buildings were, for the most part, preserved and the original central square was transformed into a small park. Although the beguines have been gone for more than a century now, the beguinage still has an enclosed, village-like feel to it.
A contemporary work of art that bears a resemblance to a gateway now stands in the place where the original gatehouse was once located. The gateway was dismantled around 1913 and relocated to the site at which the 1913 World Exhibitions was held. It was later moved to the Bijlokemuseum (now the STAM City Museum of Ghent, *see pages 108-109*), situated in Godshuizenlaan.

Rabot ❻

Opgeëistenlaan 1. **Map** 1 A1.

The Rabot, also called the Drie Torekens, is one of the few remaining structures that formed part of the 14 km-long city wall. During the 13th century, the Lieve was excavated to pass through the Wondelgemse Meersen. This canal linked Ghent to the ocean via Damme and the Zwin. Nine sluice gates – rabots – were incorporated into the canal. With the help of raising partitions, these sluice gates regulated the water level in the canal. The sluice gates were also a means of defence. When Ghent was besieged by the Roman emperor Maximilian in 1488, the grounds outside the city walls were purposely flooded using these sluice gates. Between 1489 and 1491, the first sluice gate that Ghent relied on was reinforced with the addition of two interconnected towers across the Lieve. It was possible to shut off the water using a drop-gate. When the patent laws were scrapped in 1860 and the city gateways lost their function, the Rabot was used as a gunpowder magazine, an ice-house and an inn. In 1872, the part of the Lieve behind the Rabot was filled in.

The Rabot, a sluice gate inside the city at the end of the Lieve

Gravensteen ❶

The imposing Gravensteen is a walled fortress consisting of a gatehouse, a donjon, the Huis van de Graaf and various annexes. The counts of Flanders lived in this stronghold, while judges passed sentence, suspects were tortured, convicts were imprisoned and labourers toiled in the factories here. The history of the fortress goes back to the start of the 10th century when count Arnulf I the Great commissioned the building of a simple wooden structure (castrum) on the Oudburg island. Count Philip of Alsace extended the fortress, which had meanwhile been converted to a stone structure, making it a donjon more than 30 m in height with a gatehouse and a round defensive wall with battlements. Today, an imaginary count Philip and his Portuguese wife, Mathilde, take visitors on a journey of discovery all the way from the 12th to the 21st century.

Wall-walk
The gatehouse and the wall-walk emphasise the defensive character of the castle. The wall-walk was defended with the help of 24 bastions featuring arrow loops, murder holes and battlements with hatches.

★ Audiëntiezaal
The count of Flanders received his guests in this audience room. Later, the Council of Flanders sat here. During the 19th century, this area housed the machinery for a cotton spinning mill.

STAR ATTRACTIONS

★ Audiëntiezaal

★ Bovenzaal

★ Poortgebouw

TIMELINE

1st and 2nd century Gallo-Roman settlement.

1180 Philip of Alsace (1186-1191) Motte castle with upper- and forecourt.

1355 Count's residence relocated to Hof ter Walle (the future Prinsenhof).

0-200 | 900 | 1000 | 1100 | 1200 | 1300 | 140

Start of 10th century Arnulf I the Great (918-965) Wooden structures.

End of 11th century Stone hall structure.

1216 Dedication of St.-Veerlekerk.

1407 Council of Flanders seated in Gravensteen. The Gravensteen building receives new purpose as court of justice and prison.

★ Bovenzaal
The upper hall of the donjon houses the Weapons Museum.

TIPS FOR VISITORS

St.-Veerleplein 11. **Map** 1 C2. ***Tel.*** *09-2259306.* *Apr-Sep 9am-6pm; Oct-Mar 9am-5pm.*

★ Poortgebouw
A view of the gatehouse (1870) prior to the demolishing of the houses built against it.

Suikerlade
The prisoners were held in a large metal cage (suikerlade) in the former count's chapel.

1774 Relocation of the Council of Flanders to the Jesuit monastery in Voldersstraat.

After 1850 Factories relocate to the outskirts of the city. Demolition of the Gravensteen looms.

1907 Gravensteen opened to the public.

1500 | 1600 | 1700 | 1800 | 1900 | 2000

1779 Jean Denis Brismaille purchases the Gravensteen and establishes a cotton mill and metal workshops.

1865 City of Ghent purchases the Gravensteen.

1893 Major restoration works begin.

1980 Second round of restoration works begin.

Boating on the Lieve near the Augustijnenkaai

Prinsenhof 7

Prinsenhof and surroundings. **Map** 1 B2.

The **Brug der Keizerlijke Geneugten** (bridge) across the Lieve provides access to the site Prinsenhof from the St.-Antoniuskaai (quay). Four life-size sculptures, designed by the sculptor Walter De Buck (1936), give the pedestrian bridge across the Leie an 'imperial' look. The Prinsenhof is the name given to the area around the former Hof ten Walle where, on 24 February 1500, young Charles of Luxembourg – the future emperor Charles V – was born. The Hof ten Walle court was built in the mid-14th century for the Flemish-Italian banker, Simon de Mirabello (ca. 1280-1346). In 1355, the counts of Flanders exchanged the Gravensteen for the more comfortable Hof ten Walle. After the birth of Charles V, the residence was named the Prinsenhof. The complex comprised approximately 2 ha and was completely walled in. The only evidence that remains of the Prinsenhof is the Noordpoort gate (now called the Donkere Poort). A boiler house and factory warehouses, the remains of a former cotton mill, are found not far from the gatehouse. *Also see* Princes and beguines, *pages 124-125*.

Brug der Keizerlijke Geneugten

Stroppendrager 8

Bachtenwalle. **Map** 1 A1.

This life-size statue of the *Stroppendrager* (noose bearer has stood in the park in front of the Donkere Poort since the year 2000. The sculpture was designed by Ghent artist Chris Demangel. In 1537, Charles V imposed an extra war tax on Ghent. The citizens protested and refused to pay. Irritated with the stubbornness of the citizens of Ghent, the emperor decided to personally restore order. He travelled to Ghent and, after short legal proceedings, declared the city guilty of disobedience, breach of agreement, incitement, mutiny and lese majesty. As its punishment, Ghent lost its freedoms and privileges. The city charters were surrendered and all its goods impounded. The Klokke Roeland was removed from the Belfort. In addition, the emperor demanded that the St.-Baafs abbey make way for a citadel. However, the greatest humiliation took place on 3 May 1540. On this day, a procession of prominent citizens departed from the town hall to the Prinsenhof, barefoot and clothed only in black garments. At the back of the procession were fifty 'creesers' (instigators, ringleaders) dressed only in their undershirts and with nooses around their necks. At the Prinsenhof, they had to bow down to the emperor and beg his sister, Maria of Hungary, for mercy. Every year, during the Gentse Feesten, the stroppendragers parade through the city.

Stroppendrager

Augustijnenklooster St.-Stefanus 9

Academiestraat 1. **Map** 1 B2-C2. ***Tel.*** *09-2251659.* *church: 7am-12:30pm, 2pm-6:30pm.*

The Augustijnenklooster is a well-preserved monastery. On 24 November 1296, the bishop of Doornik granted the Augustinians, who had established themselves in the city a year earlier, permission to build a monastery and a church. In 1582, the church and the monastery were almost completely destroyed during the iconoclasm. From 1621, the Augustijnenklooster was rebuilt. Between 1718 and 1720, the impressive monastery library was constructed as the final piece of the monastery. This has remained well-preserved to this day and it is possible to view it (by appointment).

Provinciaal Cultuurcentrum Caermersklooster 10

Vrouwebroersstraat 6. **Map** 1 C2. ***Tel.*** *09-2692910.* *Tue-Sun 10am-5pm.* **www**.caermersklooster.be

In 1287, the Calced Carmelites or *caermers* purchased the house of refuge of the Cambron abbey in Lange Steenstraat, where they built a monastery and church. During the time of the Calvinist Republic (1578-1584), the friars were driven from their monastery, but when they returned at the end of the 17th century, the buildings were restored. The order disbanded during the French Revolution. A few of the brothers succeeded in buying back the monastery, but they were forced to leave for good in 1841. The monastery was then converted into a factory and warehouse. Later, the Archaeological Museum and the Museum of Folklore were housed in the church. In 1977, the province of East-Flanders took over ownership of the monastery complex, after which restoration work to the church and the house of refuge was carried out. Since 1998, the monastery has been home to the Provinciaal Cultuurcentrum (Provincial cultural centre), which organises high-profile exhibitions on a regular basis. Currently, the first courtyard and the large- and small rectory are being restored.

Exhibition area in the Caermersklooster

Huis van Alijn ⓫

Kraanlei 65. **Map** 1 C2.
Tel. *09-2692350.* *Tue-Sat 11am-5pm, Sun 10am-5pm.* *puppet theatre: see page 243.* **www**.huisvanalijn.be

The museum Huis van Alijn is located within the Kinderen Alijnshospitaal (1363), the only alms-house in Ghent that has remained preserved. This museum has left behind its traditional past function as a Museum of folklore, and now presents itself as the epitome of modernisation and creativity. Through the use of everyday objects and items, the Huis van Alijn provides an overview of life in Ghent from 1900 onwards, all the way from subjects' birth to their death. Digital photo albums, audio recordings and film- and video clips with the utmost effect in order to illustrate the changes in daily life that occurred during the 20th century, the rooms, furnished in fifties, sixties and seventies style, bring back fond memories. On every Saturday afternoon, the brilliant Puppet theatre presents a performance all about the antics of Pierke (a character from Flemish folklore) watched by children as well as adults.

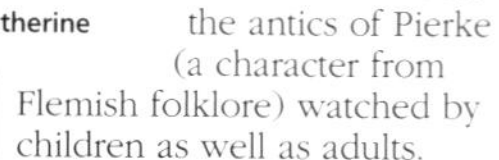

Saint Catherine

The beautiful courtyard garden of the Huis van Alijn, a former almshouse, is an oasis of peace

Jacob
Van Artevelde.

VRIJDAGMARKT AND PORTUS GANDA SITE

The Vrijdagmarkt has played an important role in the history of the city. This square was the scene for festivals, riots, executions, and since the Middle Ages, the weekly market. Historic buildings with lovely step gables and bell gables are surrounding the Vrijdagmarkt; the guildhall of the Huidenvetters ('t Toreken) is the structure that draws the most attention. The Gothic-style St.-Jacobskerk (church) dominates the small Bij St Jacobs square. A flea market is held here on Fridays and weekends. For centuries, the Scheldt and the Leie met at the Portus Ganda, the birthplace of the city of Ghent. In 1960, the Nederschelde – or the Reep – was filled in. In 2003, the first part of the Scheldt was once again connected to the Leie. Portus Ganda is now the name of the city's marina. On the opposite bank of the Leie, the forgotten ruins of St.-Baafsabdij form an oasis of peace.

SIGHTS AT A GLANCE

Churches and monasteries
St.-Baafsabdij 9
St.-Jacobskerk 6

Buildings
Hof van Ryhove 4
Huys van Oombergen 5
Ons Huis – Bond Moyson 1
RTT- or Belgacomtoren 12
't Toreken | Poëziecentrum 2
Zwembad Van Eyck 11

Museum
MIAT (Museum Industrial Archaeology and Textiles) 8

Street
Werregarenstraat 3

Park
Baudelopark 7

Harbour
Portus Ganda 10

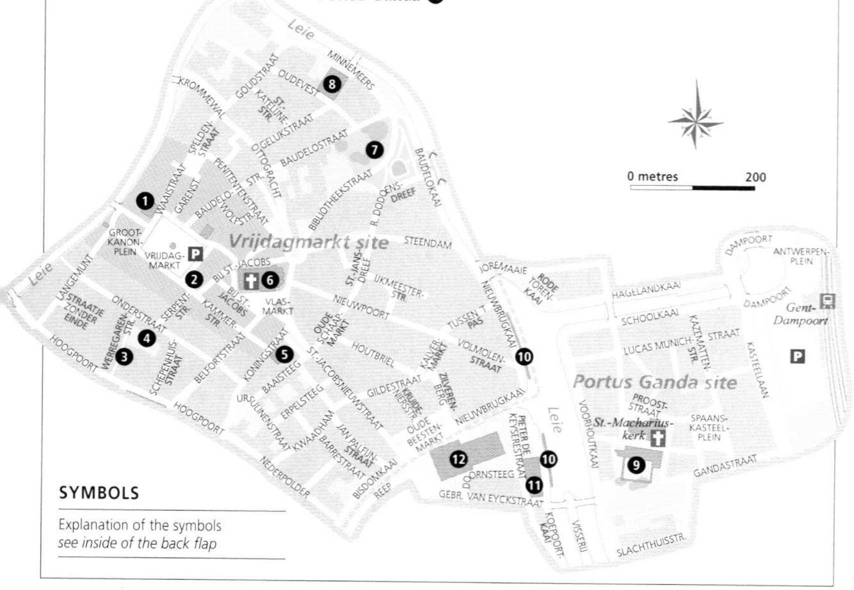

0 metres 200

SYMBOLS

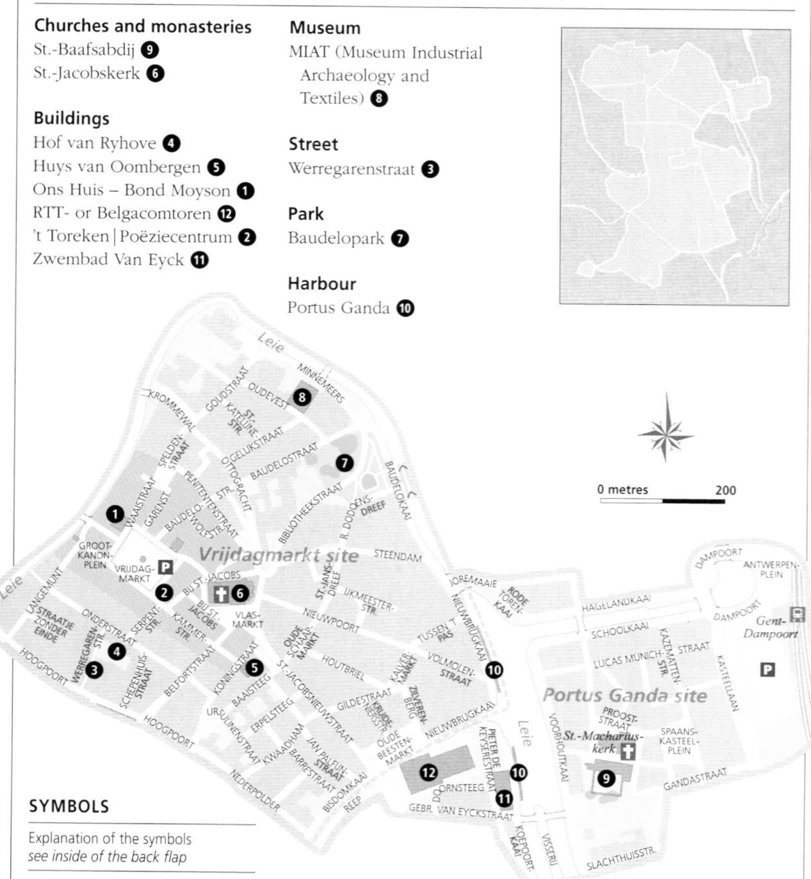

Explanation of the symbols
see inside of the back flap

◁ **Hero Jacob van Artevelde looks out over the Vrijdagmarkt**

Exploring the Vrijdagmarkt

The Vrijdagmarkt played an important role in political and social life in the city. Large festivals, jousting tournaments and joyous inaugurations of new rulers took place here, as did revolts and battles. Since the 16th century, public executions have been carried on the square, the last of which took place in 1863. The square is named after the market that's been held here since the 12th century. A life-size statue of Jacob van Artevelde, the 14th-century hero of Ghent, stands in the middle of the square. The St.-Jacobskerk is one of the oldest parish churches in the city. On weekends, a flea market is held on the church square.

Jacob van Artevelde
Van Artevelde has been pointing towards England since 1863. He succeeded in having the boycott on English textile imports lifted, but this cost him his life. ⑧

Zuivelbrug
The Zuivelbrug across the Leie links the Vrijdagmarkt to the Patershol. ②

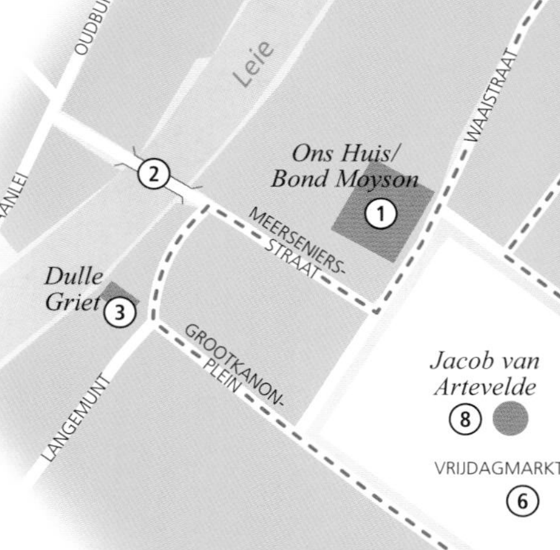

Dulle Griet
No shot was ever fired in Ghent from this cannon, weighing over 12,500 kg. Ghent locals call it Dulle Griet, or Mad Meg. ③

Ons Huis – Bond Moyson
Both of these buildings – built with the purpose of party headquarters and warehouse in mind – symbolise the power and prestige of the labour movement in Ghent. ①

SYMBOLS

– – Recommended route

Lakenmetershuis
The Lakenmetershuis, built between 1770 and 1772 for the cloth measurers, looks like a canal home in Amsterdam with its double stairway and decorative neck gable. ⑦

St.-Jacobskerk
This 12th-century church has an impressive Romanesque western façade flanked by two steeple towers. ⑤

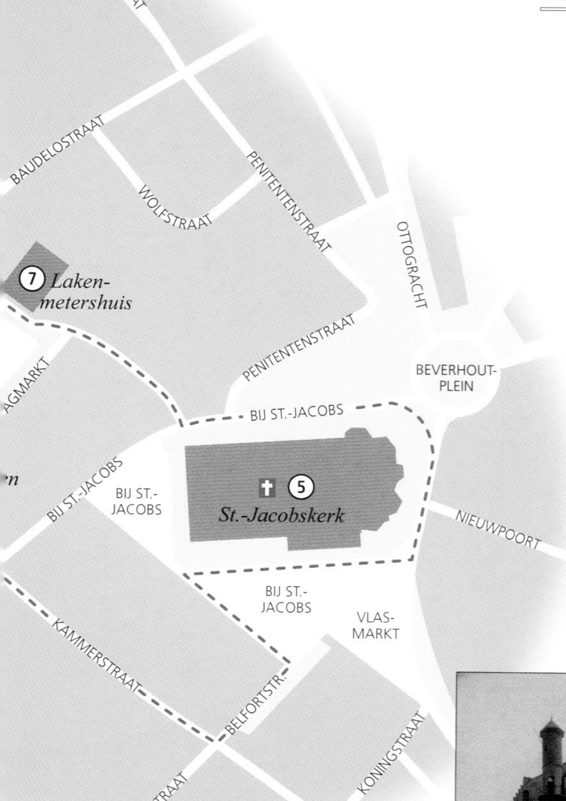

Vrijdagmarkt
Since the 12th century, Friday morning markets have been held on this square. The market bell in 't Toreken signals the opening and closing of the market. ⑥

't Toreken
This prestigious tanners' company house dates to between 1451 and 1458. Linen rejected due to poor quality was hung from the railing of the round turret as a warning signal. ④

HISTORIC CENTRE
VRIJDAGMARKT SITE

Ons Huis - Bond Moyson ❶

Vrijdagmarkt 9-10. **Map** 2 C2.

This imposing complex was designed for the 'Socialistische Werkersvereenigingen' (Socialist Workers Union) partly as a public house (Ons Huis) and partly as 'Groote Magazijnen' (the great warehouse, headquarters of the Gentse Bond Moyson since 1958). Fernand Dierckens, who also drew up the designs for the Kunstencentrum Vooruit, built it in an eclectic style between 1897 and 1902.

't Toreken | Poëziecentrum ❷

Vrijdagmarkt 36. **Map** 2 D2.
Tel. *09-2252225.* *Mon-Sat 10am-6pm.*
www.poeziecentrum.be

't Toreken was the company house of the tanners. It was constructed between 1450 and 1483 in Gothic style with a step gable and a stair tower that serves as a prominent landmark. Most of its trade was in linen. Pieces of linen that didn't meet quality and size requirements were hung from the balustrade of the tower as a warning signal. The building was sold at public sale when Charles V brought an end to the power of the guilds in 1542. The mermaid on the tower summit is *Melusine*, the spirit of fresh waters. The building now houses the Poëziecentrum, a centre which promotes the reading of poetry.

't Toreken, tanners' company house

Graffiti artist at work in Werregarenstraat

Werregarenstraat ❸

Map 1 C3.

One of the most fun streets in Ghent is the Werregarenstraat, better known as the 'graffiti alley'. Here, graffiti artists have free rein and are welcome to leave behind their *tags* (small images by which an artist is recognised by his fellows) and *pieces* (larger images). The artworks are constantly and quickly refreshed, so that the alley never looks the same for more than a week.

Hof van Ryhove ❹

Onderstraat 22. **Map** 1 C3.
garden: Mon-Fri 9am-5pm.

The history of the building goes back to the middle of the 12th century. At the start of the 13th century, existing buildings had to make way for a new residence. The gable on the garden side is one of the oldest step gables in Ghent. In 1371, this stately home came into the possession of Simon de Rijke, a descendant of a prominent family of cloth traders. Around 1518, the home was converted into a luxurious royal residence. It was taken over by the Van der Kethulle family, who played an important role in Ghent politics. During the 18th and 19th century, the interior was updated to suit the style of the time. The gate provides access to a small medieval Flemish garden with a historically accurate selection of plants. Currently, the building houses various city service offices.

Huys van Oombergen ❺

Koningstraat 18. **Map** 2 D3.

The academy 'Koninklijke Vlaamse Academie' is one of the most attractive homes from 18th-century Ghent. In 1746, David 't Kindt took ownership of the Huys van Oombergen and converted it into a beautiful stately home in the Louis XV style. In 1893, the Koninklijke Academie voor Nederlandse Taal- en Letterkunde (Royal Academy for Dutch Language and Literature) occupied the building. The dome is crowned by a celestial sphere. Much of the home's original interior has remained preserved.

Rear façade of the Hof van Ryhove

St.-Jacobskerk ❻

Bij St.-Jacobs. **Map** 2 D3. ***Tel.*** *09-2232526.* ◯ *Apr-Oct Fri-Sat 9:30am-12:30pm.*

The two massive western towers and the beautifully restored western portal give the St.-Jacobskerk a Romanesque look. The sombre stone church building, built in the honor of St James, houses an interesting collection of church treasures and 17th-century paintings. During the 12th century, the simple wooden church that had originally stood here was replaced by a stone church. This building was then modified, extended and, after the iconoclasms, restored in baroque style. The church has a Gothic-styled interior. Treasures inside the church include various paintings, the tomb of the obstetrician Jan Palfijn (1650-1730) and the sacramental tower built in 1593, one of the few that remain preserved in Flanders.

Baudelopark ❼

Map 2 D2.

The Baudelopark has always been an open and spacious area. During the 16th century, it was the garden of the Baudelo abbey. This garden formed an islet between the Leie, the Ottogracht and two other canals. During French rule, the *école centrale* (central school) was placed in the abbey and the cloister garden was reconstructed as a botanical garden. When the university relocated the garden to the outskirts of the Citadelpark in 1903, the Baudelopark became Ghent's first public park. At the start of the previous century, the city centre and the harbour were connected by a road, which divided the park into two. At the insistence of the area residents, the road was replaced with a bicycle and walking path, once again uniting the park.

LIEVEN BAUWENS

Lieven Bauwens (1769-1822), born in Waaistraat near the Vrijdagmarkt, came from a Ghent family of tanners and traders. Through his contacts in The Netherlands, Hamburg and England, he succeeded in smuggling the *mule jenny*, a spinning machine, from England.

This enabled him to become the first person on the European continent to supply mechanically spun cotton thread from his businesses in Ghent and the Oude Abdij van Drongen. In 1810, he was mayor of Ghent for a single year. Partly due to his ties to the French government, his businesses went bankrupt in 1814. Disillusioned, he passed away in Paris in 1822. Bauwens' role in Ghent's history is controversial. Some consider him a hero and an altruist, while others see him as an unscrupulous businessmen who oppressed his workers.

The Gothic-style interior of the St.-Jacobskerk creates an impression of enormous space

MIAT ❽

Minnemeers 9. **Map** 2 D2. ***Tel.*** *09-2694200.* *10am-6pmr.* **www**.miat.gent.be

No other place presents the history of Ghent as a textile city like the MIAT does. The museum describes the history of the textile industry and industrial society from 1750 to the present day. It is located in the former Desmet-Guèquier cotton mill, which was constructed to resemble a cotton mill in Manchester, England. The MIAT has an extensive collection. Authentic machines, including the famous mule jenny – the symbol of Ghent's rise as a textile city – can be viewed on the fifth floor. The new *Wereld-WijdWerken* exhibit on the fourth floor tells the story of the working and social lives of six generations of a single family from the start of the 19th century until today. The MIAT contains a reconstructed cinema, dating back to the period between the wars, in which classic movies are screened every second Sunday of the month. *Katoenkabaal* follows the cotton production process step-by-step, from cultivation on a cotton plantation to its emergence as a 'smart' textile. On the first floor, the museum presents temporary exhibitions. In the dye garden, you'll find forty indigenous plants used for the dyeing of textiles, including woad, madder and dyer's rocket. The corner of the garden features a statue of **Pierre De Geyter**, the composer of *De Internationale*, the labour movement's anthem. From the top floor, there's a lovely view over the city.

Textile machinery in the MIAT

Pierre De Geyter

HISTORIC CENTRE
PORTUS GANDA SITE

St.-Baafsabdij ❾

Entrance: Voorhoutkaai.
Map 2 E3-F3. *end Apr-start Nov. Sun 12pm-5pm.*
www.burenvandeabdij.be

The ruins of the once mighty abbey St.-Baafsabdij form an oasis of peace just a few minutes' walk from the St.-Baafskathedraal. One of Ghent's best-kept secrets is hidden behind the abbey wall. During the 7th century, Amandus founded the Ganda abbey at the confluence of the Leie and the Scheldt. After the death of Bavo van Gent in 653 (*page 57*), the abbey was named after him. The abbey church became a popular pilgrimage site where relics were worshipped, the most important being those of Bavo and Macharius. In the 9th century, the Normans destroyed the abbey. During the 10th century, it was rebuilt under the leadership of count Arnulf de Grote. Between the 12th

The romantic ruins of the St.-Baafsabdij at the confluence of the Leie and the Scheldt

The Van Eyck swimming pool with its glass roof in striking art deco style

and 15th century, the abbey was at its prime and was extended and rebuilt a number of times. In 1540, emperor Charles V ordered the demolition of large parts of the abbey building. A Spanish castle arose on the site of the abbey with the purpose of restraining the rebellious people of Ghent. Between 1827 and 1834 the castle was demolished, while the remains of the abbey were preserved as ruins. The abbey church occupied the area that is now a small park. During the 19th century, there was a slaughterhouse on this site, of which only the gatehouse remains. Now, the former abbey church has risen again with an abundance of greenery and the walls of the forgotten church laid out in hornbeam hedges. An open-air theatre has been created in the choir area and the current, overgrown abbey looks like a romantic ruin. The heart of the abbey, the cloister, has remained partly preserved, while the exterior garden and other green zones around the abbey are ecologically managed, ensuring that more than 150 species of wild plants thrive here. The refectory creates an imposing impression. A number of tombstones have been erected in this hall. The Steenmuseum, featuring extraordinary finds and objects from the abbey and other Ghent monuments, has been set up in the crypt under the refectory.

Tombstone

Portus Ganda 10

Nieuwbrugkaai, Voorhoutkaai and Rodetorenkaai. **Map** 2 E3. **www.** portus ganda.be

Portus Ganda, the recently-constructed marina in Ghent, is located at the confluence of the Leie and the Scheldt. In 1959, the Nederschelde or Reep was filled in and, 43 years down the line, the newly re-excavated Nederschelde was reconnected to the Leie prior to the complete reopening of the city waterways.

Zwembad Van Eyck 11

Veermanplein 1. **Map** 2 E3.

This swimming pool was designed in 1886 by Edmond De Vigne and was the first covered swimming facility in Flanders. The inscriptions 'Bains' and 'Badhuis' can still be read on the former entrance to the building from the Julius de Vigneplein. In past times, a nearby textile company was used to heat the water. During the 1930s, the swimming pool's interior was decorated in art deco style. Bathing cubicles, fitted with yellow and black tiles, surround the rectangular swimming pool.

RTT or Belgacomtoren 12

Keizer Karelstraat/Nieuwbrug. **Map** 2 E3.

During the 1960s and 1970s, a number of major city architectural developments were constructed that – especially due to their size and height – encroached on the skyline of the historic city centre. In 1961, the buildings around the Nieuwbrug had to make way for the RTT (now Belgacom) tower. This building, considered to be 'the ugliest building in the city' by numerous Ghent residents, will be given a complete facelift in 2012 and will converted into a trendy new apartment complex.

Boats moored in Portus Ganda, Ghent's marina

Ghent in the 19th century

During the 19th century, Ghent was a city of contrasts. It was a case of poor labourers versus wealthy bourgeoisie, French Ghent citizens versus Flemish Ghent citizens and Catholics versus liberals and secularists. These different populations lived closely together in a relatively small city. The presence of a large group of textile labourers led to Ghent becoming the birthplace of the labour movement in Flanders. Edward Anseele stood at the helm of the socialist labour movement in Flanders. His greatest achievement is undoubtedly the establishment of the union called Samenwerkende Maatschappij Vooruit (Cooperative Society).

Gravensteen and Patershol
In the 19th century, the vacant Gravensteen was converted into a spinning factory complex and metal workshops. The Patershol district changed from an influential neighbourhood to a labourers' district. These labourers lived in crowded conditions in large houses and dark beluiken *(dead-end alleys).*

Lieven Bauwens (1769-1822)
Lieven Bauwens paved the way for the mechanical textile industry in Ghent. In 1798, he smuggled components of the mule jenny, a mechanical spinning machine, from England to Paris, where he established his first cotton mill. In 1800, the first factory in Ghent opened.

MIAT
The MIAT is located in the former Desmet-Guèquier cotton mill. This 1905 mill is a fine example of a modern Manchester-style factory building with brick façades. The large steel-framed windows and saw-tooth roof – added later – ensure good interior lighting.

Beluik

A beluik is a small, dead-end ally with tiny homes on either side of it, occupied by labourers during the 19th century. These homes often had no facilities – water had to be brought from a central pump and all inhabitants of the beluik had to share one toilet.

Edward Anseele (1856-1938)

Edward Anseele was born in 1856 in Penitentenstraat (at the St.-Jacobskerk) and is considered the father of Belgian socialism. In Ghent, he established the Samenwerkende Maatschappij Vooruit and the socialist newspaper, Vooruit. He also co-founded the union Belgische Werklieden Partij (Belgian Labour Party).

MULE JENNY

The mule jenny (or spinning mule) is one of the oldest spinning machines in Belgium, brought to Ghent by Lieven Bauwens. The machine symbolises the rise of Ghent as an industrial city. During the 18th century, Ghent's position as an industrial city was under threat due to cheaper exports from England. Thanks to the arrival of this mechanical spinning machine and other machines, and the presence of cheap labour, Ghent – the 'Manchester of Europe' – developed into the most significant industrial city in all of Flanders.

MIAT (Museum for Industrial Archaeology and Textile), **www**.miat.gent.be

De Vooruit

The labour union Samenwerkende Maatschappij Vooruit was originally a bakery from which members could buy bread at a reduced price. The Vooruit became a success story. Before the start of World War I, the company owned more than 100 buildings throughout the entire city, including cotton mills, weaving mills, ironworks, pharmacies and a bank. The union had around nine thousand members.

ZUID AND ST.-PIETERSPLEIN SITE

In 1837, the laying of the first Ghent-Mechelen railway line signalled the start of the development of the Zuidwijk district. Originally, this was the Muinkmeersen, a marshy and undeveloped area that belonged to the abbey, called St.-Pietersabdij. The rail traffic at the Zuidstation, which also served as a freight station, caused a great deal of inconvenience. After the opening of the St.-Pietersstation in 1912, the Zuidstation lost its purpose and it was closed in 1928. The station building and freight yard were demolished and replaced thirty years later by the offices of the Electricity, Gas and Water Services (EGW) of the city of Ghent (which now house the City Library) and Koning Albertpark (King Albert park).

SIGHTS AT A GLANCE

Churches
- Onze Lieve Vrouw-St.-Pieterskerk ⑩
- St.-Annakerk ④

Buildings
- Boekentoren ⑫
- Klein Begijnhof Onze-Lieve-Vrouw ter Hoyen ③
- Kunstencentrum Vooruit ⑤
- Leopoldskazerne ⑬

Museums
- De wereld van Kina: het Huis ⑪
- Kunsthal St.-Pietersabdij ⑧

Streets and squares
- De Zuid ①
- St.-Pietersplein ⑦
- Waalse Krook ⑥

Parks
- Koning Albertpark ②
- Tuin van de St.-Pietersabdij ⑨

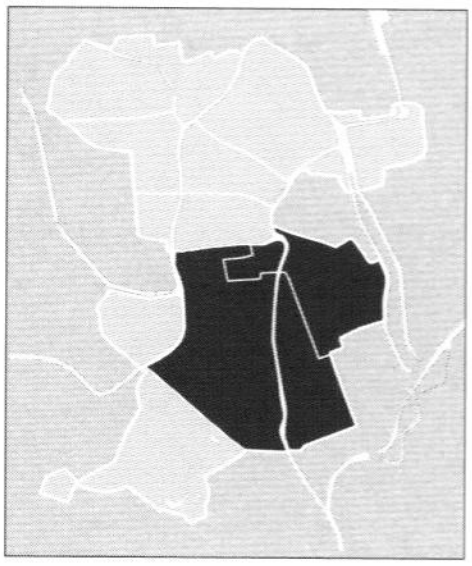

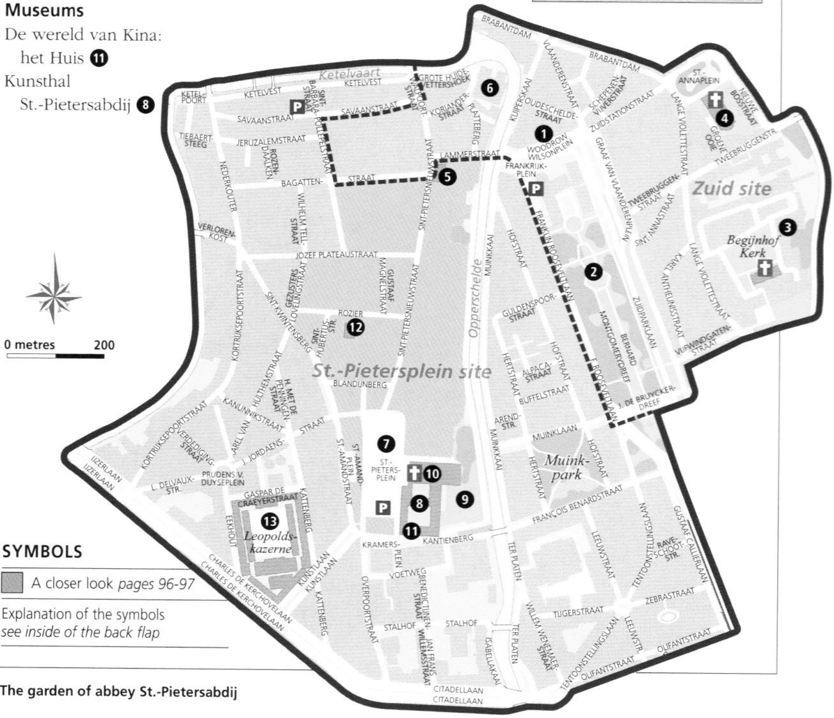

0 metres 200

SYMBOLS

A closer look *pages 96-97*

Explanation of the symbols *see inside of the back flap*

◁ **The garden of abbey St.-Pietersabdij**

ART DISTRICT

ZUID SITE

The Zuid ❶

Map 2 D5-E5

The Graaf van Vlaanderenplein, better known as the Zuid, was constructed in 1847 after the opening of the Gent-Zuid station. As a result of the building of the station, the Muinkmeersen – originally an area on the outskirts of the St.-Pietersabdij – developed into a new residential district. Keizer Karelstraat (1837-1841) and later Vlaanderenstraat (1883) connected the Zuidstation with the inner city. The station building and the railway line were demolished in 1928 and replaced with Koning Albertpark (King Albert Park) and a new office complex. The Zuid is now a busy tram- and bus line junction surrounded by the Administratief Centrum, the administrative heart of the city of Ghent, the Central City Library and the **Shopping centre Gent Zuid.**

King Albert I

Koning Albertpark ❷

Map 2 E5.

Around 1930, the Zuidpark was created in art deco style with fixed geometric lines on the site of the former Zuidstation rail yard. Only after the death of **King Albert I** in 1934 was it given the name of Koning Albertpark. The original design of the park has been affected by the construction of the city motorway (B401), the building of the Administratief Centrum (Administrative Centre) and the reconstruction of the park in 2006, after which the last remaining art deco elements disappeared.

Klein Begijnhof Onze-Lieve-Vrouw ter Hoyen ❸

Lange Violettestraat 205.
Map 2 E5.

The sisters, Johannna and Margaretha of Constantinople, the daughters of count Boudewijn IX of Flanders, founded two beguinages in Ghent. These were the Oud (Groot) Begijnhof St.-Elisabeth (1234) in the northwest, and the Klein Begijnhof (1262) in the south of the city. The Klein Begijnhof was built on the Groene Hooie (Green Hay), hence the name Onze-Lieve-Vrouw 'ter Hoyen' (Our Lady 'in the Hay'). It provided shelter to solitary women and, in its prime, housed more than three hundred beguines. In 1862, Duke Engelbert August of Arenberg purchased the beguinage, but it fell into the hands of the Belgian state after World War I, due to the duke's German nationality. The death of the last governess in 2008 heralded the end of beguine life in Ghent after eight hundred years. The Lange Violettestraat gate (1819) provides access to the attractive beguinage. Its homes and convents surround the beguinage meadow and the 17th-century beguinage church. Lime trees and hornbeams surround the square. The St.-Godelieve chapel, the home of the governess, and the former infirmary are located in the southeast corner. The front yards of most of the houses are enclosed by walls. The green gateways feature a saint's name or one of Mary's titles.

Entrance to the Gent Zuid Shopping Centre

St.-Annakerk ❹

St.-Annaplein. **Map** 2 E4-5.

A new church for the rapidly expanding Zuidwijk was planned for St.-Annaplein to

A quiet street in the more than 750 year-old Klein Begijnhof

replace the chapel of St Anna in Lange Violettestraat. City Architect Louis Roelandt worked on the design, but he was later replaced by Jacques Van Hoecke. In 1866, the church was consecrated. It was never completed, with a tower originally planned for its western side. The church was built in the so-called 'Rundbogenstijl', an eclectic style combining Romanesque, Byzantine and Gothic elements. The historic wall murals by the artist Theodoor Canneel give the interior an oriental feel.

Café Vooruit, the place to meet in the art centre

Kunstencentrum Vooruit ❺

St.-Pietersnieuwstraat 23.
Map 2 D5. ***Tel.*** *09-2672820.*
first Sat of every month. For performances, see page 237.
www.vooruit.be

The Vooruit is a Ghent art institution. This spacious art deco café with its newspaper rack, (vegetarian) meals and café performances is a popular spot amongst many (young) Ghent residents. Dance, theatre, literature and music performances are organised in its halls. The rear part of the centre, which borders on the Muinkschelde, is 12 m below the level of the main building in St.-Pietersnieuwstraat and houses a concert hall as well as a theatre. The Vooruit symbolised the Ghent labour movement. In 1910, the Samenwerkende Maatschappij Vooruit (*page 91*) purchased a lot on St.-Pietersnieuwstraat. In building the Vooruit, the socialists wanted to showcase their cultural wealth as a counterpart to the civic Vlaamse Opera and theatre. The opening celebrations that had been planned for 1914 could not be held due to the start of World War I. The Vooruit thrived during the period between the wars, but fell out of fashion after World War II. Today, the art centre Vooruit is one of Ghent's most significant cultural centres.

Waalse Krook ❻

Map 2 D5.

The Waalse Krook lies wedged between the Ketelvaart, the Nederschelde, Walpoortstraat and Lammerstraat. The area is named after the Waalse Krook, a short street that ends where it meets the Scheldt. This name refers to the 'kreuk', the bend that the Scheldt makes here. The former Wintercircus, specifically constructed in 1923 for the purpose of hosting the circus, is one of the buildings that define the image of the area. A new multimedia facility has been built within this historic area, with the Library of the Future and the Centre for New Media featuring prominently as the area's greatest attractions. A number of information technology companies have established themselves in the renovated Wintercircus.

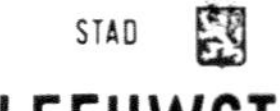

OLIFANT-, LEEUW- AND TIJGERSTRAAT

At one time, Ghent had its own zoo. In 1851, a number of influential Ghent citizens, inspired by the success of the Antwerp Zoo, founded the *Jardin Zoölogique* near the Muinkpark. This animal park was laid out with great care. Betsie the elephant was its pride and joy. However, the zoo was not a great success. It had to close in 1904, and the animals were sold and the site was subdivided. Only the street names are reminiscent of what was once here.

The interior of the St.-Annakerk with its neo-Romanesque and Gothic elements

A closer look: St.-Pietersplein

The 'young' St.-Pietersplein (square) is located in the heart of the student district. The Overpoortstraat is a cluttered student street with a range of cafés, eateries, dance venues and night shops. The street called St.-Pietersnieuwstraat connects the square to the top of the Blandijnberg on top of which stands the 64 m high Boekentoren, symbolising scientific knowledge. The university buildings are located between St.-Pietersnieuwstraat and the Muinkschelde and around the Rozier. Halfway through Lent, the square is transformed into a massive fairground called the Halfvastenfoor.

The Feestlokaal of the Vooruit
The venue for the socialist movement's events consists of two buildings, A café-restaurant on the street side and a hall on the side of the Scheldt. 5

Student district
With around 65,000 students attending the University Ghent and three other colleges, Ghent has the largest student population in Flanders. Many students live in the student district.

SYMBOLS

– – Recommended route

★ Boekentoren
In 1933, architect Henry Van de Vlede designed the Boekentoren (Book tower), which stands atop the Blandijnberg, the highest point in the city. Since its construction, the Ghent skyline has featured four towers. 12

STAR ATTRACTIONS

★ Boekentoren

★ Garden of St.-Pietersabdij

★ Kunsthal St.-Pietersabdij

★ Garden of St.-Pietersabdij
The abbey garden is wedged between the abbey church and the Muinkschelde. It is an oasis of peace with an herb garden, orchard and vineyard. 9

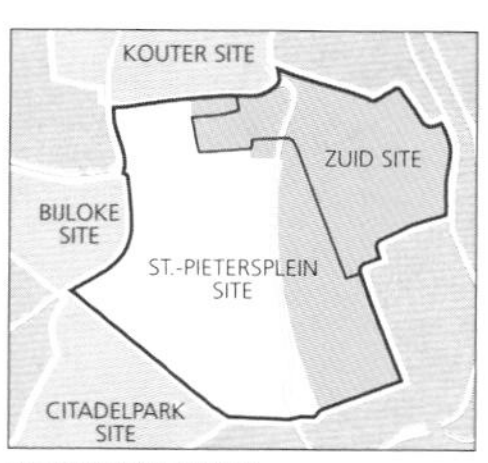

LOCATOR MAP
See Street guide, map 4.

★ Kunsthal St.-Pietersabdij
The Exhibition Hall in the St.-Pietersabdij organises major national and international exhibits. It also houses a small museum dealing with the history of the abbey. 8

ST.-PIETERSPLEIN

ST.-AMANDS-PLEIN

0 meter 100

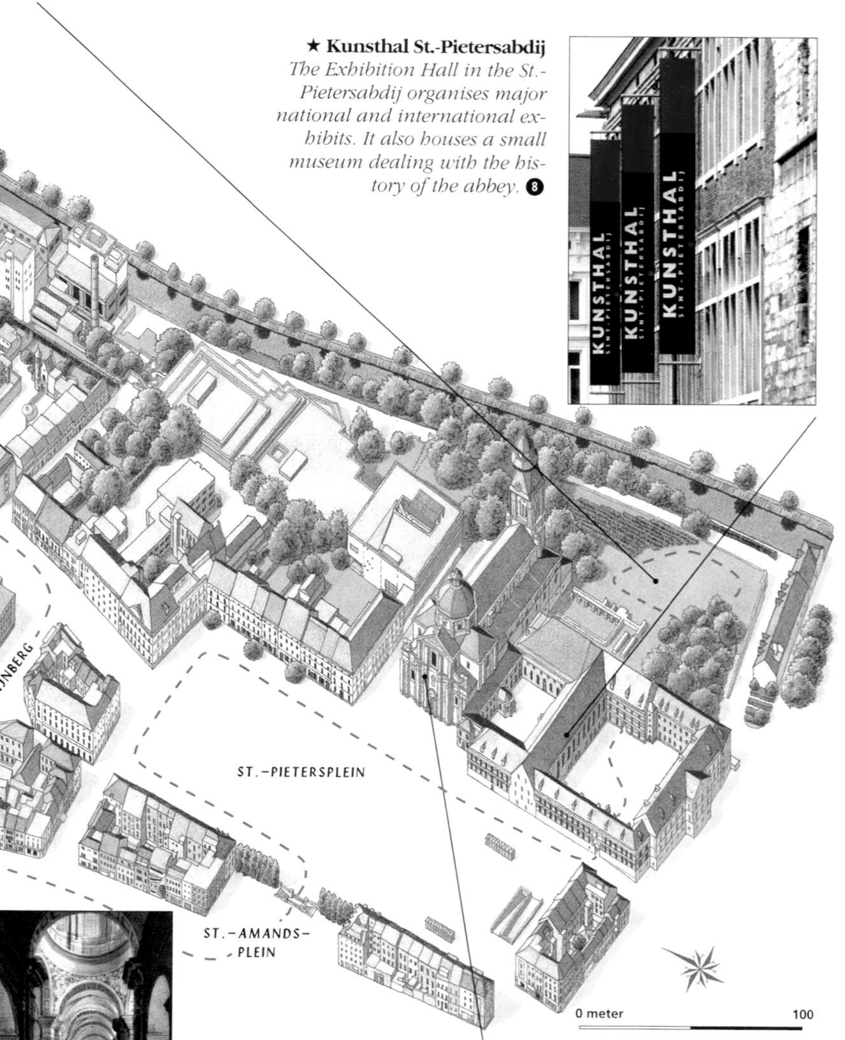

Onze-Lieve-Vrouw St.-Pieterskerk
In 1722, the new baroque-style St.-Pietersabdijkerk was completed. According to a plaque in the apse, the first counts of Flanders were buried here. 10

The Onze-Lieve-Vrouw St.-Pieterskerk is located on St.-Pietersplein, the heart of the St.-Pietersplein site

ARTS DISTRICT
ST.-PIETERSPLEIN SITE

St.-Pietersplein ❼

Map 4 D3.

St.-Pietersplein (*pages 96-97*) is a large rectangular square that resulted from the 1799 demolition of the Onze-Lieve-Vrouw parish church, the luxurious abbot's residence and various other surrounding buildings in 1811. These buildings had to make way for a large military drill area. The square received its current design in 1849 in the context of the urbanisation plan of city architect Leclerc-Restiaux.

Kunsthal St.-Pietersabdij ❽

St.-Pietersplein 9. **Map** 4 D3. ***Tel.*** *09-2439730.* *Tue-Sun 10am-6pm.* *video guide.* **www**4.gent.be/spa

The Kunsthal (art hall) arranges cultural-historical exhibitions in the St.-Pietersabdij. Alison, the virtual monk, accompanies visitors through the abbey in a video guide. The *Tussen Hemel en Aarde (Between Heaven and Earth)* exhibit explains the history of the abbey and the monks that lived here. The Kunsthal also arranges major, thought-provoking exhibitions.

Garden of St.-Pietersabdij ❾

Entrance on St.-Pietersplein. **Map** 4 D3. *Tue-Sun 10am-8pm.*

There is a lovely hidden garden located behind the walls of St.-Pietersabdij. It is wedged into the space between the abbey buildings and the Scheldt. This abbey garden has, over the years, retained its enclosed atmosphere. Kiwi vines and fig trees have been planted along the sunny southern wall and a small vineyard yields approximately one hundred bottles of wine, bearing the *In Monte Blandinio* label, on an annual basis.

FROM BLANDINIUM TO ST.-PIETERSABDIJ

In the 7th century, the missionary Amandus from Aquitaine (a district in southwestern France) founded two abbeys in Ghent. These were Ganda at the confluence of the Leie and the Scheldt (*page 88*) and Blandinium on the southern flanks of the Blandijnberg. Throughout its existence, Blandinium experienced times of prosperity, as well as times of neglect. In 879-880 the abbey, then already called St.-Pietersabdij, was plundered and destroyed by the Normans. The counts of Flanders sponsored its restoration because their ancestors were buried in the monastery church. St.-Pietersabdij became the more powerful of the two large abbeys in Ghent. During the iconoclasms (1566 and 1578) and Calvinist rule, the abbey fell into disrepair. Under the leadership of abbot Joachim Schaeyck (1615-1631), the returning monks restored the abbey to its former glory. In 1796, French rule abolished all religious orders and impounded their property. In 1810, the city of Ghent purchased the derelict buildings and the abbey was used as a barracks. The last military personnel left the barracks in 1948. The building was thoroughly restored and part of it is now used as an exhibition hall.

Onze-Lieve-Vrouw St.-Pieterskerk ⑩

St.-Pietersplein. **Map** 4 D3. *Tue-Sat 10am-12pm and 1:30pm-5pm, Sun 10am-12pm (in summer also 1:30pm-5pm).*

After the iconoclasms, the 'old' abbey church was so damaged that it could no longer be used. The construction of the new abbey church on the foundations of the medieval abbey church was the highlight of the rebuilding of the St.-Pietersabdij under the leadership of Joachim Schaeyck. Pieter Huyssens, a jesuit, designed a beautiful baroque-style church with a spacious choir and a striking dome structure. When the abbey was taken over by the French rulers in 1796, the church was preserved. In 1803, it found a new use as parish church, bearing the name Onze Lieve Vrouwe St.-Pieterskerk.

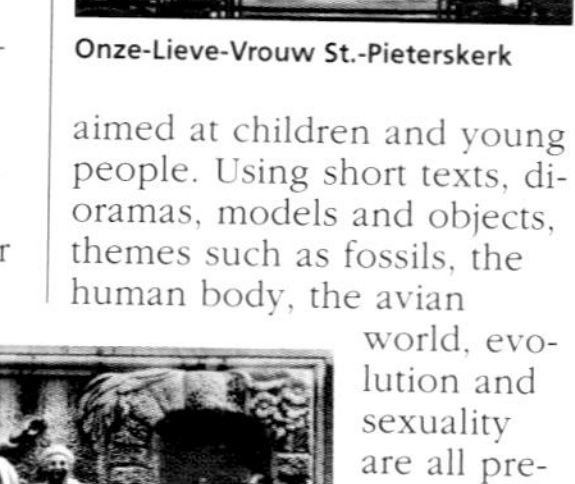

Onze-Lieve-Vrouw St.-Pieterskerk

Stone tablet above the Kina entrance

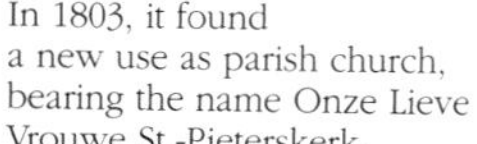

De wereld van Kina: het Huis ⑪

St.-Pietersplein 14. **Map** 4 D3. ***Tel.*** *09-2447373. Mon-Fri 9am-5pm, Sun 2pm-5:30pm.* **www**.dewereldvankina.be

De wereld van Kina is a museum dealing with humankind, nature and science aimed at children and young people. Using short texts, dioramas, models and objects, themes such as fossils, the human body, the avian world, evolution and sexuality are all presented in an interesting and educational manner. The model of Ghent during the time of emperor Charles V featuring audio and lighting effects is most certainly worth seeing.

The Wereld van Kina is a house with many rooms

Boekentoren ⑫

Rozier 9. **Map** 4 D2.

From 1933, the seventy year-old Henry Van de Velde (1863-1957) built an exceptional complex on the Blandijnberg – a new university library and institute. At the highest point in the city, he constructed a book repository as the university's landmark and as a symbol of wisdom, science and knowledge. The Boekentoren, the 'fourth tower of Ghent', is 64 m high and includes two basement floors, twenty regular floors and a belvedere that serves as a lookout platform. The tower houses more than 48 km of books, magazines and rare collections. To symbolise the modern age, Van de Velde decided to use a concrete structure. The floor plan was designed in the shape of a Greek cross. Van de Velde designed all the details, including the window profiles, furnishings, floor patterns, etc. Due to the outbreak of World War II, he was unable to realise all his plans. In 1950, the Faculty of Arts was built in a different style. During the following years, the Boekentoren was restored. In 2013, a part of the collection that has been in temporary storage in an underground depot will be returned to the tower. Work on the tower itself will be completed in 2016.

Leopoldskazerne ⑬

Gaspar de Craeyerstraat 2. **Map** 3 C3.

This impressive-looking complex of barracks has the appearance of a fortified castle. This barracks complex was constructed during the period between 1902 and 1906 on the site where the former Kattenberg infantry barracks was located. The Kattenberg barracks complex was demolished in 1830 due to the fact that it was an obstruction that spoilt the view of the city as seen from the citadel. The management of a major part of the complex is now in use by the city of Ghent, and the site now accommodates rehearsal rooms, studios, the Higher Institute for the Fine Arts (HISK) and storerooms that belong to Design Museum Gent.

AU COMTE
OSW DE KERCHOVE
DE DENTERGHEM
PRESIDENT DE LA
ROYALE
AGRICULTURE
BOTANIQUE
1906

CITADELPARK AND BIJLOKE SITE

With two leading museums – the Museum voor Schone Kunsten (MSK, Museum for Fine Arts) and the Stedelijk Museum voor Actuele Kunst (S.M.A.K.). City Museum for Contemporary Art – the Citadelpark area is the heart of the Arts district. The Citadelpark, the largest green space in the city, was created on the site of the Dutch citadel that was demolished after 1870. In 1904, the Museum of Fine Arts was constructed on the edge of the park in the style of a classic ancient temple. In 1999, the Museum for Contemporary Art was allocated its own space in the former casino and was renamed the S.M.A.K. The opening of the Stadsmuseum Gent (STAM, City Museum Ghent) breathed new life into the Bijloke site. The area became the new entrance to the city with a direct connection to the centre across the Leie.

SIGHTS AT A GLANCE

Buildings

The Bijloke Muziekcentrum Gent ❼

Building complex

Bijloke site ❻

Museums

Museum voor Schone Kunsten Gent ❶

S.M.A.K. ❷

STAM-Stadsmuseum Gent ❺

Parks

Citadelpark ❸

Plantentuin UGent ❹

SYMBOLS

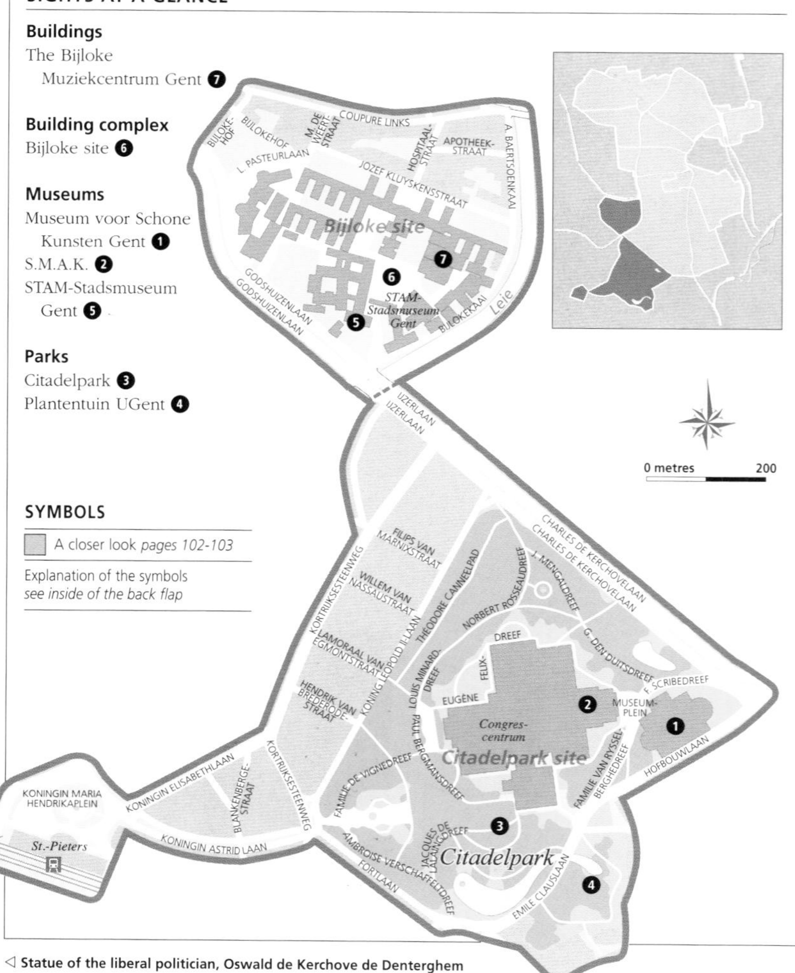

A closer look *pages 102-103*

Explanation of the symbols *see inside of the back flap*

0 metres 200

◁ **Statue of the liberal politician, Oswald de Kerchove de Denterghem**

Exploring the Citadelpark

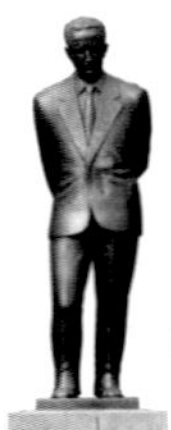

King Boudewijn

'When we say that the lovely Park laid out on the slopes of St.-Pieters stirs the pride of Ghent's citizens and and the admiration of visitors, surely no-one can accuse us of exaggeration,' wrote Willem Rogghé in 1895 in the *Gentsch Museum* magazine. With its two museums, university botanical garden, artworks in the park and the ICC (convention centre) complex, the Citadelpark is a major cultural area in addition to being a city park. The busy road that currently still bisects the area between the museums will be transformed into a museum square within a few years. The park will undergo a restoration in the near future.

Sunbathing park
On sunny days, the Citadelpark is transformed into a large sunbathing area, mostly frequented by students from the nearby student district.

Arts and culture
The Citadelpark is an important area for arts and culture. Various works of art are located throughout the park and the two Ghent art museums are situated at the park.

THEODORE CANNEELPAD
KONING LEOPOLD II-LAAN
LOUIS MINARD-DREEF
PAUL BERGMANSDREEF
FAMILIE DE VIGNEDREEF
KORTRIJKSESTEENWEG
JACQUES DE LALAINGDREEF
AMBROISE VERSCHAFFELTDREEF
FORTLAAN
PARKLAAN

TRACK 2012

The sequel to the acclaimed Over the Edges art route takes place in 2012 with TRACK. TRACK is the final part of a remarkable public art trilogy with Chambres d'amis (1986) and Over the Edges (2000) as its well-known predecessors. TRACK refers, on the one hand, to the railways around Ghent and, on the other hand, to the tracks on a CD. The S.M.A.K. has invited thirty artists to provide contributions that will be displayed outdoors and at indoor venues. For more information, visit **www**.smak.be en **www**.track.be

'Over the Edges', Jan Fabre

Museum voor Schone Kunsten Gent
The museum features a representative collection of art from the southern Low Countries encompassing the period between the Middle Ages and the first half of the 20th century.

SYMBOLS

– – Recommended route

S.M.A.K.
This is one of the most intriguing contemporary museums in Belgium, with exciting international exhibits enhanced by sculptures, paintings and items from the museum's own collection.

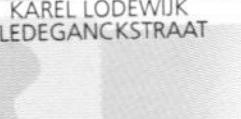

0 metres 200

Plantentuin UGent
This botanical garden features more than ten thousand plant species, outdoors and in tropical greenhouses. Two extraordinary sections are the rock- and Mediterranean gardens.

Museum voor Schone Kunsten Gent ❶

The Museum of Fine Arts opened at the Citadelpark in 1903. Charles Van Rysselberghe (1850-1920) designed the building in the style of a classic temple in honour of the fine arts. The result is an amazing building with spacious halls and ample natural light. In 1913, the museum underwent major expansion on the occasion of the World's Fair. The MSK owns a superb collection of antique paintings, 16th- and 17th-century paintings and 19th- and early 20th-century Belgian and international paintings. There is also an extensive collection of sculptures and 18th-century Brussels tapestries.

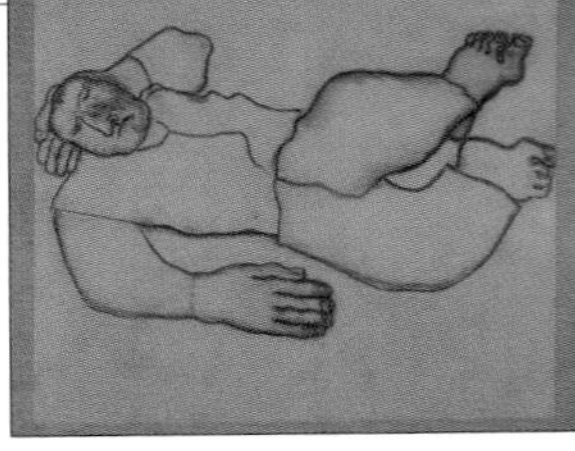

Liggende Boer *(1928)*
Constant Permeke (1886-1952) used just a few lines to sketch this curled-up, sleeping farmer. This is a prime example of Permeke's expressionist work.

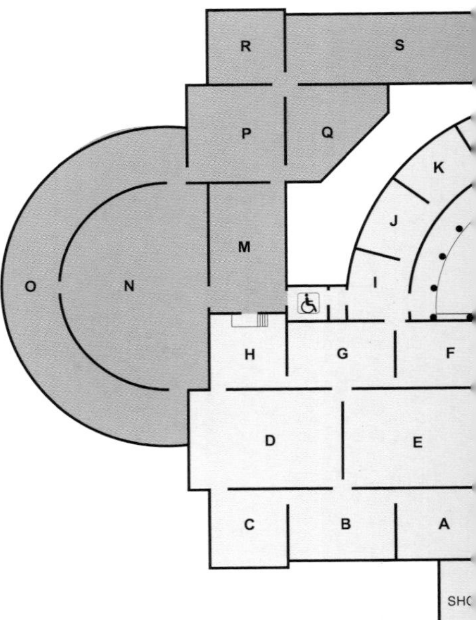

★ Christ Carrying the Cross *(1510-1516)*
The contrast between good and evil is the focal point of this work by Hieronymus (Jeroen) Bosch (ca. 1450-1516). This contrast is expressed through a cluster of sinister faces around that of Christ.

★ Seated woman *(1915)*
Rik Wouters (1882-1916) painted this sunny portrait of his favourite model, Hélène Duerinckx – also known as Nel – sitting at a window.

STAR ATTRACTIONS

- ★ Christ Carrying the Cross, Hieronymus Bosch
- ★ Seated woman, Rik Wouters
- ★ Boerinnetje, Gustave Van de Woestyne

Francis of Assisi Receiving the Stigmata *(ca. 1633)* *Peter Paul Rubens depicted a confused and pained Francis for the (former) Franciscan Recollects' monastery in Ghent.*

TIPS FOR VISITORS

Citadelpark, Fernand Scribedreef 1. **Map** 4 D4. ***Tel.*** *09-2400700.* *Tue-Sun 10am-6pm.* **www**.mskgent.be

Portrait of a Kleptomaniac *(ca. 1820)* *This masterpiece by Théodore Géricault (1791-1824) is considered a highlight of romantic-period painting.*

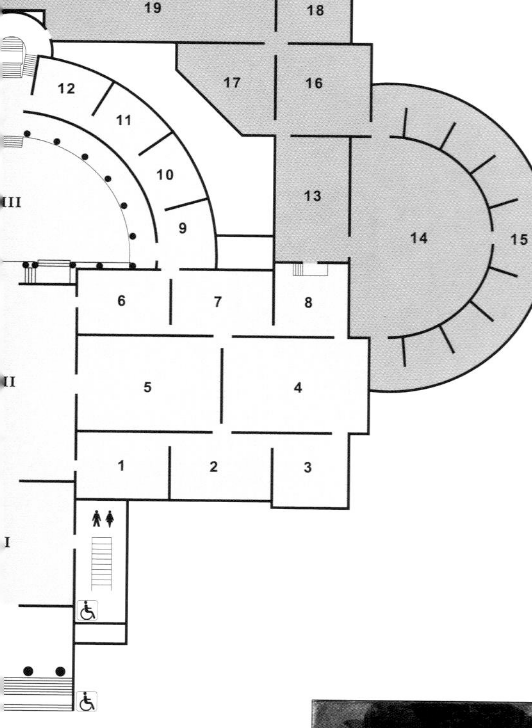

Fountain of kneeling youths *(appr. 1905 and 1927-1930)* *The most famous work by Ghent artist George Minne (1866-1941) is a sculpture of five youths kneeling on the edge of a fountain.*

THE FLEMISH ART COLLECTION is a collaboration between three art-historical museums in Antwerp, Bruges and Ghent. Together, they present an overview of the art produced in the southern Low Countries and Belgium in the period between the Middle Ages and the 20th century.
www.vlaamsekunstcollectie.be

★ **Boerinnetje** *(1913)* *Gustave Van de Woestyne (1881-1947) studied at the Ghent Academy for Fine Arts and often visited the MSK as a student. In 1900, he moved to St.-Maartens-Latem and became part of the Eerste Latemse group* *(page 151).*

Inside Installations, Jason Rhoades, PIG (Piece in Ghent), fragment 1994

ARTS DISTRICT
CITADELPARK SITE

Museum voor Schone Kunsten Gent ❶

Pages 104-105.

S.M.A.K. ❷

Citadelpark. **Map** 4 C4. ***Tel.*** *09-2407601.* *Tue-Sun 10am-6pm.*
www.smak.be

The S.M.A.K. is the life's work of Jan Hoet (also known for his involvement in acclaimed projects such as Chambres d'Amis in Ghent and Documenta IX in Kassel) who, in his time as the director of the Museum voor Hedendaagse Kunst, campaigned for an independent museum for more than twenty years. From 1975 to 1996, the museum was housed in the Museum voor Schone Kunsten. The collection systematically grew under Hoets' management and the museum became internationally renowned. In 1999, the museum relocated to its own premises in the Casino building opposite the Museum voor Schone Kunsten and was renamed the S.M.A.K., the Stedelijk Museum voor Actuele Kunst. It is an unassuming building with the bronze sculpture *The Man Measuring the Clouds* (1998) by Jan Fabre on its roof. This work is almost 4 m high, weighs 450 kg and shines like a mirror. Beyond the entrance hall, the pure-white exposition halls are spread out over two floors. The museum has an interesting collection of contemporary art dating from the 1950s to the present-day. Works by, among others: Joseph Beuys, Panamarenko, Marcel Broodthaers and Luc Tuymans, are displayed in alternating presentations in combination with temporary exhibits of works by national and international artists.

Citadelpark ❸

Map 4 C5.

In 1870-1871, the city of Ghent purchased the area around the dismantled citadel with the aim of creating a park. The park (*pages 102-103*) was designed by Hubert Van Hulle in English landscape style. In creating the greenery, ponds and slopes, clever use was made of exist-

The cast-iron bandstand in the Citadelpark was built in 1885

THE CITADEL

Demolishing the bunkers in the Citadelpark

The construction of the citadel underlined the strategic importance of the city of Ghent during the Dutch period. The citadel's design consisted of two interwoven pentagons equipped with bastions and surrounded by deep dry moats. Within its walls, the barracks and stables were built around a central square. When a fortification was constructed around Antwerp in 1870, the citadel became obsolete. In 1872, not even fifty years after building was started, large parts of the citadel were demolished. The cleared space was used for new streets, buildings and a park. The last remaining military personnel left in 1908 when the Leopold barracks was opened, and the final part of the citadel made way for the Feestpaleis for the 1913 World's Fair. Nowadays, The Feestpaleis is a dance theatre. Only the name of park, the Citadelpoort and a few old bunkers are reminiscent of the citadel. The Citadelpoort was erected in 1826 and now bears the Belgian coat of arms on its pediment instead of the Dutch coat of arms that it initially displayed. The motto 'Nemo me inpune lacesset' (no-one will mock me without being punished) adorns the gateway. After World War II, the Feestpaleis was converted into an exhibition centre for trade fairs and the Gentse Floraliën, held every five years. The fairs and the flower and plant show were relocated to the Flanders Expo in St.-Denijs-Wetrem. In 1975, the *International Convention Centre Ghent* (ICC) was built adjacent to the Feestpaleis.

ing inclines and the remains of the citadel. In the caves, a few remains of casemates (underground bunkers) can still be seen. The Citadelpark was part of the 1913 World's Fair. Various exhibitions areas were placed in the heart of the park. The park features more than one hundred tree species, including rare wingnut, catalpa and Kentucky coffee tree specimens. It is lovely to while away the time around the cast-iron bandstand, in the Rose garden and in the Swiss valley.

In the next few years, major development and restoration work is planned for the Citadelpark. The renovated Floriahal will become the backbone supporting the new Citadelpark.The area 't Kuipke is to be converted into a stadium in its own right, the museums are to be expanded, an expansion of the ICC is planned and the park will receive a general makeover.

The Victoria greenhouse with its famous giant water lilies in the Plantentuin UGent

Plantentuin UGent ❹

K.L. Ledeganckstraat 35.
Map 3 C5.
Tel. *09-2645073.*
Mon-Fri 9am-4:30pm, Sat-Sun 9am-12pm.
www.plantentuin.ugent.be

The botanical garden of Ghent's University is located on the outskirts of the Citadelpark. This garden dates back to 1794 when it was incorporated into the gardens of the Baudeloabdij as part of the *école centrale*. In 1903, the garden was relocated to the Citadelpark. The garden, the arboretum and the tropical and subtropical greenhouses contain more than ten thousand plant species. The umbrella pine (*Pinus pinea*) at the edge of the pond is the specimen that attracts the most attention, but also worth seeing are: the collection of succulents, the Mediterranean garden, the swamp with carnivorous plants and the rock garden are also worth seeing.

STAM Stadsmuseum Gent ❺

The new city museum on the Bijloke is the entrance to the city. The museum consists of a combination of the newly built 21st-century section (entrance building), the 14th-century abbey wings ('the story of Ghent') and the 17th-century monastery building (temporary exhibitions). Outside, the museum garden, the terrace and the pond immediately catch the eye. The highlight of the museum is the city of Ghent itself. The STAM is more than just a museum, it's a way of looking at the city. A chronological route, filled with objects and multimedia, sketches the development and growth of Ghent. The route includes everything that has made Ghent into what it is today. The temporary exhibitions focus on 'urbanism' and illustrate the creation of a city.

★ Refectory
The refectory (dining hall), the largest space in the abbey, has a vaulted wooden ceiling and is decorated with 14th-century murals.

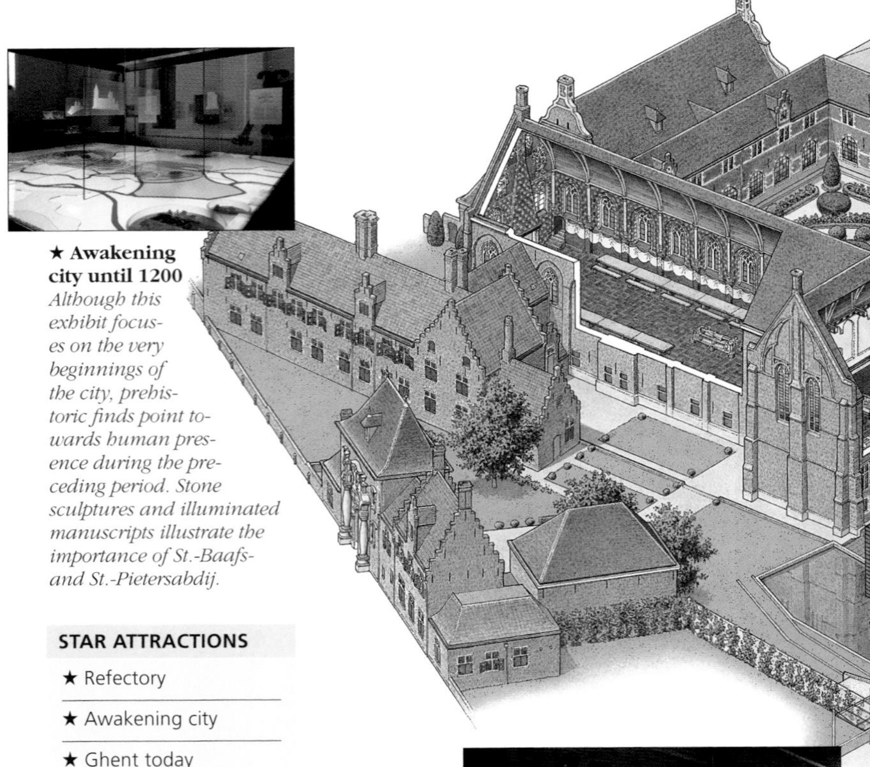

★ Awakening city until 1200
Although this exhibit focuses on the very beginnings of the city, prehistoric finds point towards human presence during the preceding period. Stone sculptures and illuminated manuscripts illustrate the importance of St.-Baafs- and St.-Pietersabdij.

STAR ATTRACTIONS

- ★ Refectory
- ★ Awakening city
- ★ Ghent today

Great city
During the medieval times, Ghent was one of the largest cities in Europe. The cloth trade and grain industry brought wealth to the city; wealth that was then transformed into castles, guild houses, public buildings, churches and monasteries.

TIPS FOR VISITORS

STAM, Bijloke site, Godshuizenlaan 2. **Map** 3 B3-C3. ***Tel.*** *09-2671400.* *Tue-Sun 10am-6pm.* **www**.stamgent.be

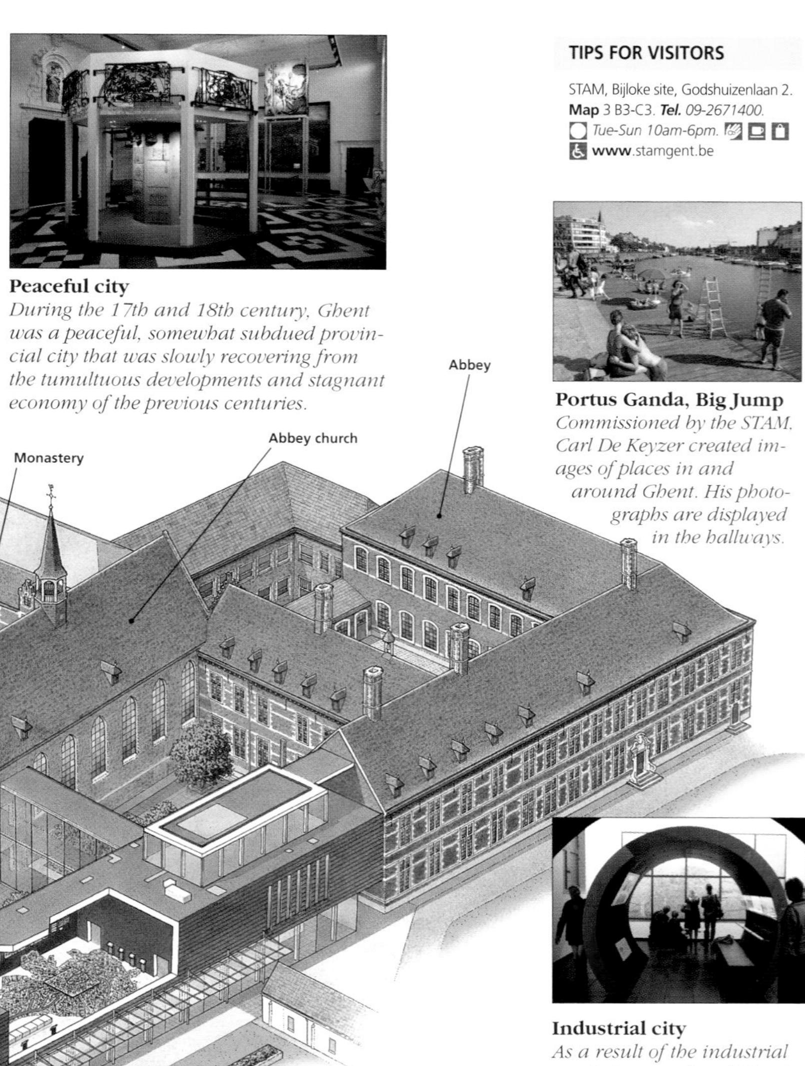

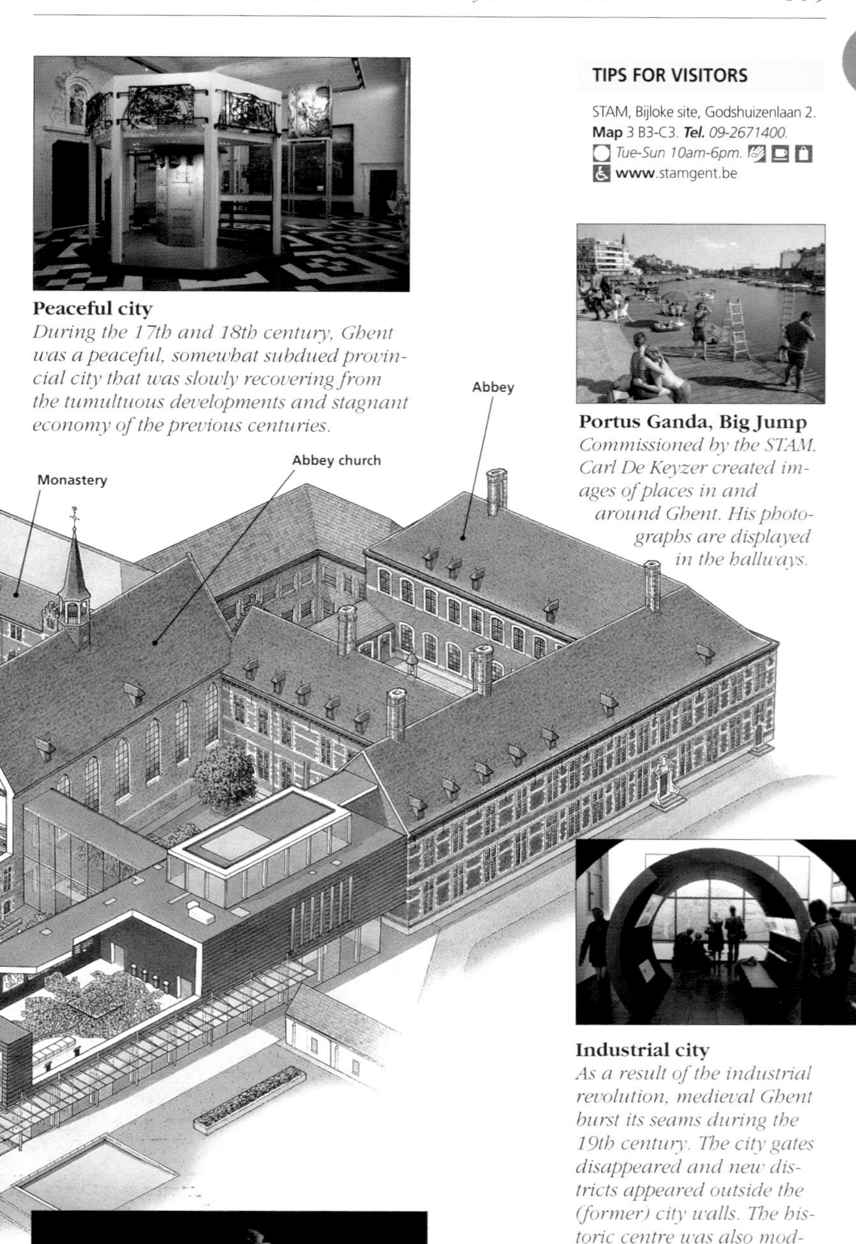

Peaceful city
During the 17th and 18th century, Ghent was a peaceful, somewhat subdued provincial city that was slowly recovering from the tumultuous developments and stagnant economy of the previous centuries.

Portus Ganda, Big Jump
Commissioned by the STAM, Carl De Keyzer created images of places in and around Ghent. His photographs are displayed in the hallways.

Industrial city
As a result of the industrial revolution, medieval Ghent burst its seams during the 19th century. The city gates disappeared and new districts appeared outside the (former) city walls. The historic centre was also modernised.

★ Introductory exhibit: Ghent today
A massive aerial photograph on the floor and a model of the historic city centre offers visitors an image of the city and a feel for the modern-day Ghent.

The Bijloke site today

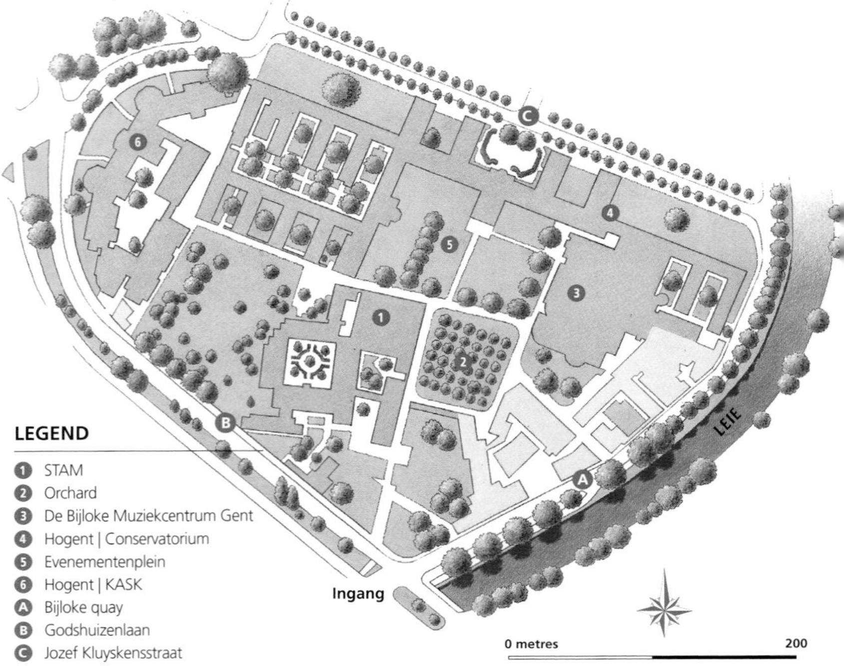

LEGEND

1 STAM
2 Orchard
3 De Bijloke Muziekcentrum Gent
4 Hogent | Conservatorium
5 Evenementenplein
6 Hogent | KASK
A Bijloke quay
B Godshuizenlaan
C Jozef Kluyskensstraat

Ingang

LEIE

0 metres 200

ARTS DISTRICT
BIJLOKE SITE

STAM-Stadsmuseum Gent 5

Pages 108-109

Bijloke site 6

Entrance: Godshuizenlaan. **Map** 3 B3.

Over the past few years, the area of Bijloke has been transformed from a deserted hospital area into a cultural haven on the banks of the Leie. Caring for the sick was the focal point here for seven centuries until the hospital was moved to a different location in 1985. First, the Hogeschool Gent college and the Conservatorium were housed in the former public hospital, followed at a later stage by the Bijloke Muziekcentrum and other cultural institutions. The opening of the STAM, the Ghent city museum, reinforced the function of the Bijloke as a cultural haven. During the next few years, the gardens will be remodelled, making the Bijloke a green gateway to the city of Ghent.

De Bijloke Muziekcentrum Gent 7

Jozef Kluyskensstraat 2. **Map** 3 B2-C2. ***Tel.*** *09-2336878.* **www**.debijloke.be **Booking agency**: *page 237.*

The music centre is housed in the former hospital complex. The historic buildings have been restored and successfully integrated into the new music centre. The 13th-century infirmary has been converted into a concert hall. It is covered with a unique roof structure for which the timber from an entire Ardennes forest was used. Concerts are also presented in the second infirmary, the 16th-century Craeckhuys. A number of 19th-century buildings have been given new purpose, including the library and the Anatomical Institute, where medical students receive training.

The audience during a concert in the medieval infirmary

From hospital to cultural area

Buildings in the Bijloke site

At the start of the 13th century, the small Onze-Lieve-Vrouw hospital in Onderbergen near St.-Michielskerk had to make way for the construction of the Dominican monastery. Johanna of Constantinople, countess of Flanders (1205-1244), donated the Bijlokemeersen, a marshy plot of land along the Leie beyond the city walls, to the hospital sisters. The Bijloke hospital formed part of the Cistercian nunnery that was built next to it. In 1511, a second infirmary, the Craeckhuys (Sick-house) was built. This ward was used as an infirmary until 1976. During the iconoclasms (1566 and 1578), the hospital and the abbey were severely affected and the sisters were forced to flee. They returned in 1585, when the buildings were repaired and new structures were built. In 1797, the abbey was disbanded and the sisters left the Bijloke site. A few years later, they returned and moved into the 17th-century abbey extension and continued their work as nurses. During the course of the 19th century, the old Bijloke hospital became too small. Adolphe Pauli (1820-1895) was instructed to develop it further. He created an extremely progressive design in an austere, neo-Gothic style, and construction took place between 1864 and 1880. Various abbey buildings served as homes for the elderly between 1805 and 1911. In 1913, the city of Ghent purchased these buildings to accommodate the Oudheidkundig Museum (Museum of Antiquities, 1928). In 1985, after more than seven hundred years of healthcare at the area, the hospital moved to the new AZ Jan Palfijn Academic Hospital.

Nun in habit

Between 1805 and 1911, the abbey buildings served as homes for the elderly

Architecture in Ghent

History has left a trail through Ghent in the form of churches, monasteries, homes and company houses. Examples of buildings from every period and in each architectural style can be found in the city. Some are pure, while others have been modified to include a number of styles. Nothing remains from the first period of habitation. The structures from this period were built using wood. Any tuff or limestone used was re-used in the construction of the abbeys. A few signs of St.-Baafsabdij, built after 940, remain. The city was spared during both World Wars, meaning that many monuments have been preserved. After 1960, Ghent underwent a phase of modernisation during which many valuable buildings were demolished.

Neo-styles from the 19th century
Revival of old architectural styles: neo-Gothic and neo-classic

Romanesque
This octagonal lavatorium with its sacrarium was built around 1170 in St.-Baafsabdij. It is a prime example of Romanesque construction. Ruins in Romanesque style can also be found in the crypt of St.-Baafskathedraal.
Romanesque characteristics: low, thick walls, small windows, vaulted arches.

Rococo and classicism
The glitzy city palaces were built in the 18th century using rococo (Louis XV style) or classicism (Louis XVI). Characteristics: rococo, with its light colours and elegant lines, is less dramatic than baroque; classicism is a return to ancient (classic) Greek and Roman techniques.

Renaissance
The Schepenbank van Ghedeele, the town hall wing on the Botermarkt.
Renaissance characteristics: application of classical style elements, horizontal lines with symmetrical structure.

Baroque

Unlike other Flemish cities, Ghent possesses few historic, baroque-style buildings. The former Berg van Barmhartigheid (1622) was the first building in Ghent constructed in the baroque style, the triumphant architectural style of the Catholics in the southern Low Countries. Baroque characteristics: abundant decorations, bold use of shapes and curved lines.

Scheldt Gothic

De St.-Niklaaskerk was built in the Scheldt Gothic architectural style and finished in Doornik limestone. The great bell tower with its detailed corner turrets is characteristic of this style. Similar smaller towers also flank the furthest wall of the transept and the front façade. Gothic characteristics: height, verticality, light, use of pinnacles, buttresses or arches and abundant brickwork.

MORE INFORMATION

Numerous public buildings can be visited on the Dag van de architectuur (Day of architecture). Discover the stories behind these buildings and learn about a number of new development projects.

BRABANT GOTHIC

After 1440, St.-Michielskerk was rebuilt in the Brabant Gothic style. Members of the Keldermans family were primarily responsible for the implementation of this regional variety of late-Gothic architecture. The churches built in this style are more modest in size than their French counterparts. The choir only has seven radiating chapels and the western wing has one tower.

Modernism

The tower called Boekentoren on the Blandijnberg, designed by the famous architect Henry Van de Velde, is the most striking example of modernism in Ghent. Van de Velde, a multi-talented artist, designed all the details, including the black steel window frames, floor patterns, door handles, furnishings and radiator covers. Modernism characteristics: sombre, geometric, basic shapes, flat roofs and the use of modern materials such as reinforced concrete.

OUTSIDE THE CENTRE

The R40, the Kleine (Inner) Ring, follows a full circle around the Ghent city centre. For much of its route, the ring road follows the old fortification that held the city in its iron grip until 1860. The abolition of patent rights started an expansion of the city beyond the medieval city limits. New districts were built and the countryside around Ghent rapidly was urbanised. In 1977, Ghent merged with the neighbouring districts of Afsnee, Drongen, Gentbrugge, Ledeberg, Mariakerke, Oostakker, St.-Amandsberg, St.-Denis Westrem, Wondelgem and Zwijnaarde, thereby becoming a metropolitan area with 249,000 inhabitants. However, each of these sub-districts has its own history with its own churches, castles and industrial developments.

SIGHTS AT A GLANCE

Churches and monasteries
Basiliek Oostakker-Lourdes 19
Oude Abdij 13
St.-Jan Baptistkerk 12

Buildings
Braemkasteel 16
Flanders Expo 15
Groot Begijnhof 10
Nieuw Gerechtsgebouw 3
Station Gent St.-Pieters 5

Museums
Illuseum 11
Museum Dr. Guislain 1
Museum voor de Geschiedenis van de Wetenschappen 7

Parks
De Assels 14
De Blaarmeersen 8
Bourgoyen-Ossemeersen 18
De wereld van Kina: de Tuin 4

Graveyards
Campo Santo 9
Westerbegraafplaats 2

District
Miljoenenkwartier 6

Football club
KAA Gent 17

SYMBOLS

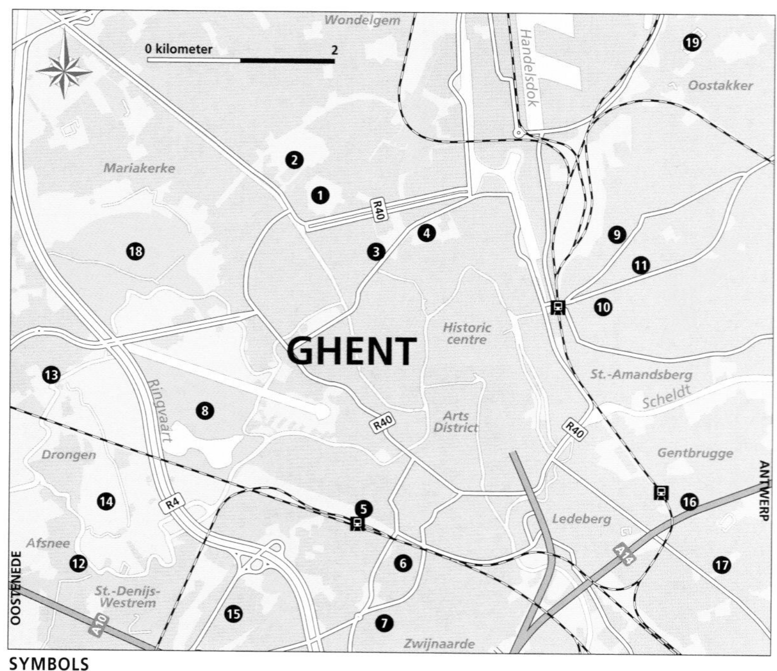

Explanation of the symbols *see inside of the back flap*

◁ **Saint's figure in a wall of the rustic St.-Elisabethbegijnhof**

The symmetric architecture of the Guislain Institute

Museum Dr. Guislain ❶

Jozef Guislainstraat 43. **Tel.** *09-2163595.* *Tue-Fri 9am-5pm, Sat-Sun 1pm-5pm.* *1.*
www.museumdrguislain.be

Jozef Guislain (1797-1860) was a medical doctor who went on to become one of the pioneers of modern psychiatry. Throughout his life, he championed the humane treatment of psychiatric patients. In 1857, the Guislaingesticht (mental hospital) opened its doors as the first psychiatric institution in Belgium. It was located in a then rural area beyond the Brugse Poort. The complex blended into the area and consisted of two rectangular wings linked by a semi-circular wing. Various other wings, outbuildings and a chapel were added later. The museum, housed in old hospital wards, portrays the history of psychiatry in Belgium and also features outsider art, the spontaneous and unconventional work by artists who ply their trade outside professional art circles. The works by these 'outsiders' are fantasy-filled, colourful and, at times, large-scale. The museum owns a large collection of psychiatry-themed photographs that is constantly being expanded, while it also presents extraordinary temporary exhibits.

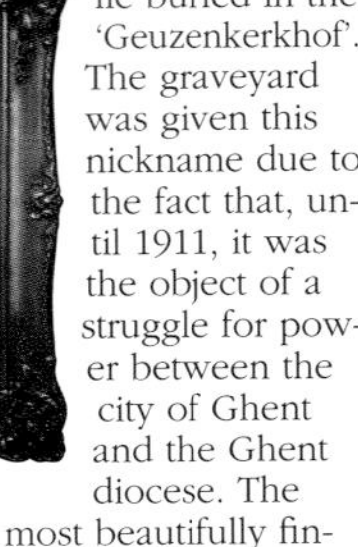

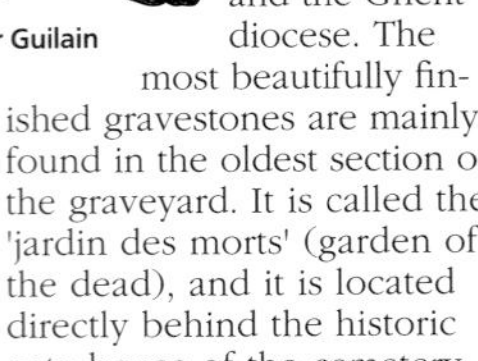
Museum Dr Guilain

Westerbegraafplaats ❷

Palinghuizen 143. **Tel.** *09-2167920.* *Mon-Sat 8am-5pm, Sun 9am-5pm.* *9.* *1.*

The Westerbegraafplaats cemetery the liberal counterpart of the Campo Santo (page 118), was opened on 1 January 1873. Mainly liberals, socialists, professors and artists lie buried in the 'Geuzenkerkhof'. The graveyard was given this nickname due to the fact that, until 1911, it was the object of a struggle for power between the city of Ghent and the Ghent diocese. The most beautifully finished gravestones are mainly found in the oldest section of the graveyard. It is called the 'jardin des morts' (garden of the dead), and it is located directly behind the historic gate house of the cemetery.

Nieuw Gerechtsgebouw ❸

Opgeëistenlaan 401.

In June 2007 the new courthouse, housing the Assize Court and various other courts, was opened. The courthouse consists of three large towers that are five storeys high. The façade along the Opgeëistenlaan is made entirely of glass. Architects Stephane Beel and Lieven Achtergael designed this building.

De wereld van Kina: de Tuin ❹

Berouw 55. **Tel.** *09-2250542.* *Mon-Fri 9am-5:30pm, Sun 2pm-5:30pm.*
www.dewereldvankina.be

De Tuin (Garden) is the life's work of teacher Michel Thiery. In 1923, he became the director of the Stedelijk Schoolmuseum, a museum that focused on nature education and study. He was a contemporary of well-known conservationists Jac. P. Thijsse and Eli Heimans. Thiery created a botanical garden around the museum featuring miniature landscapes consisting of woods, meadows, dunes and the Ardennes. Into this botanical garden, he also incorporated a greenhouse, a vegetable garden and an orchard. After his death in 1950, the garden unfortunately fell into a state of neglect.

Historic gravestones in the Westerbegraafplaats

De Tuin van Kina is reminiscent early 20th-century garden

In 1987, the garden was re-opened as Hortus Michel Thiery. The centrepiece of the garden is a Canadian poplar that is more than one hundred years old. The botanical garden is divided into sections containing medicinal herbs, ornamental plants, dye flowers and plants from various biotopes. The museum that is located in the gardens focuses on the world of bees, ants and spiders.

Station Gent St.-Pieters ❺

Koningin Maria Hendrikaplein 1.
www.projectgentsintpieters.be

The Gent St.-Pieters station, which is one of Belgium's busiest railway stations, was built in 1912 in the new Citadel district in preparation for the 1913 World's Fair. The architect Louis Cloquet (1849-1920), who was also responsible for the Postgebouw at the Korenmarkt, designed a massive, elongated station building in an eclectic style. The minaret-like eastern clock tower is an eye-catching and iconic aspect of this 'modern entrance to the city'. By 2005, the tower had subsided to such an extent that it was dismantled brick-by-brick and rebuilt using reinforced concrete. The concourse is decorated with wall and ceiling murals depicting various Belgian cities. During the upcoming years, the station will be transformed into a modern public transport hub. At the rear of the station, a second station square is being constructed. A new road connecting the station and the R4 is also being laid in the area of the Flanders Expo. This large-scale building project is expected to be finished in the year 2016.

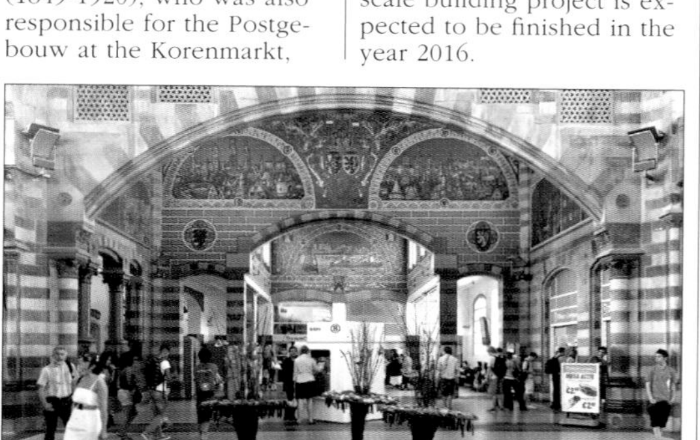
Murals in the Gent St.-Pieters station

Miljoenenkwartier ❻

5. 21/22.

After the 1913 World's Fair, the exhibition site was converted into a residential area. From Kortrijksesteenweg, Onafhankelijkheidslaan forms the 'grand entrance' to the new district where 250 homes were designed by 137 different architects between 1927 and 1939. The Miljoenenkwartier is a prime example of the architectural styles of the period between the wars. There are fine examples of the art deco, cottage and Nieuwe Bouwen architectural styles to be seen along Krijgslaan and Vaderlandstraat and around the Paul De Smet de Naeyerplein. Villa De Bondt (Krijgslaan 124B) is a residential studio (1929) in the Amsterdam School's brickwork style. Its pentagonal tower with flagpole really grabs the attention.

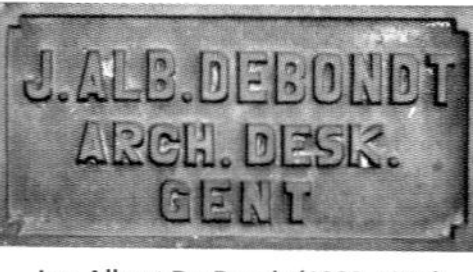

Jan-Albert De Bondt (1888-1969)

Museum voor de Geschiedenis van de Wetenschappen (Science History Museum) ❼

Krijgslaan 281 (S30).
Tel. *09-2644930.* *Mon-Fri 10am-12pm and 2pm-5pm.* *21/22.*
www.sciencemuseum.ugent.be.

This museum houses the UGent's collection of historic scientific instruments. Here, many of Ghent's scientists are placed in the limelight, such as the physicist Joseph Plateau (the inventor of the phenakastiscope, an early animation device), the chemist Lep Baekeland (the inventor of the first synthetic material) and the chemist August Kekulé, a pioneer in the field of aromatic chemistry.

Waterslide at the bathing lake of the Blaarmeersen recreational area

De Blaarmeersen 8

Zuiderlaan 5. **Tel.** *09-2668170.* *from St.-Pietersstation 41/43.* P *paid (May-Sep).* **www**.blaarmeersen.be

De Blaarmeersen is a large recreational area to the west of the city, situated between the Ringvaart (ring canal), the Leie and the Watersportbaan (water sports course). Originally, this was a marshland area along the Leie, and construction of the recreational area started after 1976. It consists of groves, sunbathing areas and walking trails surrounding a central lake with a beach, bathing area and sports facilities. Also available are boat rental, mini-golf, skating and fishing. The park offers various dining facilities, a playground and a five-star campsite.

Campo Santo 9

Visitatiestraat, St.-Amandsberg. **Tel.** *09-2167920.* *Mon-Sat 8am-5pm, Sun 9am-5pm.* *38/39.*

The Campo Santo cemetry is located on the Kapelleberg, a hill on top of which the Amanduskapel (1720) can be found. This graveyard, which was consecrated along with the chapel in 1847, has become the most important cemetry in Flanders. Firstly, author Jan Frans Willems, a prominent member of the Flemish Movement, was buried on the hill. Subsequently, many members of the Ghent Catholic elite involved in the arts, sciences and the Flemish Movement were laid to rest here. Author Hendrik Conscience came up with the honorific title of Campo Santo 'where the Flemish heroes lie'. The hundreds of historic gravestones, some severely dilapidated, designed by Ghent sculptors and architects, provide an overview of gravestone styles from 1850 to the present. Over time, the graveyard has been extended even further.

Groot Begijnhof 10

Engelbert Van Arenbergstraat, St.-Amandsberg. *Van Arenbergstraat entrance 6:30am-11pm, Schoolstraat entrance 6am-11pm.* *6.* **www**.elisabethbegijnhof.be

During the second half of the 19th century, the beguines from the Elisabeth beguinage were forced to move to a new location (pages 76-77). Duke Engelbert van Arenberg (1824-1875) purchased a site intended for the construction of a new beguinage. The new design had an English garden theme and consisted of fourteen cloisters, eighty houses, a governess residence, an infirmary, a church and a chapel all positioned around three squares and eight streets. All the buildings were designed in neo-Gothic style, making the Groot Begijnhof the largest neo-Gothic complex in Belgium. In 1874, around six hundred beguines moved in. Since 2002, no beguines have lived in the beguinage.

Shrine to Mary at Groot Begijnhof

Illuseum 11

Victor Braeckmanlaan 123, St.-Amandsberg. **Tel.** *09-2282856.* *Sun 2pm-6pm.* *17/18.* **www**.illuseum.be

The Illuseum is a small museum containing more than 120 examples of eye-trickery and optical illusions, such as moving objects that are actually stationary, depth illusions and objects that seemingly appear from nowhere.

St.-Jan Baptistkerk 12

Afsnee (village).

Until the 20th century, the village of Afsnee was primarily rural and consisted of a few scattered buildings surrounding the town centre. The village atmosphere has been best preserved around the village church, the most beautifully situated church in Ghent. This church dates back to the 12th century and was originally built in late-Romanesque style although, over the centuries, early-Gothic elements were added. When the bell rings, the ferryman transports the passengers across the Leie.

Octagonal dome on the Oude Abdij

Oude Abdij ⓭

Drongenplein 26-27, Drongen.
Tel. *09-2265226.*
www.oudeabdij.be

During the 12th century, the Norbertines settled in the Oude Abdij (Old Abbey). This abbey suffered heavy losses during the iconoclasms and the monks fled to the house of refuge in Ghent, returning in 1698. During the French Revolution, the abbey was taken over by the French. Lieven Bauwens founded his second cotton mill here. In 1837, the Jesuits made it their training institute. Currently, it is a rest home and centre for contemplation.

LEIEVALLEI

At the end of the 19th century, a young group of artists settled in St.-Martens-Latem (*page 151*). They enjoyed painting images of the natural beauty of the meandering Leie. They therefore severely objected to plans to channel the Leie River between Ghent and Deinze. Thanks in part to their efforts, the enchanting landscape has remained preserved. Drongen is an ideal point from which to embark on a cycling expedition along the marshlands and the meandering Leie. The **Langs de Leie (Along the Leie)** cycling tour focuses on nature. You will cycle along the De Assels marshlands, the Beelaertmeersen, the Latemse Meersen and the Keuzemeersen. St.-Martens-Latem and Deurle Dorp are two artist's villages where members of the two famous Latum groups visit one another and find inspiration by the surrounding landscape. Deurle has no less than three museums.

Langs de Leie
Starting point: *Drongenplein, Drongen.*
P *Drongenplein.*
Distance: *30 km.*
Route: *start* 57 62 ⛴ 63 67 74 76 86 90 88 85 72 71 61 58 57

De Assels ⓮

Asselsstraat, Drongen.
www.natuurpunt.be

The Assels formed part of the large marsh area along the Leie to which the Blaarmeersen and the Bourgoy-en Ossemeersen also belong. Due to the construction of the ring canal (Ringvaart), the Assels were separated from the other areas. In the west and the south, the Oude Leie borders the area. There is a number of natural wells along this river, including the Boterput and the Piereput. The Assels are still genuine marshlands (meadows) that are often inundated during winter. However, in the summer months, farmers use the marshlands as grass and hay meadows.

Horses grazing on the grasslands of the De Assels nature reserve along the Leie

The Flanders Expo entrance hall

Flanders Expo 15

Maaltekouter 1, St.-Denijs-Westrem. ***Tel.*** *09-2419211.* *1.*
www.flandersexpo.be

Flanders Expo is a large exhibition complex with a 54,000 m² of floor area. Every five years (next exhibition scheduled for 2015), the *Gentse Floraliën*, a major flower and plant show, is organised here. In 1820, this site was home to a military drill area. In 1830, a hippodrome was constructed here, while an airfield was created in 1910.

Braemkasteel 16

Braemkasteelstraat 1, Gentbrugge.

During the 14th century, Hughe Braem commissioned the construction of a castle on the Rietgracht, an important fortification around the city of Ghent. In the 19th century, the castle was given its current shape. In 1946, the Gentbrugge community purchased the castle to serve as its municipal headquarters. The park around it was named Frans Tochpark after the last mayor of Gentbrugge before it was incorporated into Ghent in 1977. The castle is hidden behind the A14/E17 flyover and houses the Emiel Hullebroeck Music Academy.

The Braemkasteel is located on the outskirts of Ghent

GENTSE FLORALIËN

The Gentse Floraliën is the name of the flower and plant show presented every five years by the Koninklijke Maatschappij voor Landbouw en Plantkunde (Royal Society for Agriculture and Botany). In 2015, the 35th edition will take place. The exhibition dates back to 1809, when the first

show was organised in the *Au Jardin de Frascati* along the Coupure. It was a great success and, every year, a winter and a summer exhibition was held in a hall in the Korte Meer at the Kouter and later in the lower hall of the town hall and in the auditorium of the university. In 1836, the exhibition moved to the Casino, designed by city architect Louis Roelandt. In 1839, the first quinquennial flower show was held, and it later received the name of Gentse Floraliën. In 1913, the show relocated to the Floraliënpaleis in Citadelpark. After thirteen editions, the Gentse Floraliën was moved to the Flanders Expo venue and has been held there since 1990.
www.floralien.be

KAA Gent ⓱

Jules Ottenstadion, Bruiloftstraat 42, Gentbrugge. ***Tel.*** *09-2306610.* **www**.kaagent.be

The association was established in 1864 as the 'Association Royale Athlétique Gantoise' and was originally an athletics club that was expanded with the addition of a football division in 1900. In 1913, the club was promoted to the first division. The club received its nickname – Buffalo's – thanks to a visit by the *Barnum and Bailey* circus to Ghent. During the show, the crowd shouted 'Buffalo! Buffalo!', and this cry was adopted by the football supporters. In 1920, the club moved to the Jules Otten stadium in Gentbrugge. During the 1950s, La Gantoise became embedded in Belgian football culture. In 1972, the club was renamed the KAA (Koninklijke Atletiekassociatie Gent or Royal Athletics Association of Ghent). Between 1971 and 1980, the club participated in the second division and, for just one year, in the third division. For the past few years, KAA Ghent has participated at the top of the first division, with its highlight being participation in the Belgian Cup final of 2007-2008. One season later, the club was eliminated from the Europa League by AS Roma. In the 2009-2010 season, KAA Gent finished runners-up in the Jupiler Pro League and won the Belgian Cup.

The nature and environment centre De Bourgoyen offers numerous activities

Bourgoyen-Ossemeersen ⓲

Driepikkelstraat 32. ***Tel.*** *09-2261501.* *Mon-Fri 9am-12pm and 1pm-5pm, Sat-Sun 2:30pm-6:30pm.* *3, Jutestraat stop.* **www**.natuurpuntgent.be

The Stedelijk Natuurreservaat Bourgoyen-Ossemeersen (City Nature Reserve) is located in a valley that was created by erosion caused by the Leie. It consists mainly of marshy grasslands (*meersen*) that are covered with water during winter. It is an area rich with birdlife and it is the ideal habitat for salamanders, frogs, water scorpions and water boatmen. The energy-efficient **Bourgoyen Nature and environment centre** at the main entrance is the departure point for three hiking trails.

Basiliek Oostakker-Lourdes ⓳

Onze-Lieve-Vrouwdreef 8, Oostakker. ***Tel.*** *09-2555544.* **www**.basiliekoostakker.be

In 1873, the Marquise de Courtebourne-de Nédonchel commissioned the construction of a shrine to Our Lady of Lourdes in the garden of the Slotendries castle. When a labourer from Jabbeke was miraculously healed of an open fracture to his leg, a massive influx of pilgrims followed. In order to cope with this flow of pilgrims, a new church – the Oostakker-Lourdes basilica - was built within two years in neo-Gothic style.

In 1873, the Oostakker-Lourdes basilica was built in honour of Our Lady of Lourdes

EXPLORING GHENT ON FOOT AND BY BICYCLE

The historic centre and the arts district are ideally explored on foot. The sights, the city squares and the Leie and the Scheldt are all within walking distance of one another. But there are also great off-the-beaten-track walks in the Prinsenhof, Patershol, and the arts district or along the Leie. It's almost impossible to get lost, since pedestrian signs provide directions. Those who would like to see parks, museums or graveyards outside the centre should do so by bicycle. Ghent is becoming a more cyclist-friendly city (*also see page 238*). The Prinsen en begijnen (*Princes and Beguines*) walking route takes you through the Prinsenhof district and the Oud Begijnhof St.-Elisabeth. The Gent Verlicht (*Ghent Illuminated*) walk invites you to take an evening walk through the city when it is lit up like a fairy-tale world. This is why Ghent is known as the 'Lichtstad' (city of lights). The cycling route along the Leie, Scheldt, Lieve, Sassevaart and Ketelvaart – waterways that have played a significant role in Ghent's history – is called *Stad aan het water (City on the Water)*.

0 meter 400

WALKING ROUTE
Prinsen en begijnen
(pp. 124-125)

WALKING ROUTE
Gent Verlicht
(pp. 126-127)

CYCLING ROUTE
Stad aan het water
(pp. 128-129)

SYMBOLS

--- *Prinsen en begijnen* walking route

--- *Gent Verlicht* walking route

--- *Stad aan het water* cycling route

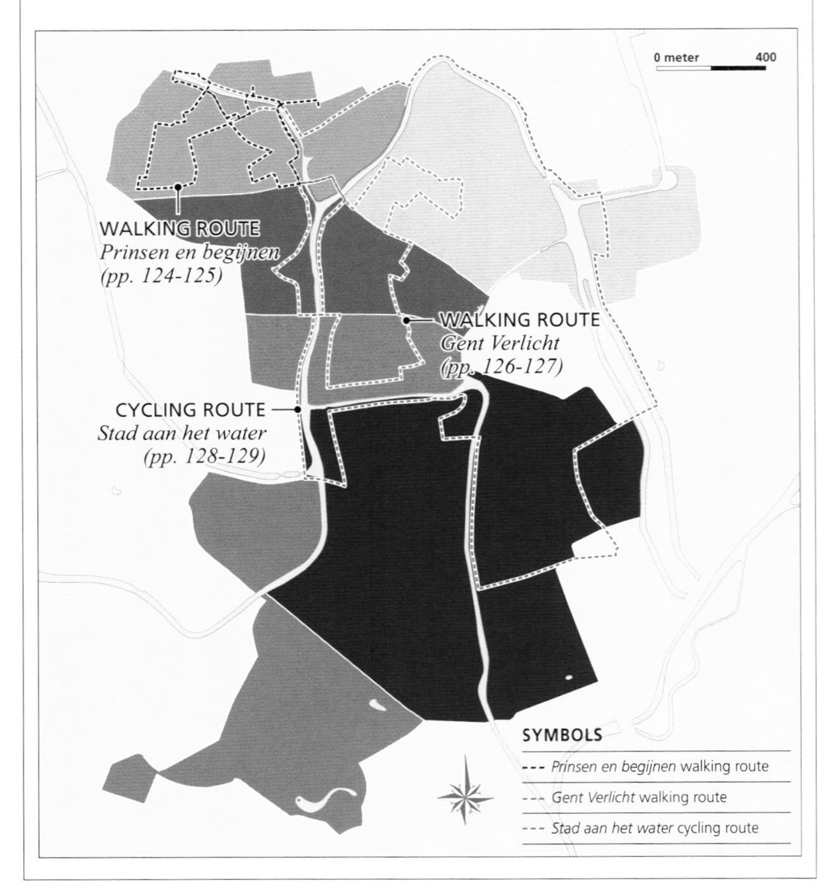

◁ **A magical view of the inner city as seen from St.-Michielsbrug**

Princes and Beguines

Karel V

The Prinsenhof is a charming district built around the former princely palace. All that remains of the palace is a gateway, parts of the castle wall and a few columns and sections of wall. A model of the Prinsenhof illustrates how the palace must have looked in its heyday. According to information handed down over the centuries, the palace had more than three hundred rooms and featured gardens and ponds. From the 17th century onwards, the Prinsenhof lost its significance, after which fires and degradation led to its complete ruin. The district now features modern architecture and traces of industrial heritage. The former St.-Elisabethbegijnhof that was developed around 1242 outside the city walls, came to be located within the defences and was dismantled at the end of the 19th century. City management forced the beguines to leave. Despite all the modifications carried out, some of the serene atmosphere remains.

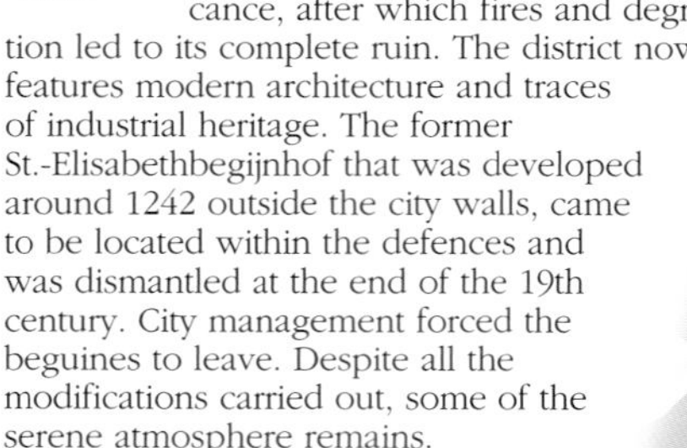

Rabot

The only remaining sluice gate on the Lieve, which can be closed with thick wooden beams. In 1492, the sluice was strengthened with the construction of two towers. ④

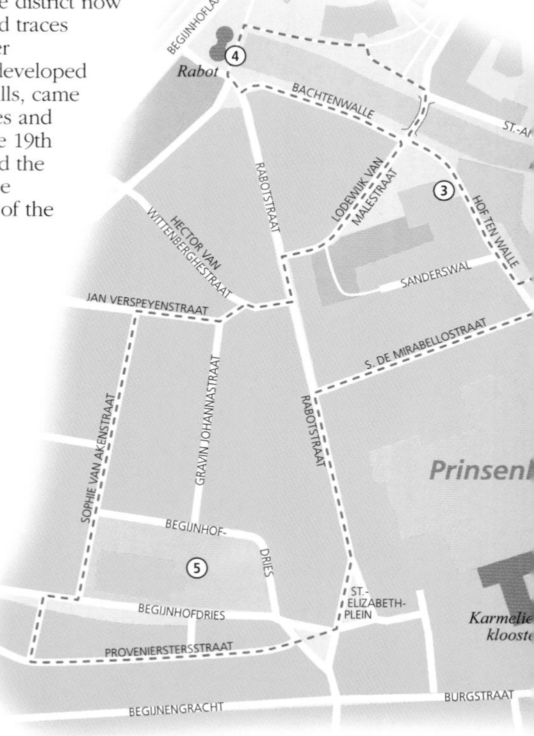

Donkere Poort

Donkere Poort is a former rear gateway into the Prinsenhof. According to tradition, emperor Charles V was born in the room above the gate. ③

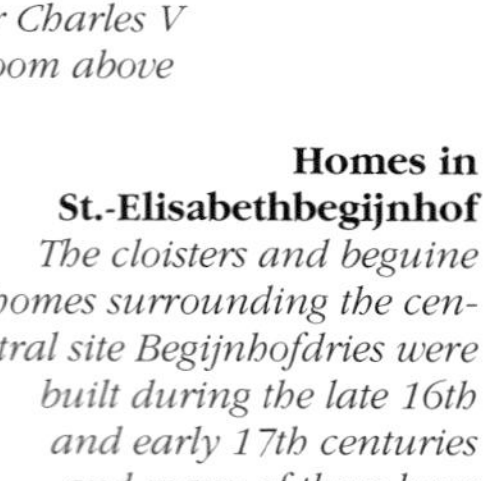

Homes in St.-Elisabethbegijnhof

The cloisters and beguine homes surrounding the central site Begijnhofdries were built during the late 16th and early 17th centuries and many of them have been painted red. ⑤

Brug der Keizerlijke Geneugten
Ghent folk singer and sculptor Walter De Buck designed this bridge – thus immortalising the extramarital activities of emperor Charles V – in honour of Keizer Kareljaar (year of emperor Charles) held in 2000. ①

FOR WALKERS

Starting point: *Corner of Burgstraat and Gewad.*
Distance: *app. 4 km.*
Duration: *1 hour.*
Getting there: *tram 1.*

Prinsenhof
The walled castle had a U-shaped ground plan. The inner courtyard was surrounded by a chapel and luxuriously appointed buildings. ②

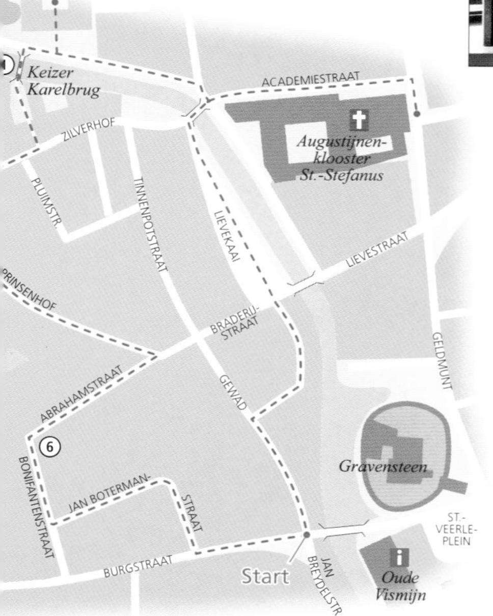

SYMBOLS

– –	Recommended route
■	Significant sights

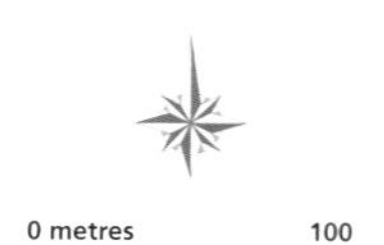

Berg van Barmhartigheid (1621-1622)
Architect Wenceslas Coeberger himself introduced and built the Bergen Van Barmhartigheid (loan offices) in Flanders. Here, loans could be taken out at low interest rates, though with the provision of collateral. ⑥

Ghent Illuminated

When night falls, the historic inner city takes on a fairy-tale-like atmosphere thanks to its unique lighting system. The formerly overpowering lighting provided by spotlights has been replaced with more discreet white light emitted by indirect wall lighting. This lighting system was designed by the famous French lighting designer Roland Jéol in conjunction with environmental designer Filip Vanderhavenbeke from Brugge. The reflection of the Graslei and Korenlei in the water of the Leie is an extraordinary sight. Besides this, other historic buildings and streets are tastefully lit. Make sure you take a walk before midnight, because when the clock strikes twelve, this atmospheric lighting is replaced with traditional lighting.

***The Graslei**, still the most beautiful street in Ghent, even at night.* ⑥

***The Korenlei** reflected in the Leie.* ⑤

***The Gravensteen**, the residence of the counts of Flanders in the medieval city.* ④

***The Vlaamse Opera** on Schouwburgstraat.* ⑦

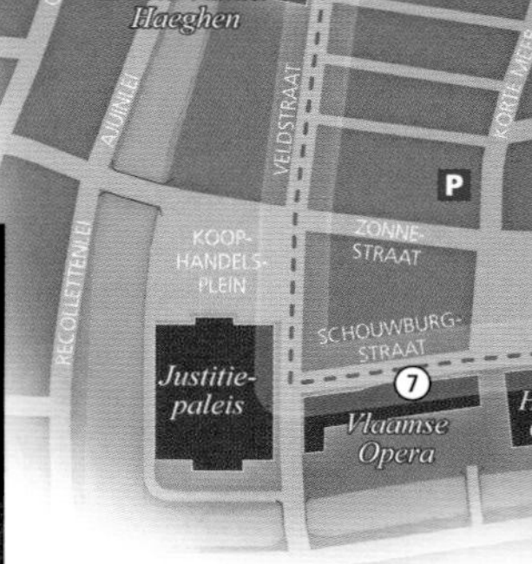

Lichtfestival Gent
At various locations along the course, works by prominent lighting artists and designers can be viewed during Light Festival Ghent.
www.lichtfestivalgent.be

FOR WALKERS

Starting point: *Kouter*
Distance: *app. 1 km.*
Duration: *1 hour.*
Getting there: *tram 1.*

SYMBOLS

– – Recommended route

Significant sights

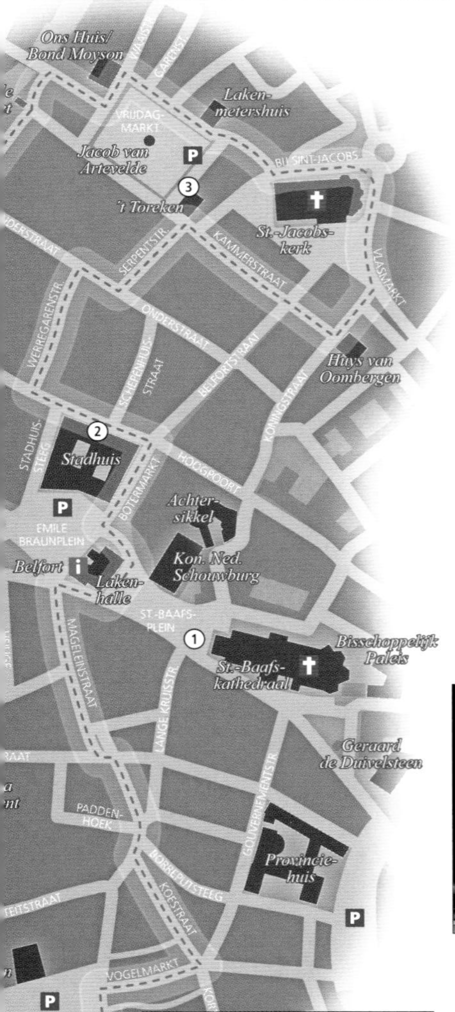

Ons Huis/ Bond Moyson
Laken-metershuis
Vrijdag-markt
Jacob van Artevelde
Bij Sint-Jacobs
't Toreken
St.-Jacobs-kerk
Serpentstr.
Kammerstraat
Vlasmarkt
Onderstraat
Werregarenstr.
Schepenhuis-straat
Belfortstraat
Huys van Oombergen
Koningstraat
Stadhuis-steeg
Stadhuis
Botermarkt
Hoogpoort
Achter-sikkel
Emile Braunplein
Belfort
Laken-halle
Kon. Ned. Schouwburg
St.-Baafs-plein
St.-Baafs-kathedraal
Bisschoppelijk Paleis
Mageleinstraat
Lange Kruisstr.
Geeraard de Duivelsteen
Gouvernementstr.
Padden-hoek
Provincie-huis
Borreputsteeg
Koestraat
Vogelmarkt
Start
Ketelvaart

***'t Toreken**, the tanners' company house, on the Vrijdagmarkt.* ③

***The town hall at the Botermarkt** with its Gothic wing (right) and Renaissance wing (left).* ②

***St.-Baafsplein** with the Koninklijke Nederlandse Schouwburg and St.-Baafs-kathedraal.* ①

City on the water

The Scheldt and the Leie rivers have played an important role in the development and growth of Ghent. The city developed at the confluence of these two rivers. They brought wealth and prosperity to Ghent. Grain and wool were transported by boat, stored and traded at the markets here. When access to the North Sea became limited, the Lieve, the Brugse Vaart and the Sassevaart (Canal between Ghent and Terneuzen) created a solution. At the end of the 19th century, open water disappeared from the city. Canals, waterways and tributaries of the Scheldt and the Leie were filled in or covered. But open water is slowly making a comeback to the city. The filled-in Nederschelde (or Reep) has been re-excavated. The cycling route through the city often passes historic areas that are – not by coincidence – located near water.

Industry
From the 18th century, many industries were established on the Lieve banks. ⑥

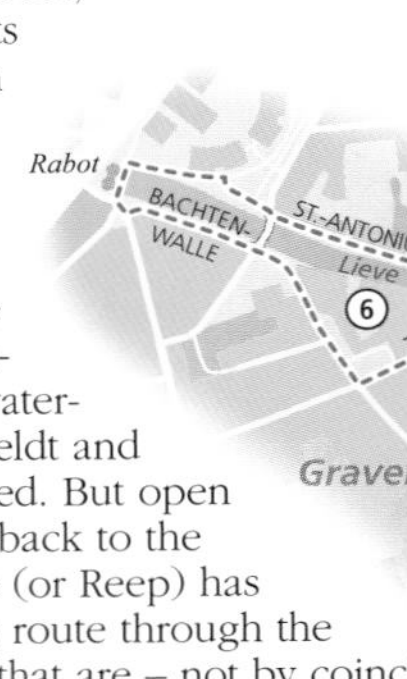

Tusschen Brugghen
Grain was stored in the old Ghent harbour. Buildings like the Korenmetershuis, Korenstapelhuis, Tolhuis and the company houses of the Vrije and Onvrije Schippers are reminders of this period. ①

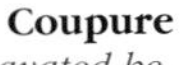

Coupure
The Coupure, excavated between 1751 and 1753, connects the Brugse Vaart to the old Ghent inner harbour (Tusschen Brugghen) via the Leie. Initially, the area through which it flowed was rural. ②

Lock

The lock at the Reke bridges the difference in water level between the Leie and the Scheldt. It also acts as a barrier to prevent flooding during spring tides. ⑤

FOR CYCLISTS

Starting point: *Graslei*
Distance: *10 km.*
Duration: *2 hours.*

SYMBOLS

– – Recommended route

Significant sights

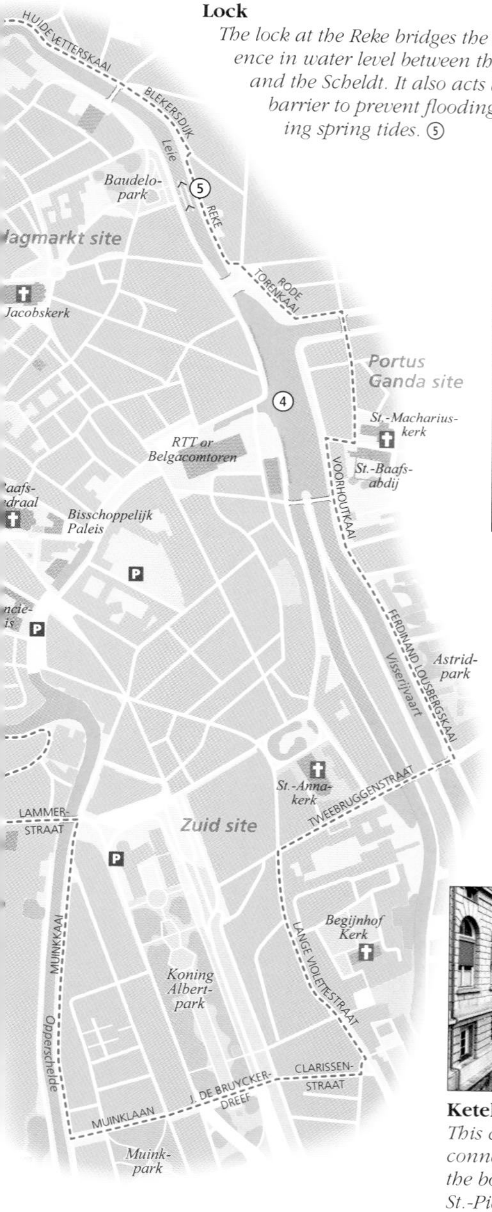

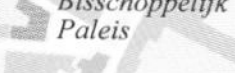

Confluence of the Leie and the Scheldt

For centuries, the Leie and the Scheldt have met here. In 1960, the Nederschelde or Reep was filled in. In 2003, a section of the re-excavated Scheldt was reconnected to the Leie. ④

SYMBOLS

– – Recommended route

Ketelvaart

This canal, excavated around 1100 to connect the Leie and the Scheldt, formed the boundary between the city and St.-Pietersdorp. ③

Street Name Index

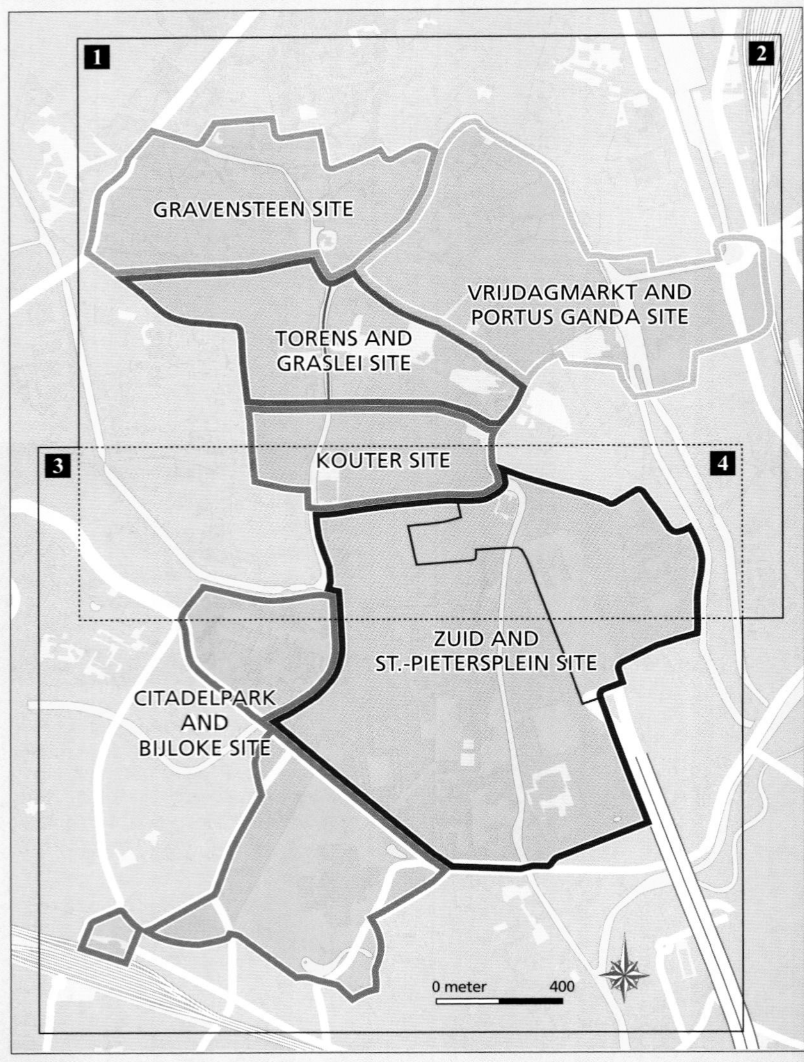

C

D

E

F

G

H

I

J

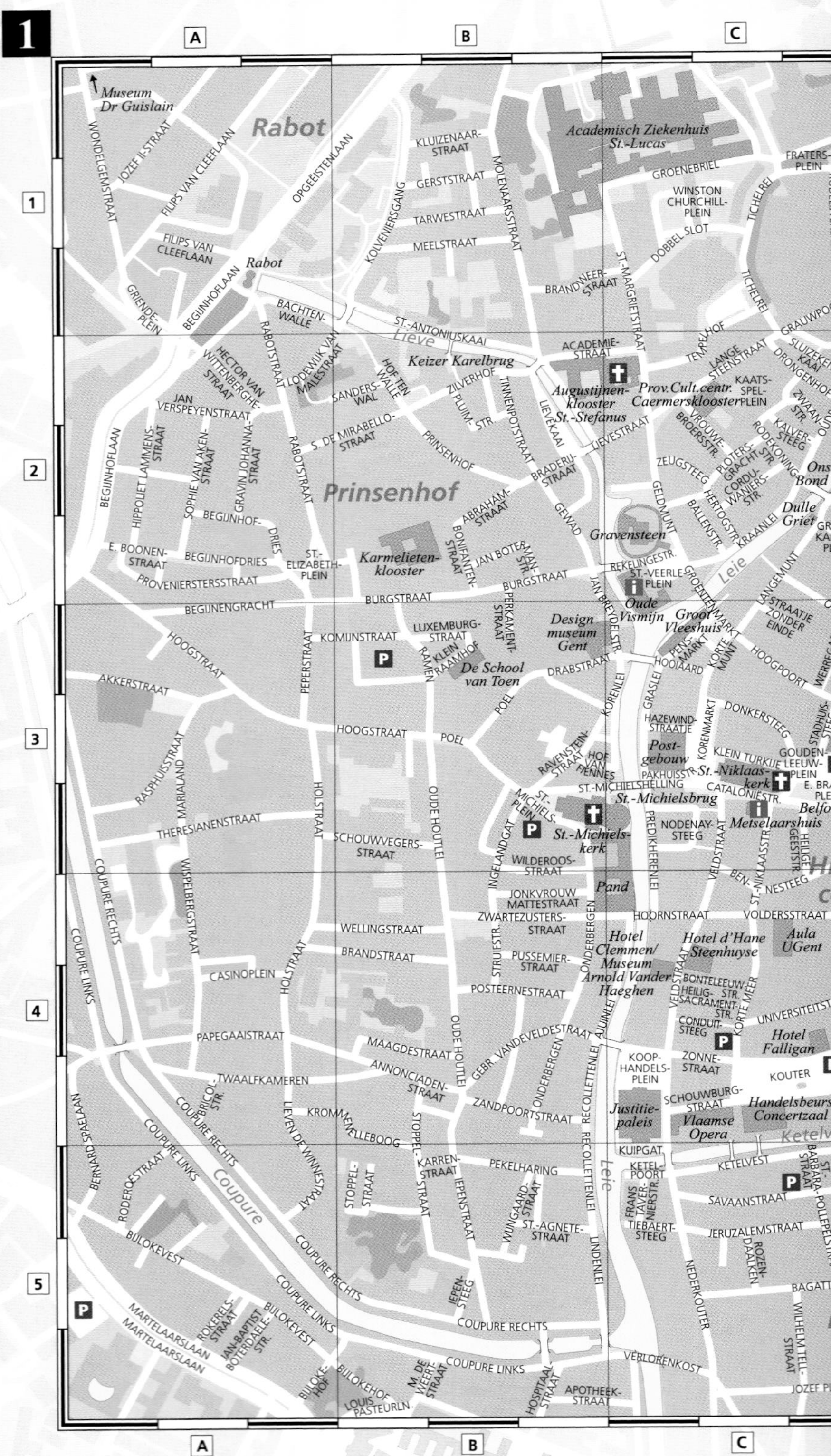
1
A
B
C
Museum Dr Guislain
Rabot
WONDELGEMSTRAAT
JOZEF II-STRAAT
FILIPS VAN CLEEFLAAN
OPGEËISTENLAAN
KLUIZENAARSTRAAT
GERSTSTRAAT
TARWESTRAAT
MEELSTRAAT
KOLVENIERSGANG
MOLENAARSSTRAAT
Academisch Ziekenhuis St.-Lucas
FRATERSPLEIN
GROENEBRIEL
WINSTON CHURCHILL-PLEIN
TICHELREI
DOBBEL SLOT
FILIPS VAN CLEEFLAAN
Rabot
BEGIJNHOFLAAN
GRIENDEPLEIN
BACHTENWALLE
RABOTSTRAAT
ST.-ANTONIUSKAAI
Lieve
BRANDWEERSTRAAT
ST.-MARGRIETSTRAAT
TEMPELHOF
GRAUWPOORT
SLUIZEKEN-KAAI
DRONGENHOF
ACADEMIESTRAAT
LANGE STEENSTRAAT
KAATSSPEL-PLEIN
ZWAANSTR.
Keizer Karelbrug
HECTOR VAN WITTENBERGHESTRAAT
LODEWIJK VAN MALESTRAAT
HOF TEN WALLE
SANDERSWAL
ZILVERHOF
PLUIMSTR.
TINNENPOTSTRAAT
LIEVEKAAI
Augustijnenklooster St.-Stefanus
Prov.Cult.centr. Caermersklooster
VROUWEBROERSSTR.
KALVERSTEEG
RODEKONINGSTR.
JAN VERSPEYENSTRAAT
S. DE MIRABELLOSTRAAT
PRINSENHOF
LIEVESTRAAT
BRADERIJSTRAAT
ZEUGSTEEG
PLOTERSGRACHT
CORDUWANIERSSTR.
Ons Bond
BEGIJNHOFLAAN
HIPPOLIET LAMMENSSTRAAT
SOPHIE VAN AKENSTRAAT
GRAVIN JOHANNASTRAAT
RABOTSTRAAT
Prinsenhof
ABRAHAMSTRAAT
GEWAD
GELDMUNT
HERTOGSTR.
BALLENSTR.
KRAANLEI
Dulle Griet
BEGIJNHOFDRIES
BONIFANTENSTRAAT
JAN BOTERMANSTR.
Gravensteen
REKELINGESTR.
E. BOONENSTRAAT
BEGIJNHOFDRIES
ST.-ELIZABETHPLEIN
Karmelietenklooster
ST.-VEERLEPLEIN
Leie
PROVENIERSTERSSTRAAT
BURGSTRAAT
BURGSTRAAT
JAN BREYDELSTR.
GROENTENMARKT
LANGEMUNT
BEGIJNENGRACHT
Oude Vismijn
Groot Vleeshuis
STRAATJE ZONDER EINDE
HOOGSTRAAT
PEPERSTRAAT
KOMIJNSTRAAT
LUXEMBURGSTRAAT
RAMEN
KLEIN RAAMHOF
PERKAMENTSTRAAT
Design museum Gent
PENSMARKT
HOOIAARD
KORTE MUNT
HOOGPOORT
De School van Toen
DRABSTRAAT
AKKERSTRAAT
POEL
KORENLEI
GRASLEI
DONKERSTEEG
HAZEWINDSTRAATJE
KORENMARKT
HOOGSTRAAT
POEL
Postgebouw
RASPHUISSTRAAT
MARIALAND
RAVENSTEINSTRAAT
HOF VAN FIENNES
KLEIN TURKIJE
PAKHUISSTR.
St.-Niklaaskerk
GOUDENLEEUWPLEIN
E. BRAUNPLEIN
ST.-MICHIELSHELLING
CATALONIËSTR.
HOLSTRAAT
OUDE HOUTLEI
ST.-MICHIELSPLEIN
St.-Michielsbrug
Belfort
THERESIANENSTRAAT
INGELANDGAT
St.-Michielskerk
PREDIKHERENLEI
NODENAYSTEEG
Metselaarshuis
SCHOUWVEGERSSTRAAT
WILDEROOSSTRAAT
VELDSTRAAT
ST.-NIKLAASSTR.
HEILIGE GEESTSTR.
BENNESTEEG
WISPELBERGSTRAAT
COUPURE RECHTS
COUPURE LINKS
JONKVROUW MATTESTRAAT
Pand
HOORNSTRAAT
VOLDERSSTRAAT
WELLINGSTRAAT
ZWARTEZUSTERSSTRAAT
Aula UGent
BRANDSTRAAT
STRUIFSTR.
ONDERBERGEN
Hotel Clemmen/ Museum Arnold Vander Haeghen
Hotel d'Hane Steenhuyse
PUSSEMIERSTRAAT
CASINOPLEIN
HOLSTRAAT
BONTELEEUWSTR.
HEILIG-SACRAMENTSTR.
POSTEERNESTRAAT
CONDUITSTEEG
KORTE MEER
UNIVERSITEITSTRAAT
PAPEGAAISTRAAT
GEBR. VANDEVELDESTRAAT
AJUINLEI
Hotel Falligan
MAAGDESTRAAT
KOOPHANDELSPLEIN
ZONNESTRAAT
ANNONCIADENSTRAAT
KOUTER
TWAALFKAMEREN
BRICOLSTR.
OUDE HOUTLEI
ONDERBERGEN
RECOLLETTENLEI
Justitiepaleis
SCHOUWBURGSTRAAT
Handelsbeurs Concertzaal
LIEVEN DE WINNESTRAAT
KROMMENELLEBOOG
ZANDPOORTSTRAAT
Vlaamse Opera
Ketelvest
BERNARD SPAELAAN
COUPURE RECHTS
STOPPELSTRAAT
KARRENSTRAAT
PEKELHARING
KUIPGAT
KETELPOORT
KETELVEST
ST.-BARBARASTRAAT
RODEROESTRAAT
COUPURE LINKS
STOPPELSTRAAT
IEPENSTRAAT
WIJNGAARDSTRAAT
ST.-AGNETESTRAAT
RECOLLETTENLEI
Leie
FRANS TAVERNIERSTR.
SAVAANSTRAAT
POLEPELSTRAAT
Coupure
TIEBAERTSTEEG
JERUZALEMSTRAAT
BIJLOKEVEST
LINDENLEI
NEDERKOUTER
ROZENDAALKEN
IEPENSTEEG
COUPURE RECHTS
BAGATTENSTRAAT
COUPURE LINKS
MARTELAARSLAAN
ROKERELSTRAAT
BIJLOKEVEST
JAN-BAPTIST BOTERDAELESTR.
COUPURE RECHTS
WILHELM TELLSTRAAT
MARTELAARSLAAN
VERLORENKOST
COUPURE LINKS
BIJLOKEHOF
BIJLOKEHOF
LOUIS PASTEURLN.
M. DE WEERTSTRAAT
HOSPITAALSTRAAT
APOTHEEKSTRAAT
JOZEF PLATEAUSTRAAT
2
3
4
5

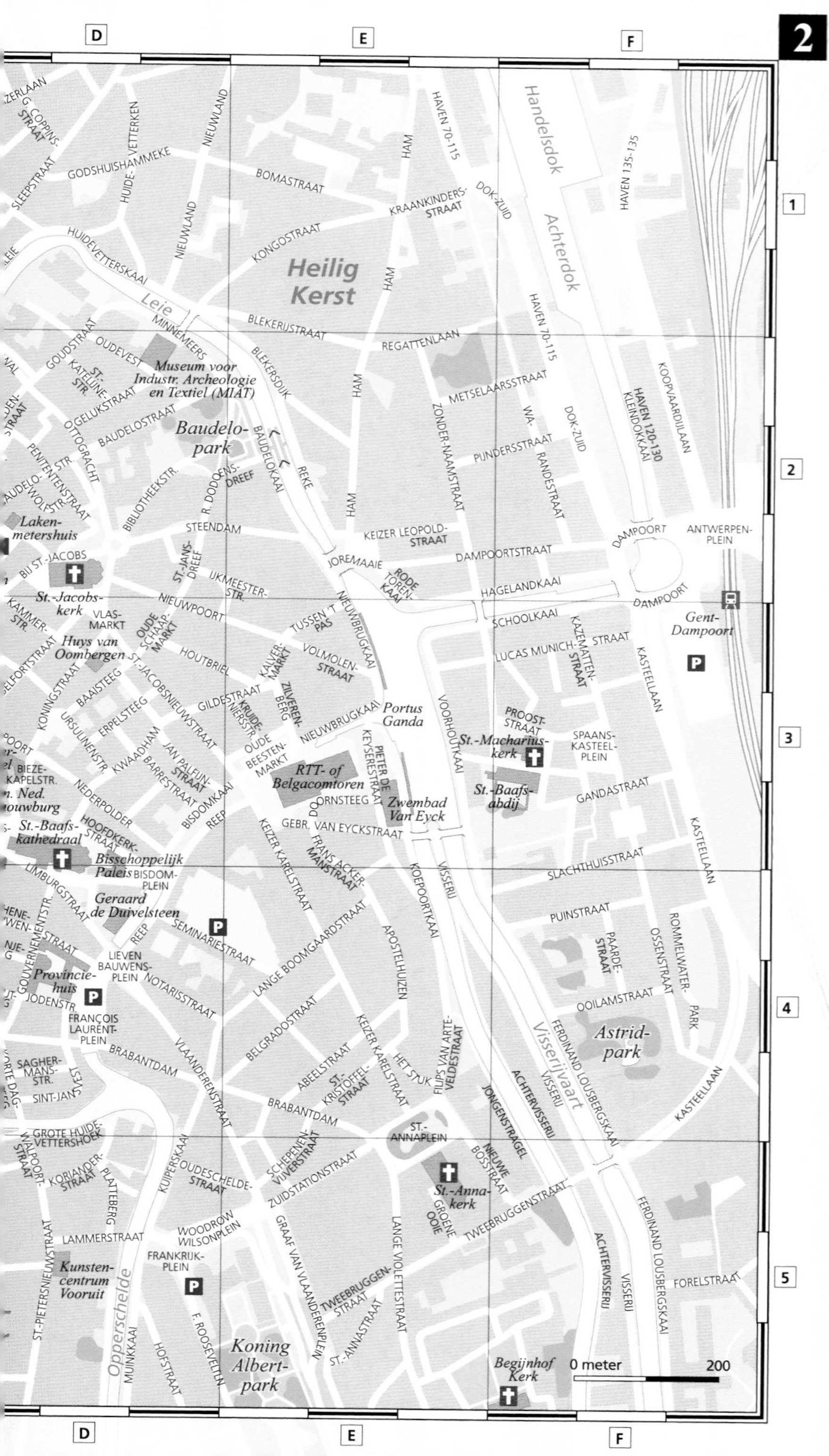

2
D
E
F
1
2
3
4
5
Heilig Kerst
Handelsdok
Achterdok
Leie
Visserijvaart
Opperschelde
Museum voor Industr. Archeologie en Textiel (MIAT)
Baudelopark
Lakenmetershuis
St.-Jacobskerk
Huys van Oombergen
Portus Ganda
RTT- of Belgacomtoren
Zwembad Van Eyck
St.-Machariuskerk
St.-Baafsabdij
Gent-Dampoort
St.-Baafskathedraal
Bisschoppelijk Paleis
Geraard de Duivelsteen
Provinciehuis
Astridpark
St.-Annakerk
Kunstencentrum Vooruit
Koning Albertpark
Begijnhof Kerk
0 meter
200
BOMASTRAAT
KONGOSTRAAT
KRAANKINDERSSTRAAT
DOK-ZUID
HAVEN 70-115
HAVEN 135-135
HAVEN 120-130 KLEINDOKKAAI
KOOPVAARDIJLAAN
HAM
NIEUWLAND
GODSHUISHAMMEKE
HUIDEVETTERKEN
HUIDEVETTERSKAAI
SLEEPSTRAAT
G. COPPINSSTRAAT
BLEKERIJSTRAAT
REGATTENLAAN
MINNEMEERS
OUDEVEST
GOUDSTRAAT
ST.-KATELIJNESTR.
BLEKERSDIJK
METSELAARSSTRAAT
WARANDESTRAAT
ZONDER-NAAMSTRAAT
PIJNDERSSTRAAT
BAUDELOSTRAAT
OGELUKSTRAAT
OTTOGRACHT
PENITENTENSTRAAT
BAUDELOKAAI
REKE
R. DODOENSDREEF
BIBLIOTHEEKSTR.
STEENDAM
KEIZER LEOPOLDSTRAAT
DAMPOORTSTRAAT
DAMPOORT
ANTWERPENPLEIN
JOREMAAIE
RODE TORENKAAI
HAGELANDKAAI
SCHOOLKAAI
ST.-JANSDREEF
IJKMEESTERSTR.
BIJ ST.-JACOBS
NIEUWPOORT
VLASMARKT
OUDE SCHAAPMARKT
TUSSEN 'T PAS
NIEUWBRUGKAAI
VOLMOLENSTRAAT
KALVERMARKT
HOUTBRIEL
LUCAS MUNICHSTRAAT
KAZEMATTENSTRAAT
KASTEELLAAN
ST.-JACOBSNIEUWSTRAAT
BAAISTEEG
GILDESTRAAT
KRUIDENIERSSTR.
ZILVERENBERG
KONINGSTRAAT
ERPELSTEEG
URSULINENSTR.
KWAADHAM
JAN PALFIJNSTRAAT
BARRESTRAAT
OUDE BEESTENMARKT
KEYSERESTRAAT
PIETER DE
VOORHOUTKAAI
PROOSTSTRAAT
SPAANSKASTEELPLEIN
GANDASTRAAT
BIEZEKAPELSTR.
NEDERPOLDER
BISDOMKAAI
REEP
DOORNSTEEG
GEBR. VAN EYCKSTRAAT
HOOFDKERKSTRAAT
LIMBURGSTRAAT
BISDOMPLEIN
KEIZER KARELSTRAAT
FRANS ACKERMANSTRAAT
KOEPOORTKAAI
VISSERIJ
SLACHTHUISSTRAAT
PUINSTRAAT
PAARDESTRAAT
OSSENSTRAAT
ROMMELWATERPARK
SEMINARIESTRAAT
LANGE BOOMGAARDSTRAAT
APOSTELHUIZEN
GOUVERNEMENTSTR.
LIEVEN BAUWENSPLEIN
NOTARISSTRAAT
OOILAMSTRAAT
JODENSTR.
FRANÇOIS LAURENTPLEIN
BELGRADOSTRAAT
FILIPS VAN ARTEVELDESTRAAT
FERDINAND LOUSBERGSKAAI
BRABANTDAM
VLAANDERENSTRAAT
ABEELSTRAAT
ST.-KRISTOFFELSTRAAT
HET SLIJK
ACHTERVISSERIJ
SAGHERMANSSTR.
SINT-JANSVEST
GROTE HUIDEVETTERSHOEK
ST.-ANNAPLEIN
JONGENSTRAGEL
NIEUWE BOSSTRAAT
WALPOORTSTRAAT
KORIANDERSTRAAT
PLATTEBERG
KUIPERSKAAI
OUDESCHELDESTRAAT
SCHEPENENVIJVERSTRAAT
ZUIDSTATIONSTRAAT
GROENE OOIE
TWEEBRUGGENSTRAAT
LAMMERSTRAAT
WOODROW WILSONPLEIN
FRANKRIJKPLEIN
GRAAF VAN VLAANDERENPLEIN
LANGE VIOLETTESTRAAT
FORELSTRAAT
ST.-PIETERSNIEUWSTRAAT
MUINKKAAI
HOFSTRAAT
F. ROOSEVELTLN
TWEEBRUGGENSTRAAT
ST.-ANNASTRAAT

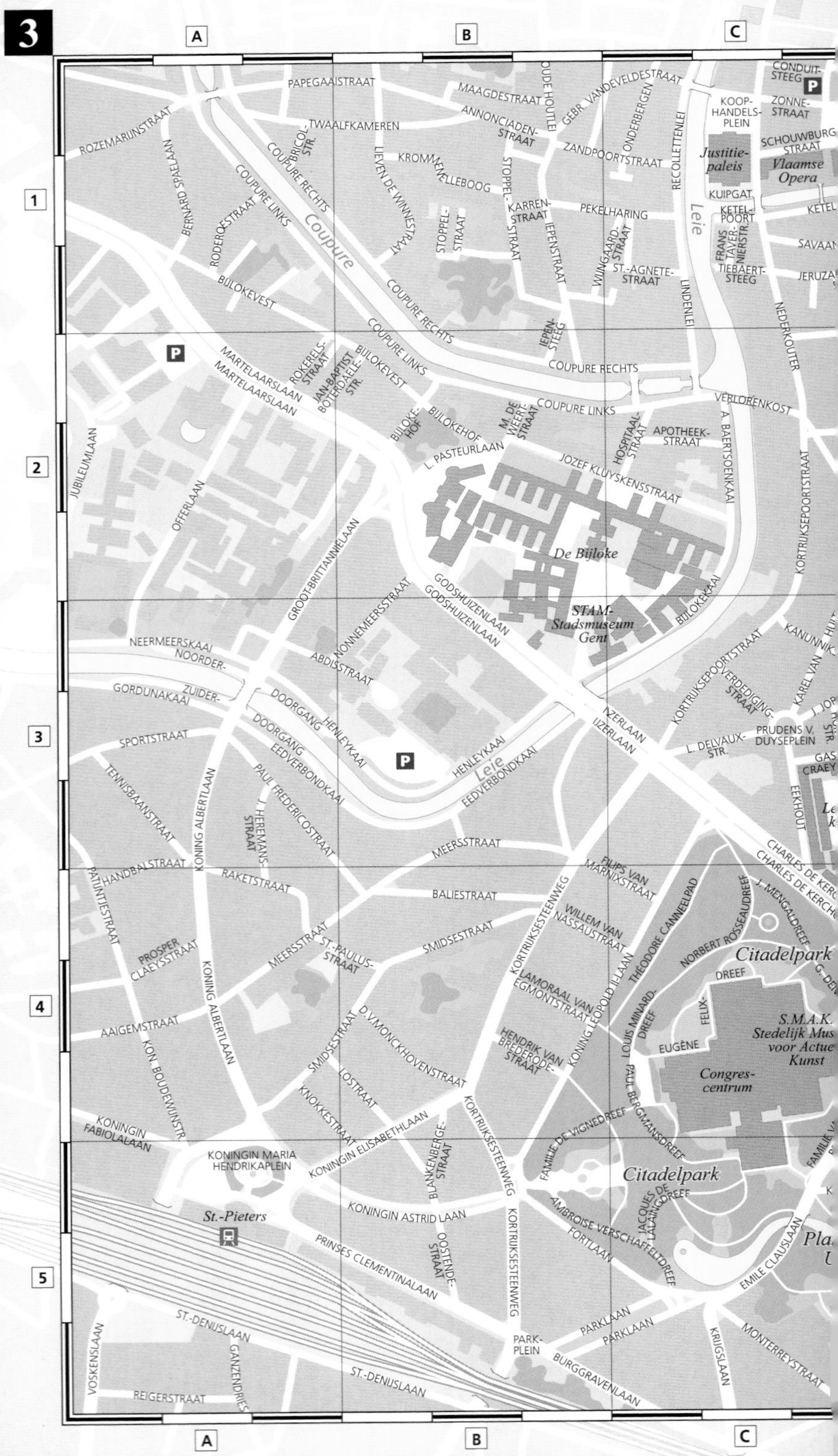
3
A
B
C
1
2
3
4
5
Coupure
Leie
Justitie-paleis
Vlaamse Opera
De Bijloke
STAM-Stadsmuseum Gent
Citadelpark
S.M.A.K. Stedelijk Mus voor Actue Kunst
Congres-centrum
St.-Pieters
PAPEGAAISTRAAT
MAAGDESTRAAT
GEBR. VANDEVELDESTRAAT
ANNONCIADEN-STRAAT
TWAALFKAMEREN
ROZEMARIJNSTRAAT
BERNARD SPAELAAN
COUPURE LINKS
COUPURE RECHTS
RODEROESTRAAT
BULOKEVEST
LIEVEN DE WINNESTRAAT
KROMMEWELLEBOOG
STOPPELSTRAAT
KARRENSTRAAT
IEPENSTRAAT
ZANDPOORTSTRAAT
ONDERBERGEN
RECOLLETTENLEI
PEKELHARING
WIJNGAARDSTRAAT
ST.-AGNETESTRAAT
LINDENLEI
IEPENSTEEG
KOOPHANDELSPLEIN
CONDUITSTEEG
ZONNESTRAAT
SCHOUWBURGSTRAAT
KUIPGAT
KETELPOORT
FRANS TAVERNIERSTR.
TIEBAERTSTEEG
NEDERKOUTER
MARTELAARSLAAN
ROKERELSSTRAAT
JAN-BAPTIST BOTERDAELESTR.
BIJLOKEHOF
M. DE WEERTSTRAAT
HOSPITAALSTRAAT
APOTHEEKSTRAAT
VERLORENKOST
A. BAERTSOENKAAI
JUBILEUMLAAN
OFFERLAAN
L. PASTEURLAAN
JOZEF KLUYSKENSSTRAAT
KORTRIJKSEPOORTSTRAAT
GROOT-BRITTANNIËLAAN
NONNEMEERSSTRAAT
GODSHUIZENLAAN
BIJLOKEKAAI
NEERMEERSKAAI
NOORDER-
ZUIDER-
GORDUNAKAAI
ABDISSTRAAT
DOORGANG
HENLEYKAAI
EEDVERBONDKAAI
IJZERLAAN
VERDEDIGINGSTRAAT
PRUDENS V. DUYSEPLEIN
L. DELVAUXSTR.
KANUNNIK
KAREL VAN
SPORTSTRAAT
TENNISBAANSTRAAT
KONING ALBERTLAAN
J. HEREMANSSTRAAT
PAUL FREDERICQSTRAAT
MEERSSTRAAT
EEKHOUT
CHARLES DE KERCHOVE
HANDBALSTRAAT
PATIJNTJESTRAAT
RAKETSTRAAT
BALIESTRAAT
FILIPS VAN MARNIXSTRAAT
J. MENGALDREEF
THEODORE CANNEELPAD
NORBERT ROSSEAUDREEF
KORTRIJKSESTEENWEG
WILLEM VAN NASSAUSTRAAT
PROSPER CLAEYSSTRAAT
ST.-PAULUSSTRAAT
SMIDSESTRAAT
LAMORAAL VAN EGMONTSTRAAT
KONING LEOPOLD II-LAAN
LOUIS MINARDDREEF
FELIX-DREEF
EUGÈNE
AAIGEMSTRAAT
KON. BOUDEWIJNSTR.
D.V.MONCKHOVENSTRAAT
HENDRIK VAN BREDERODESTRAAT
PAUL BERGMANSDREEF
LOSTRAAT
KNOKKESTRAAT
KONINGIN FABIOLALAAN
KONINGIN MARIA HENDRIKAPLEIN
KONINGIN ELISABETHLAAN
BLANKENBERGESTRAAT
FAMILIE DE VIGNEDREEF
JACQUES DE LALAINGDREEF
KONINGIN ASTRID LAAN
AMBROISE VERSCHAFFELTDREEF
FORTLAAN
PRINSES CLEMENTINALAAN
OOSTENDESTRAAT
EMILE CLAUSLAAN
ST.-DENIJSLAAN
GANZENDRIES
VOSKENSLAAN
REIGERSTRAAT
PARKPLEIN
PARKLAAN
BURGGRAVENLAAN
KRIJGSLAAN
MONTERREYSTRAAT

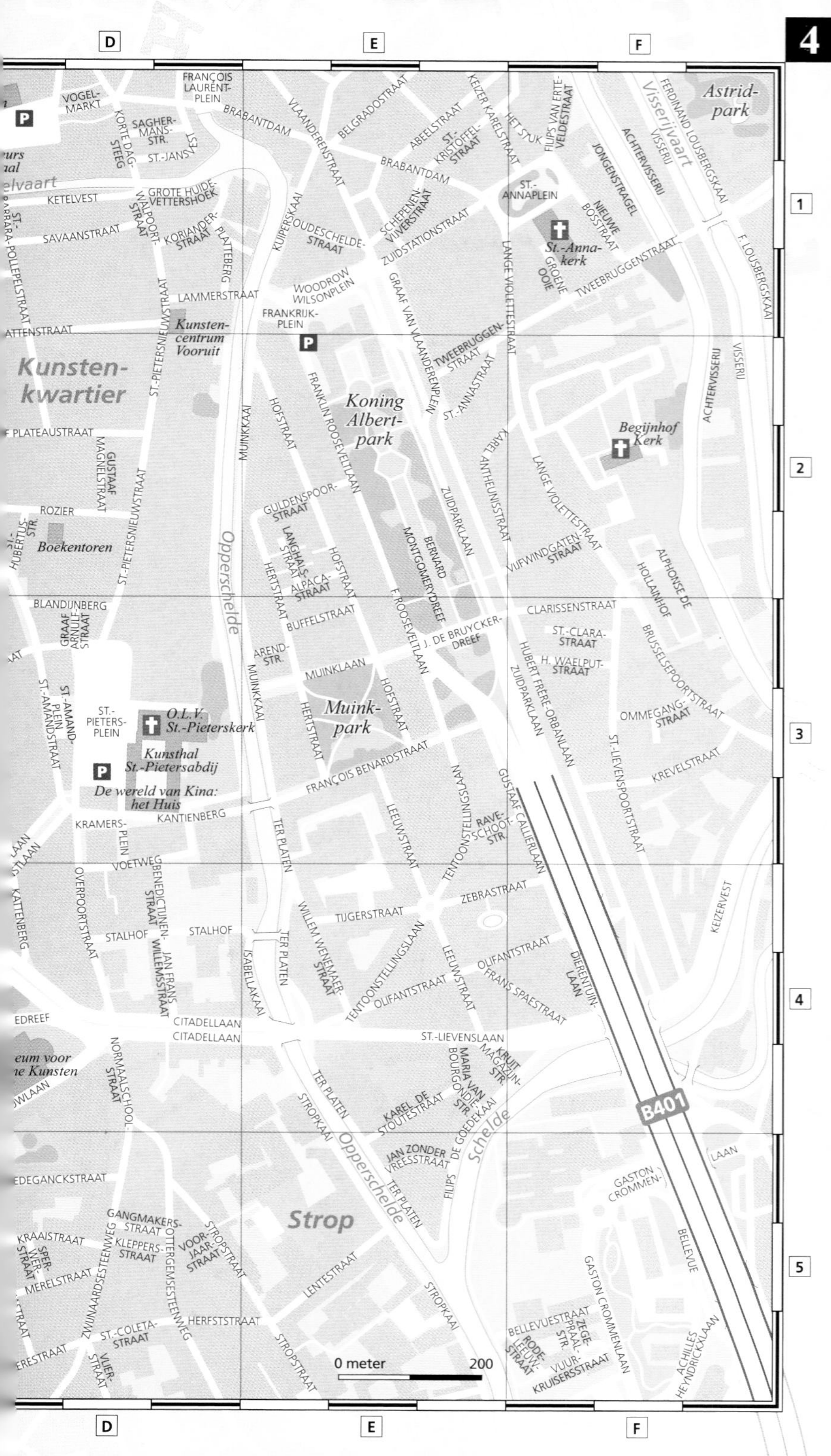

4
D
E
F
1
2
3
4
5
FRANÇOIS LAURENT-PLEIN
VOGEL-MARKT
P
SAGHER-MANS-STR.
KORTE DAG-STEEG
ST.-JANSVEST
BRABANTDAM
VLAANDERENSTRAAT
BELGRADOSTRAAT
ABEELSTRAAT
ST.-KRISTOFFEL-STRAAT
KEIZER KARELSTRAAT
HET STUK
FILIPS VAN ERTE-VELDESTRAAT
Visserijvaart
FERDINAND LOUSBERGSKAAI
VISSERIJ
Astrid-park
ACHTERVISSERIJ
JONGENSTRAGEL
NIEUWE BOSSTRAAT
ST.-ANNAPLEIN
St.-Anna-kerk
GROENE OOIE
TWEEBRUGGENSTRAAT
F. LOUSBERGSKAAI
KETELVEST
GROTE HUIDE-VETTERSHOEK
WALPOORT-STRAAT
ST.-BARBARA-POLLEPELSTRAAT
SAVAANSTRAAT
KORIANDER-STRAAT
PLATTEBERG
KUIPERSKAAI
OUDESCHELDE-STRAAT
SCHEPENEN-VIJVERSTRAAT
ZUIDSTATIONSTRAAT
LANGE VIOLETTESTRAAT
LAMMERSTRAAT
WOODROW WILSONPLEIN
FRANKRIJK-PLEIN
GRAAF VAN VLAANDERENPLEIN
ST.-PIETERSNIEUWSTRAAT
Kunsten-centrum Vooruit
Kunsten-kwartier
TWEEBRUGGEN-STRAAT
ST.-ANNASTRAAT
ACHTERVISSERIJ
VISSERIJ
MUINKKAAI
HOFSTRAAT
FRANKLIN ROOSEVELTLAAN
Koning Albert-park
Begijnhof Kerk
PLATEAUSTRAAT
GUSTAAF MAGNELSTRAAT
KAREL ANTHEUNISSTRAAT
LANGE VIOLETTESTRAAT
ZUIDPARKLAAN
ROZIER
GULDENSPOOR-STRAAT
ST.-HUBERTUS-STR.
Boekentoren
Opperschelde
LANGHALS-STRAAT
HERTSTRAAT
ALPACA-STRAAT
HOFSTRAAT
BERNARD MONTGOMERYDREEF
VIJFWINDGATEN-STRAAT
ALPHONSE DE HOLLAINHOF
BLANDIJNBERG
GRAAF ARNULF-STRAAT
BUFFELSTRAAT
F. ROOSEVELTLAAN
CLARISSENSTRAAT
J. DE BRUYCKER-DREEF
ST.-CLARA-STRAAT
BRUSSELSEPOORTSTRAAT
AREND-STR.
MUINKLAAN
H. WAELPUT-STRAAT
HUBERT FRERE-ORBANLAAN
ST.-AMANDSTRAAT
ST.-AMAND-PLEIN
ST.-PIETERS-PLEIN
O.L.V. St.-Pieterskerk
MUINKKAAI
Muink-park
HERTSTRAAT
HOFSTRAAT
ZUIDPARKLAAN
OMMEGANG-STRAAT
Kunsthal St.-Pietersabdij
FRANÇOIS BENARDSTRAAT
GUSTAAF CALLIERLAAN
ST.-LIEVENSPOORTSTRAAT
KREVELSTRAAT
De wereld van Kina: het Huis
KRAMERS-PLEIN
KANTIENBERG
TER PLATEN
LEEUWSTRAAT
TENTOONSTELLINGSLAAN
RAVE-SCHOOT-STR.
VOETWEG
BENEDICTIJNEN-STRAAT
OVERPOORTSTRAAT
KATTENBERG
ZEBRASTRAAT
TIJGERSTRAAT
KEIZERVEST
STALHOF
STALHOF
JAN FRANS WILLEMSSTRAAT
TER PLATEN
ISABELLAKAAI
WILLEM WENEMAER-STRAAT
TENTOONSTELLINGSLAAN
LEEUWSTRAAT
OLIFANTSTRAAT
OLIFANTSTRAAT
FRANS SPAESTRAAT
DIERENTUIN-LAAN
CITADELLAAN
CITADELLAAN
ST.-LIEVENSLAAN
KRUIT-MAGAZIJN-STR.
MARIA VAN BOURGONDIË-STR.
NORMAALSCHOOL-STRAAT
TER PLATEN
STROPKAAI
KAREL DE STOUTESTRAAT
DE GOEDEKAAI
Schelde
B401
Opperschelde
JAN ZONDER VREESSTRAAT
FILIPS
LAAN
GASTON CROMMEN-
EDEGANCKSTRAAT
GANGMAKERS-STRAAT
OTTERGEMSESTEENWEG
KLEPPERS-STRAAT
VOOR-JAAR-STRAAT
STROPSTRAAT
Strop
TER PLATEN
KRAAISTRAAT
SPER-WER-STRAAT
ZWIJNAARDSESTEENWEG
MERELSTRAAT
BELLEVUE
GASTON CROMMENLAAN
LENTESTRAAT
STROPKAAI
HERFSTSTRAAT
ST.-COLETA-STRAAT
BELLEVUESTRAAT
ZEGE-PRAAL-STR.
RODE-LEEUW-STRAAT
VUUR-KRUISERSSTRAAT
ACHILLES HEYNDRICKXLAAN
VIJER-STRAAT
STROPSTRAAT
0 meter
200

3

EAST FLANDERS AREA BY AREA

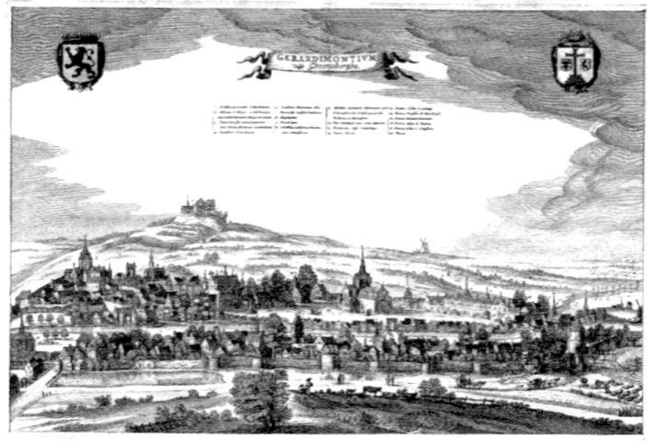

East Flanders at a glance

East Flanders is divided into five tourist regions surrounding the capital, Ghent. The Leie forms the backbone of the Leie district. At the start of the 20th century, the rural simplicity of St.-Martens-Latem attracted artists, sculptors and poets to the area. Meetjesland consists of creek areas in the north and swathes of forest in the south. In Waasland, one can follow in the footsteps of Reynaert de Vos (Reynard the fox) and the world-famous cartographer, Gerard Mercator. Scheldt Country, with its numerous lakes and ponds and the river Scheldt, is the region in Flanders with the most water. The cities of Dendermonde, Aalst and Ninove are certainly worth a visit. The best way to see the Flemish Ardennes, known as the 'most beautiful landscape in Flanders' for a reason, is by hiking or cycling. Four charming towns: Oudenaarde, Ronse, Geraardsbergen and Zottegem are located in these hills.

Meetjesland *is an area of contrasts. The north features polder meadows and creek areas, while the south has swathes of forest and peaceful watercourses.*

MEETJESLAND
pp. 152-161

GHENT

LEIESTREEK
pp. 142-151

FLEMISH ARDENNES
pp. 184-203

In the **Leie district**, *the meandering Leie inspired many artists. With their reminders of the Latemse Group, St.-Martens-Latem, Deurle and Machelen-aan-de-Leie are genuine artist's towns.*

Waasland *is ideally explored by bicycle, on foot or in a canoe. Rupelmonde, Fort Liefkenshoek and the castle of Wissekerke in Bazel are well worth a visit.*

WAASLAND
pp. 162-171

Scheldt

CHELDT COUNTRY
pp. 172-183

In **Scheldt Country**, *pontoon ferries transport cyclists and hikers across the Scheldt and the Dender. The three 'Dender cities' possess a wealth of historic buildings, festivals and folklore.*

0 kilometres 10

The **Flemish Ardennes** *are made up of a pleasant, flowing landscape with forested hills, steep climbs, areas of stunning natural beauty, inviting towns and small, scattered villages.*

LEIESTREEK

The source of the Leie is found near Lisbourg in northern France and it enters Flanders at Wervik. After flowing for 109 km, the river meets the Scheldt in Ghent. The section of the Leie between Deinze and Ghent is particularly beautiful. Here, the river still follows its original course through friendly villages and green pastures. The Leiestreek is the home of the Latem artists' groups.

Traditionally, the river is known for its role in flax processing. The river water is rich in lime and iron and is therefore ideal for the retting of flax. During this process, the pectin that binds the flax fibres is broken down. The river received the nick–name 'Golden River' due to its golden-yellow colour resulting from the retting process. In 1943, flax processing along the river was banned and water quality slowly improved. The Leiestreek of East Flanders forms part of the region that stretches along both banks of the Leie in the provinces of West and East Flanders. Inspired by Albijn Van den Abeele, painters, sculptors and poets settled in the towns along the Leie. St.-Martens-Latem and Deurle developed into small artists' colonies. The works of these artists and those of contemporary artists can be viewed in the museums of Deinze and Deurle. The eye-catching Roger Raveel Museum in Machelen-aan-de-Leie pays homage to the painter Roger Raveel. Ooidonk castle is located at one of the many bends in the Leie. This castle, which is still inhabited, is quite charming. Many of its chambers are richly furnished and it is surrounded by a large park.

More than anything else, the Leiestreek is an area through which to cycle and walk, with the Leie River as your guide. Various cycling and walk–ing routes connect Ghent to the towns along the river. Pontoons ferries at Astene, Bachte, Baarle and Afsnee transport cyclists and pedestrians across the Leie.

Sculpture *Muur der Verbeelding* by Roger Raveel in Machelen-aan-de-Leie

◁ The stunning Leie, winding its way through the flat landscape, inspired many artists

Exploring the Leiestreek

The Leiestreek, one of the most beautiful parts of East Flanders, is located between Zulte and Ghent on both sides of the Leie. It is a paradise for art lovers, nature enthusiasts, hikers and cyclists. Here, the Leie winds through the flat Flanders landscape. Over time, bends in the river have been cut off, creating oxbow lakes that linger on as reminders. The river is best explored from the water. Cruise boats sail between Ghent and Deinze during the summer months. You can also take a kayak tour from the Astene locks to Ghent. Besides various museums, the Leiestreek also features numerous historic buildings, including the famed Ooidonk castle.

The Ooidonk castle in Deinze is one of Belgium's most beautiful castles

MUNICIPALITIES

Deinze ❶
St.-Martens-Latem ❸
Zulte ❷

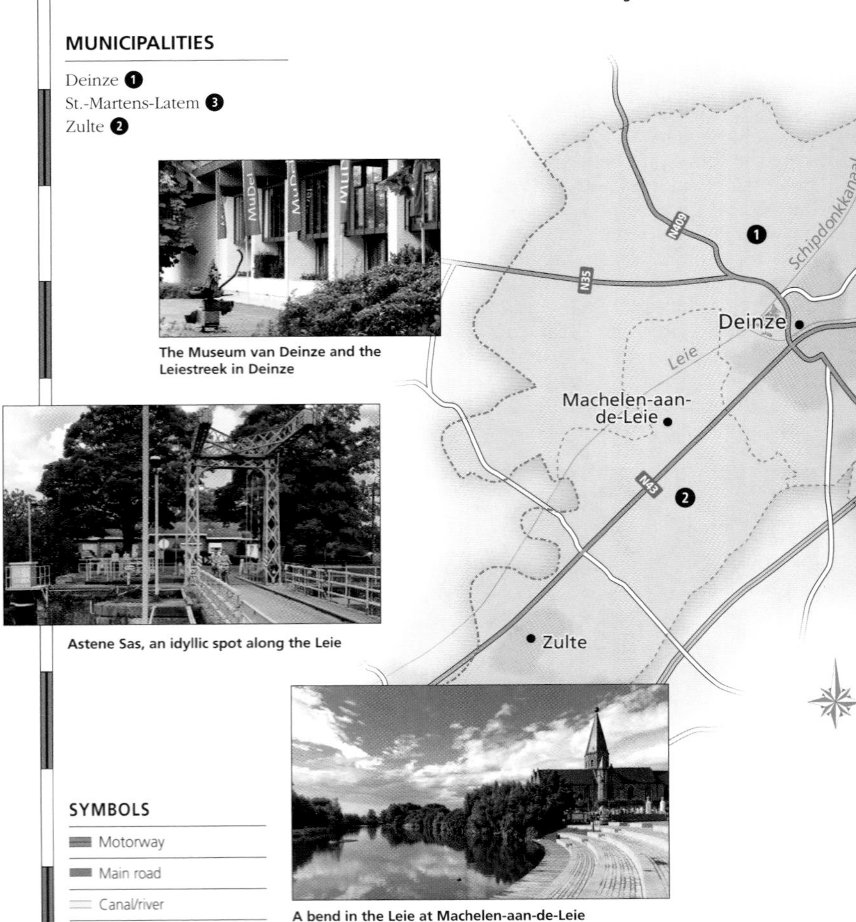

The Museum van Deinze and the Leiestreek in Deinze

Astene Sas, an idyllic spot along the Leie

A bend in the Leie at Machelen-aan-de-Leie

SYMBOLS

Motorway
Main road
Canal/river

ART HIGHLIGHTS ALONG THE LEIE

Starting point: *Deinze en de Leiestreek museum, Deinze.*
Distance: *28 km.*
Route: *junctions 5>3>4>9>11>12>90>86>20>14>13>11>9>6>5.*

Artists like Emile Claus, Albijn Van den Abeele, Leon and Gustave De Smet and Roger Raveel found inspiration along the Leie. This art-themed tour consists of two routes. The northern loop takes a route that passes Astene Sas, Ooidonk castle, the Dhondt-Dhaenens and Gustave De Smet museums and the Deurle town centre.

SEE ALSO

- ***Accommodation*** page 211
- ***Restaurants and cafés*** pages 219, 226

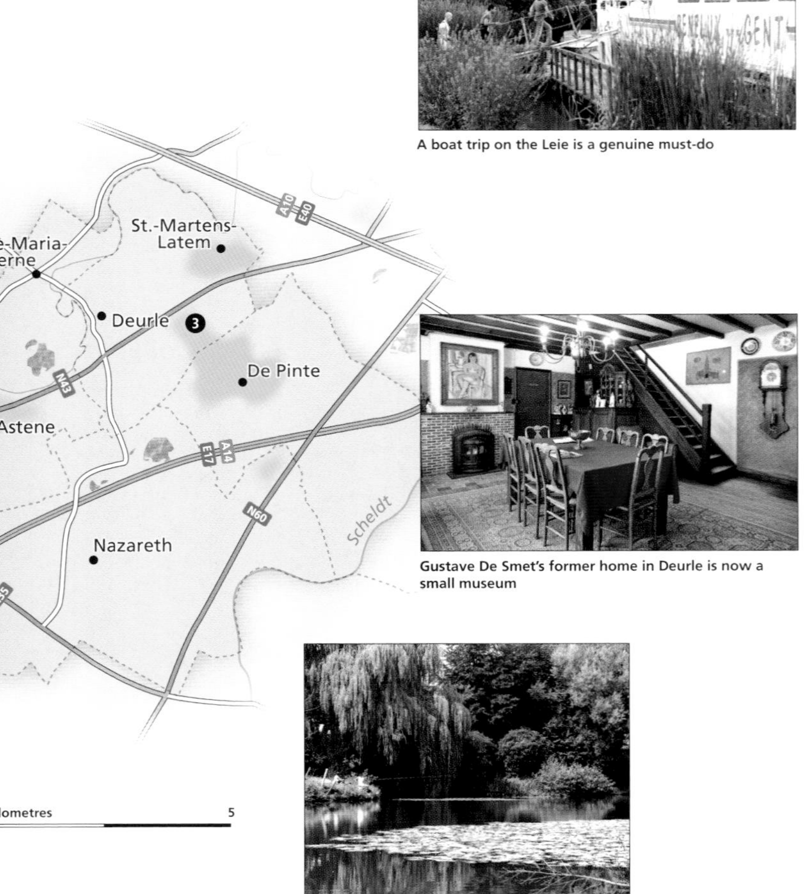

A boat trip on the Leie is a genuine must-do

Gustave De Smet's former home in Deurle is now a small museum

The Leie between Astene and Bachte

Leiestreek Tourism
www.toerisme-leiestreek.be

CITY OF DEINZE ❶

Road map B3. *29,000.*
www.deinze.be *Deinze.*
Emiel Clausplein 4 (09-3804601,
www.vvvleiestreek.be,
www.toerisme-leiestreek.be).

Deinze

The old industrial town of Deinze is the centre of the East Flanders Leiestreek. The Onze Lieve Vrouwekerk (Church of Our Lady) at the Markt is one of the historic buildings found in the town. This originally Romanesque church was rebuilt during the 14th century in the Scheldt-Gothic style. The austere **Museum van Deinze en de Leiestreek**, beautifully situated in a park along the Leie, provides an overview of the artists from the First and Second Latem group who lived and worked in the Leiestreek from 1900-1930 (*page 151*). Art displayed includes works by **George Minne,** Albijn Van den Abeele, Constant Permeke, Leon and Gustave De Smet and Roger Raveel. The **De Bietenoogst** by Emile Claus is one of the museum's greatest works. In addition to its permanent collection, the museum organises temporary exhibitions. The museum also features a small cultural-historical section.

Sculpture by George Minne

Museum van Deinze en de Leiestreek

Lucien Matthyslaan 3-5, Deinze.

Blauwe Poort of Ooidonk castle

Tel. *09-3819670. Tue-Fri 2pm-5:30 pm, Sat-Sun 10am-12pm and 2pm-5pmr.*
www.museumdeinze.be

Bachte-Maria-Leerne

The castle town of Bachte-Maria-Leerne is located along the Leie, the Oude Leie (an oxbow lake) and near the Schipdonk canal that flows towards Meetjesland.
From the centre, an attractive, tree-lined lane leads to the Blauwe Poort (Blue Gate), the entrance to Ooidonk castle *(pages 148-149).*

Astene

Astene Sas, a lock complex from 1861 with a drawbridge and lock house, is a romantic spot along the Leie. Until 1870, shipping traffic was forced to sail a few extra kilometres around a bend in the Leie. When this bend was canalised, the meander became an oxbow lake. A lock was constructed in the canal. The ***Bathio***, a self-service pontoon ferry, transports cyclists and pedestrians across the Leie to Bachte.

Cycling along marshes and river bends

Starting point: *Drongenplein, Drongen (Gent).*
Distance: *41,5 km (can be shortened to 30 km or 19 km).*
Route: *junctions 57>62>63>67>74>76>86>20>14>13>11>12>90>88>85>72>71>61>58>5.*
Leaflet: *available at Dienst voor Toerisme (tourism office).*

The Leiestreek between Drongen and Astene is an area of stunning natural beauty with the winding Leie serving as a guide. Along the riverbanks are the 'meersen', marsh areas that are seldom covered in water. This is an area of pristine natural beauty consisting of flowery

De Bietenoogst by Emile Claus (1890)

HISTORY OF DEINZE

Donsa, a 'raised area in the marshlands', was first mentioned in 840. The town originated along the Leie at the junction between two important trade routes (Oudenaarde-Bruges and Kortrijk-Ghent). In the 13th century, the small but prosperous town of Deinze was granted city status. Once in 1485 and again at the end of the 16th century, this walled city was completely destroyed, but rose again from the ashes both times. Deinze developed into an important centre for the silk and children's pram industry. After World War II, many livestock feed companies were established along the Leie. The Schipdonkkanaal, the diversion canal for the Leie, sent excess water from the Leie straight to the North Sea.

The Bathio self-service pontoon ferry transports cyclists across the Oude Leie

grasslands that create a rainbow of colours, especially during the spring. Between Deinze and Ghent, the Leie has retained its meandering character and has not been straightened, as it has south of Deinze, to aid shipping and provide more effective drainage.

ZULTE MUNICIPALITY ❷

Road map A4. 15,000.
www.zulte.be
(**www**.vvleiestreek.be, **www**.toerisme-leiestreek.be).

Machelen-aan-de-Leie

The town centre of Machelen developed along an old branch of the Leie. There is a great view of the river bend from the small amphitheatre on Kerkplein (Church Square). The modern-style **Roger Raveel Museum**, designed by Stéphane Beel, is located behind the church. The museum combines a new building with the adjacent, recently restored parsonage. Roger Raveel (1921), one of the greatest post-war Belgian artists, opened a museum in his hometown in 1999. This personalised museum, in which daylight and the relationship with the town play an important role, owns a rich collection of paintings, sketches and items belonging to the artist. The route through the museum presents a broad overview of the development of Raveel's body of work, from his initial 1950s works to his colouristic works of the 1980s and 1990s. Besides the works on permanent display, temporary exhibits are presented in the parsonage. There is more of Roger Raveel's work to be seen in the town. *De Muur der Verbeelding* (*wall of imagination*) on the Plein De Nieuwe Visie (square of new vision) is a concrete structure that is almost 40 m long. It consists of sculptures, mirrors, white squares, white poles and grass-green doors. The refreshing interior of the modern Maria Hulp der Christenen chapel at Posthoornstraat 70A (appr. 2 km outside the town centre) was also designed by the artist in its entirety. Author Gerard Reve (1923-2006) rests in the new graveyard. His gravestone reads, *U heb ik lief* (*You are the one I love*). Reve moved to Machelen in 1993, where he occupied the former doctors' mansion.

Roger Raveel Museum

Gildestraat 2-8, Machelen-aan-de-Leie. ***Tel.*** *09-3816000.*
Wed-Sat 11am-5pm.
www.rogerraveelmuseum.be

Roger Raveel Route

Starting point: *Roger Raveel Museum.*
Distance: *3,5 km.*
Leaflet: *available at Dienst voor Toerisme (Tourist Office).*

This walking route offers a look into the world of artist Roger Raveel. The route was planned in honour of his ninetieth birthday in 2011. Walkers follow in Raveel's footsteps through Machelen-aan-de-Leie as they pass the museum, the municipal school where his studio was located around 1960, and the Muur der Verbeelding. Raveel objected to plans to fill in the old branch of the Leie at Machelen. Thanks to him, the town kept its relationship with the river intact.

The Roger Raveel Museum presents more than 300 paintings and 2500 sketches by the artist

Ooidonk castle

The castle is located on a natural rise (*donk*) in the marshy Leiemeersen on a bend in the Leie. The current castle dates back to the 16th century, but the history of Ooidonk goes back much further than that. A homestead was built on the rise and it was later fortified. During the 14th century, Jan de Fosseux, lord of Nevele, ordered the conversion of the castle homestead into an imposing moated fortress. In 1592, Maarten della Faille replaced the medieval fortress with a luxurious castle built in Flemish-Spanish renaissance style. In 1864, the castle came to be owned by the t'Kint de Roodenbeke family. Its interior features rare furnishings, historic objects, rugs and a unique porcelain collection.

Ooidonk in 1735
Ooidonk depicted in a painting from 1735, when the castle was owned by the prominent della Faille family.

★ Castle garden
The French gardens surrounding the castle are very well kept. Extensive lawns, attractive flowerbeds and centuries-old trees create pleasant surroundings for a stroll.

STAR ATTRACTIONS

- ★ Castle garden
- ★ Round drawing room

Ooidonk castle
The castle is located on an expansive 300 ha estate, 45 ha of which are parks and ponds.

★ Round drawing room
Drawing room in the eastern tower containing Louis XV period furniture and a French bureau Mazarin. Large windows provide diffused light.

TIPS FOR VISITORS

Ooidonkdreef 9, Bachte-Maria-Leerne (Deinze). ***Tel.*** *09-2823570. castle: Apr-mid Sep Sun 2pm-5:30pm (Jul-Aug incl. Sat); Gardens: Tue-Sun 9am-6pm.* **www**.ooidonk.be *end Apr: Lifestyle Garden shows*

Castle at the end of the 16th century
Open renaissance view of the inner façade of the castle.

OOIDONK WALKING ROUTE

Starting point: *P Ooidonkdreef, Bachte-Maria-Leerne (Deinze).*
Distance: *7 km.*
Signposted*.*
Leaflet: *From Bachte-Maria-Leerne, the walking route passes through the Blauwe Poort and along the lane to the castle park. The return route follows the Oude Leie (Leiemeersen) and passes the Ter Meere castle on its way back to the departure point.*

Ooidonk wandelroute

ST.-MARTENS-LATEM MUNICIPALITY ❸

Road map B3. *8,300.* **www**.sint-martens-latem.be. *Dorp 1, St.-Martens-Latem (09-2821770,* **www**.vvleiestreek.be, **www**.toerisme-leiestreek.be).

St.-Martens-Latem

This flat region on the banks of the calm Leie, seems as if held in the outstretched arms of a mother: what is its secret, why can nobody resist its beauty, its noble charm?

Karel van de Woestijne, 1917

St.-Martens-Latem is a picturesque town on the banks of the Leie. Cruise boats from Ghent moor at the quay at this bend in the river that has been immortalised on canvas many times. From here, it is a short walk to the Dorp, the rustic town centre. The whitewashed **St.-Martinuskerk** was built in 1121 by order of the bishop of Doornik and, over the centuries, it has been repeatedly rebuilt and extended. It was last restored in 1990. The painter Albijn Van den Abeele and the sculptor George Minne and others lay buried in the small walled church graveyard. A bronze bust of poet **Karel van de Woestijne** (1878-1929), who lived in Latem between 1900 and 1906, is located in front of the new town hall. While living here, he wrote the parable called the *Laetemsche brieven over de lente* (Laetem Letters about Spring).

A boat trip on the Leie

In the town, street names, artists' homes and galleries draw attention to the artists who were members of the First and Second Latem groups (*see text box*).

Albijn Van den Abeele walk

Starting point: *Latem Dorp.*
Distance: *9 km.*
Signposted.
The route starts in the Latem town centre and passes the spots where artists liked to set up their easels. Information boards are located along the route.

Karel van de Woestijne

Deurle

For centuries, lovely Deurle has also been an inspiration to artists. In 1860, Xavier De Cock settled in the town as its first painter. He was followed by numerous artists who worked in the tradition of the Latem group. The town atmosphere has been especially well preserved around Dorpsstraat with the St.-Aldegondiskerk, around the parsonage hidden behind a white wall and around the two village pubs. Amongst the town's inhabitants buried in the church graveyard are Xavier de Cock, painter Jenny Montigny, brothers Leon and Gustave (Gust.) De Smet and Albert Claeys. A narrow path (Cyriel Buyssepad) leads up the hill between the orchard and the church. On top of this hill, writer Cyriel Buysse built a windmill on stilts, giving him an uninterrupted view over the Leie. The **Museum Gust. De Smet**, in the former home studio of the painter, is located in the prosperous neighbourhood on the other side of Philippe de Denterghemlaan. This home is full of reminders of the life and work of this famous Latem artist. The **Museum Dhont-Dhaenens**, abbreviated to MDD, is the life's work of the married couple, Jules Dhondt and Irma Dhaenens. Throughout their lives, they collected works by modern and contemporary Flemish artists. In 1967, the couple decided to allow public access to their collection in a newly built museum. Erik Van Biervliet designed a modernistic building. The museum does not have a fixed exhibit. Instead, it organizes a number of so-called focus exhibitions each year. These exhibitions concentrate on the works of a specific artits.

Gemeentelijk Museum Gust. De Smet

Gustaaf De Smetlaan 1, Deurle. ***Tel.*** *09-2827742.* *May-Sep Wed-Sun 12pm-6pm (Oct-Apr until 5pm).* **www**.sint-martens-latem.be

Museum Dhondt-Dhaenens

Museumlaan 14, Deurle. ***Tel.*** *09-2825123.* *Tue-Sun 10am-5pm.* **www**.museumdd.be

The whitewashed town church of St.-Martens-Latem

Art along the Leie

Between 1900 and 1930, the Leie region with its epicentre of St.-Martens-Latem was the scene of a concentration of a large number of well-known painters, sculptors and authors. They had all become disillusioned with big city life and felt a yearning for the simplicity offered by the countryside. Together, they formed a group of artists who were representative of the current artistic trends of symbolism, impressionism and expressionism in Flanders.

First Latem group

The brothers **Xavier** and César **De Cock** were the first to settle in the rural town of Deurle around 1860. They were quite familiar with the town clerk and future mayor of St.-Martens-Latem, **Albijn Van den Abeele**, the core figure within the artists colony. In 1883, Emile Claus also settled along the Leie in Astene.

Weide in de lente – Veldweg, Albijn Van den Abeele

Around 1900, young artists like the brothers Karel and **Gustave van de Woestyne**, George Minne and Valerius de Saedeleer moved to St.-Martens-Latem.

De Leie te Latem by Gustave van de Woestyne

Second Latem group

After 1904, a second group of artists from Ghent that included Gust. and Leon de Smet, Frits van den Berghe, as well as Constant Permeke from Oostende, relocated themselves to St.-Martens-Latem. They were called the Second Latem group. World War I led to an interruption of Latem art. Many of the artists fled to the safety of England and The Netherlands. After the war, they returned to Flanders. The economic crisis and the resulting failure of a number of galleries dealt the Second Latem group another blow.

Portret van mevrouw Van Hecke, Léon De Smet

Overtocht van het veer op de Leie te Latem, Xavier de Cock

MEETJESLAND

Meetjesland consists of two contrasting regions. The north is the land of polders and creeks. The Sente and Asseneed creeks are areas with valuable natural resources. It is a fertile agricultural area where beets and potatoes are cultivated. The south is covered by an expansive belt of forest that stretches from St.-Maria-Aalter to Oosteeklo. These forests are interspersed with fields and pastures.

There are a number of explanations for how the name Meetjesland came to be. 'Meetjes' could have been derived from the French word *métiers* (looms) or from small plots of measured land. However, the most obvious explanation is that 'meetje' also means an older lady or grandmother. During the 17th and 18th centuries, large amounts of linen were produced in the northwestern corner of East Flanders, and this process required the labour of many girls, women and 'meetjes'. The name Meetjesland confirms the relation between the region and the textile industry. Meetjesland is the land of the Lieve. The Lieve canal was excavated during the 13th century to provide Ghent with access to the sea. Commercial shipping on the *'t Liefken* ended a long time ago and the remainders of the original course of the Durme, formed an extended area of natural beauty. The Ghent-Brugges canal (the Brugse Vaart), the Schipdonk canal and the Leopold canal also pass through the region. The former towing paths along the canals have been converted into superb cycling tracks. The open polder landscape and forests form a superb background for cycling and walking. The Meetjesland network of cycling routes and the walking trail networks of St.-Maria-Aalter and St.-Laureins offer hours and hours of walking and cycling enjoyment. Meetjesland is a rural area with Eeklo as its central town. Its heritage is made up of unassuming historic buildings, small museums, landscapes, townscapes and the stories told by the locals.

It's great to spend some time on the patio of the Drongengoedhoeve

◁ **The creek area of St.-Laureins (Sente) features an idyllic landscape with kilometres of channels**

Exploring Meetjesland

Between the small centres of the Krekengebied, the Houtland and the urbanised towns is a patchwork of pastures, fields and forests, criss-crossed by creeks and canals. Historical churches, narrow streets, interesting museums and castle parks give Eeklo and Maldegem a city-like feel. Watervliet, Boekhoute and Kaprijke have retained their village atmosphere. A ride on the steam train in Maldegem, a walk through Middelburg or a visit to the Bezoekerscentrum Boekhoute (visitors' centre) allows the visitor to relive old times. The Drongengoed and the Leen and the Lembeekse forests are superb walking destinations.

The church of St.-Jan-in-Eremo

MUNICIPALITIES

- Aalter 1
- Assenede 2
- Eeklo 3
- Evergem 4
- Kaprijke 5
- Knesselare 6
- Maldegem 7
- Nevele 8
- St.-Laureins 9

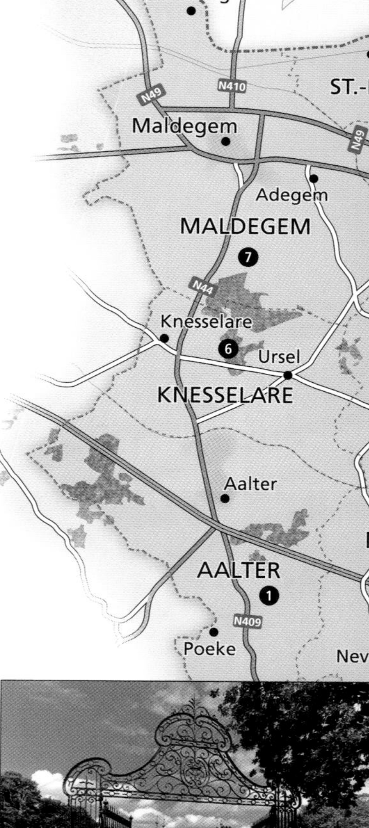

Interior of Maldegem steam train

Oud Schepenhuis (tourist office) in Maldegem

Entrance gate to the Poeke castle

The Lieve flowing through Meetjesland

MEETJESLAND AND WATER

Meetjesland has always been associated with water. At a number of places, the landscape is exceptionally beautiful, like at the Stoktevijverbrug bridge where the Lieve flows into the Schipdonk canal. It is just as beautiful around Driesselken in Merendree (Nevele), where you'll find the virtually untouched the valley of Kalevallei. The lovely, meandering Oude Kale is best viewed at the Vlaenderensmolen (windmills) in Vinderhoute (municipality Lovendegem).

Krulbollen match on the Doornzele common

Town hall and belfry in Eeklo

Meetjesland Tourism
www.toerismemeetjesland.be

SEE ALSO

- ***Accommodation*** page. 211
- ***Restaurants and cafés*** page. 219, 226

SYMBOLS

- Motorway
- Main road
- Canal/river

The Poeke castle, a proud moated fortress in a beautifully appointed park

AALTER MUNICIPALITY ❶

Road map A3. *19,000.* **www**.aalter.be *Aalter.* www.toerismemeetjesland.be

Poeke

Poeke castle is situated beyond a high cast-iron gate. With its light-pink walls, it looks like a French castle along the Loire. Poeke has an eventful history dating back to the 12th century. Over the centuries, this fortified knights' castle was expanded into a luxurious fortress. A lovely park surrounds the castle. The front garden has been laid out the French style, while the rear garden is in the English landscape style with a star-shaped lane pattern of lanes.

Poeke castle

Kasteelstraat 26, Poeke. ***Tel.*** *051-688300. Castle: by appointment; park: sunrise to sunset.*

ASSENEDE MUNICIPALITY ❷

Road map C2. *13,500.* **www**.assenede.be *Boekhoutedorp 3, Boekhoute (09-3736008,* **www**.toerismemeetjesland.be).

Boekhoute

The fishing vessel, BOU 8 (*Isabella*), moored at the foot of the town church is a reminder of the town's fishing history. Until 1952, Boekhoute had its own harbour and fishing fleet. The town traditionally had open access to the sea via the Braakman. Due to silting and the construction of dikes, the harbour was relocated a number of times. During the late Middle Ages, the harbour was moved to the northwest of town and at a later stage even further to the northwest, right into Dutch territory. Boats then accessed the Braakman along the specially excavated Isabella canal. When this access to the sea was closed off, it meant the end of fishing activities for the town. The fishing boats moved to the Dutch towns of Terneuzen and Breskens and now the fleet consists of just two vessels. Boekhoute calls itself the 'fishing town without a harbour'. The **Bezoekerscentrum Boekhoute** (visitors' centre) keeps the history of this fishing town alive through multimedia and interactive displays.

The 'fishing town without a harbour'

Bezoekerscentrum Boekhoute

Boekhoutedorp 3, Boekhoute. ***Tel.*** *09-3736008. Wed-Fri 9am-12pm and 1:30pm-4:30 pm (also Sat 1:30pm-4:30pm during Jul and 1st half of Sep, also Sun 1:30pm-4:30pm during 2nd half of Jun and Aug).*

Meetjesland walking route networks

The Bulskampveld walking network presents a blend of nature and culture amongst the West Flanders towns of Wingene, Ruiselede and Aalter in Meetjesland. This network, more than 120 km in length and with 110 junctions, takes walkers through the forests to a series of sights, including the Ghent-Oostende canal, the Oude Vaart, the town centre of St.-Maria-Aalter and many castles. Walking routes are also being developed in the Krekengebied (scheduled completion: autumn of 2011).

A small farmstead on the Meetjesland meadows

KREKENGEBIED

Creeks created by flooding

Nowhere in Meetjesland is the effect of the sea as tangibly evident as in the area Krekengebied. On 8 October 1375, fate struck and water from the Western Scheldt streamed into Meetjesland at full force. Similar disasters occurred in 1404, 1420, 1440, 1510 and 1530. Every time this happened, new layers of fertile soil were laid down and deep gullies were cut. Today, Krekengebied is predominantly an agricultural region with areas of natural beauty. Birds like reed warblers, blue throats and brown harriers thrive in the reedlands. The brackish grasslands are home to salt-loving plant species such as glasswort, salty marsh grass, sea rushes and sea spurrey. White-fronted geese, small swans, greylag geese and bean geese spend their winters on the polders. Between 1846 and 1849, the Leopold canal was excavated to drain the polders and to combat polderkoorts ('polder fever': malaria).

TOWN OF EEKLO ❸

Road map B2. *20.000.*
www.eeklo.be
Toerisme Meetjesland, Stationsstraat 21 (09-3778600, **www**.toerismemeetjesland.be).

Eeklo, the main town of Meetjesland, developed on a dune ridge that runs from Maldegem to Stekene. Until well into the 20th century, Eeklo's prosperity was due to the flourishing wool industry. Between 1960 and 1970, the textile industry ceased to exist here. The Grote Baan (N9), the busy road between Ghent and Bruges, splits the town in half. The Markt (market-square) features the 17th-century town hall in Flemish renaissance style with its belfry and – somewhat further to the rear – the neo-gothic St.-Vincentiuskerk with its 99 m tower. Although the Eeklo belfry only dates from 1932, it has been declared a UNESCO world heritage site along with 55 other towers in Belgium and France. The neo-gothic Paterskerk (Minderbroederskerk) is located on the other side of the Markt. Not far from the Markt, a statue of **Karel Lodewijk Ledeganck** (1805-1847), one of the great Flemish champions during the 19th century, looks out over the busy intersection. The Heldenpark is a pleasant town park surrounding a castle. During the summer, a world music festival is held here over four Thursdays.

The **Provinciaal Domein Het Leen** (265 ha), a former military ammunition depot to the south of the town, has been converted into a large recreational forest with paved roads and unpaved walking trails. The permanent exhibition called *Bos, Boom en Hout (Forest, Trees and Wood)* can be viewed in the **Bosinfocentrum** (forest info centre). The **Heemmuseum** features a collection of old tools of the trade and historical reconstructions of old Eeklo shops. The **arboretum** (6 ha) possesses more than 7,000 plants including many species of magnolias, rhododendrons and camellias. **Huysmanhoeve**, a recently renovated centuries-old farm on the Expresweg (A11), functions as a visitors' centre from which to further discover the history, culture and nature of Meetjesland.

Karel Lodewijk Ledeganck

Provinciaal Domein Het Leen

Entrance on Gentsesteenweg, Eeklo **Tel.** *09-3767474. property: from 9am to sunset; Forest info centre: Tue-Sun 9am-12pm and 1pm-5pm (May-Oct Sat-Sun to 6pm); Arboretum: daily 9am-4:30pm.*
www.hetleen.be

Heemmuseum

Gentsesteenweg 80, Eeklo. **Tel.** *09-3781222. Tue-Fri 10am-5pm, Sun 2pm-5pm (also Sat 2pm-5pm Jun-Aug). mon*

Streekcentrum Huysmanhoeve

Bus 1 (side road off Peperstraat), Eeklo. **Tel.** *09-3270447. Apr-Sep Wed and Sun 11am-6pm.*
www.huysmanhoeve.be

'Bos, Boom en Hout' exhibition in the Bosinfocentrum

EVERGEM MUNICIPALITY 4

Road map C2. *32,500.*
www.evergem.be *Evergem.*
1 from Ghent St.-Pieters.
www.toerismemeetjesland.be

Doornzele

The Doornzele Dries (common) is an elongated square – the largest common in Flanders – in the heart of Doornzele, a small town along the Ghent-Terneuzen canal. Homes, windmills and the church surround 'den dries'. During the Middle Ages, this square served as a communal pasture and field. From the common, farmers drove their livestock along the herding trails to the fields around the town. Today, the common is home to a football pitch, a playground, an archery range and krulbollen lanes. Krulbollen is a popular pastime in Meetjesland. It is played by two teams who try to throw their krulbol (a thick disc with rounded edges) as close as possible to the stek (a wooden stake just a few centimetres high). A small exposition about the history of krulbollen has been set up in the **Doornzelemolen**, a stone windmill.

Doornzelemolen (Krulbolmuseum)

Doornzeledries, Evergem.
summer months Sat-Sun afternoons. ***Tel.*** *0476-466002.*

KAPRIJKE MUNICIPALITY 5

Road map B2. *6200.*
www.kaprijke.be
Plein 1 (09-3239054, **www**.toerismemeetjesland.be).

Kaprijke

The former Kaprijke 'town hall' on the Plein

During the late Middle Ages, Kaprijke was a prosperous town with a flourishing textile industry. War and plundering during the 16th century ended this prosperity and the industry. The Plein, the largest green town square in Flanders, is a big rectangular open space with a double row of chestnut and ash trees and a bandstand. The lovely 17th-century **town hall** overlooks the town's meadows on which cloth was traditionally washed, dried and dyed. The artwork named **De Omroeper/Beeld voor Vlaanderen** by Philip Aguirre y Otegui was made in honour of Hippoliet Van Peene and Karel Miry, writer and composer respectively of *De Vlaamse Leeuw*, the anthem of the Flemish community.

The Omroeper

Lembeke

The St.-Egidiuskerk has a gothic-style tower (late 13th, early 14th century). The present-day church was built around 1755. A beautiful 1642 painting by Bruges artist Lodewijk de Deyster is displayed in the church. The annual Meetjesland gingerbread festival also takes place in this town.

THE LIEVE, THE OLDEST CANAL IN FLANDERS

The Lieve was excavated between 1251 and 1269. The canal was 45 km long and ran from the Gravensteen in Ghent to Damme, where it flowed into the Zwin. For centuries, the canal was of great economic significance. It could be used by boats up to 2,3 m wide, 7 m long and with a draught of as much as 1 m. A number of sluice gates were installed in the canal to regulate its water level. As the Zwin silted up, this canal lost its importance. In 1547, emperor Charles V granted permission for the Sassenvaart to be excavated (the future Ghent-Terneuzen canal), giving Ghent direct access to the North Sea via the Western Scheldt, In 1847, the Schipdonk canal between Stoktevijver and Damme was constructed, following the route of the Lieve.

De Lieve vertelt

Starting point: *P at the sports hall, Sportstraat, Waarschoot.*
Distance: *40 km.*
Leaflet: *available at information office.*

KNESSELARE 6

Road map A2. 8000.
www.knesselare.be
www.toerismemeetjesland.be

Ursel

Drongengoed-Maldegemveld (770 ha) is the largest uninterrupted forest area in East Flanders. During the 13th century, the Norbertines from the Drongen abbey established a farmstead to develop the wild meadowlands of the Maldegemveld. Their first attempts were unsuccessful. Only in the 18th century did the enterprising abbot Antoine De Stoop succeed in converting the meadows into a forest plantation with a triangular pattern of lanes. The present-day buildings date back to 1746. Fifty years later, the abbey property was sold. The Drongengoedhoeve, with its café and gallery, is a pleasant place at which to stop in this expansive forest area. The **Landschapsinfocentrum Drongengoedhoeve** (landscape info centre) provides an overview starting from the development of the Maldegemveld (1200-1750) and continuing to the reforestation of the 'field' and its conversion to an agricultural area (from 1750).

Landschapsinfocentrum Drongengoedhoeve

Drongengoedhoeve, Drongengoedweg 9, Ursel. ***Tel.*** *09-3250980.* *see website.*

Drongengoed route

Starting point: *Drongengoedhoeve, Ursel.* ***Distance:*** *44 km.* ***Route markings:*** *red.*
Cycling route along the lanes through the heart of the Drongengoed forest passing the former NATO airfield, the Prinseveld castle and the Maldegemveld nature reserve. This cycling route also passes through two other Meetjesland forests, the Leen and the Keigat forest. The slighty hilly nature of the Meetjesland takes one by surprise on this route.

Steam train ready for departure to Eklo

MALDEGEM MUNICIPALITY 7

Road map A2. 22,000.
www.maldegem.be
Oud Schepenhuis, Marktstraat 38 (050-728622, **www**.toerismemeetjesland.be).

Maldegem

Maldegem is a friendly town in the northwestern corner of Meetjesland. Its large double Marktplein forms the heart of the city. The municipal hall with its projecting tower is located here. It was constructed in 1907 in neo-gothic style and was extended in 2010 with the addition of a modern sunken wing. The church

St.-Barbarakerk

St.-Barbarakerk, established in 1074, is somewhat hidden behind the information office in the former Schepenhuis (city hall) in Marktstraat. The church, with its massive bell towers, has a closed courtyard atmosphere. St.-Annapark is a pleasant park with centuries-old trees and numerous artworks. This park is part of the St Anna castle, a former town hospital that now houses the police station. Maldegem's major attraction is the **Stoomcentrum (steam centre)**. Historic steam and diesel trains, like the well-known 'kamielkes', now run along the former Maldegem to Eeklo railway line, which was closed in 1988. A narrow-gauge line links the steam centre to Donk. Various steam locomotives and -machines are displayed in the museum shed. A walking- and cycling trail now runs along the former Maldegem to Bruges via Donk line.

Stoomcentrum Maldegem

Stationsplein 8, Maldegem. ***Tel.*** *050-716852.* *May-Sep Sun (Jul-Aug also Wed and Fri) 11am-5pm.*
www.stoomcentrum.be

Poëzieroute Maldegem (poetry route)

This walking route follows poetry posted on panels set through the Maldegem municipality. These boards contain poems by Belgium poets inspired by fables and legends from Maldegem.

Adegem

The **Canada-Poland War II Museum** honours the Canadian, Polish and British forces that liberated Meetjesland from German occupation in the autumn of 1944. Its dioramas with soldiers and authentic war material provide a realistic rundown of *Operation Switchback*, the battle for the Scheldt. A free Scheldt was necessary in order for Antwerp, liberated in 1944, to act as a supply harbour for the allied forces. Next to this museum are the **Tuinen van Adegem (Gardens of Adegem)** that include of a romantic French garden with thousands of roses, an English landscape garden with ponds and waterfalls, a Japanese garden with rocks that symbolise a person's life journey, and an exotic garden with menhirs and a druid ring.

Information board

Canada-Poland War II Museum | Tuinen van Adegem

Heulendonk 21, Adegem. ***Tel.*** *050-710666.* *museum: Apr-Sep Tue-Sun 10am-6pm; Oct-Mar Wed-Sun 12pm-6pm; garden: Apr-Sep Tue-Sun 1pm-4:30pm.* **www**.canada-museum.be

Middelburg

Middelburg is a quiet town on the border between Belgium and The Netherlands, best explored on foot. Eight **information panels** at historic buildings of archaeological importance highlight the town's turbulent history. With the aid of archaeological finds, a 3D display and a film, the **bezoekerscentrum** (visitors' centre) sketches the medieval history of the town. Middelburg was established around 1450 by Pieter Bladelin, a prominent Bruges citizen. He passed away in 1472 without any children and he was buried in his own church. Middelburg never developed into a prosperous town, falling prey to the conflicts between Spain and the Low Countries.

Bezoekerscentrum Middelburg

Groene Markt 8A, Middelburg. ***Tel.*** *050-728622.* *May-Sep Thu-Sun 1:30pm-5pm.*

Bladelin walking route

Starting point: *Bezoekerscentrum Middelburg.* ***Distance:*** *6,5 km.* ***Signposted. Leaflet:*** *available at Dienst voor Toerisme.*

A walk through the 'pearl of Meetjesland' past the castle built in 1448 by Pieter Bladelin, through the Meulekreek scenic area and along the old smuggling routes. Between World War I and World War II, a great deal of smuggling activity took place in the border area between The Netherlands and Belgium.

THE 'STINKER' AND THE 'BLINKER'

From Strobrugge (to the north of Maldegem), the Schipdonk canal (the 'Stinker') and the Leopold canal (the 'Blinker') flow fraternally side by side. These canals are separated by a dike on which rows of poplars grow. The Schipdonk canal was excavated in 1852 for the purpose of draining the water from the Leie, polluted due to the retting of flax (the 'Stinker'). The Leopold canal between Boekhoute and Damme was opened in 1854 and its purpose was to drain the polders of the Krekengebied. Because the canal carried away pure rainwater, it was nicknamed the 'Blinker' (sparkling).

The Schipdonk- and Leopold canal flow parallel to one another

NEVELE MUNICIPALITY 8

Road map B3. *11.500.* **www**.nevele.be Landegem, Hansbeke.
www.toerismemeetjesland.be

Nevele

St.-Mauritiuskerk, originally a 12th-century Romanesque church, dominates the small market square. The author **Cyriel Buysse** was born in Nevele in 1859. The **Streekmuseum Rietgaverstede**, the treasure-house of Nevele, has a small literary section with photographs, documents and items that belonged to the author and his aunts, Rosalie and Virginie Loveling *(see text box)*.

Streekmuseum Rietgaverstede

C. Van der Cruyssenstraat 60, Nevele. ***Tel.*** *09-3718339.* *May-Sep Sun 2pm-6pm.*

CYRIEL BUYSSE

Cyriel Buysse was born in 1859 in the Lange Munt and lived in number 38 of the present-day Cyriel Buyssestraat (formerly Tieltstraat) from 1865 to 1896. His father managed the local chicory factory. His mother was the sister of authors Rosalie and Virginie Loveling. He was destined to succeed his father but, encouraged by both his aunts, showed more interest in literature. His first novel, *Het recht van de sterkste (The right of the strongest)*, was released in 1892. In 1896, he married Nelly Tromp-Dyserinck, a wealthy widow. He is regarded as the author who introduced naturalism to Flanders. In his books, Buysse described daily life in a realistic, sometimes ironic, way, showing more sympathy and understanding towards the lower than towards the higher social classes. He had a plain writing style, ensuring that his works are still readable to-day. Buysse's most famous work is the play, *Het gezin van Paemel (The Van Paemel family)* written in 1902. Cyriel Buysse passed away in 1932.

MUNICIPALITY ST.-LAUREINS ❾

Road map B1. *6500.*
www.sint-laureins.be
Dorpsstraat 87 (09-2187647, **www**.toerismemeetjesland.be).

St.-Laureins

In the north of Meetjesland are five towns right next to the Dutch border. They are St.-Laureins (Sente), Watervliet, St.-Jan-in-Eremo, St.-Margriete and Waterland-Oudeman. The Sentse Kreken (creeks) are a reminder of the many floods that affected the area centuries ago. When the border between The Netherlands and Belgium was established in 1843, the Dutch created a straight boundary and left the marshy area to the young country of Belgium. St.-Laureins is dominated by the huge **Godshuis**. In 1843, the wealthy and godly governess Antonia Van Damme ordered the construction of the complex to serve as a convent, care home, orphanage and hospital. Now restored, the Godshuis is used as a hotel. The **Plattelandscentrum Meetjesland (rural centre)** provides a behind-the-scenes look at present-day agriculture in the area.

Plattelandscentrum Meetjesland

Leemweg 24, St.-Laureins.
Tel. *09-3797837.*
Thu-Fri 1:30pm-4pm.
www.plattelandscentrum.be

Surroundings

Taking a detour to visit the small **St.-Jan-in-Eremo** is well worth the trouble. The 17th-century whitewashed town church with its churchyard is somewhat hidden behind a row of high trees. The town is located in a vast polder landscape with five creeks and a number of dikes, the most significant of which is the St.-Jansdijk that was constructed during the rule of duke 'Jan without fear'. The old town of Watervliet was washed away in 1377. Thanks to Hiëronymus Lauwerijn, the town was rebuilt around 1500. The first homes were situated around the church and the harbour. The new town of **Watervliet** featured a town square, the former harbour, a bandstand and a butter store. The Stee square is surrounded by 18th-century homes, the former town hall and the town church. The Onze-Lieve-Vrouw-Hemelvaartkerk (church of Our Lady of the Ascension) was constructed in 1501. The *Nood Gods* triptych, a painting by the 'master from Frankfurt' who presumably worked in Antwerp between 1480 and 1518, is displayed in the church. The Onze-Lieve-Vrouw-Hemelvaartkerk is sometimes nicknamed the **'cathedral of the North'** by chauvinists.

The 'cathedral of the North'

The Godshuis was constructed as a charitable act

MERCATORI
RUPELMUNDA
PRINCIPI
RECENTIORIS
CONDITORI
VIXIT ANNOS
ANN MDXCIV

WAASLAND

Waasland is a historic region in the northeast of the province of East Flanders. The meaning of the word Waas can be attributed to the Germanic 'wasu' that means 'marshy land', or to an old Teutonic word that means 'mud'. However, it could also have originated from the Middle Dutch work 'wastin(n)e', that means 'wasteland' or 'uncultivated land'.

In the north, the vast polders of the Scheldt determine the landscape. Due to the increased tidal nature of the Scheldt and floods resulting from land reclamation, the low-lying bogs had to be surrounded by dikes and drained during the late Middle Ages (1250-1500). The polders were only given their present-day form after large-scale flooding towards the end of the 16th century. Sandy areas with typical 'raised fields' surrounded by pollard willows are found in the south. Large parts of Waasland are covered by the *Koningsforeest*, an expansive forest area that belonged to the Carolingian kings and later to the counts of Flanders. From the 11th century, St.-Pieters abbey (Ghent) and the abbey in Boudelo (Klein-Sinaai) received large areas of forest on loan. Under abbey management, the *Koningsforeest* was greatly exploited. By the 16th century, the forest had largely disappeared. Waasland is the land of Reynard the Fox and the well-known cartographer, Mercator. The town of St.-Niklaas boasts the largest market square in Belgium, a modern city museum, a large shopping centre and an extended cultural network. With towns and villages like Rupelmonde, Bazel, Temse and Lokeren, the restored Fort Liefkenshoek and the Scheldt, Waasland has much to offer its visitors. The small town of Rupelmonde is proud to be associated with Gerardus Mercator, one of the greatest cartographers of the 16th century. He developed a world map that proved to be of great importance to shipping.

Canoeists hard at work during the tour of Waasland at Wachtebeke

◁ **Statue of the cartographer Mercator on the Rupelmonde town square**

Exploring Waasland

Reynard the Fox, the core character from the medieval beast epic, is inextricably linked to Waasland. The characters from the Reynard fable are the focal point of the info.waasland visitor's centre on the Grote Markt in St.-Niklaas. Lokeren is a pleasant town along the Durme. The Wissekerke castle in the old centre of Bazel is certainly worth a visit. Rupelmonde is a romantic town along the Scheldt that is lovely to walk through. Fort Liefkenshoek has stood for centuries in the middle of the impressive industrial landscape to the north of Antwerp.

Reynard the Fox

Lokeren town centre

MUNICIPALITIES

Beveren ❹
Kruibeke ❻
Lokeren ❸
St.-Niklaas ❶
Temse ❺
Wachtebeke ❷

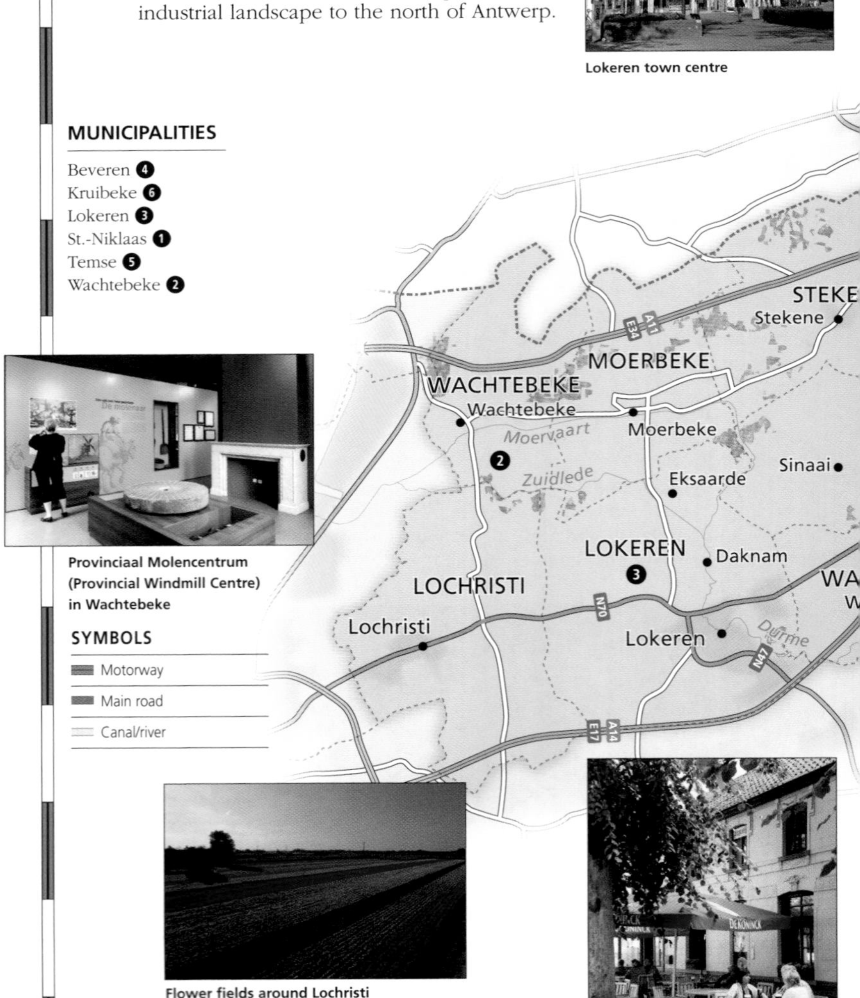

Provinciaal Molencentrum (Provincial Windmill Centre) in Wachtebeke

SYMBOLS

Motorway
Main road
Canal/river

Flower fields around Lochristi

Outdoor cafés in Daknam

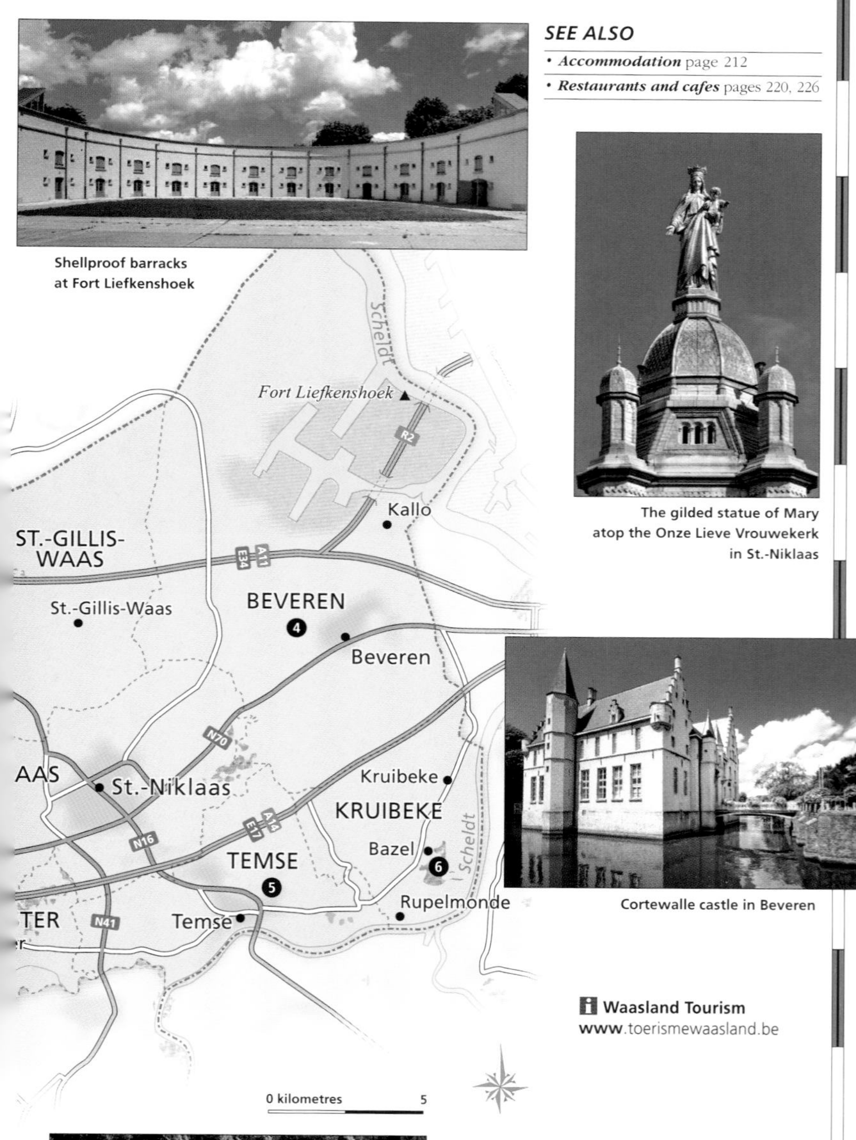

Shellproof barracks at Fort Liefkenshoek

SEE ALSO

• ***Accommodation*** page 212

• ***Restaurants and cafes*** pages 220, 226

The gilded statue of Mary atop the Onze Lieve Vrouwekerk in St.-Niklaas

Scheldt
Fort Liefkenshoek
R2
Kallo
ST.-GILLIS-WAAS
E34 A11
St.-Gillis-Waas
BEVEREN
4
Beveren
N70
AAS
St.-Niklaas
Kruibeke
KRUIBEKE
E17 A14
N16
Bazel
6
Scheldt
TEMSE
5
Rupelmonde
TER
N41
Temse
0 kilometres 5

Cortewalle castle in Beveren

Waasland Tourism
www.toerismewaasland.be

Crossing the Scheldt by ferry at Rupelmonde

TIBEERT ROUTE

Starting point: *Pastoor Verwilghenplein, Haasdonk (Beveren).*
Distance: *50 km.*
Leaflet: *available at Dienst voor Toerisme.*

Tibeert route

Tibeert, the tomcat from the Reynard epic, takes you to the banks of the Scheldt. The route starts in Beveren and passes through Kruibeke, Bazel and Temse on its way back to the departure point.

The rich interior of St.-Nicolaaskerk, the 'oldest church of St Nicholas'.

CITY OF ST.-NIKLAAS 1

Road map E2. 71.000.
www.sint-niklaas.be
Grote Markt 45 (03-7609260, www.toerismewaasland.be).

St.-Niklaas

At 3.19 ha, the Grote Markt (Great Market) is the largest market square in Belgium. In 1248, countess Margaretha of Constantinople donated 8 ha of unused land to city management. The donation conditions determined that the completed square had to remain here permanently. Over the course of the centuries, part of the land was lost. From the start of the 19th century, the Grote Markt became the scene for public demonstrations, city festivals, balloon festivals, parades and mass games. In 2004, the Stationsbuurt (station district) was given a drastic facelift during which an expansive esplanade with a double row of nineteen plane trees was constructed. Stationsstraat, the link between the Grote Markt and Stationsplein, is a chic shopping street with elegant buildings.

Neo-gothic town hall with belfry

Grote Markt

Besides being the largest, the Grote Markt is also the most beautiful market square in Belgium. The new multipurpose square is fringed by a tropical hardwood promenade and various artworks. The neo-gothic **city hall**, designed by Ghent architect P. Van Kerkhove, was constructed in 1878 to replace the old city hall that was destroyed by fire in 1874. The belfry in the centre of the front facade is 40 m high. A statue of **Sinterklaas**, the patron saint of the city, guards the entrance to the city hall. In the foyer, a large statue of cartographer Mercator welcomes visitors. The interior is elegant and the wedding room offers a beautiful view over the vast market square. The Dienst voor Toerisme and the visitor's centre are located in the 17th century Cipierage (court of justice).

Statue of St Nicholas

Onze-Lieve-Vrouwekerk

Grote Markt, St.-Niklaas.
information available at Dienst voor Toerisme

The church Onze-Lieve-Vrouwekerk, constructed between 1840 and 1896 and containing colourful wall murals, is located behind the city hall. A 6-m-tall gilded statue of Mary is perched on top of the church tower.

St.-Nicolaaskerk

St.-Nicolaasplein, St.-Niklaas.
information available at Dienst voor Toerisme.

The gothic-style St.-Nicolaaskerk is located on the square with the same name at a stone's throw from the Grote Markt. This church dates back to the 13th century and has a lovely interior and a rich trove of church treasures, including important relics, liturgical gold and silver, ironwork and religious garments.

The working SteM Zwijgershoek knitting studio

Stedelijk Musea St.-Niklaas (City Museums)

SteM Zwijgershoek, Zwijgershoek 14; **Salons voor Schone Kunsten**, Stationsstraat 85; **Mercatormuseum**, Zamanstraat 49. ***Tel.*** *03-7603750. Tue-Sat 2pm-5pm, Sun 11am-5pm.*

The **SteM Zwijgershoek** offers a refreshing look at the history of St.-Niklaas and Waasland.

Gem of the art deco style

In a converted factory, themes such as 'man and material' (12,000 BC-18th century), 'man and machine' (late 18th century-early 20th century) and 'man and body' (from 19th century) come to life through the use of objects, photographs, documents and audio clips. Numerous machines, from the time in which the knitting industry played a major role in the Waasland economy, can be viewed in the **Breiatelier (knitting studio)**. The Salons voor Schone Kunsten (Fine Arts Suites) are housed in a stately historic home commissioned by textile producer Edmond Meert in 1928. The museum accommodates more than one hundred paintings dating from the 16th century to around 1950. The Mercator museum introduces its visitors to the history of cartography prior to and after Mercator (1512-1594). The original earth- and sky globes and the world- and European wall maps produced by Mercator are the most popular displays.

Art deco walking route

Starting point: *Grote Markt, St.-Niklaas.* ***Distance:*** *5.3 km.* ***Leaflet:*** *available at Dienst voor Toerisme.*

During the period between the world wars, the textile industry experienced enormous growth. Many new homes were built in the art deco style, the major art trend during this period. Take an artistic walk past some of the gems of this 'modern style'.

Sinaai

In the centre of the green Dries (common) is the Vrijheidsboom (freedom tree), a venerated oak from 1830. The (former) municipal building, the St.-Catharinakerk with its lovely churchyard and the parsonage all surround the leafy town square.

Fondatie van Boudelo

Starting point: *Liniedreef, Sinaai.* ***Distance:*** *6.5 km.*
www.vzwdurme.be

When the Cistercian abbey of Boudelo was established in 1197, it received land to the north of Sinaai as a gift. The area was named the Fondatie (foundation) of Boudelo. The abbey has disappeared, but the natural area still bears the same name. It consists of coppices, deciduous forest to walk around, meadowlands, a timber plantation and lovely pools.

WACHTEBEKE MUNICIPALITY 2

Road map C2. *7000.*
www.wachtebeke.be
Dr. J. Persynplein 6 (09-3427165, **www**.toerisme.wachtebeke.be, **www**.toerismewaasland.be).

Wachtebeke

Wachtebeke is located along the Moervaart, a canal excavated between Ghent and Durme around 1300 for the transport of peat. A canoeing- and kayaking course has been laid out on the Moervaart and the Zuidlede. The Provinciaal Domein Puyenbroeck is a large recreational area that includes a miniature town and a water fun park. Mola is located in the Puyenbrug castle. **Mola** (Latin for mills) is the mill heritage centre in East Flanders. The exhibits focus on milling techniques, the history of the Flemish stake or post mills and the future of windmills as a source of 'green' energy.

Mola – Provinciaal Molencentrum (Provincial windmill centre)

Puyenbrug castle, Puyenbrug 5, Wachtebeke. ***Tel.*** *09-3424240.* *Apr-Sep Wed-Fri 9:30am-5pm, Sat-Sun 10:30-6pm; Oct-Mar Wed-Sun 9:30am-5pm.*

Moervaart and Zuidlede

Starting point: *Kalvebrug 1, Wachtebeke.* ***Distance:*** *32 km.* ***Signposted.***

Canoeing and kayaking along the De Reepkens scenic area, the drawbridges of the Moervaart and the Provinciaal Domein Puyenbroeck.

Model of a windmill in Mola

CITY OF LOKEREN ❸

Road map D3. *38.500.*
www.lokeren.be
Markt 2 (09-3409474, **www**.toerismewaasland.be).

Lokeren

Lokeren, meaning 'land-locked', developed on a bend of the Durme. During the mid-18th century, the city was centre of the rabbit hide industry. In 35 felt factories, rabbits and hares were skinned and (Lokeren) hats were made from the hides. Sights include St.-Laurentiuskerk, dating back to 1719-1725, with its nearly 70 m high tower.

Marshy beauty in Het Molsbroek

The **Stadsmuseum** (city museum) describes the history of the city through the use of objects, photographs and film clips. The rabbit hide industry is also explained in detail. Huis Thuysbaert, a 19th-century home on Stationsplein, is a branch of the museum. The **Het Molsbroek** nature reserve is located within walking distance of the station. A 4.5 km walking dike crosses this marshland made up of marsh Alderwoods, river dunes, reed lands and marshy grasslands.

The Romanesque church at the pleasant Daknam town square

Stadsmuseum

Markt 15A, Lokeren. ***Tel.*** *09-3454458.* *Wed-Sat 2pm-5pm, Sun 10am-12pm and 2pm-5pm.*

Bezoekerscentrum Molsbroek (visitors' centre)

Molsbergenstraat 1, Lokeren. ***Tel.*** *09-3483020.* *Feb-Oct Sun 2pm-6pm, Wed 1pm-5pm (Jun-mid Sep Tue-Fri 1pm-5pm Sat-Sun 2pm-6pm; Nov-Jan Sun 2pm-5pm).* **www**.vzwdurme.be

Surroundings

In **Daknam**, the 12th-century **town church** and its low whitewashed wall determine the atmosphere of the intimate town square with its tall trees. The **Kruiskapel (cross chapel)** along the Kruiskapeldreef in **Eksaarde** was constructed in 1626 at the spot where two crosses, believed to have miraculous powers, were discovered in 1317. This pilgrim's chapel is located in the fields and is surrounded by majestic red birch trees. A sandstone cross adorns its forecourt.

BEVEREN MUNICIPALITY ❹

Road map E2. *46,000.*
www.beveren.be
Grote Markt 2 (03-7501580, **www**.toerismewaasland.be).

Beveren

The **Cortewalle castle**, originally a 15th-century moated fortress, is situated in a large park within walking distance of the Grote Markt. In 1856, the castle was rebuilt in the French style that was fashion–able at the time. The most eye-catching feature here is the restored 19th-century *Aubussontapijt*, a huge Aubusson rug (9.5 m by 6 m) that is displayed under a glass floor. The castle's basement houses the Heemkundig Museum that describes the art of making bobbin lace and displays traditional tools.

Cortewalle castle

Zwarte Dreef 1, Beveren. ***Tel.*** *03-7751508.* *May-Aug 1st and 3rd Sun of the month 3pm.*

The Kruiskapel is surrounded by mighty birch trees

Kallo

Fort Liefkenshoek is located on the left bank of the Scheldt and forms one of the last remaining green areas in the industrial landscape of Antwerp's harbour. Along with fort Lillo, located on the opposite side of the river, Fort Liefkenshoek safeguarded shipping traffic into and out of Antwerp for more than two centuries. In 1577, the city of Antwerp constructed a bulwark on Liefkenshoek which was later expanded into a fort. After the fall of Antwerp, the fort remained in the hands of the United Netherlands. After 1795, the French destroyed all the buildings here and constructed a new fort. From 1839 to 1960, the fort was the property of the Belgian state and acted as a barracks, quarantine hospital, naval base and holiday resort. In 1980, the Beveren Municipality purchased the fort and a long restoration process began. A superb multimedia exhibition was installed in four rooms of 'De Kat', a semi-circular shellproof building. Themes like the battle against water, the polders, war and peace and infectious diseases are brought to life through the use of life-size panels with photographs, text, maps, as well as an audio guide. The former Belgian naval lookout tower offers a magnificent view of the Scheldt and the surrounding industrial landscape.

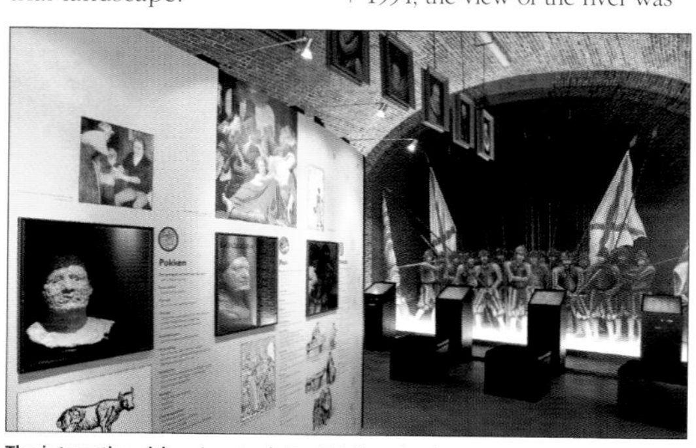

The interactive visitors' centre in Fort Liefkenshoek

A crane left behind as a reminder of Temse's shipbuilding past

Fort Liefkenshoek
Ketenislaan 4, Kallo. ***Tel.*** *03-7501290. Easter-Oct Wed-Sun 10am-6pm; Nov-Easter Sat-Sun 1pm-5pm. May-Aug every 2nd and 4th Sun 3pm.*

TEMSE MUNICIPALITY 5

Road map E2. *26,000.*
www.temse.be
Markt 1 (03-7715131, **www**.toerismewaasland.be).

Temse

Temse is situated along the Scheldt and is famous for the Scheldt bridges that connect Waasland to Klein-Brabant in the province of Antwerp. The first Scheldt bridge, designed by Eiffel, was taken into use in 1870. The present-day bridges were constructed in 1955 and 2009. With a length of 374 m, the 'new' bridge is the longest span across a waterway in Belgium. Both bridges have a 50 m section that can be raised. Until 1994, the view of the river was dominated by Boelwerf, previously Belgium's largest shipbuilding company. The De Zaat residential- and office district was built on the site of this shipyard. The Wilfordkaai (quay) offers a lovely view of the Scheldt and the bridges. Cruise boats also depart on river trips from this quay.

STROPERSBOS-ROUTE

Starting point: *Fort Sint-Jan, De Stropersstraat, Kemzeke (Stekene).*
Distance: *2 x 4 km.*
Leaflet: *available at Dienst voor Toerisme.*

Northern Waasland is one of the less forested areas of East Flanders. The Stropersbos (500 ha) on the boundary between Stekene and St.-Gillis-Waas formed part of the *Koningsforeest* *(page 163)*. This forest was divided by the Bedmar line, an important line of defence constructed during the War of the Spanish Succession (1701-1714). The line runs from the Moervaart to fort Sint-Jan and then through the Stropersbos towards fort Bedmar on the border between Belgium and The Netherlands. More information: **www**.natuurenbos.be, **www**.staatsspaanselinies.eu

A walk through Rupelmonde

Rupelmonde is nestled up close to the bank of the Scheldt across from the mouth of the Rupel. This is the birthplace of the world-famous cartographer Gerard de Cremer, better known as Mercator. From the 12th century, Rupelmonde developed into an important fishing, trade and industry centre. During the 16th century, the town suffered as a result of conflicts. In the 19th century, Rupelmonde flourished again thanks to its brick firing kilns and salt works. These industries came to an end towards the latter part of the 20th century.

MUNICIPALITY KRUIBEKE ❻

Road Map E2. *15,000.*
www.kruibeke.be
Nederstraat 2, Rupelmonde (03-7441013, **www**.toerismewaasland.be).

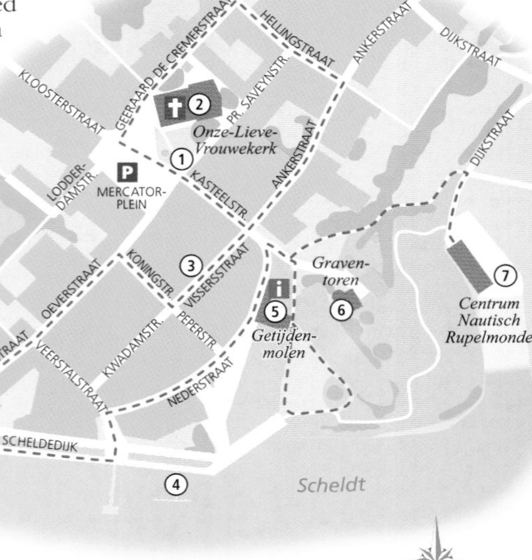

WALKING ROUTE

Mercator statue ①
Onze-Lieve-Vrouwekerk ②
Wijk Het Schelleke ③
Lichtschip Westhinder ④
Getijdenmolen ⑤
Graventoren ⑥
Centrum Nautisch Rupelmonde ⑦

SYMBOLS

······ Recommended route

Mercatorplein

Taking centre stage on the square is the life-size **statue** ① of the most famous citizen of Rupelmonde, cartographer and philosopher Mercator, who was born in 1512 as Gerard de Cremer in Kloosterstraat. The statue's meridian and its co-ordinates are indicated on its pedestal.
The **Onze-Lieve-Vrouwekerk** ②, constructed between 1751 and 1758, is located at the square. Visserstraat is the heart of **Het Schelleke** ③, the oldest fishing district in Rupelmonde, featuring narrow uphill side streets. Residents follow a medieval tradition in using colourful house numbers. The **Lichtschip Westhinder** ④ is moored at the Scheldt quay. In 1950, this ship left the yard as the first of a series of three lighthouse ships. These ships protected the shipping lines along the West-Hinderbank and in the North Sea. The Scheldt quay offers a lovely view over the river, and a pedestrian and bicycle ferry also travels between this quay and Wintam.

Het Schelleke

Getijdenmolen

The 16th-century **tidal mill** ⑤ is situated in the mouth of the Vliet. The Vliet, the tidal harbour of Rupelmonde, was partly walled off after the 1990 floods. A gear, 6 m in diameter, is driven by the force of the water as the tide recedes. This gear, in turn, drives four large millstones. Inside the mill, there is a small exposition explaining the workings of the water-driven mill.

Interior workings of the Getijdenmolen

Mercatoreiland

A small bridge at the *kapel Weg-om* (1864) provides access to the island Mercatoreiland. The statue named *Reinaert, pilgrim en torenwachter (pilgrim and tower watchman)* and the *Reynaertmuur (wall)* are also located here. The **Graventoren** ⑥ dominates the island. This tower was built in 1817 on the ruins of the medieval moated castle and served as a hunting hide. This castle was used for the collection of toll from passing vessels. It was destroyed in 1678. The tower now houses a small museum that tells the story of Mercator. Historic vessels are restored in the demonstration shed on the yard of the former Chantier Naval de Rupelmonde, now called the **Centrum Nautisch Ruplemonde** ⑦. The repair slipway has been newly equipped to enable the restoration of historic vessels.

Lichtschip Westhinder
Scheldekade, Rupelmonde.
Jul-Aug 9am-5pm.

Getijdenmolen | Graventoren
Nederstraat 2-4, Rupelmonde.
Easter-Oct Tue-Fri 1pm-5pm, Sun 11am-5pm (Jul-Aug Tue-Sun 11am-5pm).

Centrum Nautisch Rupelmonde CNR
Dijkstraat, Rupelmonde.
Thu-Sat 9am-5pm (Jul-Aug Sat 9am-5pm).

The Graventoren

Kasteel Wissekerke is surrounded by a beautifully landscaped park

Bazel

The St.-Pieterskerk dominates the small town square. Various historic buildings surround the charming square, such as De Eenhoorn (former court of justice), the Klein Kasteeltje (Small Castle) and the Old Municipal Building of Bazel. The gothic-style church with its bell tower replaced an older Romanesque-style chapel in around 1364. The church welcomes visitors with a virtual tour. Two brickwork towers form the gateway to the park of the **Wissekerke castle** that is located between the town centre and the Scheldt polders. A castle, that formed part of the fortifications around the Scheldt, has stood in this place since the 10th century. In 1562, troops under the command of Marnix of St.-Aldegonde, the right-hand man of Willem of Orange, destroyed the castle. It was rebuilt and modernised in 1803 by order of count Philippe Vilain XIIII. Currently many of its chambers have been restored, including the neo-gothic chapel, the reception hall, the hall of mirrors, the great drawing room and the Egyptian hall. A cast-iron drawbridge added in 1820 links the two sections of the park to one another.

Wissekerke castle
Koningin Astridplein 17, Kruibeke.
Tel. *03-7400400.* *Mon-Thu 8:30am-12pm and 1pm-5pm, Fri 8:30am-1pm.* *Apr-Oct Sun 2pm-5pm (every two weeks).*

GFlood control area Kruibeke – Bazel – Rupelmonde

The Sigma plan is the Flemish version of the Dutch Delta plan. In order to protect areas along the Zeeschelde (from Ghent to the Dutch border), the height of dikes along the Scheldt, amongst others, is being increased. The polders of Kruibeke, Bazel and Rupelmonde are being designated as flood control areas. Shortly you'll be able to enjoy extensive cycling and walking routes in this area of natural beauty.

Sigmaplan
ontmoet de Schelde

GOG Kruibeke - Bazel - Rupelmonde
Scheldelei info hut, on the ferry to Hoboken, Kruibeke. *Tel. 03-8990562.* *Mon-Fri 9am-5pm.* *by appointment.*
www.gogkbr.be

NEC SPE 1900 NEC METU

SCHELDT COUNTRY

This region is located inside the triangle formed by Ghent, Antwerp and Brussels and it stretches along the Scheldt, Dender and Rupel rivers. Water forms the 'blue thread' running through Scheldt Country. Traffic-free dikes and towing paths along the rivers and canals make it an excellent area for cycling and walking. Pontoon ferries transport pedestrians and cyclists across the Scheldt at no cost.

Scheldt Country stretches along the mighty Scheldt, the beautiful Rupel and the changeable Dender rivers in the provinces of East Flanders and Antwerp. With 277 km of navigable waterways and many lakes and ponds, Scheldt Country is a region rich in water.

The effects of ebb and flow are manifested far inland. The Dender is closed off from the Scheldt by sluice gates. As recently as November 2010, the volatile Dender made its presence felt. After heavy rainfalls, the river burst its banks at various spots. The three 'dender' cities of Dendermonde, Aalst and Ninove are located along the Dender. These three cities have lengthy histories, interesting city centres with beautiful historic buildings, lovely museums and delicious regional specialities, such as Dendermondse kop (a type of brawn) Aalsterse vlaaien (a type of flan, a recognized regional product) and Witkap (beer). Typical towns along the Scheldt include Vlassenbroek and Baasrode.

There is no better way to view Scheldt Country than from the water. As you sail down the meandering Dender, it will yield its secrets and show you a varied landscape with sluices and bridges that are still operated by hand. The river is at its prettiest between Ninove and Geraardsbergen. Sports enthusiasts can paddle along the river in canoes or kayaks. Cyclists can explore Scheldt Country by following the Scheldeverentocht or the Denderende Stedentocht. Both of these routes are part of the Scheldt Country cycle route network.

Donkmeer has been associated with boat hire for a long time

◁ Statue of the printer Dirk Martins in front of the belfry, the Oud-Schepenhuis and the Gebiedshuisje in Aalst

Exploring the Scheldt Country

Dendermonde, Aalst and Ninove are linked by the Dender. Every year, Aalst exuberantly celebrates carnival. On the Sunday before Ash Wednesday, a colourful carnival parade passes through the streets. However, it is also a city with a rich history, a lovely Grote Markt (square) and many statues telling the story of the social struggles. Dendermonde is proud of its world heritage, which includes Ros Beiaard, the three Gildenreuzen (giants), the Belfort (belfry) and the beguinage Alexiusbegijnhof. There is a real medieval atmosphere around the abbey church in Ninove, the smallest of the three Dender cities.

The Twijnster (Spinster), Ninove

The centuries-old Bareldonkkapel at the summit of the 'donk' (dune)

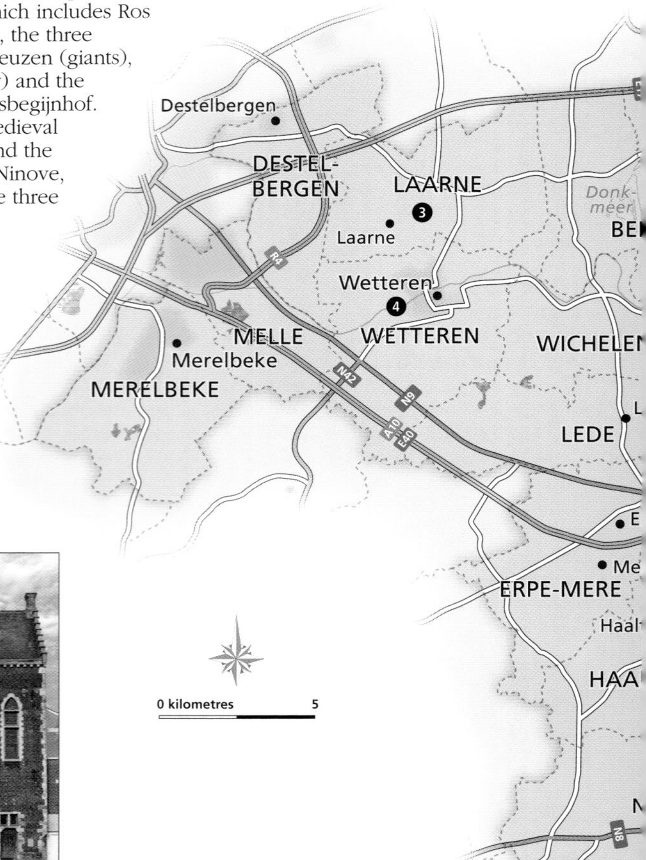

MUNICIPALITIES

Aalst ❶
Berlare ❺
Buggenhout ❻
Dendermonde ❷
Laarne ❸
Ninove ❼
Wetteren ❹

0 kilometres 5

Old city gateway in Ninove

Laarne castle

SYMBOLS

Motorway
Main road
Canal/river

Cyclists riding on the Scheldt dike

SEE ALSO

- ***Accommodation*** page 212
- ***Restaurants and cafés*** pages 220-221, 227

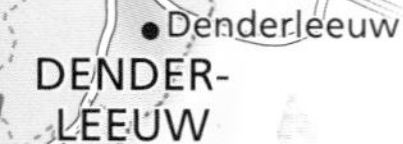

The expansive Buggenhoutforest

No other city in Flanders celebrates carnival as enthusiastically as 'Oilsjt' (Aalst)

Dender winding though Scheldt Country

DENDER

The 65 km long Dender River has its source in Ath in the province of Henegouwen. The Dender was a rain-fed river and was therefore not very navigable. As far back as the 10th century, its water level was regulated using sluice gates. In 1854, the river was canalised from its source to its mouth. The vessels that subsequently used the river transported coal, bluestone, bricks and grain. Numerous factories sprung up along the river. Since World War II, tourist boat cruises have generated most of the traffic on the Dender.

A walk through Aalst

CITY OF AALST 1

Road map D4. 80,000. **www**.aalst.be *Aalst.* *Molenstraat 45 (053-732270,* **www**.scheldeland.be).

During the 19th century, the city rapidly developed from a medieval fortress into a strong, industrialised city. This former textile city is now a commuter town serving its neighbours, Brussels and Ghent. Aalst was the home of printer Dirk Martens, politician-priest Adolf Daens, the painter Valerius de Saedeleer and author and painter Louis Paul Boon. However, Aalst is best known as the city of carnival. In 2010, UNESCO added the Aalst Carnival to its Representative List of Intangible Cultural Heritage.

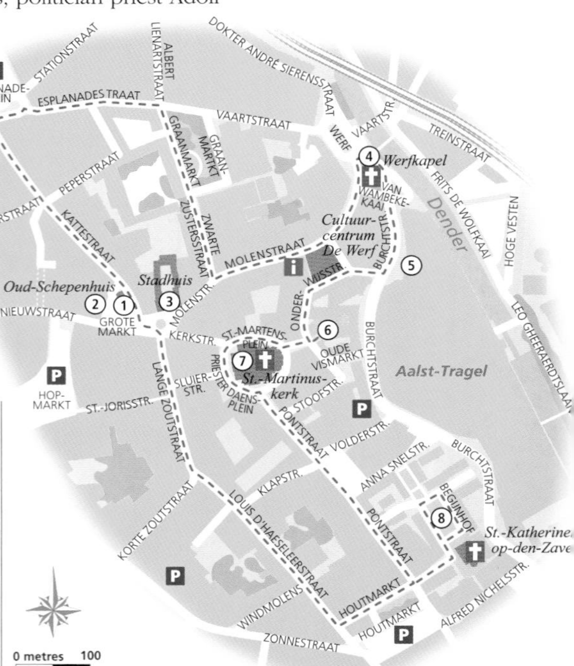

WALKING ROUTE

Oud-Schepenhuis ①
Borse van Amsterdam ②
Stadhuis ③
Werfplein ④
Het eiland Chipka ⑤
't Gashuys-Stedelijk Museum Aalst ⑥
St.-Martinuskerk ⑦
Begijnhof ⑧

SYMBOLS

······ Recommended route

Around the Grote Markt

The **Oud-Schepenhuis** ① (1225), presumably the oldest Alderman's bench in the Low Countries, is located at the Grote Markt. After being destroyed by fire, it was rebuilt in gothic style. The belfry, mockingly called the 'tettentoren' (teats tower) due to the half-spheres used in the clock, was added to the Alderman's bench in 1460. The front gable bears the inscription *Nec Spe, Nec Metu* (neither through hope, nor through fear), the motto of Spain's Philip II adopted by the lords of Aalst. The Gebiedshuisje (house of decrees), from which the bailiff decreed the laws, was built adjoining the Alderman's bench. The statue in front of the Gebiedshuisje honours Dirk Martens, the pioneer of printing in the southern Low Countries, who was born in Aalst in 1446. The **Borse van Amsterdam** ② is a renaissance-style building with a row of columns supporting its front façade. The **Stadhuis** (city hall) ③ consists of a neoclassic main building from 1828 along the Grote Markt, and the 17th-century former Landhuis (stately home) that was partly reconstructed in rococo style along the courtyard.

The front façade of the Borse van Amsterdam rests on twelve columns

The Werf

The robust monument to Adolf Daens (1839-1907), the driving force behind the Christene Volkspartij (Christian People's Party), is found on **Werfplein** ④. He devoted himself to achieving better working and living conditions for factory workers in Aalst and in the rest of Flanders. Because of his radical stance, Daens received much criticism from the well-established Catholic Party and the Catholic Church. In 1992, the film *Daens*, made by director Stijn Coninx and based on the novel by Louis Paul Boon about Adolf's brother Pieter Daens, was released. The De Werf cultural centre took its name from the former shipyard along the Dender.

Stedelijk Museum

Between the Oude Dender – filled in in 1964 and now called Burchtstraat – and the canalised Dender, lies **Chipka Island** ⑤, where the starch production and – processing company Syral, formerly known as Amylum, is located. The **'t Gasthuys-Stedelijk Museum Aalst** ⑥ can be found in the Oud Hospitaal. This museum succesfully combines historic buildings and new development and has an astonishing collection that deals with the Aalst carnival celebrations. It includes archive pieces, photographs and information about the *voil jeanet* (men dressed as women and vice versa), the Aalst Gilles and the giants. Other topics include the landscape paintings of **Valerius de Saedeleer**, the life and political struggles of Adolf Daens, the Louis Paul Boon collection and the city collection.

St.-Martinuskerk

Construction of the imposing **St.-Martinuskerk** ⑦ started in 1480 but was never completed. Its designers – Herman De Waghemakere and Laurens II Keldermans – had a much larger church in mind. With the 'provisional' closing of the western façade in 1730, construction came to an end. The church interior features stained-glass windows, frescos, paintings and no less than 21 shrines devoted to various religious fraternities. The only trace that remains of the original begijnhof, **beguinage** ⑧ is the St.-Catharinakerk (church). The beguinage homes were demolished in 1952 and replaced with social housing.

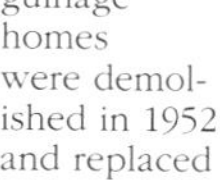

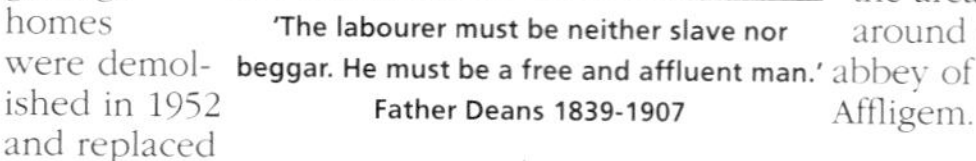

'The labourer must be neither slave nor beggar. He must be a free and affluent man.'
Father Deans 1839-1907

't Gasthuys - Stedelijk Museum Aalst

Oude Vismarkt 13, Aalst. ***Tel.*** *053-732345. Tue-Fr 10am-12pm and 13pm-17pm, Sat-Sun 14pm-18pm.*

Surroundings

The four towns to the north-east of Aalst – **Baardegem, Herdersem, Meldert** and **Moorsel** – together form the Faluintjes-streek region. The name *Faluintjes* refers to the scenic area with the same name, located between Moorsel and the abbey of Affligem. Due to the influence of the abbey, the region developed into Flanders' hops-growing region. Hops are the main ingredient in beer. After 1950, hops cultivation ceased to exist in the region. The farming of hops, with its characteristic poles, stakes and overhead wires, has made a comeback in various areas. The Hoppetocht (hops tour), a themed cycling tour, passes through the Faluintjes-streek and the area around the abbey of Affligem.

Faluintjesstreek routes

Starting point: *St.-Margaretakerk, Baardegem-Dorp.*
Distance: *12.5 km.*
Signposted.
Walking map: *available at Dienst voor Toerisme.*

The St.-Walburga walk is one of the four walking routes that together form the Faluintjesstreek walking route. This walk passes through Baardegem, the most rural municipality of the region. The walk follows paved and unpaved trails.
In Baardegem, a statue honours its most famous resident, Jan-Frans Vonk. He was born in the town in 1743 and became the greatest driving force behind the Brabant Revolution (1789). Using the walking map, this walk and others can be shortened or extended.

Sneeuwlandschap met ondergaande zon by Valerius de Saedeleer

A closer look: Dendermonde

The proud city of Dendermonde, located at the confluence of the Dender and the Scheldt, is a small provincial city. The pleasant Grote Markt with the city hall, the Vleeshuis museum, the many historic buildings and the Onze-Lieve-Vrouwekerk (Our Lady's Church) are proof of the economic prosperity of the city during the rule of the Burgundians. Dendermonde is the city of the legendary Ros Beiaard en de Vier Heemskinderen (see text box). Once every ten years, the famous horse returns to parade through the streets of the city. The festive parade Ros Beiaardommegang and the annual folkloristic event 'Katuit' Reuzenommegang have been added to the UNESCO Representative List of Masterpieces of Oral and Intangible Cultural Heritage.

★ City hall with belfry
The former Lakenhalle with belfry, the present-day city hall, is a prime example of Flemish medieval construction and dominates the Grote Markt.

★ Romanesque baptismal font
The showpiece of the Onze-Lieve-Vrouwekerk is this 12th-century Romanesque baptismal font made of Doornik limestone. The Last Supper is depicted on one of its sides.

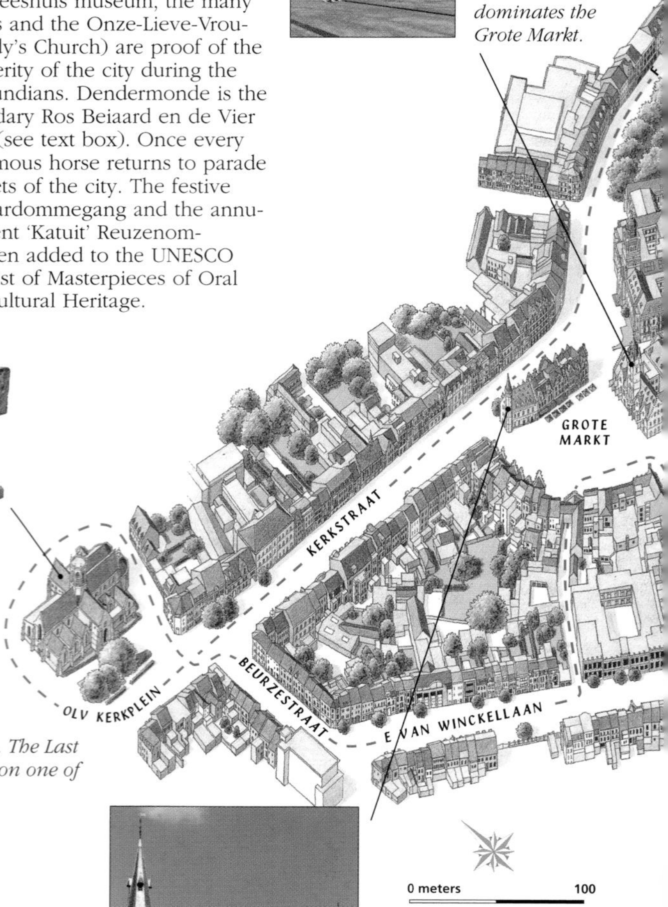

GROTE MARKT
KERKSTRAAT
OLV KERKPLEIN
BEURZESTRAAT
E VAN WINCKELLAAN

0 meters 100

Vleeshuis
This museum, home to objects and documents about the city, is housed in the Vleeshuis, a gothic-style building from the 15th century.

SYMBOLS

– – Recommended route

STAR ATTRACTIONS

★ City hall with belfry

★ Romanesque font

★ Ros Beiaard

Vlasmarkt

The Zwartzusterklooster and the neo-gothic Abbey church of the St.-Pieters en Paulusabdij, the only remaining monastery in East Flanders, dominate the square.

TIPS FOR VISITORS

Road map E3.
www.dendermonde.be Dendermonde. *Stadhuis, Grote Markt (052-213956).*
last Thu in Aug. Reuzenommegang Katuit.

★ ROS BEIAARD

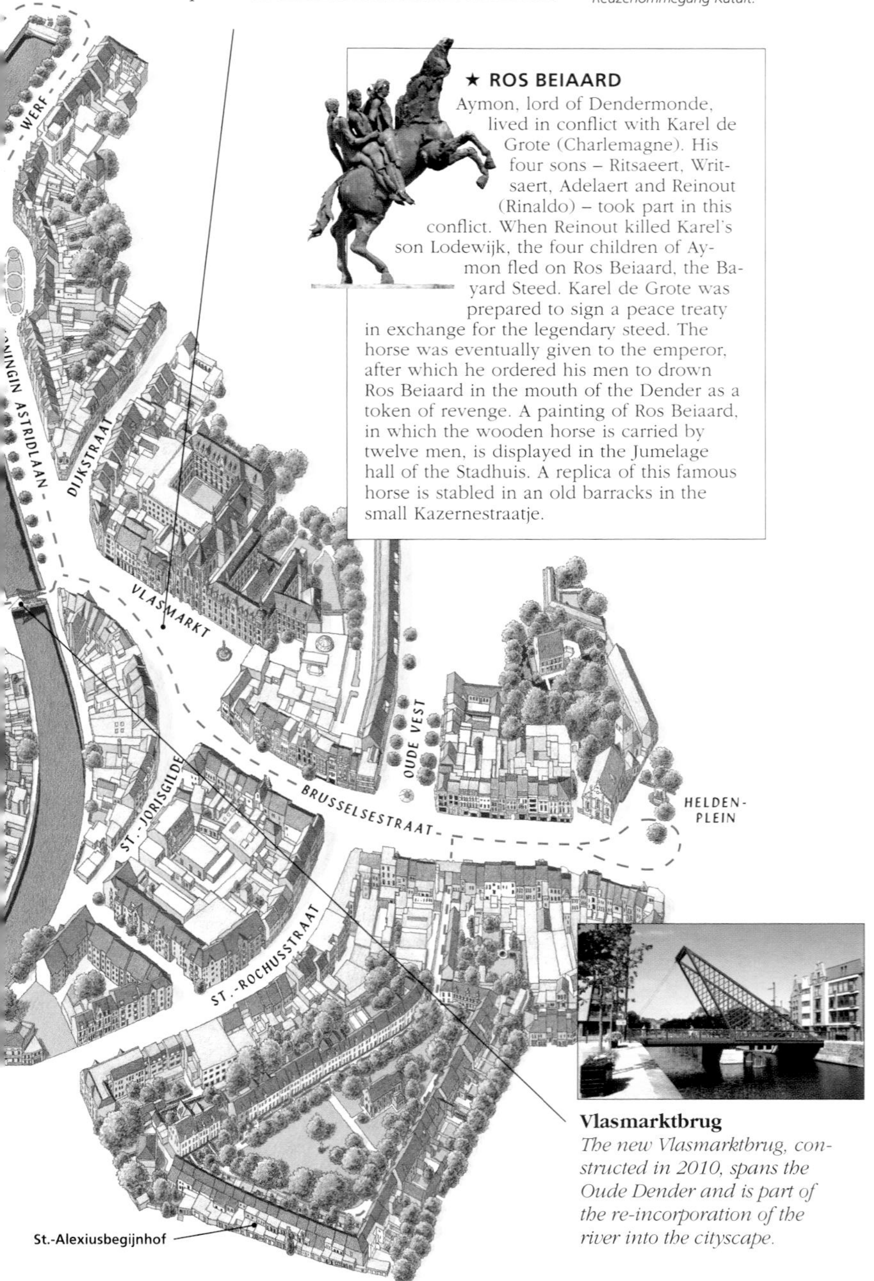

Aymon, lord of Dendermonde, lived in conflict with Karel de Grote (Charlemagne). His four sons – Ritsaeert, Writsaert, Adelaert and Reinout (Rinaldo) – took part in this conflict. When Reinout killed Karel's son Lodewijk, the four children of Aymon fled on Ros Beiaard, the Bayard Steed. Karel de Grote was prepared to sign a peace treaty in exchange for the legendary steed. The horse was eventually given to the emperor, after which he ordered his men to drown Ros Beiaard in the mouth of the Dender as a token of revenge. A painting of Ros Beiaard, in which the wooden horse is carried by twelve men, is displayed in the Jumelage hall of the Stadhuis. A replica of this famous horse is stabled in an old barracks in the small Kazernestraatje.

WERF
KONINGIN ASTRIDLAAN
DIJKSTRAAT
VLASMARKT
OUDE VEST
BRUSSELSESTRAAT
HELDEN-PLEIN
ST.-JORISGILDE
ST.-ROCHUSSTRAAT

Vlasmarktbrug

The new Vlasmarktbrug, constructed in 2010, spans the Oude Dender and is part of the re-incorporation of the river into the cityscape.

St.-Alexiusbegijnhof

CITY OF DENDERMONDE 2

Road map E3. *43,500.* **www**.dendermonde.be *Dendermonde.* *Stadhuis, Grote Markt (052-213956,* **www**.scheldeland.be).

The Grote Markt is the heart of the historic city centre

Dendermonde

A closer look: pages 178-179.

Grote Markt

The traffic-free, half-moon-shaped Grote Markt, reconstructed in 2004, is located at the heart of the historic city centre. The beauty of this square is due to the successful marriage between historic buildings and newly developed structures. Many of the original buildings were destroyed by the Germans in 1914. The elegant Vlasmarktbrug (2010) spans the Oude Dender and links the Grote Markt to the Vlasmarkt. In years to come, the Oude Dender will be reconnected to the Scheldt and passable for leisure vessels.

Stadhuis, lakenhalle and belfry

Grote Markt, Dendermonde. *Tue-Fri 9am-12pm and 1:30pm-4:30 pm (Apr-Sep Sat-Sun 10am-12pm and 1:30pm-6pm; Oct-Mar Sun 10am-12pm and 2pm-4:30pm; Jul-Aug Tue-Fri 9am-6pm Sat-Sun 10am-6pm).*

The **Stadhuis** (city hall) and belfry, of which the front façade is decorated with eleven heraldic flags in the summer months, is the most striking building on the Grote Markt. This 14th-century building, originally a cloth-makers' hall, was almost completely destroyed by fire in 1914. It was restored between 1920 and 1922 and extended with the addition of a neo-gothic wing. The weavers, who originally shared their hall with the butchers, moved to their own cloth-makers' hall in 1340. The city council also relocated to its own accommodation towards the end of the 14th century. When the textile industry languished. The City Council took over the entire building. The city hall houses an extraordinary collection of paintings by artists from the Dendermondse School, including Franz Courtens, Isidoor Meyers and Jacques Rosseels.

Onze-Lieve-Vrouwekerk

Onze-Lieve-Vrouwekerkplein, Dendermonde. *Apr-Sep Sat-Sun 2pm-4:45pm (Jul-Aug Tue-Sun 2pm-4:45pm).*
The 13th-century

Art gallery in the city hall

HISTORY OF DENDERMONDE

Dendermonde developed around 1050 at the foot of a castle at the confluence of the Scheldt and the Dender. In 1233, the flourishing settlement was granted a city charter. During this period, the Vleeshuis, the Lakenhalle with its belfry and the Onze-Lieve-Vrouwekerk were constructed. The barracks, bastions and

walls with the Brussels and Mechelen gate remind one of the city's military history. The city was largely destroyed by the Germans during World War I. A total of 1,252 homes and buildings were destroyed, many hundreds were severely damaged and only 98 were spared. During the following years, a new city arose from the ashes and the Lakenhalle and the Benedictine abbey were rebuilt. After 1950, the Oude Vest (medieval moat) was filled in and the Dender was rerouted around the outside of the centre.

The Onze-Lieve-Vrouwekerk is located near the Grote Markt

Onze-Lieve-Vrouwekerk, a prime example of Scheldt-gothic architecture, is located a few hundred metres from the Grote Markt. The church tower is missing its steeple. It was dislodged from the tower during a storm in 1940 and was never replaced. The church possesses a wealth of artworks, including paintings by Antoon van Dyck and David Tenier, lovely wall murals, stained-glass windows and a richly sculpted pulpit. Its showpiece is a beautifully decorated baptismal font made of Doornik limestone.

Vleeshuismuseum

Grote Markt, Dendermonde. ***Tel.*** *052-213018.* *Apr-Oct Tue-Sun 9:30am-12pm and 1:30pm-6pm.*

The history of the city is brought to life in the gothic-style Vleeshuis (1460-1462). It presents subject matter ranging from elements from the legendary Ros Beiaard parades to the skeleton of a mammoth that died 28,000 years ago. The 'story of the city' consists of chapters titled 'guilds and trades', 'faith and devotion', 'guest houses and cloisters' and 'daily life in Dendermonde'.

Zwijvekemuseum

Nijverheidsstraat 1, Dendermonde. ***Tel.*** *052-213018.* *Mon-Fri 9am-12pm and 1pm-4pm (also Sun 2pm-6pm Apr-Oct).*

The story of the city is continued with the chapters 'Dendermonde during the 19th and 20th century housed in the outbuildings of the **former Zwijveke abbey**, which was occupied by Cistercians from 1223 to 1797. Gravestones are displayed in the colonnade.

St.-Alexius-begijnhof

Entrance via Brusselsestraat, Dendermonde.
see Vleeshuismuseum.

This small beguinage, which is surrounded by 61 homes dating back to the 16th, 17th and 18th century, was established in 1288. The gardens in front of the homes are not enclosed by walls as is the case with most other beguinages. The church was destroyed in 1914 and was replaced with a smaller chapel. After the death of the last governess in 1975, the infirmary building was converted to a folklore museum. The small beguinage museum is housed in a former beguine home.

Beguine

St.-Pieters- en Paulus-abdij

Vlasmarkt, Dendermonde.
Whit Monday 2pm-6pm.
www.abdijdendermonde.be

In 1837, the Benedictines moved into the former Capuchin monastery. This monastery was destroyed by fire in 1914, but was later rebuilt in neo-gothic style. Abbey beer and a number of abbey wines are available at the gateway to the abbey.

Fortress

Dendermonde, strategically located at the confluence of the Dender and the Scheldt, was an important military stronghold from 1200 until after World War I. At the start of the 19th century, the city became a fortress with eleven bastions and six ravelins. Gates, barracks, arsenals and ammunition dumps were also constructed here. The heavy military presence severely impeded the effective economic development of the city. The fortress was dismantled in 1906 and only then was Dendermonde able to expand beyond its fortifications.

History room in the former Zwijveke abbey

Construction of an eel boat at the turn of the 19th century

Baasrode

By the 15th century, Baasrode was a busy trading harbour along the Scheldt at which ships from Antwerp moored on a daily basis. As a result, a flourishing shipbuilding industry developed here. The last shipyard here, Van Praet-Dansaert, was shut down in 1986. The **museum** in the former manager's residence focuses on the construction of wooden and steel ships and on the lives of the shipbuilders. Much attention is paid to the *Bostroëneir*, a ship's lamp that remained alight even during the most violent storms. The Baasrode palingbotter (eel boat) was built in this yard. The shipyards have gradually developed into a maritime heritage site.

Scheepswerven Baasrode
Sint-Ursmarusstraat 137, Baasrode. ***Tel.*** *052-333426.* *Sat 2pm-6pm (Apr-Oct. also Sun 2pm-6pm).*

Vlassenbroek

Vlassenbroek, a small, picturesque town at the foot of the Scheldt dike is known as an artist's town. Bars, restaurants, outdoor cafés and galleries are concentrated around the late-gothic style St.-Gertrudiskerk. Various walks along the polders and marshes start from the church square. Walking maps are available at local information offices.

LAARNE MUNICIPALITY 3

Road map C3. *12,000.*
www.laarne.be
www.scheldeland.be

Laarne

The Kasteeldreef, a beautiful, long lane lined with chestnuts, leads from the town to the imposing **Laarne castle**. The oldest part of the castle, the best-preserved moated castle in Belgium, dates back to the 13th century. The castle was built in a pentagonal shape and has three round towers, a square dungeon and a gatehouse. The building was given its current form during the 17th century. It features a rich collection of silver and beautifully appointed rooms, it is not always open to the public.
In 1607, four women were sentenced to be burnt at the stake after being accused of witchcraft. The Heksengilde (Guild of witches) keeps Laarne's heritage as a town of witchcraft alive.

Laarne castle
Eekhoekstraat 5, Laarne. ***Tel.*** *09-2309155.* *May-Sep. Sun 3pm (Jul-Aug also Thu 3pm).*
www.slotvanlaarne.be

WETTEREN MUNICIPALITY 4

Road map C3. *23,000.*
www.wetteren.be
De Poort, Markt 27 (09-3663104, **www**.scheldeland.be).

Wetteren

Wetteren is split in two by the Scheldt. Its market square is dominated by the huge neo-Romanesque St.-Gertrudiskerk (1861-1866) built in eclectic style and designed by Ghent architect Louis Minard. Wetteren is located at the heart of the ornamental plant cultivation region. Decorative trees and fruit trees, roses, azaleas, conifers and ornamental shrubs are cultivated in greenhouses and planted in the fertile soil. Adolf Papeleu (1811-1859) made Wetteren famous in the world of ornamental plants. The **Provinciaal Domein Den Blakken** is a promotional garden with incredible trees and plants from the region, a smell-and-taste garden and a small maze. The garden is located on the Warandeduinen, old river dunes, along the Scheldt.

Provinciaal Domein Den Blakken
Wegvoeringstraat 308, Wetteren. ***Tel.*** *09-3663104.* *sunrise to sunset.*

Domein Den Blakken with the 1931 former doctor's residence

BERLARE MUNICIPALITY 5

Road map D3. *14,500.* **www**.berlare.be *Donklaan 123, Donk (09-3429240,* **www**.scheldeland.be).

Donk

The **Donkmeer** (86 ha) developed from a bend in the Scheldt that was naturally cut off from the river ten thousand years ago. The dead branch of the river became a marshland from which peat was cut from the 17th century onwards. This created a large lake, called the Donkmeer. The lake has been converted into a large water sports and recreational area. The Bareldonkkapel, located on a low hill, is an often-visited pilgrimage chapel.

BUGGENHOUT MUNICIPALITY 6

Road map E3. *14,000.* **www**.buggenhout.be, **www**.scheldeland.be

Buggenhout

Buggenhout is one of the few towns in Flanders that still has two breweries. For more than two hundred years and for seven generations, *Tripel Karmeliet, Pauwel Kwak* and *Deus* have been brewed at the Bosteels brewery in the heart of the town. The De Landtsheer brewery is considerably newer and sells *Malheurbieren (Malheur beers)*. The Buggenhout forest forms part of the medieval Buckenholt forest, which used to cover thousands of hectares. The forest is now used for recreational purposes. The arboretum features all the trees and shrubs found in the Buggenhout forest, marked with name tags. A small monument in Opdorp, in the furthest corner of East Flanders, marks the geographic centre point of Flanders.

Former peat pit, now the domain of water sports enthusiasts

CITY OF NINOVE 7

Road map D4. *36,500.* **www**.ninove.be *Ninove.* *Stadhuis. Centrumlaan 100 (054-313285,* **www**.scheldeland.be).

Ninove

Ninove, the 'Oudste, de Stoutste en de Wijste der Steden' (Oldest, Boldest and Wisest of Cities)' is a friendly town on the banks of the Dender. It is the *oldest* because the name Ninove strongly resembles the name of the Assyrian city of Nineveh, the *boldest* because the city gates were always open and the city did not fear its enemies, and the *wisest* because the city did not employ a (paid) city jester. Until after World War II, Ninove was an important textile-producing city and the centre of match production. This town invites its visitors to take a walk through the city centre and along the banks of the Dender. The former abbey church, the baroque-style **Onze-Lieve-Vrouw Hemelvaartkerk**, also known as Our Lady of the Ascension church, the Couberg, is one of the few remaining reminders of the mighty Norbertine abbey that once controlled life in and around Ninove. After the forced closure of the abbey in 1794, the abbey church was received a new purpose as a parish church. The tower was added to the church in 1834, but it is rapidly subsiding. During archaeological digs, the former cloister hallway along the Kloosterweg road was exposed. The Koe gate is the only one of the four city gates to have survived. At the Graanmarkt square, four stones mark the site of the former grain hall. Not far from the market is the Oud-Stadhuis (old town hall), a striking neo-classic structure. Centrumlaan divides the 'new' Ninove with its shops, offices and town hall. The *Oeversteksen* spans the Dender. A small marina has been constructed on the left bank and a visitor's centre is being planned for the future.

Ferdinand Vander Haeghem designed the former abbey church in 1716

sky
sky

FLEMISH ARDENNES

The Flemish Ardennes, a region that differs vastly from the rest of East Flanders, starts not even 20 km south of Ghent. The boundaries of this region are not clearly outlined and, according to the author Omer Wattez – who coined the term 'Flemish Ardennes' – it is the 'schoone streek' (beautiful region) surrounding the cities of Oudenaarde, Ronse, Geraardsbergen and Zottegem.

The Flemish Ardennes landscape consists of soft, rolling hills with forest-covered inclines, open fields, rivers and brooks interspersed with historic towns and charming villages. Pollard willows, pools, sunken lanes, chapels, well-ordered fields and windmills dot the landscape. Its highest point, the Hotondberg in Zulzeke (Kluisbergen), is 150 m above sea level. In contrast to the 'real' Ardennes, there are no expansive forests here. It is a predominantly open landscape with forest only on the tops of the hills. The Kluisbos (Kluis forest) is the largest uninterrupted forest. The summit of the Kluisberg (141 m in height) is located precisely on the border between Flanders and Wallonia. The Zwalm River winds its way through the Flemish Ardennes and flows into the Scheldt at Nederzwalm. The Mijnwerkerspad (Miner's road), a cycling track that follows the former Zottegem to Ellezelles railway line, passes through the Zwalm valley between Opbrakel and Zottegem. The Flemish Ardennes are famous for the cobbled roads that turn cycling up the climbs of Oude Kwaremont (4.2-11%), the Muur van Geraardsbergen (9.2-19.8%) and the Bosberg (5.8-11%) into a true challenge. Every year, thousands of cycling fans line the Muur van Geraardsbergen to witness the culmination of Tour of Flanders. Nestled amongst the hills are many small towns that, with their intimate little town squares, emphasise the charm of the Flemish Ardennes landscape.

The rolling landscape and beautiful vistas of the Flemish Ardennes

◁ **Cycling up the road called Muur van Geraardsbergen**

Exploring the Flemish Ardennes

The Flemish Ardennes are best explored on foot or by bicycle. The Fietsnetwerk Vlaamse Ardennen (Flemish Ardennes Cycling Network) offers cyclists more than 830 km of cycling pleasure, from leisurely valley roads along the Scheldt or the Zwalmbeek to steep leg killers. Most of the inclines have a 5-6% gradient and there are many 'false flats'. Signposted walking routes can be found in most of the towns and cities. Whether you are cycling or walking, the views en route are often breathtaking. Oudenaarde, Geraardsbergen, Ronse and Zottegem are four cities with many historic buildings, museums, delicious regional foodstuffs and long histories. The many towns and villages offer a wealth of unexpected surprises.

Tour of Flanders centre in Oudenaarde

MUNICIPALITIES

- Geraardsbergen 1
- Horebeke 4
- Kluisbergen 5
- Oosterzele 6
- Oudenaarde 2
- Ronse 3
- Zottegem 7
- Zwalm 8

The Oudenaarde town centre

The Flemish Ardennes around Ronse

Coarse Balegem sandstone

SEE ALSO

- ***Accommodation*** page 213
- ***Restaurants and cafés*** pages 221, 227

Toerisme Vlaamse Ardennen
www.toerismevlaamseardennen.be

Oosterzele
OOSTERZELE
6
Balegem
ST.-LIEVENS-HOUTEM
St.-Lievens-Houtem
A10
E40
N42
Herzele
Velzeke
Zottegem
Zwalm
WALM
8
7
ZOTTEGEM
HERZELE
ria-Horebeke
St.-Maria-Lierde
N8
N42
Brakel
LIERDE
Dender
BRAKEL
Geraardsbergen
1
GERAARDSBERGEN

Statue of Lamoraal, count of Egmont, in Zottegem

0 kilometres 5

Market square with the 15th-century Marbol in Geraardsbergen

CASTLE RUIN HERZELE

For centuries, the lords of Herzele controlled the splendid 'Hersele'. The history of this castle goes back to the 7th century. During the course of the 11th century, it was constructed in stone. Its ruins are located in a park.

SYMBOLS

- Motorway
- Main road
- Canal/river

Vlaanderens Mooiste Landschap

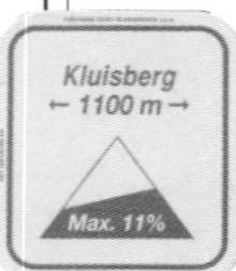

At one time, the sea regularly flooded this area, leaving behind alternating layers of sand and clay. Once the sea had subsided for good, the soft layers were eroded by wind and rain. However, the harder sandstone layers resisted and remained part of the landscape (getuigenheuvels) as testimony to this previous activity.

These hills were covered with forest and later they were turned into farmland. The rolling landscape, with its meadows, forests, fields and towns, is the showpiece of the Flemish Ardennes. This extraordinary landscape deservedly bears the title of *Vlaanderens Mooiste landschap (Flanders' most beautiful landscape).*

Walking
There are more than 25 walking routes in the Flemish Ardennes along which walkers can enjoy stunning views, sunken lanes, forests and open fields.

Ooievaar lookout tower
This 30 m lookout tower is located at one of the highest points of the region. At 140 m above sea level, it offers a unique view over the Flemish Ardennes.

By bike
Its forested hills, lovely views and sharp climbs make the Flemish Ardennes a cyclist's paradise.

OMER WATTEZ AND THE FLEMISH ARDENNES

Omer Wattez was born in 1857 in Schorisse (Maarkedal). He devoted much of his time as a writer to praising his birthplace. In his work, he dedicated himself to the emancipation of Flanders. Towards the end of the 19th century, he used the term 'Flemish Ardennes' for the first time. In 1890, his travel guide, *De Vlaamsche Ardennen, een tochtje in het Zuiden van Vlaanderen (The Flemish Ardennes, a tour through the South of Flanders)* was released.

TIPS FOR VISITORS

Toerisme Vlaamse Ardennen
www.toerismevlaamse ardennen.be

Regionaal Landschap Vlaamse Ardennen
www.rlva.be

Molen Ten Hotond
At the summit of the Hotondberg (150 m), the highest point of the Flemish Ardennes and of East Flanders, is the shell of the 18th-century Ten Hotond windmill. It has been converted into a lookout with an orientation map and offers a stunning view of the Flemish Ardennes and Pays des Collines (hill country).

ROLLING LANDSCAPE

Its steep hills, wide valleys and untouched nature makes the Flemish Ardennes one of the most beautiful landscapes in Flanders.

GETUIGENHEUVELS VLAAMSE ARDENNEN WALKING NETWORK

The Getuigenheuvels Vlaamse Ardennen walking network is a signposted network of walking routes totalling 300 km found within the Kluisbergen-Oudenaarde-Brakel-Ronse area. Using the junctions, you can plan your own walking routes. A walking map is available from Toerisme Oost-Vlaanderen and from local information offices in the Flemish Ardennes.

A walk through Geraardsbergen

Manneken-Pis

Geraardsbergen is a charming town on the banks of the Dender. Its medieval town centre between the Dender and the Oudenberg is ideally explored on foot. Narrow and occasionally steep streets, historic architecture and amazing views give the city a genuine Arden–nes atmosphere. Brugstraat climbs the hill towards the Markt after which it winds further upwards and becomes the fearsome Muur van Geraardsbergen, the steep climb to the summit of the Oudenberg. It is tough for walkers and cyclists alike, but the one-of-a-kind view from the Molen ten Hotond overlook at 110 m makes it all worthwhile.

CITY OF GERAARDSBERGEN ❶

Road map C5. *31,500.* **www**.geraardsbergen.be *Geraardsbergen.* *Markt (054-437289),* **www**.toerismevlaamseardennen.be *Krakelingenworp and Tonnekensbrand (UNESCO World Heritage List), penultimate Sun before the first Mon of March.*

SYMBOLS

······ Recommended route

WALKING ROUTES

Markt ①
St.-Adriaansabdij ②
Muur van Geraardsbergen ③
Oudenberg ④
Dierkosttoren ⑤
St.-Bartholomeuskerk ⑥
Dender ⑦
Geraardsbergse Musea ⑧

Around the Markt

In front of the neo-gothic town hall with its towers at the **Markt** ① is a replica of the 15th-century **Marbol**, a bastardisation of the word 'marktbron' (spring). Inside an alcove in the town hall staircase, **Manneken-Pis** has been urinating nonstop since 1459. He is 160 years older than his famous Brussels lookalike. The Marbol and Manneken-Pis are two manifestations of the underground spring water network that supplied the town with water in the past. The **De Permanensje**, located in the former cloth-makers hall of the town hall, is the city and regional tourist information office. Here, visitors can view photographs, maps and multimedia presentations and familiarise themselves with the cultural heritage and nature of *Flanders' most beautiful landscape.* All that remains of the once-mighty **St.-Adriaansabdij** ② are the gatehouse, the abbey wing, the abbot's home and the coach house. The abbey is located in a park with a pond, an arboretum and a playground. The collections

The 15th-century Marbol in Geraardsbergen

Oudenbergkapel

from the city museums have been placed in temporary storage in Kollegestraat in preparation for the renovation of the abbot's home.

The Muur

The **Muur van Geraardsbergen** ③ also called the Muur and the Kapelmuur, is very well known in the cycling world. This dreaded cobblestone road has a 92 m altitude difference, a length of 1,075 m and an average gradient of 9.2%. Its steepest section has a gradient of 19.8%. The Muur is the deciding factor at various cycling events, the most famous being the Tour of Flanders. It ends at the summit of the **Oudenberg** ④ where the **Oudenbergkapel** (1905), dedicated to Our Lady, is located. The walls of the chapel are covered in votive plates giving thanks for blessings received. Behind the chapel, the orientation map area offers a stunning view of the Flemish Ardennes.

Around St.-Bartholomeuskerk

The Grupellopark (or Stadspark) lies on the western slope of the Muur. The recently restored 14th-century **Dierkosttoren** ⑤ formed part of the city fortifications that were demolished during the 19th century. The Boerenhol is a narrow street with a gateway that linked the Markt to the fortifications. The large **St.-Bartholomeuskerk** ⑥ dominates the Markt. It has a baroque-style interior. Within the church, the wall murals created by Louis Bert-de l'Arbe attract the most attention.

Benedenstad

The **Dender** ⑦ bisects Geraardsbergen. It contains a sluice-gate that regulates the Dender's water level. Freight vessels on the Dender have made way for leisure yachts moored in the yacht harbour. The **Geraardsbergen Museums** ⑧ have been temporarily accommodated in a stately mansion in Kollegestraat. The various 'robes' worn by Manneken-Pis on festival days can be seen here, as well as at the De Permanensje tourist information office. The museum is further dedicated to the match industry, Chantilly lace, breweries and the cigar industry, topics that are closely linked to the industrial history of this interesting and historical city.

In November 2010, the Dender flooded the Geraardsbergen streets

HISTORY OF GERAARDSBERGEN

Geraardsbergen developed during the 11th century due to its strategic position on the border between Flanders and Brabant. In 1096, the Benedictines established the St.-Pietersabdij along the Dender. With the arrival of the relics of St Adriaan, a saint worshipped during the time of the plague, the name was changed and St.-Adriaansabdij became a much-visited pilgrimage site. In the 12th century, the city flourished thanks to the textile industry. After centuries of conflicts and economic decline, the textile industry recovered in the 17th century. Black silk Chantilly lace from Geraardsbergen became world-famous. During the 19th and 20th centuries, Geraardsbergen was an important centre for the tobacco- and match industry.

De Permanensje

Markt, Geraardsbergen. ***Tel.*** *054-437289.* *Jun-Sep. Mon-Fri 9am-12:30pm and 1:30 pm-5pm (Oct-May. 9am-12pm and 1:30pm-4pm), Sat-Sun 10am-12pm and 1pm-4:30pm.*

Geraardsbergse Museums

Kollegestraat 26, Geraardsbergen. ***Tel.*** *054-411394.* *Apr-Sep. Mon-Fri 2pm-5pm, Sat-Sun 2pm-6pm (Oct-Mar 2pm-5pm).*
www.de-abdij.be

Surroundings

The **Provinciaal Domein De Gavers** is located between the hills of the Flemish Ardennes and the Dender valley. The area offers many day-activity options, including swimming and wall climbing.

Provinciaal Domein De Gavers

Onkerzelestraat 280, Geraardsbergen. ***Tel.*** *054-416324.*
www.degavers.be

A closer look: Oudenaarde

Oudenaarde, with a lovely location along the Scheldt and surrounded by the hills of the Flemish Ardennes, is a city with a long history. The flamboyant city hall, the imposing St.-Walburgakerk and the historic buildings around the Grote and Kleine Markt are reminders of the rich history of this city of tapestry weavers and beer brewers. The verdures, well-known wall tapestries from Oudenaarde, brought the city worldwide fame. Oudenaarden brown ale was known throughout Flanders. The present-day Centrum Ronde van Vlaanderen, Tour of Flanders Centre, is an interactive museum. Not far from the city is the Ename abbey, the birthplace of Oudenaarde.

★ City hall with belfry
The large rectangular market square, presumably constructed during the 14th century along with the belfry and cloth-makers, hall on it northern side, defines the Oudenaarde centre.

0 metres 100

★ Centrum Ronde van Vlaanderen
The centre provides a unique interactive experience, features an astonishing image archive and allows one to experience the Tour of Flanders from a rider's point of view.

SYMBOLS

– – Recommended route

STAR ATTRACTIONS

- ★ City hall with belfry
- ★ Centrum Ronde van Vlaanderen
- ★ St.-Walburgakerk

★ St.-Walburgakerk
The 88-m-high tower of this gothic-style church, dedicated to Walburgis, patron saint of the city, is a landmark that can be seen from a distance.

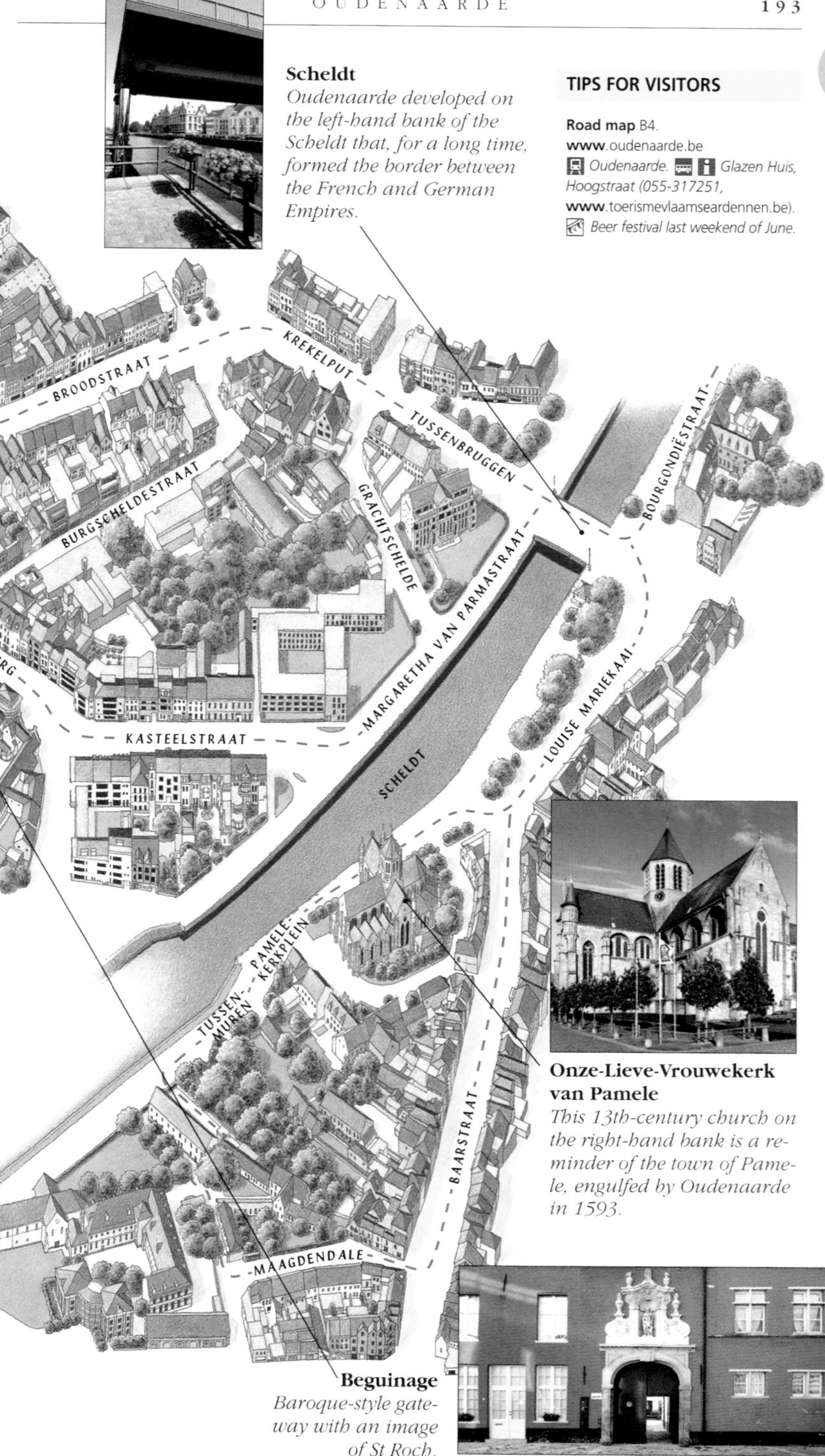

Scheldt
Oudenaarde developed on the left-hand bank of the Scheldt that, for a long time, formed the border between the French and German Empires.

TIPS FOR VISITORS

Road map B4.
www.oudenaarde.be
Oudenaarde. *Glazen Huis, Hoogstraat (055-317251,* **www**.toerismevlaamseardennen.be).
Beer festival last weekend of June.

Onze-Lieve-Vrouwekerk van Pamele
This 13th-century church on the right-hand bank is a reminder of the town of Pamele, engulfed by Oudenaarde in 1593.

Beguinage
Baroque-style gateway with an image of St Roch.

CITY OF OUDENAARDE ❷

Road map B4. *29,000.*
www.oudenaarde.be *Oudenaarde.* *Glazen Huis, Hoogstraat (055-317251,* **www**.toerismevlaamseardennen.be).

A closer look: pages 192-193.

Historic buildings around the pleasant Kleine Markt

Markt

Around the large square, historic buildings with names like *De Maenen, De Rebbe* and *De Gulden Cop*, jostle for space. The royal fountain, given to the city's residents by Louis XIV in 1677-1678, is located in front of the city hall. At the pleasant **Kleine Markt**, the former yarn market, there are many stunning historic buildings, such as a home named after Margaret of Parma. She was the offspring of a brief dalliance between Charles V and Johanna van der Gheynst, a chambermaid belonging to countess de Lalaing, who lived in the Burgundian castle that is no longer in existence. In 1559, Margaret was named governess of the Low Countries. The castle was demolished in 1970 when the Scheldt was widened. In the 12th century, the Boudewijntoren was built onto a city dwelling as a status symbol. Other buildings, including the 18th-century Vleeshuis (now the city library), strengthen the historical character of the Kleine Markt.

Hanske de Krijger

City hall, clothmakers' hall and belfry

Markt, Oudenaarde. *visitors' centre-museum: Tue-Sun, see website.* *only museum.*

The proud city hall, designed by Brussels architect Hendrik Van Pede, is a prime example of Brabant late-gothic style architecture. It was constructed between 1526 and 1538 adjoining the clothmakers' hall on the site of the former Alderman's bench. With its fine decoration, the façade resembles lacework. The crown on the belfry is in honour of Charles V. On the crown stands a sculpture of the 16th-century guardsman, Hanske de Krijger. The visitors' centre in the lower clothmakers' hall provides information about the city and the region. Historic characters take visitors on a tour through the history of the city. The famous Oudenaarde wall tapestries, called *verdures* because of their predominantly green-blue colour *(see text box)*, are hung in the upper clothmakers' hall. A rich collection of silverware is displayed in an adjacent hall. The **schepenzaal** features a lovely enclosed patio in renaissance style, a gallery of paintings and other artworks.

Centrum Ronde van Vlaanderen

Markt 45, Oudenaarde. ***Tel.*** *055-339933.* *Feb-Dec. Tue-Sun 10am-6pm.*
www.crvv.be

A superbly designed interactive museum with many reminders of the greatest cycling competition in Flanders. After watching the introductory film, featuring unique footage visitors experience what the tour must be like for its riders. Besides the photographs, information panels and memorabilia, there are hands-on attractions, such as simulators that give people a cobblestone- or Flemish hill climbing cycling experience. *See also pages 24-25.*

St.-Walburgakerk

Markt, Oudenaarde. *Jun-Sep. Tue-Sat 2:30pm-5pm (Thu also 10am-12pm), Sun 2pm-6pm; Oct Tue, Thu and Sat 2:30pm-5pm (Thu also 10am-12pm).*

The painting 'Panorama van Oudenaarde' is displayed in the schepenzaal

Homes in the beguinage

St.-Walburgakerk (church) and its tower without a spire dominate the city. Of the 12th-century early-gothic church, all that remains is the choir. During the 15th century, the church was rebuilt in Brabant-gothic style, but only the tower and the nave were completed. In 1534, construction was halted. Inside, it is easy to distinguish between the 'old' (dark-grey Doornik stone) and the 'new' church (white Balegem sandstone). The church contains a wealth of treasures, including life-size sculptures of the apostles, paintings and tapestries.

Historic city walk

Distance: *4 km per loop.*
Leaflet: *available at Dienst voor Toerisme.*
This city walk consists of two loops. The first passes through the historic area with the most important historic buildings and the **Pamelewijk** on the right-hand bank of the Scheldt. The second loop passes through the city park and the industrial and station district of 19th-century Oudenaarde.

Maagdendale

Maagdendale 13, Oudenaarde.
In 1234, the Cistercians established themselves in the Maagdendale abbey. All that remains of the original abbey are the 13th-century abbey church and the home of the abbess. The buildings now house the city archives and the arts academy.

Begijnhof

Achterburg, Oudenaarde.
summer until 9pm, winter until 7pm.
The gateway, which features an image of St.-Rochus, St Roch or Rocco, provides access to this small city within the city. Surrounding the square and the 16th-century chapel are whitewashed homes from the 17th century and later.

Pamelewijk

The new Scheldebrug (bridge) connects the old city to the Pamele district. From the 12th century, an independent city centre, managed by the lords of Pamele, developed on the right-hand bank of the Scheldt. The lords ordered the construction of the Onze-Lieve-Vrouwekerk van Pamele and established the Maagdendale abbey. In 1593, Pamele became part of Oudenaarde.

Huis de Lalaing

Bourgondiëstraat 9, Oudenaarde.
Tel. *055-314863.* *Tue-Fri 1:30pm-4:30pm.*
Huis de Lalaing, a stately 17th-century aristocrat's home, was named after city governor Philips de Lalaing who lived here during the 16th century. Inside the home, a restoration workshop makes sure that the long-standing tradition of Oudenaarde tapestries is maintained. The restoration process can be followed in the workshop and by means of a display. In the VASA weaving workshop, modern wall hangings are produced using old techniques.

View of the Scheldt bridges and the Pamelewijk

Restoration workshop

OUDENAARDE WALL TAPESTRIES

From the 15th century onwards, Oudenaarde had a flourishing wall tapestry industry. Its greatest period was during the 16th century, when more than half of the population worked in the workshops. The last tapestry weaver closed shop in 1772. The precious tapestries were exported to all parts of the world. These tapestries usually contained images of gardens and trees, and every leaf was woven with the utmost precision. The most famous tapestries are the decorative green verdures onto which a range of green shades were woven. The most famous series consists of three 16th-century tapestries that illustrate the most significant periods in the life of Alexander the Great.

Interior of the Onze-Lieve-Vrouwkerk of Pamele

Onze-Lieve-Vrouwekerk van Pamele

Louise-Mariekaai/Spei, Oudenaarde.
Jun-Aug. Sat 2:30pm-5pm.
This early-gothic style church dominates the view of the Scheldt. Because it was constructed over a relatively short period of time thirty years, it is a textbook example of the Scheldt-gothic style, and was built using Doornik limestone. A bronze plaque in the upper choir mentions the name of Arnulf van Binche, the church's architect, and the year of its completion, 1234. The light entering through the windows in the south chapel, created in 1909 by J. Dobbelare, emphasises the intimate nature of the church. Behind the church are the two tombs of the lords of Pamele.

Cycling route – In the footsteps of Adriaen Brouwer

Starting point: *Markt.* ***Distance:*** *35 km.* ***Leaflet:*** *available at Dienst voor Toerisme.*
This cycling route combines the very best of what the Flemish Ardennes have to offer. The impressive Flemish Ardennes landscape provides one-of-a-kind views. After climbing a steep 'leg killer', catch your breath at an authentic outdoor café and enjoy an Oudenaarde brown ale. Oudenaarde painter Adriaen Brouwer (1605-1638) was the kind of person who really enjoyed the good life.

Kerselare

The pilgrimage site of Onze-Lieve-Vrouw van Kerselare developed around a statuette of Our Lady and a kerselaar (cherry tree) on the summit of the Edelareberg. The 30 cm high miraculous image of Mary is found in a modern chapel built to replace the 16th-century chapel that was completely destroyed by fire in 1961. During the 3 km *Lange ommegang* also known as the Long procession, pilgrims walk along peaceful trails past fifteen small chapels. The annual blessing of cars takes place on Ascension Day.

Mullem

Mullem, as is said by the inhabitants of the area themselves, is 'tenden de weireld': the end of the world. It is a small picturesque town with a church, a modest **town square** and a castle hidden in a park. This cosy town attracts a lot of visitors who populate the cafés and patios on weekends.

Rooigemsebeekroute

Starting point: *Mullem.*
Distance: *3, 6 of 13 km.*
Signposted.
This route passes through the town centres of Mullem and Wanegem-Lede, visiting two castles (De Ghellinck and De Gerlache), the Huisekouter mill in Zingem and the Schietsjampetter mill in Kruishoutem. Both mills were originally located in West Flanders, but have since been relocated to their present-day home. The relocation of the Schietsjampetter mill was opposed by the local *sjampetter* (village policeman), who did not hesitate to draw his weapon and fire; hence the name.

Town square with the St.-Hilariuskerk in the castle town of Mullem

Ename

In Ename, a town a few kilometres upstream from the Oudenaarde centre, the Provinciaal Archeologisch Museum (Provincial Archaeological Museum), the archaeological park, the St.-Laurentiuskerk and the Bos t'Ename illustrate the story of the thousand year-long history of this strategic town on the banks of the Scheldt.

During the early Middle Ages, the Scheldt formed the boundary between the French and German Empires. Around 974, the German emperor constructed a castle on the right-hand bank. A flourishing trading town developed at the foot of this fortress. In 1033, the castle was occupied and destroyed by count Boudewijn (Baldwin) IV of Flanders and only the Ottonian St.-Laurentiuskerk was spared. The residents of the trade town moved to the newly-established Oudenaarde. Amongst the remnants of the German settlement, Boudewijn V, the son of the count of Flanders, established a Benedictine monastery. This monastery existed for seven centuries until the French brought an end to the order in 1794. The monastery was destroyed. Its foundations have been exposed in the archaeological park.

Feest van Duizend Jaar museum display

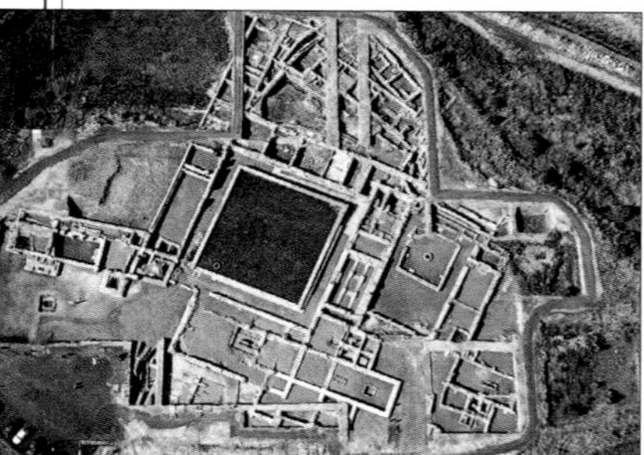

Labyrinth of archaeological remains

Archaeological Park

With the aid of information panels and the *Tijdvenster* (Time window), the labyrinth – that is the foundations of the Benedictine abbey – is explained to visitors. This abbey dominated life in Ename between 1063 and 1795.

St.-Laurentiuskerk

This church, constructed around the year 1000, was originally a double-choir imperial church, a style that reflected loyalty to the German emperor. The eastern choir section is especially unusual. The arch area in the eastern choir is decorated with a Byzantine-style mural representing the *Majestas Domini* from approximately 1010. The *Tijdvenster* uses an interactive storytelling technique to explain various aspects of the building.

Altar of the St.-Laurentiuskerk

Bos t'Ename

To the south of Ename, there is an expansive forest area that was closely related to the harbour town and later the Ename abbey.

Provinciaal Archeologisch Museum (pam)

Contemporary museum in which one thousand years of history is brought to life in words, images and archaeological finds. Lords and servants, abbots and monks and countesses and archaeologists enjoy a feast together and tell the stories of their lives.

Mariette Tielemanspad (route)

Starting point: *pam Ename.*
Distance: *6 km.*
Signposted.

From the museum, the Mariette Tielemanspad passes traces of human presence, as well as extraordinary plants and animals.

TIPS FOR VISITORS

pam Ename
Lijnwaadmarkt 20, Ename.
Tel. *055-309040. Tue-Sun 9:30am-5pm; archaeological park: daily; St.-Laurentiuskerk, via museum. 41 from the Markt in Oudenaarde.*
www.pam-ename.be

St.-Hermescrypte in Ronse

The relics of St Hermes, patron saint of the mentally ill, have been safeguarded in the Romanesque crypt of St.-Hermeskerk (church) since 860. The crypt was dedicated in 1089. Pilgrims came from far and wide to find help and healing. Mentally ill persons were bathed (men and women separately) in the two small side rooms of the crypt.

Meanwhile, a priest presented a special bath mass in a nearby chapel. In 1267, the collapsing of a church tower resulted in destruction as 9 columns and almost all of the walls were severely damaged. At the start of the 16th century, the crypt was extended towards the east and, since then, has had 32 columns.

Hermes of Rome
St Hermes was portrayed as a Roman officer on horseback leading the devil on a chain. He and his company fell into the hands of judge Aurelianus, after which they died martyrs.

★ Water well
A well in the crypt was important because, as far back as can be remembered, water has been a symbol of life, redemption and healing.

Fiertelommegang
In order to be eligible for healing, the mentally ill had to perform a physical effort (pilgrimage) in return. For this reason, the residents of Ronse form a procession with the reliquary around the town in the hope of protecting themselves and the town from mental illness. On Trinity Sunday, the Sunday after Pentecost, the fiertelommegang is held, and the relics are carried along the city boundaries. The word fiertel is derived from the Latin word *ferebrum*, meaning reliquary.

★ Romanesque columns
The crypt originally had 24 columns of which 15 dated back to the first (Romanesque) period. They were each hewn from a single piece of natural stone and support typical cubic- or die chapiters (capitals).

★ Bathing rooms
While the ill were bathed in the bathing rooms, a 'bath mass' was held in the adjacent chapel.

TIPS FOR VISITORS

Kaatsspelplein, Ronse. **Tel.** 055-211735. *Mar-Sep Tue-Sun 2pm-5pm; Oct-Nov Sat-Sun 2pm-5pm.* *Dec-Feb.* **www**.ronse.be *Fiertelommegang Sun after Pentecost; St. Hermes holiday 28 Aug.*

Reliquary
Relics of St Hermes are safeguarded in this beautifully-made reliquary in the St.-Hermeskerk.

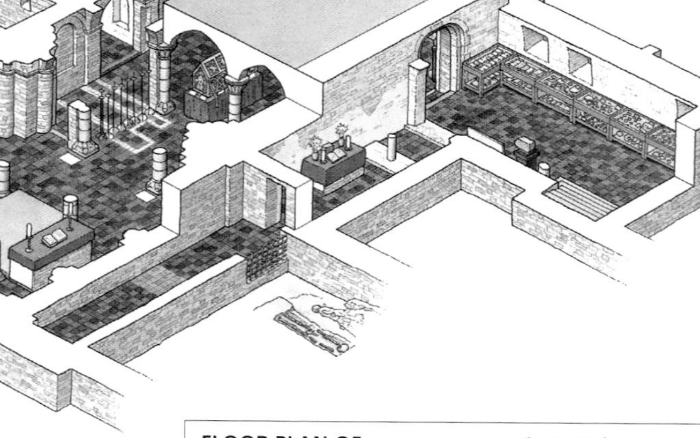

STAR ATTRACTIONS

- ★ Water well
- ★ Romanesque columns
- ★ Bathing rooms

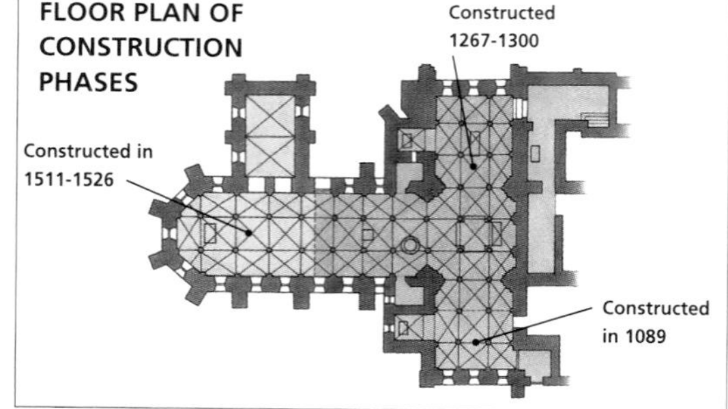

CITY OF RONSE 3

Road map B5. *24,500.* **www**.ronse.be *Ronse.* *Hoge Mote, de Biesestraat 2 (055-232816,* **www**.ontdekronse.be, **www**.toerismevlaamseardennen.be).

Ronse

Grote Markt

In the centre of the rectangular Grote Markt (Great Market) is the public fountain with its 12 m bluestone needle. This fountain formed the final part of the 19th-century water network. The town hall was rebuilt after World War II in neo-classic style. Priesterstraat links the Grote Markt to the more subdued and charming Kleine Markt (Small Market).

Tower of the Oude St.-Martinuskerk

St.-Hermeskerk

Kleine Markt, Ronse. *kerk: Mon-Sun 8am-7:30pm; tower: via Dienst voor Toerisme.*

This late-gothic style church features an elegant choir pew and an impressive sculpture of St Hermes on horseback. Across from the altar, hooks hang from the wall to which the difficult-to-restrain mentally ill were chained while a priest bathed them to bring on healing. The 79 m tall St Hermes tower is built against the church. Climb the 208 steps to the top and – on clear days – enjoy the panoramic view that stretches well into France. The foundations of a predecessor of this church, demolished in 1843, are found in the adjacent park.

One of the functional looms in the MUST Werken

St.-Hermescrypte

Pages 198-199.

Oude St.-Martinuskerk

St.-Martinusstraat, Ronse.

All that remains of the old church, built next to the St. Hermes church during the 11th century, is its 15th-century tower. The present-day church dates back to 1829, but was closed in 1896 after the new red-brick St.-Martinuskerk at Kerkplein was taken into use. Because it was threatening to collapse, the choir section was demolished in 1996.

MUST Wonen

Bruulpark, Ronse. ***Tel.*** *055-232806.* *Apr-Oct Tue-Sun 10am-12pm and 2pm-5pm; Nov-Mar Tue-Sun 10am-12pm and 2pm-4pm.*

This museum deals with the influence that the textile industry had on the development of the then small town of Ronse. Architecture, culture and art flourished thanks to the growing textile industry. But there were also side-effects to this textile boom, including poverty, poor housing and alcoholism. In video images, famous characters from the history of Ronse guide visitors around the museum. *Den Dragonder* is an authentic folk café that dates to 1900.

MUST Werken

Hoge Mote/De Biesestraat 2, Ronse. ***Tel.*** *055-232816.* *Apr-Oct Tue-Sun 10am-12pm and 2pm-5pm; Nov-Mar Tue-Sun 10am-12pm and 2pm-4pm.*

The *Werken* (Work) section of the Stedelijk Musea Ronse, Ronse city museums, is housed in the old 'Cambier-Robette' textile factory, a side wing of **the Hoge Mote**. The pride and joy of the museum is the weaving mill, where forty functional looms stand, giving visitors an overview of the technical developments that took place between 1900 and 2000.

Inner courtyard of De Hoge Mote

Art deco style home

Art deco ten voeten uit

Starting point: *Dienst voor Toerisme, Hoge Mote, De Biesestraat 2.*
Distance: *4 km.*
Leaflet: *available at Dienst voor Toerisme.*

During the period between the two world wars, Ronse experienced turbulent growth. Upper management at the factories and textile barons built new homes on the edge of the city in the art deco style fashionable at the time. Many homes were built in this style, that is especially prominent in Léopold Sturbautstraat. The beautiful Villa Carpentier (1899), designed by Victor Horta – art nouveau's leading figure – is located in the middle of a small park.

HISTORY OF RONSE

One hundred years ago, Ronse was a prosperous textile-producing city. It was home to numerous textile companies both large and small. The textile barons had mansions built for them, while the labourers lived in cramped conditions in *beluiken* (dead-end streets). In 1861, Ronse was linked to the railway network. The new station building was brought here from Brugge-Zand, transported in sections to Ronse by rail, and rebuilt brick by brick. Between the two world wars, Ronse developed into the second textile centre of Flanders. This industry started to decline after World War II. Today, Ronse (Renaix in French) is a small provincial city in the south of the Flemish Ardennes on the linguistic frontier with Wallonia.

HOREBEKE MUNICIPALITY ❹

Road map C4. *2000.*
www.horebeke.be,
www.toerismevlaamseardennen.be

St.-Maria-Horebeke

A small community of protestants has lived in Korsele since 1554. Besides a handful of homes, De Geuzenhoek has two churches, a graveyard, a former school and a Protestant parsonage. For centuries, the descendants of Jacob Blommaert (1534-1572), an army captain, met here. Secretly at first and – after 1795 – in a conventicle far from the street and without a tower. In 1820, the protestants ('geuzen') were given their own school and – in 1824 – a graveyard. A memorial stone was added to the wall of the graveyard with the inscription *Even after his death, Willem I, King of the Low Countries, still cares for his subjects. MDCCCXXIV*. In 1872, the 'New Church', was completed. A **small museum**, devoted to the history of the Geuzenhoek, is located in the former protestant school. The museum was established in remembrance of folk author Abraham Hans (1882-1939), who wrote numerous children's books known as 'Hanskes' in Flemish.

Memorial stone

Protestants Historisch Museum Abraham Hans

Abraham Hansstraat 1, Horebeke.
mid Feb to mid Mar. Sun 3pm-5:30pm.
www.museumabrahamhans.be

Geuzenhoek

Starting point: *P at church in Dorpsstraat.*
Distance: *8-14 km.*
Signposted.

A walk along trails and paved roads through a beautiful part of the Flemish Ardennes. The protestant community has lived here from the 16th century. En route, visit the **graveyard** and the museum.

Het Burreken

www.burreken.be

Het Burreken, located at the point where Brakel, Maarkedal and Horebeke meet, is one of the most beautiful spots in the Flemish Ardennes. This area of natural beauty consists of three small valleys with extraordinary fauna and flora, including the fire salamander, the rare golden-winged dragonfly, wood anemones and wild garlic. Two different walking routes have been set out in Het Burreken – *Eikelmuis route* (7.5 km) and *Vuursalamander route* (4 km).

Weeping willow in the Geuzenhoek protestant graveyard

The 1787 St.-Amanduskerk in the town of Kwaremont

KLUISBERGEN MUNICIPALITY 5

Road map B5. 6400.
www.kluisbergen.be
Kluisbergen.
www.toerismevlaamseardennen.be

Kwaremont

The artist's town of Kwaremont draws a lot of visitors, especially on weekends. The modest whitewashed little church of **St Amandus** dates back to 1787. Following in the footsteps of the Kwaremont-born 17th-century painter Jan Van den Hecke, many Flemish artists settled in this picturesque Ardennes town right around 1940. Every year, the cobbled section of the *Oude Kwaremont* (altitude 111 m) tests the riders participating in the Tour of Flanders and other cycling classics. The first 600 m of the climb takes place on a narrow asphalt road, after which 1,600 m of cobbles follow. A monument to Karel Van Wijnendaele, journalist and founder of the Tour of Flanders, is located in the street bearing the same name.

Ruien

The **Kluisbos** is located at the top of the Kluisberg-Mont de l'Enclus (141 m) and is approximately 300 ha in size. The language border runs through this forest. On the Walloon side of the summit is the 19th-century brick tower used as a lookout and signal tower during the time of Napoleon.

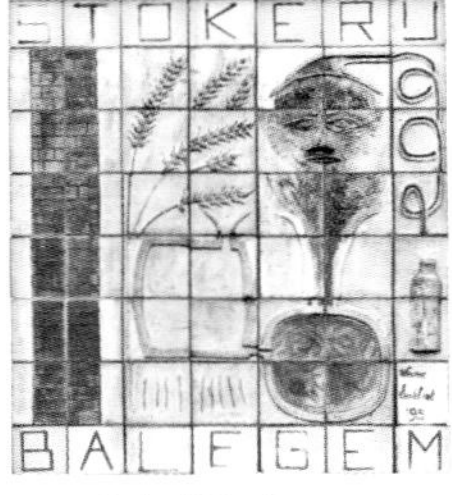

Stokerij Van Damme

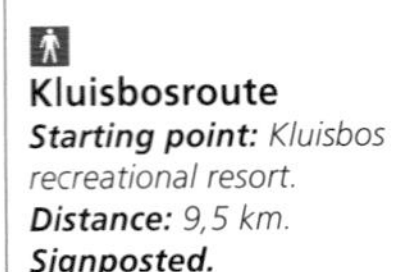

Kluisbosroute
Starting point: *Kluisbos recreational resort.*
Distance: *9,5 km.*
Signposted.

A walk along narrow trails that constantly rise and fall. The route passes the former De Vierschaar open-air courtroom and goes through the village of Pensemont, passing the Calmont castle and the former *Yzermijn-Mine de Fer* inn that had separate entrances for Flemings and Walloons.

The Kluisbos forest on the Kluisberg-Mont de l'Enclus at Ruien

OOSTERZELE MUNICIPALITY 6

Road map C4. *13.000.*
www.oosterzele.be
www.toerismevlaamseardennen.be

Balegem

Balegem is part of the Oosterzele municipality, a rural municipality between Ghent and Zottegem. With a wooden windmill, two stone windmills and two water mills, Oosterzele is a genuine mill area. The distillery **Stokerij Van Damme** was established in 1862 in Balegem and, to this day, still distills traditional grain jenever (gin). During the 14th and 15th centuries, Balegem stone – strong, calciferous sandstone – was very popular for use in the construction of churches, homes and public buildings because it was easy to process. After the mid-18th century, Balegem stone was seldom used. This stone was formed in the Eocene (56-34 million years ago) when Flanders was flooded by the sea. Balegem stone is still quarried on a limited scale.

Balegem sandstone
Starting point: *Stokerij Van Damme, Issegem 2, Balegem.*
Distance: *54 km, or 35,5 km shortened.*
Signposted.
A cycling tour that passes buildings and small monuments constructed using Balegem sandstone.

The city of Zottegem and the count of Egmont have a close bond

CITY OF ZOTTEGEM 7

Road map C4. *25,075.* **www**.zottegem.be *Zottegem.* *Stadhuis, Markt 1 (09-3646464,* **www**.toerismevlaamseardennen.be).

Zottegem

Zottegem is the city of Egmont. Two statues – one on the Markt and one in the Egmont castle park – honour **Lamoral, count of Egmont** and lord of Zottegem (1522-1568) who, along with Willem of Orange and count Horne, was one of the leading figures during the initial years of the Opstand (Eighty years' war). On 5 June 1568, he and count Horne were beheaded on the Grote Markt in Brussels by order of the duke of Alba. Egmont's final resting place was the Zottegem church and, in 1857, he was transferred to the crypt on the Markt side of the church. One of his neck vertebraes, bearing signs of the execution, was safeguarded in the city hall. The castle, only a shadow of what it must have been during the 16th century, houses the city library. The eight rooms of the **Museum voor Folklore** in an old parsonage transport visitors back to the time of their grandmothers. It's a museum full of reminders of the old history of Zottegem.

Lamoral, count of Egmont

Museum voor Folklore

Grotenbergestraat 162, Zottegem. ***Tel.*** *09-3457773. Mon, Wed-Fri 10am-12pm and 2pm-4pm (Easter-Aug first and third Sun of the month 3pm-6pm).*

Velzeke

The **Provinciaal Archeologisch Museum Velzeke** (Provincial Archaeological Museum) is located in Paddastraat, part of a former Roman road between Boulogne-sur-Mer and Cologne. The 2,400 m cobbled stretch is an infamous part of the Tour of Flanders. Along Paddastraat, numerous archaeological finds have been made. The museum uses finds and information panels to create an image of daily life during the prehistoric age, the Gallo-Roman period and the Merovingian era, thus spanning more than 300,000 years.

PAM Velzeke

Paddestraat 6, Velzeke. ***Tel.*** *09-3606716. Mon-Fri 9am-12pm and 2pm-5pm, Sat-Sun 2pm-6pm.*
www.pam-velzeke.be

ZWALM MUNICIPALITY 8

Road map C4. *8000.* **www**.zwalm.be *Munkzwalm and St. Denijs-Boekel* **www**.toerismevlaamseardennen.be

The Zwalm, a tributary of the Scheldt, flows through an undulating landscape. The Zwalm valley is an area of incredible natural beauty. This valley is asymmetrical and has a steep eastern incline and a gradual western incline. Because the Zwalm drops 60 m over a distance of 19 km, it releases so much energy that, in the past, it was gladly utilised by many watermills. The Zwalm valley is a superb walking destination.

Waterkersgrachtenroute

Starting point: *Dorpsplein, Roborst.*
Distance: *7–11 km.*
Leaflet: *Toerisme Oost-Vlaanderen.*
This route starts at the Roborst town square near the 13th-century St.-Denijskerkje. It then passes through the rolling Zwalm valley landscape. Organic watercress is cultivated in Roborst. The water in which this medicinal vegetable grows comes from a source near Fonteinstraat.

The Roman section of the Provinciaal Archeologisch Museum Velzeke

Resta

TIPS FOR TRAVELLERS

WHERE TO STAY

The city of Ghent and the province of East Flanders have a wealth of places to stay. From a luxurious hotel on the Korenlei site to a comfortable B&B in a large farmhouse in the East Flanders countryside. Most of the hotels in Ghent are to be found in the historic centre; guest rooms are more widely spread throughout the town. You will find hotels around the St.-Pieters station and its environs and there is a huge choice accommodation just outside Ghent whether you prefer a long or short stay. You will find hotels as well as B&Bs, camp sites and holiday homes out in the countryside. On *pages 208-213* you can see and read a selection of all the different kinds of places to stay.

HOTELS

There are 35 hotels in Ghent itself, ranging from luxurious four star hotels to good medium-class hotels. In the historic centre, there are several large and stylish hotels, carefully designed to fit in with their surroundings. You will also find a good selection of cheaper and more basic accommodations. During the week, many hotels cater mainly to business people and then offer special breaks during the weekends and holiday periods for tourists. There are plenty of places to stay just outside Ghent, ranging from four-star hotels to comfortable B&Bs. You can spend a night in the Flemish Ardennes, soaking up the atmosphere of the Tour of Flanders, or enjoying the beautiful view of the surrounding hills from your room. Take a look at the websites of **Toerisme Ghent** and **Toerisme Oost-Vlanderen** which have the recognised accommodations sorted by region, name, star rating and price.

PRICES AND RESERVATIONS

The average price of a room per night in a threestar hotel is € 80-100. The price for a hotel room includes breakfast, tourist tax and VAT, but does not include a parking space (€ 10-15 per night). Increasingly, breakfast is no longer included in the cost of the room, and some hotels have a surcharge for using the (WiFI) internet, (€ 5-20 per 24 hours). Consequently a stay can be more expensive than the price stated in the guide or on the Internet. Many hotels allow pets but you must let them know in advance when you make the booking because there can be a surcharge in that case.

Atrium of the Ghent Marriott Hotel

The price can vary depending on whether it is high- or low season, Monday to Friday or weekend. Many hotels offer attractive weekend breaks. Some hotels still have fixed prices, but the prices for most of the large (business) hotels are determined by supply and demand. You can reserve a room via the website or in the Ghent Tourist Information Office, via a booking site or by contacting the hotel directly.

HOTEL CLASSIFICATIONS

The hotels have not only been assessed by Toerisme Vlaanderen on the basis on the facilities on offer, but also with a view to hygiene, the state of repair and the atmosphere. These classified hotels can be recognised by a plaque from 'Toerisme Vlaanderen'. The

One of the two charming, spacious suites at the Accipio, Ghent

◁ Pop in to the terrace at the Borse van Amsterdam in Aalst

Unusual designs and original features in Het Godshuis (St.-Laureins)

classification is as follows: simple (one star), standard (two stars), medium-class (three stars), first class (four stars) to luxurious (five stars). Guesthouses and B&Bs with fewer than four rooms can voluntarily request a classification.

BED & BREAKFASTS

There are over 190 rooms in B&Bs in Ghent. They are often situated in historic buildings, residences, art galleries and even on a boat. Rooms are given a comfort classification, ranging from one to five stars (in the city of Ghent, they are also classified into basic, comfort and deluxe); holiday homes are also classified into basic, comfort and deluxe. B&Bs offer one or more rooms for guests. More and more B&Bs have ensuite bathrooms, but sometimes you will have to share a toilet and shower. B&Bs are famous for their hearty breakfasts as well as their personal service. They can range from offering a luxurious suite with its own entrance to a simple room in a family home. The prices per night vary from € 35-195 for a two-person room including breakfast. You can book a room via **Bed & Breakfast Gent**. There are plenty of charming B&Bs in other towns and in the countryside of East Flanders. They can be found in historical buildings, farms or country houses, and many of them welcome walkers and cyclists, These B&Bs can easily be recognised by the plaque Fietsvriendelijke logies: 'Cycle friendly accommodation'.

The Clethyl Hotel in Maldegem is a lovingly restored farmhouse

ACCOMODATION ON A BUDGET

Ghent offers various types of accommodation for those travellers who are on a budget. **De Draecke** is a modern hostel in the city centre near the Gravensteen which is open all year round. **Hostel 47** is a trendy hostel just outside the city centre. **Ecohostel Andromeda** is an ecological hostel on a barge moored alongside the Bargiekaai. You can enjoy an organic beer on the sunny deck. In the summer holidays, from about mid-June to September, the empty rooms in the university's student accommodation are available for use by anyone. Blaarmeersen is a good camping site (*see pages 240-241*). Aside from those in Ghent, there are five hostels and two caravan parks in East Flanders.

ADDRESSES

HOTEL RESERVATIONS

Tourism Ghent
www.visitgent.be

Tourism Oost-Vlaanderen
www.tov.be

Bed & Breakfast Ghent
www.bedandbreakfast-gent.be

Countryside tourism
www.hoevetoerisme.be

ACCOMODATION ON A BUDGET

De Draecke
St.-Widostraat 11.
Tel. *09-2337050.*
www.vjh.be

Ecohostel Andromeda
Bargiekaai 35.
Tel. *0486-678033.*
www.ecohostel.be

Hostel 47
Blekerijstraat 47.
Tel. *0478-712827.*
www.hostel47.com

Tourism Oost-Vlaanderen (East Flanders Tourist Office)
www.tov.be

Choosing a hotel or guest room

The overview below will help you to find accommodation in Ghent and East Flanders. The accommodation has been selected on the basis of its luxurious design, unique location or the interesting history of the building itself. Unless indicated otherwise, all the guest rooms have ensuite facilities and bicycle parking.

PRICE CATEGORIES for a standard double room, including breakfast, VAT, and services during the high season (recommended price).

€ less than € 60
€€ € 60 - € 90
€€€ € 90 - € 120
€€€€ € 120 - € 150
€€€€€ more than € 150

GHENT

Aanaajaanaa €€€
Hoogpoort 25, 9000 Ghent ***Tel.*** *0476-755255* ***Rooms*** *3* ***Map*** *1 C3-2 D3*
Aanaajaanaa means to come and to go in Hindi. B&B in a former rectory in de Hoogpoort, the oldest street in Ghent. Wonderful Oriental atmosphere. Breakfast with organic and fair-trade products. You will feel quite welcome. **www**.aanaajaanaa.be

Absolute Home €€
Beukelaarstraat 33, 9000 Ghent ***Tel.*** *0475-242411* ***Rooms*** *1*
You will be staying on the ground floor of a manager's house of a former brickyard. The entrance to the house is on the street. The room (36 m^2) has been tastefully decorated. Ensuite bathroom. **www**.absolutehome.be

Accipio €€€
St.-Elisabethplein 26, 9000 Ghent ***Tel.*** *0486-559498* ***Rooms*** *2* ***Map*** *1 A2*
Stylish, recently renovated town house in the Historic Centre of Ghent, adjacent to the St.-Elisabethbegijnhof. Two spacious, attractive suites one on the ground floor and the other on the first floor. Comfortable, plenty of room and rather quirky. **www**.accipio.be

Allegra-Nova €€
Ramen 24, 9000 Ghent ***Tel.*** *0475-960737* ***Rooms*** *2* ***Map*** *1 B3*
Two rooms with ensuite bathrooms in a recently renovated 19th century house in the centre of the city. Solar panels provide green, ecological energy. The Fatima Room is decorated in Oriental style, and the Allegra Room in a modern Belgian style. **www**.allegra-nova.be

Alphabed B&B €€
Jan Palfijnstraat 26, 9000 Ghent ***Tel.*** *0497-689108* ***Rooms*** *3* ***Map*** *2 D3*
Three stylish, idiosyncratic rooms with ensuite bathroom. Conveniently situated in the city centre. Minimum two nights on the weekend. Breakfast is served on the patio or in the rooms. Has the personal touch. **www**.alphabed.be

Atlas €€
Rabotstraat 40, 9000 Ghent ***Tel.*** *0473-279309* ***Rooms*** *3* ***Map*** *1 A1-A2*
Three large, romantic rooms in a 19th-century town house in the centre of Ghent. Each room is decorated in a different ethnic style. The guests can enjoy a separate breakfast room and a drawing room with an open fire. Babysitter available. **www**.atlasbenb.be

B^3 - Bed and Breakfast Boat €€€
Zuidkaai 43, 9000 Ghent ***Tel.*** *09-3355140 / 0477-540003* ***Rooms*** *2*
Spend the night on board a ship. The captain's suite measures 26m^2 and consists of three rooms: bedroom, sitting room and toilet. You also have a private terrace. The sailor's suite is smaller but has the same facilities. **www**.bnbtripleb.be

Baeten's €€
Burgstraat 11, 9000 Ghent ***Tel.*** *09-2230617 / 0496-266894* ***Rooms*** *2* ***Map*** *1 B2*
Two guest rooms in a 16th-century townhouse which has an antiques and second-hand store on the street side. The rooms are on the ground floor at the rear of the house and overlook a terrace and the municipal gardens. Breakfast is served in the rooms. **www**.baetenbnbgent.be

Best Western Residence Cour St. Georges €€€-€€€€
Botermarkt 2, 9000 Ghent ***Tel.*** *09-2242424* ***Rooms*** *31* ***Map*** *1 C3-2 D3*
The hotel is opposite the Town Hall and consists of two 18th-century town houses that have been renovated and brought up to modern standards without losing their original charm. All of the rooms are luxuriously appointed. **www**.courstgeorges.be

Boutique Hotel Onderbergen TV W €€€
Onderbergen 69, 9000 Ghent ***Tel.*** *09-2236200* ***Rooms*** *22* ***Map*** *1 B4, 3 C1*
This hotel offers its guests a very comfortable, with its high ceilings, original features, attractive decor and quiet yet central location.
www.hotelonderbergen.be

Cathedral TV W P €€€
St.-Jacobsnieuwstraat 87, 9000 Ghent ***Tel.*** *09-3295608* ***Rooms*** *5* ***Map*** *2 D3*
Right in the centre of the city. Trendy, totally renovated hotel with five rooms. The owner will greet you herself. The rooms are designed with comfort in mind. You can dine in the Santiago restaurant.
www.hotelcathedral.be

Chambreplus TV W €€€
Hoogpoort 31, 9000 Ghent ***Tel.*** *09-2253775 / 0496-748129* ***Rooms*** *3* ***Map*** *1 C3-2 D3*
Three tastefully designed, themed rooms (Sultan, Congo and Côté Sud) at the rear of the house looking out onto the garden, completely protected from the bustle of the city. Breakfast is served in the conservatory or on the terrace. Two night minimum on the weekend. **www**.chambreplus.be

Engelen aan de Waterkant TV W €€€€
Ter Platen 30, 9000 Ghent ***Tel.*** *0476-402523* ***Rooms*** *2* ***Map*** *4 E3-5*
A charming house in the Kunstenkwartier. On the first floor, there is an ensuite room and on the second floor is a spacious double bedroom, also with bathroom. Both rooms look out over the Scheldt. Only a 10 minute stroll from the city centre. **www**.engelenaandewaterkant.be

Faja Lobi TV €
Tarbotstraat 31, 9000 Ghent ***Tel.*** *09-2235533* ***Rooms*** *3*
Unpretentious B&B in a 19th-century house, just a 10-15 minute stroll from the historic centre. Each room has a small sitting area. There is a small municipal garden just behind the house. Faja Lobi also has a B&B in the Vlaanderenstraat. **www**.fajalobi.be

Four Corners W P €€
Abdisstraat 8, 9000 Ghent ***Tel.*** *09-2342951 / 0475-891389* ***Rooms*** *2* ***Map*** *3 A3-B3*
Two peaceful, airy rooms in a house dating from the 1930s (Le Corbusier style) in the Kunstenkwartier. The rooms are on the second floor and share a bathroom. Breakfast is served in the rooms or in the living room. **www**.bedandbreakfast-gent.be

Ghent Marriott Hotel TV W P €€€€-€€€€€
Drabstraat, 9000 Ghent ***Tel.*** *09-2339393* ***Rooms*** *150* ***Map*** *1 B3-C3*
First-class hotel in the most beautiful location in Ghent: the Korenlei. The hotel is a combination of designer and historic styles. The rooms are ranged around the atrium, the central hall with restaurant and lounge. Bargain weekend breaks. **www**.marriottghent.be

Ghent River Hotel TV W P €€€€€
Waaistraat 5, 9000 Ghent ***Tel.*** *09-2661010* ***Rooms*** *77* ***Map*** *2 D2*
Modern hotel on the Leie and just a stone's throw from the Vrijdagmarkt. Actually two buildings: a Renaissance house dating from 1518 and a rice-husking plant built on the foundations of a sugar refinery in 1857. All rooms are of contemporary design. **www**.ghent-river-hotel.be

Gravensteen TV W P €€€€€
Jan Breydelstraat 35, 9000 Ghent ***Tel.*** *09-2251150* ***Rooms*** *49* ***Map*** *1 B2-C3*
The Gravensteen Hotel has been incorporated into a 19th-century town house that has been brought back to its former glory. The beautiful eclectic Empire interior, the marble entrance hall and the staircase have been completely restored (2009). Located in the city centre. **www**.gravensteen.be

Harmony TV W P €€€€-€€€€€
Kraanlei 37, 9000 Ghent ***Tel.*** *09-3242680* ***Rooms*** *17* ***Map*** *1 C2*
Truly welcoming family hotel near the Patershol, one of the city's oldest districts.
The hotel is actually two buildings connected by a garden. The rooms overlook the city.
www.hotel-harmony.be

Holiday Inn Gent Expo TV W P €€€-€€€€€
Maaltekouter 3, 9051 St.-Denijs-Westrem ***Tel.*** *09-2202424* ***Rooms*** *169*
A modern hotel with renovated atrium near the Flanders Expo on the outskirts of the city. Good connection to the city by tram. The rooms each have a large bed and a desk. Cycle-friendly address.
www.holiday-inn-gentexpo.be

Hotel Astoria Gent TV W P €€€
Achilles Musschestraat 39, 9000 Ghent ***Tel.*** *09-2228413* ***Rooms*** *25*
Centrally located family hotel in the Kunstenkwartier, with 25 stylishly decorated rooms. Unique municipal garden. Attractive bargain breaks including Vive le vélo: get to know Ghent by bike.
www.astoria.be

See inside of the back flap for an explanation of the symbols

Hotel de Flandre €€€€€
Poel 1-2, 9000 Ghent ***Tel.*** *09-2660600* ***Rooms*** *47* ***Map*** *1 B3*
This hotel is located in a 19th-century building right in the heart of the city. The classical features have been carefully preserved and combined with modern design. The rooms are tastefully decorated and each has a fully-equipped bathroom. **www**.hoteldeflandre.be

Ibis Gent Centrum St.-Baafs Kathedraal €€
Limburgstraat 2, 9000 Ghent ***Tel.*** *09-2330000* ***Rooms*** *120* ***Map*** *2 D4*
In the city centre with the St.-Baafs Kathedral on the doorstep. The rooms are functionally designed in the standard Ibis-chain style. Good value for money.
www.ibishotel.com

Het Kouterhof €€
Afsneekouter 10, 9051 Afsnee (Ghent) ***Tel.*** *09-2217896* ***Rooms*** *2*
Two comfortable guest rooms, in a recently restored country house in Afsnee, just a short distance from Ghent. Ideal starting point for visits to the city (excellent bus service) or long bike rides through lovely surroundings. **www**.hetkouterhof.be

Logidenri €€€
Brabantdam 201, 9000 Ghent ***Tel.*** *09-3288093* ***Rooms*** *3* ***Map*** *2 D4-E4, 4 D1-E1*
Two guest rooms on the first and second floors of this typical Ghent mansion. The rooms have been designed by an interior designer in keeping with the originality of the house itself and have all modern comforts. **www**.logidenri.be

Monasterium PoortAckere €€€
Oude Houtlei 56, 9000 Ghent ***Tel.*** *09-2692210* ***Rooms*** *54* ***Map*** *1 B3-B4, 3 B1*
Have a simply heavenly night's sleep! Stay in a monastery with a history going back to 1278. The simple, austere rooms are perfectly suited to their environment. Special weekend breaks.
www.monasterium.be

NH Gent Belfort €€€€€
Hoogpoort 63, 9000 Ghent ***Tel.*** *09-2333331* ***Rooms*** *174* ***Map*** *1 C3-2 D3*
Modern hotel in the city centre opposite the Town Hall. Ideal base for exploring the city. Stylish rooms in three categories. Garden terrace.
www.nh-hotels.nl

NH Gent St.-Pieters €€€
Koning Albertlaan 121, 9000 Ghent ***Tel.*** *09-2226065* ***Rooms*** *49* ***Map*** *3 A3-A4*
Comfortable four star hotel near St.-Pieters station. Practically designed rooms. Good tram service to the historical city centre. The hotel has its own parking facilities.
www.nh-hotels.nl

Novotel Gent Centrum €€
Goudenleeuwplein 5, 9000 Ghent ***Tel.*** *09-2242230* ***Rooms*** *117* ***Map*** *1 C3*
Modern hotel in the heart of the old town. The rooms are designed in the usual Novotel style. Dine by the pool or on the terrace. City Breaks is good value for money (minimum two nights).
www.novotel.com

Puerto Patershol €€€
Kraanlei 55, 9000 Ghent ***Tel.*** *09-2257532 / 0476-645557* ***Rooms*** *2* ***Map*** *1 C2*
Perfectly situated B&B. Two very spacious, sunny rooms looking out over the Leie. At the rear, both rooms border a peaceful inner courtyard with a southern atmosphere. The rooms have a contemporary design. **http**://patersholbb.ceciliajaime.com

Rustpunt €€
Burgstraat 46, 9000 Ghent ***Tel.*** *09-2259571* ***Rooms*** *28* ***Map*** *1 B2*
The Rustpunt forms part of the Carmelite Monastery on the Burgstraat. A simple hotel, with rooms designed for comfort in the Zen style. It is a green oasis in the city, ideal for those seeking peace and quiet. **www**.rustpunt.net

Snooz Inn €€€
Ham 89, 9000 Ghent. ***Tel.*** *0496-241426* ***Kamer*** *1* ***Map*** *2 E1-E2*
In the Snooz room you'll find all the ingredients for a wonderful break: a rain shower with colour therapy, private cinema, king-size bed, wellness and breakfast on your private terrace.
www.snoozinn.be

De Waterzooi €€€€€
St.-Veerleplein 2, 9000 Ghent ***Tel.*** *09-3307721 / 0475-436111* ***Rooms*** *2* ***Map*** *1 C2*
Luxurious B&B in a renovated town house built in 1787 opposite the Gravensteen. Two beautifully designed suites – Felix and Phara – have every comfort. A peaceful oasis in the bustling heart of Ghent. Minumum of two nights on the weekend. **www**.dewaterzooi.be

LEIESTREEK

Aan de Leie €€€€

Wakkense Heirweg 26, 9800 Deinze **Tel.** *0497-702702* **Rooms** *3* **Road map** *B3*

At 'Aan de Leie' the keywords are rest and tranquillity. This B&B has three chic, attractively designed rooms decorated in the rustic style. Body & Balance offers a comprehensive programme of physical treatments and massages. **www**.aandeleie.be

In 't Boldershof €€€

Dorpsstraat 37, 9831 Deurle (St.-Martens-Latem) **Tel.** *09-2827545* **Rooms** *5* **Road map** *B3*

The hotel In 't Bolderhof has a long history; it has been a popular bar/café since before 1800. The five rooms on the first floor are decorated with Laura Ashley designs. For the two standard rooms, there is a toilet in the corridor. **www**.boldershof.com

Auberge du Pêcheur €€€€€

Pontstraat 41, 9830 St.-Martens-Latem **Tel.** *09-2823144* **Rooms** *32* **Road map** *B3*

You will find the Auberge du Pêcheur on the banks of the Leie. The Orangerie restaurant has a Michelin star. The spacious rooms are elegantly designed in the boutique style. Attractive bargain breaks. **www**.auberge-du-pecheur.be

B&B 't Eiernest €€€

Latemstraat 82, 9830 St.-Martens-Latem **Tel.** *09-2826231* **Rooms** *3* **Road map** *B3*

The three rooms are in the annexe, each with a view of the garden and its own entrance. The rooms are elegantly designed with durable, warm materials, adorned with works of art by the Latem painter Jacobert. Breakfast with local- and home-made produce. **www**.eiernest.be

B&B Anno 1756 €€

Ketelstraat 2, 9800 Vinkt (Deinze) **Tel.** *09-3863498 / 0479-731616* **Rooms** *3* **Road map** *B3*

Anno 1756 is an old farmhouse with whitewashed walls, a red-tiled roof and tiny windows with painted shutters. The three rooms and the breakfast room are, like the rest of the house, beautifully decorated with antique toys: a reminder of the Deinze toy industry. **www**.anno1756.be

MEETJESLAND

De Waeterhoek €€€

Nieuwendam 7, 9880 Aalter **Tel.** *0475-652734* **Rooms** *4* **Road map** *A3*

De Waeterhoek is a renovated farmhouse, built in 1870 with four large, comfortable, warm and cosy rooms. Each room has a beautiful country view, from which you can see all kinds of animals wandering about. **www**.waeterhoek.be

Casabelle €€€

Boekhoutedorp 17, 9961 Boekhoute (Assenede) **Tel.** *09-3243067 / 0474-338066* **Rooms** *4* **Road map** *C1*

Casabelle is in the heart of the tiny village of Boekhoute. This B&B has three rooms and one apartment, spread out over four floors, accessible by lift or staircase. There is also a swimming pool. 'Provence in Meetjesland'. **www**.casabelle.be

Cleythil Hotel €€€

Kleitkalseide 193, 9990 Maldegem **Tel.** *050-300100* **Rooms** *19* **Road map** *A2*

This is a designer hotel in a centuries-old location, where you will receive a warm welcome. The spacious rooms (24 m²) are comfortable and tastefully decorated. The large breakfast room gives you a panoramic view over the lovely fields and woods of Drongengoed. **www**.cleythil.be

Huyze Bladelin €€

Kasteelstraat 2, 9992 Middelburg (Maldegem) **Tel.** *050-397426 / 0475-577050* **Rooms** *4* **Road map** *A1*

Four modern guest rooms with all the comforts and fully equipped bathrooms. The rooms all adjoin a sun terrace that leads to the garden and orchard. Breakfast is served in a 19th-century country cottage. **www**.huyzebladelin.com

Het Godshuis €€€€€

Leemweg 11, 9980 St.-Laureins **Tel.** *09-2231510* **Rooms** *64* **Road map** *B1*

Het Godshuis is a 19th-century restored monastery which combines the original features such as thick walls and wood beam ceilings with a modern design. There is a wellness centre in the cellar. The rooms are all beautifully decorated. **www**.godshuis.be

See inside of the back flap for an explanation of the symbols

WAASLAND

Casa-Cosi €€€
Ward de Bockstraat 21b, 9160 Lokeren ***Tel.*** *09-3563979* ***Rooms*** *4* ***Road map*** *D2-3*

This is a B&B showing a true passion for interior design, wellness and hospitality. The three large guest rooms and the apartment with kitchenette are beautifully decorated and have all the facilities. There is also a wellness pavilion for guests. **www**.casa-cosi.be

De Pastorie €€€
Patershof 33, 9160 Lokeren ***Tel.*** *09-3605878* ***Rooms*** *3* ***Road map*** *D2-3*

There are three guest rooms in this former rectory are on the first floor.The Alpha room is decorated in an art deco style; the Beta room is rather more eclectic while the Gamma room has features from the 1950s. **www**.bb-depastorie.be

Het Schaliënhuis €€€-€€€€
Appelstraat 54, 9120 Melsele (Beveren-Waas) ***Tel.*** *0476-307169* ***Rooms*** *3* ***Road map*** *F2*

A step-gabled farmhouse dating from 1564 with two spacious guest rooms in the farmhouse and a large apartment in the lodge. The farmhouse is surrounded by a huge garden, and guests can enjoy a cupboard full of toys, jigsaws and books. Extremely child-friendly. **www**.hetschalienhuis.be

Malpertuus €€
Weststraat 64, 9180 Moerbeke-Waas ***Tel.*** *0479-380275* ***Rooms*** *3* ***Road map*** *D2*

Located in the Waasland polders, this former stable has been revamped so it offers three large country-style guest rooms, two of which have a mezzanine with a desk. Very child-friendly. **www**.benbmalpertuus.be

Meirlaenhof €
Wijnstraat 26, 9170 St.-Pauwels (St.-Gillis-Waas) ***Tel.*** *03-7769694 / 0474-985586* ***Rooms*** *4* ***Road map*** *E2*

Four sunny rooms, each with its own bathroom, in a bungalow tucked away in the countryside. Ideal location between Antwerp and Ghent. The garden is a haven of peace. Breakfast is served in the breakfast room overlooking the garden. **www**.meirlaenhof.be

SCHELDT COUNTRY

Boskapelhoeve €€€
Kasteelstraat 214, 9255 Buggenhout ***Tel.*** *0474-774192* ***Rooms*** *15* ***Road map*** *E3*

This is a charming hotel on the fringes of the Buggenhout forest. There are seven rooms in the country house itself and eight rooms in the 'large stable'. All rooms have wooden floors and have views over the woods or the inner courtyard. **www**.boskapelhoeve.be

Cosy Cottage €€€
Eegene 38, 9200 Dendermonde ***Tel.*** *052-428443 / 0475-461393* ***Rooms*** *6* ***Road map*** *E3*

Each of the three guest rooms in this distinctive Cosy Cottage are decorated in a country style and have lovely views over the Scheldt. There are also three studio/apartments in the annexe. Very English. **www**.cosycottage.be

Het Zoete Water €€€
Damstraat 64, 9220 Hamme ***Tel.*** *052-470092* ***Rooms*** *8* ***Road map*** *E3*

The hotel is situated near the heart of the village. The renovation faithfully kept to the art deco style. The rooms are stylishly decorated.
www.hetzoetewater.be

Hof Selmussen €€€
Blektestraat 140, 9308 Hofstade (Aalst) ***Tel.*** *053-215053 / 0477-611871* ***Rooms*** *3* ***Road map*** *D4*

The Hof Selmussen has been converted into a guest house surrounded by an ecological garden and has three charming guest rooms. Breakfast made with home-made and locally produced products is served in the spacious living room. **www**.hofselmussen.be

Nova Zembla €€
Dries 69, 9255 Opdorp (Buggenhout) ***Tel.*** *052-550008* ***Rooms*** *3* ***Road map*** *E3*

This B&B is located in a hundred-year-old, completely renovated smithy. The three charming rooms (North, South and West) offer every comfort. Breakfast is served in the breakfast room overlooking the village square, or in the inner courtyard. **www**.nova-zembla.eu

FLEMISH ARDENNES

Stokerij Van Damme €€
Issegem 2, 9860 Balegem (Oosterzele) ***Tel.*** *09-3625025* ***Rooms*** *4* ***Road map*** *C4*
Here you will be staying in a gin distillery and farmhouse. The four guest rooms are in the annexe of the Van Damme gin distillery. The rooms are all very comfortable. Breakfast is served in a common room with an open fire. **www**.stokerijvandamme.be

De Groene Weg €€
Groeneweg 3, 9660 Brakel ***Tel.*** *0473-863512* ***Rooms*** *4* ***Road map*** *C5*
The four guest rooms overlook the sheltered inner courtyard of this small courtyard farm surrounded by an orchard and fields. The rooms are decorated using natural materials from floor to ceiling. De Groene Weg is all about simplicity, peace and nature. **www**.degroeneweg.be

Hotel Grupello €€€
Verhaegenlaan 17, 9500 Geraardsbergen ***Tel.*** *054-416007* ***Rooms*** *11* ***Road map*** *C5*
This is a small, family-run hotel in the centre of Geraardsbergen. The hotel has been renovated, but the original art deco features of the interior have been carefully preserved.
www.hotel-grupello.be

Het Leerhof €€€
Hollebeekstraat 6, 9661 Parike (Brakel) ***Tel.*** *055-420243* ***Rooms*** *10* ***Road map*** *C5*
This hotel lies in the middle of the Flemish Ardennes. The rooms, all named after birds, are in the former hay and grain loft above the workplace. Breakfast is served in the dining room, the farmer's 'best' room, or in the new Vivaldi room. **www**.leerhof.be

Huis Minne €€€
Kafhoek 2, 9681 Nukerke (Maarkedal) ***Tel.*** *055-213220 / 0478-477633* ***Rooms*** *6* ***Road map*** *B5*
Huis Minne is a villa built in 1920, the former home of a textile baron. Romantic rooms in the Victorian style. The house is surrounded by a lovely garden with ancient trees and a swimming pool. The shop and tea room are open at the weekends. **www**.huisminne.be

Refuge Kapelleberg €€
Kapelleberg 16, 9680 Maarke-Kerkem (Maarkedal) ***Tel.*** *0474-607608* ***Rooms*** *6* ***Road map*** *B5*
This courtyard farmhouse was completely renovated a few years ago. The farmhouse has six guest rooms, two of which have a kitchenette, and a communal room with an open fire. The farm is surrounded by the gorgeous natural scenery of the Flemish Ardennes. **www**.refugekapelleberg.be

Hof Ter Kammen €€
Schapendries 53, 9700 Oudenaarde ***Tel.*** *055-303558 / 0497-460837* ***Rooms*** *4* ***Road map*** *B4*
Absolutely charming house at the foot of the Koppenberg. The guest rooms have names such as De Koppenberg and De Taalenberg. Looking at the many photos of racers on the walls, the cyclist will feel right at home. Child-friendly. **www**.hofterkammen.be

Gastenverblijf Steenhuyse €€€
Markt 37, 9700 Oudenaarde ***Tel.*** *055-232373 / 0485-834790* ***Rooms*** *7* ***Road map*** *B4*
These guest rooms are in a historic 16th-century building in the centre of Oudenaarde. It is wonderful to relax in the bar/lounge or on the terrace in the old walled garden. The rooms look out over the market or the inner garden. **www**.steenhuyse.info

Au Mazet €€€€
Boskant 17, 9790 Elsegem (Wortegem-Petegem) ***Tel.*** *0486-640141* ***Rooms*** *3* ***Road map*** *B5*
Au Mazet spoils its guests with pure Provençal hospitality. The bathrooms are fitted with a Turkish bath, bubble bath or sauna. Every detail lovingly thought out.
www.aumazet.be

't Heufke €€
Vredesplein 26, 9630 St.-Denijs-Boekel (Zwalm) ***Tel.*** *055-496957* ***Rooms*** *5* ***Road map*** *C4*
't Heufke is a renovated almshouse dating from the 18th-century, bursting with character. It has five stylishly restored rooms, each of which remind you of the painter Vincent van Gogh who travelled through St.-Denijs-Boekel on his way to the Protestant village of Korsele. **www**.theufke.be

De Kollebloem €€
Doornstraat 30, 9550 St.-Lievens-Esse (Herzele) ***Tel.*** *054-343682* ***Rooms*** *3* ***Road map*** *D4*
The Kollebloem is a biological horticultural company, situated in the foothills of the Flemish Ardennes. The three rooms are on the first floor. In the morning you can tuck into a hearty breakfast buffet.
www.kollebloem.be

See inside of the back flap for an explanation of the symbols

RESTAURANTS AND CAFÉS

Ghent has hundreds of restaurants, bistros, brasseries and snack bars. You could enjoy a wonderful dinner for two in a gourmet restaurant, a simple dish of the day in a pleasant café, or try the famous Ghent chicken casserole or other specialities in a typical local restaurant. You can let yourself be guided by your mood, the look of the kitchen, the atmosphere or a review in **Zone 09**, or a write-up in any of the countless restaurant sites. Most restaurants in Ghent follow the classic French cooking style, enriched with a dash of Belgian flair. With more than ten (100%) vegetarian restaurants and countless veggie-friendly restaurants that have at least one vegetarian dish on the menu, Ghent is the Eastern vegetarian capital of Europe. East Flanders has twelve restaurants with Michelin stars (2011).

RESTAURANTS

Going out for a meal in Ghent couldn't be easier. Alongside the traditional restaurants there are numerous snack bars, fast food outlets, chips shops, pizzerias and exotic restaurants. Many restaurants have an attractively-priced daily menu between noon and 2pm. Most restaurants open for dinner at 6pm and the kitchens close around 10pm. The formal restaurants have a rotation system where reservations can be made at 8pm and 9.30pm. A brasserie is a more casual restaurant where the locals pop in for a cup of coffee, a leisurely lunch or a beer. A lot of the bakeries have a lunch room where you can have breakfast, lunch or just a cup of coffee or tea with a slice of cake. The culinary heart of Ghent is Patershol, with its restaurants in various price classes serving mouthwatering dishes from all over the world.

Waterzooi, a typical Ghent dish made with chicken or fish

LOCAL PRODUCTS

East Flanders has a rich tradition when it comes to local specialities, such as the locally produced beers, gin, cheeses, mustard and chocolate. Fresh produced and local products are sold in small speciality shops in Ghent and other towns and villages in East Flanders as well as at various Diensten voor Toerisme (Tourist information) and in the Groot Vleeshuis (meat market) in Ghent. See *pages 222-223* for an overview of the local specialities.

Belga Queen gives a typical impression of Belgian gastronomy

GHENT: VEGETARIAN CAPITAL

Ghent is an absolute paradise for vegetarians, offering a multitude of choices amongst its countless vegetarian, vegan and vegetarian-friendly restaurants, bakeries, fast food restaurants and organic food shops. Local government offices and schools even have regular meat-free days. At **Renaissance**, you can enjoy the most delicious veggie sandwich in Ghent. It is filled with shredded carrot garnished with cress, tomato, cucumber and white cabbage.

MICHELIN STARS

THREE STARS
Hof van Cleve, Kruishoutem
ONE STAR
't Huis van Lede, Wannegem-Lede (Kruishoutem)
't Overhamme, Aalst
't Truffeltje, Dendermonde
Apriori, Haaltert
C. Jean, Gent
Clandestino, Haasdonk (Beveren)
Auberge du Pêcheur, St.-Martens-Latem
Herbert Robbrecht, Vrasene (Beveren)
Hof ter Eycken, Ninove
Jan Van den Bon, Gent
Lijsterbes, Berlare

CAFÉS

There are over three hundred cafés in the centre of Ghent, ranging from simple local cafés to trendy lounge cafés. There are also cafés for special target groups such as those for the gay community, students, night owls, music lovers, thirty-somethings, theatre goers and beer lovers. The cafes and terraces on the Korenmarkt and Klein Turkije are very popular. You will also find lots of cafés near the Vrijdagmarkt.
Students tend to congregate in the Overpoortstraat where the cafés are open early in the morning.
As soon as the sun comes out the town squares (Vrijdagmarkt, Botermarkt, St.-Baafsplein) and the Gras and Korenlei on the banks of the Leie metamorphose into one gigantic terrace. Many cafés have roadside- or inner terraces, or a shady garden. The most beautiful terrace is to be found in the Restaurant d'Oude Leie in Deinze. The shady terrace overlooks a quiet branch of the river Leie. **Caféplan Ghent** has made a chart of all the cafés in Ghent and classified them according to the type (brown pub, local café, music café, etc.) what kind of tap beer they serve, what kind of music is played and the type of clientele. You can pick up the chart at the Tourist Office. **Volkscafés** preserve the traditions of the Flemish local cafés. There is an overview of all the cafés on the website. *See pages 224-227* for an overview of the special cafés and terraces in Ghent and East Flanders.

'**t Galgenhuisje, the smallest café in Ghent**

The Brooderie specializes in Breakfast, coffee and tea

ADDRESSES

For a delicious breakfast or lunch
How about starting your day off properly with a hearty breakfast or – maybe later – a long, leisurely lunch? The addresses below are the places in Ghent where you can do just that.

Brooderie
Jan Breydelstraat 8.
Tel. *09-2250623.*
www.brooderie.be

Brood-Huys
Jacobijnenstraat 12.
Tel. *09-2257765.*

Le Pain Quotidien
Kalandeberg 10.
Tel. *09-2241879.*
www.lepainquotidien.be

Oud Huis Himschoot
Koningin Elisabethlaan 57.

Le Pain Perdu
Walpoortstraat 9.
Tel. *09-2241825.*

Renaissance
Lange Violettestraat 42.
Tel. *09-2251762.*

Simon says
Sluizeken 8
Tel. *09-2330343.*
www.simon-says.be

Restaurants and cafés

Zone 09
www.zone09.be

Dinnersite
www.dinnersite.be/gent

PocketResto
www.pocketresto.be/restaurant-gent

Caféplan Gent
www.cafeplan.be

Volkscafés
www.volkscafes.be

Choosing a restaurant

The restaurants listed below vary in price class and have been selected for their high quality, excellent cuisine, pleasant atmosphere and good service. The symbols above the descriptions tell you what kind of facilities to expect. It is advisable to make reservations in advance at many of the restaurants, especially on the weekend.

PRICE CATEGORIES per person for a three course meal, including VAT and services

€ up to € 30
€€ € 30 - € 45
€€€ € 45 - € 60
€€€€ from € 60

GHENT

De 3 biggetjes — €€

*Zeugsteeg 7, 9000 Ghent **Tel.** 09-2244648 **Covers** 36 **Map** 1 C2*

Cuisine: French. There are two dining rooms and a patio in this renovated town house. The chef, who comes from Vietnam, cooks like a French culinary genius. Friendly welcome. Kitchen open: 12 midday-2pm and 7pm-9pm. Closed: Wed, Sat afternoon and Sun. **www**.de3biggetjes.com

A Food Affair — €€€

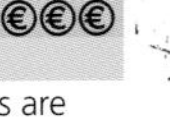

*Korte Meer 25, 9000 Ghent **Tel.** 09-2241805 **Covers** 30 **Map** 1 C4*

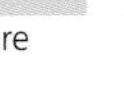

Cuisine: Eastern, world cuisine. Not your everyday wok restaurant. The interior is dark red. The walls are covered with photos of smiling Asian children. Delicate dishes and full of surprises. Kitchen open: 12 midday-2pm and 6:30-10pm. Closed: Mon, Sat afternoon and Sun. **www**.afoodaffair.be

Allegro Moderato — €€-€€€

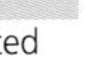

*Korenlei 7, 9000 Ghent **Tel.** 09-2332332 **Covers** 80 **Map** 1 B3-C3*

Cuisine: classic. Original 18th-century house on the Leie with stylish interior design. Beautifully decorated dining rooms, quayside terrace. Classic and classy. The second dining room is candlelit. Kitchen open: 11:15am-3pm and 6pm-10pm. Closed: Mon and Sun. **www**.restoallegro.com

Amadeus — €

*Plotersgracht 8-10, 9000 Ghent **Tel.** 09-2251385 **Covers** 200 **Map** 1 C2*

Cuisine: American, spareribs. Amadeus' speciality is 'Spareribs à la volonté', all-you-can-eat spareribs with salad and jacket potato with herb butter. They also have Ghent waterzooi. There is also a branch on the Goudenleeuwplein. Kitchen open: Mon-Thu 6:30pm-11:00pm and Fri-Sun 6pm-11:30pm. **www**.amadeusspareribrestaurant.be

Avalon — €

*Geldmunt 32, 9000 Ghent **Tel.** 09-2243724 **Map** 1 C2*

Cuisine: organic-vegetarian. Dishes with grains, fresh seasonal vegetables and legumes. Almost all ingredients are organic. Kitchen open: Tue-Sat 11:30am-2:30pm. Closed: Mon, Sun and Bank Holidays. **www**.restaurantavalon.be

Belga Queen — €€

*Graslei 10, 9000 Ghent **Tel.** 09-2800100 **Covers** 150 **Map** 1 C3*

Cuisine: Belgian. Antoine Pinto has transformed the old Korenstapelhuis into a modern brasserie. Belga Queen's menu offers Belgian specialities using top quality products from the Belgian soil. Kitchen open: Mon-Sun 12 midday-11pm. **www**.belgaqueen.be

Bij den wijzen en den zot — €€

*Hertogstraat 42, 9000 Ghent **Tel.** 09-2234230 / 0475-666239 **Cover** 50 **Map** 1 C2*

Cuisine: Belgian-French. The oldest restaurant in Ghent in an old guildhall in the Patershol. Inside, it's pure nostalgia with the little inglenooks and staircases. Belgian specialities menu with Ghent stew and fish casserole. Kitchen open: 12 midday-2pm and 6:30pm-10pm. Closed: Sun and Mon. **www**.bijdenwijzenendenzot.be

De Blauwe Zalm — €€€

*Vrouwebroersstraat 2, 9000 Ghent **Tel.** 09-2240852 **Covers** 35 **Map** 1 C2*

Cuisine: French. Most famous fish restaurant in Ghent. Very smart interior in grey and aubergine. Classic dishes lovingly prepared. Decorative lighting takes pride of place in the dining room. Kitchen open: 12 midday-1:30pm and 7pm-9.30pm. Closed: Mon, Sat afternoon and Sun. **www**.deblauwezalm.be

Bord'eau — €€

*St.-Veerleplein 5, 9000 Ghent **Tel.** 09-2232000 **Map** 1 C2*

Cuisine: fish. Mainly fish on the menu – but what else would you expect in the Oude Vismijn (fishmarket)? There is an eye-catching fish bar in the very modern interior, but the old cast-iron columns are still intact. Kitchen open: 12 midday-2:30pm and 7pm-10pm. **www**.oudevismijn.be/bordeau

· SALONS CARLOS QUINTO

Brasserie deus €€

Vlaanderenstraat 128, 9000 Ghent ***Tel.*** *09-2336606* ***Covers*** *70* ***Map*** *2 D4-E4, 4 E1*

Cuisine: Belgian-French fusion. A brasserie with wooden floors named after DeuS, the symbiosis of beer and sparkling wine. The menu offers over 150 types of beer and 100 wines. Kitchen open: 12 midday-10pm. Closed: Sun evening. **www**.brasseriedeus.be

Brasserie HA' €€

Kouter 29, 9000 Ghent ***Tel.*** *09-2659181* ***Map*** *1 C4, 3 C1-4 D1*

Cuisine: Belgian-French. Enjoy lunch or dinner in lovely surroundings. In the summer you can dine on the unique terrace on the waterfront. Kitchen open: Mon-Sat 11am-3pm and 6pm-11pm, Sun 9am-12 midday. Closed: Sun evenings. **www**.brasserieha.be

Brasserie Pakhuis €

Schuurkenstraat 4, 9000 Ghent ***Tel.*** *09-2235555* ***Covers*** *200*

Cuisine: French-Italian. The Portuguese architect Pinto has given this former warehouse a beautiful new look. The menu offers oyster- and shellfish platters as well as classic French dishes. Kitchen open: Mon-Sat 12 midday-2:30pm and 6:30-11pm (Fri-Sat until midnight). Closed: Sun. **www**.pakhuis.be

Café Parti €€

Koningin Maria Hendrikaplein 65a, 9000 Ghent ***Tel.*** *09-2423291* ***Covers*** *75* ***Map*** *3 A4-A5*

Cuisine: fusion. Bustling brasserie near the St.-Pieters station in Ghent. Smart interior with a travellers theme. Varied menu including pasta, salads, wok dishes and the classics. Kitchen open: Tue-Fri 11:30am-11pm, Sat and Mon 11am-3pm and 6pm-10pm, Sun 11am-3pm and 6pm-10pm. **www**.cafeparti.be

Café Theatre €€

Schouwburgstraat 5-7, 9000 Ghent ***Tel.*** *09-2650550* ***Covers*** *150*

Cuisine: Belgian-French. The trendy Café Theatre has been hailed by Trends magazine as the best brasserie in Belgium. Kitchen open: Mon-Fri 12 midday-2:15pm and 7pm-11pm (Fri until midnight), Sat 7pm-12 midnight, Sun 12 midday-2pm and 7pm-11pm. Closed: Sat afternoon. **www**.cafetheatre.be

C-Jean €€€€

Cataloniëstraat 3, 9000 Ghent ***Tel.*** *09-2233040* ***Covers*** *32* ***Map*** *1 C3*

Cuisine: Belgian, global. Awarded a Michelin star. Elegant tables, subdued atmosphere. We highly recommend the lunch menu for €35, and the à la carte menu. Kitchen open: 12 midday-2pm and 7pm-9pm. Closed: Mon, Sun and Bank Holidays. **www**.c-jean.be

Domestica €€

Onderbergen 27, 9000 Ghent ***Tel.*** *09-2235300* ***Covers*** *46* ***Map*** *1 B4, 3 C1*

Cuisine: French. This restaurant in a renovated town house also has a garden terrace. The elegant interior with its chandeliers remind you of its former glory. Kitchen open: Mon and Sat 6pm-10pm, Tue-Fri 12 midday-2pm and 6pm-10pm. Closed: Mon and Sat afternoons, Sun. **www**.domestica.be

Du Progrès €€

Korenmarkt 10, 9000 Ghent ***Tel.*** *09-2251716* ***Map*** *1 C3*

Cuisine: Belgian-French. A gem of a place on the Korenmarkt. Behind its red façade you will find a classic brasserie with panelling, brown tables and mirrors. Du Progrès has been run by three generations of the De Baets family. Excellent cuisine. Kitchen open: Thu-Mon 11:30am-10:30pm. Closed: Tue and Wed. **www**.duprogres.be

Facon €€

Hoogstraat 23, 9000 Ghent ***Tel.*** *09-2342402* ***Covers*** *50* ***Map*** *1 A3-B3*

Cuisine: Belgian-French. Modern restaurant in a renovated 19th-century town house with three dining rooms that lead one to the other. For menu suggestions, look at the daily specials. Kitchen open: Wed-Fri 12 midday-2pm and 6pm-10pm (Fri until 11pm), Sat 6pm-11pm. Closed: Sat afternoon, Sun-Tue. **www**.excelsior-facon.be

Grade €€

Charles de Kerchovelaan 79-81, 9000 Gent ***Tel.*** *09-92244385* ***Covers*** *70* ***Map*** *3 C3-4 D4*

Cuisine: Belgian-French. A brasserie with an up-to-date bar, where modernity and nostalgia are harmoniously woven together behind a stately façade. Cosy garden terrace in summer. Kitchen open: Tue-Sat 12 midday-2pm and 7:30pm-10:30pm (Fri-Sat until 11:30pm). Closed: Mon and Sun. **www**.grade.be

Le Grand Bleu P €€

Snepkaai 15, 9000 Ghent ***Tel.*** *09-2205025* ***Covers*** *60*

Cuisine: Fish. Popular fish restaurant on the banks of the Leie just on the outskirts of the city. Simple, homey design. Enjoy fish, crabs and shellfish fresh from the day's catch. The Bauwe Kiosk on the Kouter is run by the same owners. Kitchen: Mon-Sun 12 midday-1:30pm and 7pm-8:30pm. **www**.legrandbleu.be

Grand Café Godot €€

Hooiaard 8, 9000 Ghent ***Tel.*** *09-3298208 / 0473-676266* ***Covers*** *60* ***Map*** *1 C3*

Cuisine: international. Godot stands for young and modern, white and black, trendy and attractive with music that fits all these characteristics. The menu is truly international: tapas, stew with trappist beer, pasta and so on. The white terrace is a big surprise. Kitchen open: 11am-1am. **www**.godotgent.be

See inside of the back flap for an explanation of the symbols

Greenway €
Nederkouter 42, 9000 Gent ***Tel.*** *09-2690769* ***Map*** *1 C5, 3 C1-2*
Cuisine: International, vegetarian. Veggie restaurant. 'Taste the world' is Greenway's motto: global cuisine with a trendy facelift. As well as the monthly recommendations there is also a fixed, fresh-daily menu. Kitchen open: Mon-Sat 11am-9pm. Closed: Sun. **www**.greenway.be

The House of Eliott €€€
Jan Breydelstraat 36, 9000 Gent ***Tel.*** *09-2252128* ***Covers*** *40* ***Map*** *1 B2-C3*
Cuisine: French. Based on the English TV series of the same name. Design and decorations hark back to the roaring 1920s. Contemporary food in a pleasant atmosphere. Kitchen open: Mon and Fri-Sun 12 midday-2pm and from 6pm, and Thu from 6pm. Closed: Tue-Wed. **www**.thehouseofeliott.be

Jan van den Bon €€€
Koning Leopold II-Laan 43, 9000 Gent ***Tel.*** *09-2219085* ***Covers*** *30* ***Map*** *3 B4-C4*
Cuisine: French. Townhouse opposite the S.M.A.K. (Art Museum), Contemporary cuisine served in the three dining rooms. Awarded a Michelin star. Kitchen open: Mon-Sat 12 midday-2:30pm and 7:30pm-9pm. Closed: Sat afternoon, Sun and Bank holidays. **www**.janvandenbon.be

Korenhuis P €€€
Korenlei 10, 9000 Gent ***Tel.*** *09-2697744* ***Covers*** *60* ***Map*** *1 B3-C3*
Cuisine: Belgian. The Korenhuis has four small rooms quite separate from each other. They serve Flemish dishes with a modern, international twist. Kitchen open: Mon-Sat 12 midday-3pm and 6:30pm-2am, Sun 12 midday-3pm. Closed: Sun evening. **www**.korenhuis.be

Korenlei Twee €€€
Korenlei 2, 9000 Gent ***Tel.*** *09-2240073* ***Map*** *1 B3-C3*
Cuisine: Belgian. Immaculate interior with elegant furniture and modern art adorning the walls. Enclosed terrace overlooking the confluence of the Leie and the Lieve. Heated lounge. Kitchen open: Tue-Sat 12 midday-2:30pm and 6:30pm-10pm, Sun 12 midday-2:30pm. Closed: Mon-Sun evening. **www**.korenleitwee.be

Martino €
Vlaanderenstraat 125, 9000 Gent ***Tel.*** *09-2250104* ***Map*** *2 D4-E5, 4 E1*
Cuisine: Belgian. Martino, a monument in Ghent and the meeting place for students and well-known Ghent residents, has a smart interior. The long bar allows plenty of room for solo-eaters. Famous for its classic dishes: steak Martino, cheese, egg and chips. Kitchen open: Wed-Sun 6pm-1pm. Closed: Mon-Tue.

Mosquito Coast €
Hoogpoort 28, 9000 Gent ***Tel.*** *09-2243720* ***Covers*** *100* ***Map*** *1 C3-2 D3*
Cuisine: international, fusion. Café with a global touch. On the menu you will find food and beverages (including Belgian beers) from all corners of the earth, as well as traditional Flemish fare. It boasts the sunniest terrace in Ghent. Kitchen open: 12 midday-2pm and 6pm-10:30pm. Closed: Mon. **www**.mosquitocoast.be

Passion €€
Emile Braunplein 1, 9000 Gent ***Tel.*** *09-2256886* ***Covers*** *155* ***Map*** *1 C3*
Cuisine: Flemish. Drink-lunch-dessert-dinner. Mainly specialities from Ghent, such as pan-fried eel with fresh-made tartar sauce and lemon, Ghent beef stew and Ghent waterzooi: chicken casserole. Kitchen open: 11:30am-9:30pm. Closed: Wed-Thu. **www**.resto-passion.be

De Tempelier €€
Meerseniersstraat 9, 9000 Gent ***Tel.*** *09-2330305*
Cuisine: Belgian-French. Cosy, intimate restaurant with a long wooden counter and a long couch ranged against the wall. The menu changes every day and offers a modest selection of appetizers, main courses and desserts. Kitchen open: Wed-Sun 6pm-10pm. Closed: Mon-Tue. **www**.brasseriedetempelier.be

Toi et moi €€€
St.-Michielsstraat 31, 9000 Gent ***Tel.*** *09-2258633* ***Covers*** *40*
Cuisine: French. Not really trendy, but it does have three open-plan rooms. No real surprises on the menu but a variety of the classics and contemporary dishes. Kitchen open: Thu-Fri 6pm-10pm, Sun also 12 midday-2pm. Closed: Wed. **www**.restotoietmoi.be

Volta €-€€€
Nieuwe Wandeling 2b, 9000 Gent ***Tel.*** *09-3240500* ***Covers*** *45*
Cuisine: French-Belgian. This isn't your classic brasserie but an ambitious restaurant with a lovely yet functional design. Modern twists to classic dishes with imaginative use of seasonal produce. Kitchen open: From 10am. Closed: Mon and Sun. **www**.volta-gent.be

't Vosken €€
St.-Baafsplein 19, 9000 Gent ***Tel.*** *09-2257361* ***Map*** *1 C3-2 D3*
Cuisine: Ghent specialities, traditional. Typical Ghent brasserie (with a brand new black and white interior) where you can sit and eat in comfort all day long. Large terrace on the St.-Baafsplein. Kitchen open: Mon-Sun 11:30am-10:30pm (Sat-Sun until midnight). **www**.tvosken.be

LEIESTREEK

't Veer €€
Achterstraat 61, 9800 Astene (Deinze) ***Tel.*** *09-3800460* ***Road map*** *B3*
Elegant restaurant on the banks of the Leie. You can choose from the brasserie menu or à la carte. Kitchen open: 12 midday-2pm and 6pm-10pm. Closed: Mon evening, Tue and Sat afternoon. **www**.brasserietveer.be

d'Oude Leie €€
Bachtekerkstraat 9, 9800 Bachte-Maria-Leerne (Deinze) ***Tel.*** *09-3870300* ***Road map*** *B3*
Cuisine: classic bistro cuisine. Spacious bistro that boasts the most beautiful terrace in and around Ghent, on quiet stretch of the Leie. Menu based on seasonal produce. A tribute to good taste. Kitchen open: Wed-Sun 12 midday-2:30pm and 6pm-10pm. Closed: Mon-Tue. **www**.oudeleie.be

D'Ouwe Hoeve €€
Dorpsstraat 48, 9831 Deurle (St.-Martens-Latem) ***Tel.*** *09-2823252* ***Road map*** *B3*
Cuisine: French-Belgian. Family-run, farmhouse style, friendly welcome. Peaceful and lovely surroundings in the heart of Deurle. Specialities are T-bone steak and lobster. Large terrace. Kitchen open: daily until 11pm. **www**.ouwehoeve.be

Marlin's Eetwinkel €
Kerkplein 5, 9810 Eke (Nazareth) ***Tel.*** *09-3854033* ***Road map*** *B4*
Cuisine: Belgian. This restaurant is in a former butcher's shop. Extensive menu with a choice of anything from sandwiches to wok dishes, vegetarian to meat specialities. Kitchen open: Mon and Thu 11am-9pm, Fri-Sun 11am-11pm. Closed: Tue-Wed.

De Afspanning €€
Machelendorp 4, 9870 Machelen-aan-de-Leie (Zulte) ***Tel.*** *09-3864124* ***Road map*** *B4*
Cuisine: French. You will find this restaurant in the village of Machelen in a former 17th-century tavern. Child-friendly. Kitchen open: Wed-Thu 11:30am-2pm, Fri-Sat 11:30am-2pm and 5:30pm-10pm, Sun 11:30am-9pm, July-Aug from 11am. Closed: Mon-Tue. **www**.deafspanning.be

L'homard Bizarre €€€
Dorp 12, 9830 St.-Martens-Latem ***Tel.*** *09-2812922* ***Cover*** *25* ***Road map*** *B3*
Cuisine: French. A small restaurant in the centre of the village with an attractive monthly menu of four courses. The menu includes the classics as well as some more adventurous dishes. Kitchen open: Mon and Thu-Sun 12 midday-2pm and 7pm-9pm. Closed: Tue-Wed. **www**.homard-bizarre.be

MEETJESLAND

Stadhuis van Raverschoot €€
Raverschoot 14, 9991 Adegem (Maldegem) ***Tel.*** *09-3772432* ***Road map*** *B2*
Cuisine: Belgian. In this modernised kitchen, they use produce fresh from the market. Fish dishes are prepared on a special Tepan plate. A tearoom is open in the afternoons. Large, sunny terrace. Kitchen open: Wed-Sun from 11am (July-Aug also Mon). Closed: Mon-Tue. **www**.stadhuisvanraverschoot.be

De Warande €€€
Warande 10, 9982 St.-Jan-In-Eremo (St.-Laureins) ***Tel.*** *09-3790051* ***Road map*** *B1*
An exceptional restaurant in a country village. On the menu you will find a 'Meetjeslandse Tafel' with a variety of local dishes. The veranda opens onto a lovely terrace and gorgeous garden. Kitchen open: Mon and Thu-Sun 12 midday-2pm and 6:30pm-9pm. Closed: Tue-Wed. **www**.dewaranderestaurant.be

Drongengoedhoeve €
Drongengoedweg 9, 9910 Ursel (Knesselare) ***Tel.*** *09-3250980* ***Road map*** *B2*
A pleasant hostelry in the middle of the wide Drongengoed forest. Kitchen open: April-Sept. Tue-Fri 11am-7pm, Sat-Sun 10am-7pm (July-Aug also Mon 11am-8pm); Oct-Mar. Wed-Thu 1:30am-7pm, Sat-Sun 10am-7pm. Closed: Mon-Tue (Oct-March also Friday). **www**.drongengoedhoeve.be

De Roste Muis €
Drijdijk 2, 9988 Waterland-Oudeman (St.-Laureins) ***Tel.*** *09-3798560* ***Road map*** *B1*
Quiet restaurant with playground, large outdoor terrace and an authentic interior. De Roste Muis was an illicit café in the 19th century. Speciality: stewed eel in creamed chervil sauce or prepared to the chef's recipe. Kitchen open: Thu-Mon from 12 midday (July-Aug daily). Closed: Tue-Wed. **www**.rostemuis.be

See inside of the back flap for an explanation of the symbols

WAASLAND

De Eenhoorn €€
Koningin Astridplein 20, 9150 Bazel (Kruibeke) ***Tel.*** *03-7440061* ***Road map*** *F2*
Cuisine: French-Belgian. Romantic restaurant with a crackling fire and parquet floor. The cuisine is a wonderful mix of traditional French-Belgian dishes and produce available from the market. Kitchen open: Wed-Sun 12 midday-3pm, Sat-Sun 6pm-10pm. Closed: Mon-Tue. **www**.restaurant-deeenhoorn.be

Koetshuis Cortewalle €€€
Essendreef 2, 9120 Beveren-Waas ***Tel.*** *03-7755385* ***Road map*** *E2*
Cuisine: Belgian-French. The Koetshuis is in the gardens of the Cortewalle castle. Gastronomic monthly menu. Seasonal dishes with fresh daily produce.
Closed: Wed (also on Tue from 3pm in the winter).

Tiecelijn €€€
Daknam-dorp 34, 9160 Daknam (Lokeren) ***Tel.*** *09-3480059* ***Road map*** *D2*
Cuisine: Belgian-French. Classic dishes with modern and multicultural influences. Very private terrace. Warm welcome and friendly service. Kitchen open: Mon, Thu-Fri, Sun 12 midday-2pm, Thu-Mon 6:30pm-8:30pm. (Sat 9pm). Closed: Tue-Wed and Sat afternoon. **www**.tiecelijn.be

Kasteel Walburg €€
Walburgstraat 35, 9100 St.-Niklaas ***Tel.*** *03-7662115* ***Road map*** *E2*
Cuisine: Belgian-French. With its combination of a wide-ranging menu and a lovely decor, Kasteel Walburg is simply not to be missed. Kitchen open: Wed-Sun.
Closed: Mon-Tue. **www**.kasteelwalburg.be

Palingshuis €€€
Wilfordkaai 17, 9140 Temse ***Tel.*** *03-7710370* ***Road map*** *E2*
Cuisine: Belgian-French. Fish dishes. Eel in chervil sauce has appeared on the menu at the Palingshuis for over one hundred years. The terrace on the embankment has a beautiful view over the Scheldt. Kitchen open: Mon-Wed 11:45am-3pm and 6pm-10pm, Sat-Sun from 11:45am. Closed: Thu-Fri. **www**.palingshuis.be

SCHELDT COUNTRY

De Kapelaan €€
Zwarte Zustersstraat 6A, 9300 Aalst ***Tel.*** *053-416634/0475-805187* ***Road map*** *D4*
Cuisine: Belgian-French. The smartly designed brasserie offers more than one hundred covers spread out over three levels. The seasonal menu is supplemented by original Tapalaantjes (delicate appetizers). Kitchen open: Tue-Sat 11:30am-2pm and 6pm-10pm. (Fri-Sat until 10:30pm). Closed: Sun-Mon. **www**.dekapelaan.be

't Overhamme €€€
Brusselsesteenweg 163 B, 9300 Aalst ***Tel.*** *053-778599* ***Road map*** *D4*
Cuisine: Belgian-French. This restaurant is in a stately home with a charming modern interior, with lots of wood and bluestone. In the summer, enjoy your meal on the terrace. Kitchen open: 12 midday-2pm and 7pm-9pm. Closed: Sat afternoon, Sun evening, Mon and 1st Tue in the month, mid-July to mid-Aug. **www**.toverhamme.be

't Laurierblad €€€
Dorp 4, 9290 Berlare ***Tel.*** *052-424801* ***Road map*** *D3*
Cuisine: Belgian. Gastronomic restaurant where Guy Van Cauteren, well-known author and TV chef, holds sway. Class without pretence. Kitchen open: Wed-Sun 12 midday-2pm, Wed-Sat 7pm-9:30pm. Closed: Sun evening, Mon-Tue. **www**.laurierblad.com

De Heeren van Liedekercke €€€
Kasteelstraat 33, 9470 Denderleeuw ***Tel.*** *053-680888* ***Road map*** *D4*
Cuisine: Belgian. The beer restaurant De Heeren van Liedekercke offers a special monthly beer menu, alternating the beers from East Flanders and Flemish Brabant. Kitchen open: Mon 11:30am-2:30pm, Thu-Sun from 11:30am. Closed: Mon evening, Tue-Wed. **www**.heerenvanliedekercke.be

Huis van Cleophas €€€
Sint-Gillislaan 47, 9200 Dendermonde ***Tel.*** *0497-575655* ***Road map*** *E3*
Cuisine: Belgian-French. Trendy brasserie in the formers mayor's residence. During the summer, you can enjoy your meal on the veranda overlooking the garden. Kitchen open: Tue-Thu 11:30am-4pm and from 6:30pm, Fri-Sun from 11:30am. Closed: Mon. **www**.cleophas.be

Thooftgerecht €€€
Hundelgemsesteenweg 57, 9820 Merelbeke ***Tel.*** *09-3243347* ***Road map*** *C3*
Cuisine: Belgian. Brasserie-tearoom in a grand town house with three charming, intimate dining rooms. Extensive menu with 29-minute lunch. Kitchen open: Mon, Thu-Fri and Sun 11:30am-10pm, Tue 11:30am-2:30pm, Sat 12 midday-2pm and 6pm-10pm. Closed: Tue afternoon and Wed. **www**.thooftgerecht.be

FLEMISH ARDENNES

De Soetekoeke €€
Issegem 14, 9860 Balegem (Oosterzele) ***Tel.*** *09-3248874 / 0476-815676* ***Road map*** *C4*
Cuisine: Belgian-French. Restaurant with three dining rooms decorated in the English style. The south-facing terrace has a real holiday atmosphere. Kitchen open: Wed-Sat 11:30am-2pm and 6pm-9:30pm, Sun 11:30am-2pm. Closed: Sun evening, Mon-Tue. **www**.desoetekoeke.be

De Zwalmmolen €€
Rekegemstraat 28, 9630 Beerlegem (Zwalm) ***Tel.*** *055-498933* ***Road map*** *C4*
Cuisine: Belgian-French. A retro-style restaurant with terrace at the front and a dining area inside. Cuisine using traditional local produce, including pigeon, hare, asparagus and spinach, strawberries, raspberries and Balegem gin. Kitchen open: Thu-Mon from 12 midday. Closed: Tue-Wed. **www**.dezwalmmolen.be

Hof van Weenen €€
Markt 16-18, 9550 Herzele ***Tel.*** *053-630354* ***Road map*** *D4*
Cuisine: grill. This former hospital is now a comfortable restaurant. The interior has been renovated recently. Kitchen open: Tue, Thu and Fri 11:30am-2:30pm and from 5:30pm, Wed 8:00am-2:30pm, Sat from 5:30pm, Sun from 11am. Closed: Mon, Wed evening, Sat afternoon. **www**.hofvanweenen.be

Het Genot op den Berg €€
Bovenstraat 4, 9690 Maarke-Kerkem (Maarkedal) ***Tel.*** *055-303556* ***Road map*** *B5*
A wine restaurant in a formerly deserted farmhouse. The cuisine radiates quietness and country style with dishes such as Flemish casserole and fisherman's stew. Kitchen open: Thu-Sun 12 midday-3pm and 6pm-9pm. Closed: Mon-Wed. **www**.genotopdenberg.be

Margaretha's €€€
Markt 40, 9700 Oudenaarde ***Tel.*** *055-210101.* ***Road map*** *B4*
Cuisine: Belgian-French. Restaurant in the grand property known as Huis Margaretha van Parma. Wine bar, salon and restaurant, tastefully designed. Good-value gastronomic menu.
Kitchen open: from 11:30am. Closed: Mon-Tue. **www**.margarethas.be

De Mouterij €€
Markt 42, 9700 Oudenaarde ***Tel.*** *055-304810* ***Road map*** *B4*
Cuisine: Belgian. Restaurant with a lovely walled terrace in a former malt-house. Traditional cuisine specializing in grilled food. Kitchen open: 12 midday-2pm and 6pm-10pm. Closed: Wed. **www**.de-mouterij.be

Margriet €€€
Den Bos 36 (N60), 9750 Ouwegem (Oudenaarde) ***Tel.*** *09-3848016* ***Road map*** *B4*
Cuisine: French. Classic dishes are central here. Fresh produce every day. Exceptional value for money. Kitchen open: from 12 midday-6pm. Closed: Tue and Sun evening, Wed and Sat afternoon. **www**.restaurantmargriet.be

De Pikardijn €
Cotthem 6, 9520 St.-Lievens-Houtem ***Tel.*** *09-3605128* ***Road map*** *C4*
Cuisine: Belgian. Café, tavern and restaurant specialising in local Belgian beers and dishes. The terrace is divided into different garden rooms. Situated along walking- and cycle paths. Kitchen open: Thu-Fri 7pm-11pm, Sat 6pm-10pm, Sun 12 midday-9pm. Closed: Mon-Thu.

Den Gulzigen Bok €€
Gentweg 48, 9890 Vurste (Gavere) ***Tel.*** *09-3847572* ***Road map*** *C4*
Cuisine: local produce. Peacefully situated along walking- and cyding paths. The café is in the middle of a beautiful garden with some lovely intimate corners. Homely yet contemporary. Kitchen open: Thu-Sun from 11am (July-Aug also Wed from 5pm). Closed: Mon-Wed. **www**.dengulzigenbok.com

Kasteel van Breivelde €€€
Parkstraat 1, 9620 Zottegem ***Tel.*** *0475-861131* ***Road map*** *C4*
Cuisine: French-Belgian. Dine in a castle: a dream location with a lovely terrace. Dishes based on local produce. Have a walk in the park, then pay a visit to the restaurant. Kitchen open: Mon-Thu 11:30am-4pm, Fri-Sun 11:30am-11pm. **www**.restaurantkrant.be

SPECIALITIES FROM EAST FLANDERS

In the rather grand Groot Vleeshuis on the Groentenmarkt in Ghent, you can find the Promotion Centre for East Flanders local produce. Here they sell local beers, gins, fruit juices, mineral water, ham, bacon, cheeses, 'Geraardsbergs mattentaart', a sort of cheesecake-gingerbread, cakes, chocolates and jams. Just as in the olden days when the covered meat market was held here every day, you will find the famous Ghent Ganda hams hanging from the wooden supports to age. Along with smoked horse meat sausage, Ghent hotch potch and Ghent stew, Ghent waterzooi (casserole) is the most famous dish of the city. Inhabitants of Ghent adore cuberdons, the reddish-purple raspberry-flavoured sweets.

Mustard

Geraardsberg mattentaart has been recognised by the European Union as a local product. (Protected Designation of Origin or PDO).

GHENT WATERZOOI

This is undoubtedly the best known speciality of East Flanders. In the middle ages this soup would be made using fish from the Leie and the Scheldt. When fish later became hard to come by due to river pollution, the dish was made with chicken instead.

TIERENTEYN MUSTARD

The poet Willem Elsschot sang the praises of the Tierenteyn mustard house, the pride of Ghent, in many of his works. The company *firma Vve Tierenteyn-Verlent* has been selling its mustard in the shop on the Groentenmarkt since 1790, where it is still made behind closed doors in the cellar in the traditional way. Ferdinand Tierenteyn started his family business in 1818 and the 'yellow gold' is still made according to his own tried and tested recipe.

CUBERDONS

These reddish-purple raspberry-flavoured sweets are hard on the outside but have a soft centre. These 'neuzen' (noses) can only be kept for three weeks, after which the centres turn to sugar, which means that these sweets cannot be exported.

Red-purple cuberdons

MATTENTAART

Geraardsbergen mattentaart (curd or cheesecake) is recognised by the EU as a local product. It has a long history and a rich tradition. Curds were already being used in cakes as far back as the 17th century. The round cakes have a diameter of 8 to 10 cm. They are made from puff pastry, filled with a cheesecake mixture (a mixture of full cream milk and buttermilk) eggs and almonds.

FLANS

Belgian flans come in so many sizes, weights and sorts. They are a very popular dessert in East Flanders. Every family, village, town and baker has their own recipe. You'll find flans with syrup and maslin (a type of cinnamon-flavoured donut) as well as flans made with gingerbread and spices. The Aalster flan has recently been awarded the status of a recognised local product.

ROOMER

This is a traditional Ghent drink, based on elderflowers and contains 14% alcohol. The elderflowers are cultivated on the Koppenberg. The drink comes in small, round bottles containing white elder blossoms.

The shops at the Promotion Centre for East-Flanders products

O'DE FLANDER

Eleven of the gin distilleries in East Flanders have marketed their authentic gin under the quality lable *O'de Flander*. These gins have a minimum alcohol content of 35% and are distilled from a mash made of different grains (wheat, rye, barley and corn).

EAST FLANDERS BEERS

During the first half of the last century in the 'beer town' of Oudenaarde, there were twenty breweries all making the same beer: Oudenaards Old Brown. This beer is dark brown, bitter and incredibly refreshing and thirst quenching. These days, only three breweries in the Oudenaarde area still brew the original beer: *Liefmans, Roman* and the smaller *Cnudde*. There are still twenty large and small breweries in East Flanders producing beers with charming names like

The dark brown Adriaen Brouwer beer

Kwak, Deua, Gruut, Malheur, Adriaen Brouwer, Pater Lieven and Buffalo. Most of the breweries offer a guided tour, after which you can taste the house beer in the local pub. The closure of Riva signaled the end of the Ghent breweries. In 2009, the brewery Stadsbrouwerij Gruut opened its doors on the Ketelvaart. Gruut is made from 'gruut' a blend of dried spices and plants that was once used in place of or in addition to hops and that gives the beer its distinctive taste.

Mattentaart

THE GHENT AZALEA

It isn't just foodstuffs that have been awarded the status of local produce – some plants have that distinction as well. In 2010 the Ghent Azalea was recognised as a European local product. Market gardeners from Ghent brought the plant back from China and Japan at the end of the 18th century and started to cultivate the azalea in Ghent and its surroundings.

The Ghent Azalea

ADDRESSES

Het Groot Vleeshuis Promotioncentre Eastern Flemish local products
Groentenmarkt 7, Gent.
Tel. *09-2232324.*
www.grootvleeshuis.be

MUSTARD

Tierenteyn-Verlent
Groentenmarkt 3, Gent.
Tel. *09-2258336.*
www.tierenteyn-verlent.be

Ferdinand Tierenteyn
www.tierenteyn.be

BREWERIES

Bosteels
Kerkstraat 92,
Buggenhout.
Tel. *052-332323.*
www.bestbelgianspecialbeers.be

De Landtsheer
Mandekensstraat 179,
Buggenhout.
Tel. *052-333911.*
www.malheur.be

Brouwerij Slaghmuylder
Denderhoutembaan 2,
Ninove.
Tel. *054-331831.*
www.slaghmuylder.be

Cnudde
Fabriekstraat 8, Eine
(Oudenaarde).
Tel. *055-311834.*

Van den Bossche
Sint-Lievensplein 16,
St.-Lievens-Esse (Herzele).
Tel. *054-500411.*
www.paterlieven.be

Liefmans
Aalststraat 200,
Oudenaarde.
Tel. *03-8609400.*
www.liefmans.be

Roman
Hauwaert 105,
Oudenaarde.
Tel. *055-455401.*
www.roman.be

Stadsbrouwerij Gruut
Grote Huidevettershoek
10, Gent.
Tel. *09-2690269.*
www.gruut.be

Van Steenberge
Lindenlaan 25, Ertvelde.
Tel. *09-3445071.*
www.vansteenberge.com

GERAARDSBERGEN MATTENTAART

Nevens Mattentaartenbakkerij
Boelarestraat 38,
Geraardsbergen.
Tel. *054-411823.*
www.mattentaart.be

Olavs Mattentaartenhuis
Brugstraat 1,
Geraardsbergen.
Tel. *054-417887.*

Choosing a café, bar or terrace

Ghent has hundreds of cafés with a rich history, local cafés, snack bars, grand cafés and cafés with inviting terraces. In the snack bars you will find simple meals, salads or more interesting dishes. This applies to the whole of East Flanders, where there are small, traditional cafes, which are often near a riverbank or canal. A no-smoking policy came into force on 1st January 2010 for all places that serve food. There are separate smoking rooms, where food will not be served.

GHENT

Brooderie

Jan Breydelstraat 8, 9000 Ghent ***Tel.*** *09-2250623* ***Map*** *1 B2-C3*

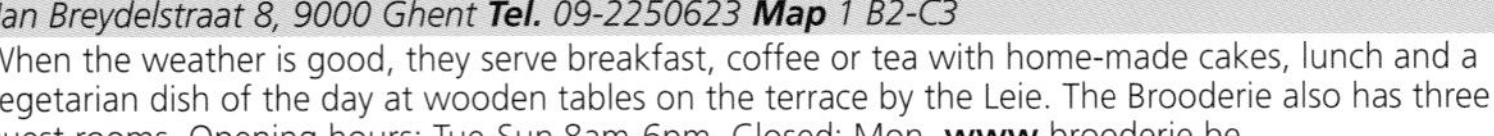

When the weather is good, they serve breakfast, coffee or tea with home-made cakes, lunch and a vegetarian dish of the day at wooden tables on the terrace by the Leie. The Brooderie also has three guest rooms. Opening hours: Tue-Sun 8am-6pm. Closed: Mon. **www**.brooderie.be

Café De Loge

Annonciadenstraat 5, 9000 Ghent ***Tel.*** *09-2253438* ***Map*** *2 B4, 3 B1*

The cosy atmosphere simply invites good conversation, a favourite book or party games. Breakfast on Sat and Sun (9am-2pm), there is a free concert on Wednesday evenings. Opening hours: Mon-Sun 11:30am-1am (Sat-Sun from 9am). **www**.deloge.be

Café René

Gebroeders Vandeveldestraat 2-4, 9000 Ghent ***Tel.*** *09-2232700* ***Map*** *1 B4, 3 B1-C1*

Trendy, modern snack bar in the centre of Ghent. The menu offers children's meals, pasta salads and a huge selection of sandwiches and toasties. Friendly service. Opening hours: Mon-Thu 10am-11pm, Fri-Sat from 10am, Sun 9am-6pm. **http://**cafe-rene.tumblr.com

Charlatan

Vlasmarkt 6, 9000 Ghent ***Tel.*** *09-2242457* ***Map*** *2 D3*

Music café Charlatan has been at the epicentre of Ghent's nightlife for years. It has three different rooms, a summer terrace, various performances during the week and DJs, and is one of the city's most popular entertainment venues. Opening hours: Tue-Sun from 7pm. Closed Mon. **www**.charlatan.be

Chez de Beir

Onderbergen 33, 9000 Ghent ***Tel.*** *0475-590487* ***Map*** *1 B4, 3 C1*

Chez de Beir is a trendy place with a modern interior and a relaxed atmosphere, with over thirty types of champagne and tapas. Opening hours: Wed-Thu and Sat 5:30pm-1.00am, Fri 4:30pm-1am, Sun 11am-2pm. Closed: Mon-Tue. **www**.champagnebar.biz

't Dreupelkot

Groentenmarkt 12, 9000 Ghent ***Tel.*** *09-2242120* ***Map*** *1 C2-3*

Unique café with more than two hundred kinds of gin, including some of their own make such as the famous vanilla gin. Opening hours: daily from 4pm.
www.dreupelkot.be

Dulle Griet

Vrijdagmarkt 50, 9000 Ghent ***Tel.*** *09-2242455* ***Map*** *1 C2, 2 D2*

The Dulle Griet Inn is worth a visit for its selection of over 250 varieties of beverages, including all of the Trappist beers and a good assortment of traditional Brussels' beers and cherry beers.
Opening hours: Mon 4:30pm-1am, Tue-Sat 12 midday-1am, Sun 12 midday-7:30pm. **www**.dullegriet.be

Galgenhuisje

Groentenmarkt 5, 9000 Ghent ***Tel.*** *09-2334251* ***Map*** *1 C2-3*

The smallest intimate cafés in Ghent since 1776 (thirty people spread out over three floors), the Galgenhuisje attracts visitors from all over the world. The bar is just 1 m long. The terrace is bigger than the café. Opening hours: Mon-Sun 10pm-1am.

De Geus van Gent

Kantienberg 9, 9000 Ghent ***Tel.*** *09-2207825* ***Map*** *4 D3*

Cosy café where everyone feels comfortable in a homely setting (café, salon and billiards room). There are free jam sessions on Wednesday evenings (not during holiday periods). Opening hours: Mon-Fri from 4pm, Sat from 7pm. Closed: Sun. **www**.geuzenhuis.be

Hot Club de Gand

Schuddevisstraatje (Groentenmarkt 15b), 9000 Ghent ***Tel.*** *0486-288051* ***Map*** *1 C2-3*

Well hidden, this jazz café has a heated terrace. The Hot Club de Gand was set up by several enthusiasts in May 2005. It has acoustic live music, jazz as well as other genres. Open: daily from 3pm. **www**.hotclubdegand.be

Jazz café Damberd

Korenmarkt 19, 9000 Ghent ***Tel.*** *09-3295337* ***Map*** *1 C3*

Authentic pure-bred brown pub and jazz café. Perfect for a game of chess, a live concert or a good natter. Colourful Ghent café for people from all walks of life.
Opening hours: Mon-Fri 11am-4pm, Sat 1pm-4pm, Sun 12 midday-4pm. **www**.damberd.be

Marimain

Walpoortstraat 17, 9000 Ghent ***Tel.*** *09-3243766* ***Map*** *2 D5, 4 D1*

Theater café next to the Minard theatre with bustling terrace. The name is a combination of the names of the manager Mary Brouillard and the Ghent comedian Romain Deconinck.
Opening hours: Mon-Fri from 10am, Sat from 12 midday and Sun from 2pm.

Max

Goudenleeuwplein 3, 9000 Ghent ***Tel.*** *09-2239731* ***Map*** *1 C3*

Max is an icon in Ghent. For generations, Max has been serving Brussels waffles in the kind of surroundings that take you right back to yesteryear. They also have apple beignets on the menu.
Opening hours: Mon, Wed-Thu 9am-6pm, Fri-Sun from 9am.

Mokabon

Donkersteeg 35, 9000 Ghent ***Tel.*** *09-2257195* ***Map*** *1 C3*

The 'coffee house of coffee houses'. Pleasant, timeless coffee house where those who know will tell you they serve the best coffee in Ghent (from their own roasting house).Take-away coffee and Mokabon coffee beans available at the Mokabon Takeaway. Opening hours: Mon-Sat 8am-7pm. Closed: Sun. **www**.mokabon.be

Pink Flamingo's

Onderstraat 55, 9000 Ghent ***Tel.*** *09-2334718* ***Map*** *1 C3-2 D3*

Kitsch and Lounge Bar. Pink Flamingo's was a theme before the term was coined. The interior and the music provide a link between past and present. Opening hours: Mon-Wed 12 midday-midnight, Thu-Fri 12 midday-3am, Sat 2pm-3am, Sun 2pm-midnight. **www**.pinkflamingos.be

Puur

Hoogpoort 35, 9000 Ghent ***Tel.*** *09-2252600* ***Map*** *1 C3-2 D3*

Coffee house (and restaurant) with a stylish look and functional interior. Ideal for a cup of coffee with your newspaper in the mornings, lunch, a tea break in the afternoon or just to pop in while you are shopping. Opening hours: Mon, Thu and Sun 10am-8:30pm, Fri-Sat 10am-10pm. Closed: Tue-Wed.

Quetzal

St.-Pietersnieuwstraat 99, 9000 Ghent ***Tel.*** *09-2241527* ***Map*** *2 D5, 4 D1-2*

Quetzal refers to Quetzalcoatl, the god of chocolate. Inside the chocolate bar, the colours shout chocolate and simply exude the smell of chocolate. Chocolate milk, chocolate shakes and chocolate cocktails. Opening hours: Mon-Fri 12 midday-10pm, Sat-Sun 10am-6pm. **www**.chocoladebar.be

Simon Says

Sluizeken 8, 9000 Ghent ***Tel.*** *09-2330343* ***Map*** *1 C1-2*

The orange, yellow, blue and green façade of this art deco building just can't help catching your eye. Two Brits run this coffee bar, snack bar and B&B. The menu has quiches, home-made cakes and a generous selection of coffees. Opening hours: Tue-Fri 9am-6pm, Sat-Sun 10am-6pm. Closed: Mon. **www**.simon-says.be

Souplounge

Zuivelbrugstraat 6, 9000 Ghent ***Tel.*** *09-2236203*

Restaurant for a quick – or just a relaxed bowl of vegetable soup, (four kinds) with a choice of fillings, vegetables, chives, cheese or meatballs. Also salads and sandwiches (mostly meat or fish). Dine at tables or at the bar. Always busy at lunchtime. Opening hours: Mon-Sun 10am-7pm. **www**.souplounge.be

De Vooruit

St.-Pietersnieuwstraat 23, 9000 Ghent ***Tel.*** *09-2672848* ***Map*** *2 D5, 4 D1-2*

This is the beating heart of the Vooruit Kunstencentrum. Café with newspapers, beverages, (vegetarian) meals, fresh soup and café concerts (always at 10pm and free).
Opening hours: Mon-Tue 11:30am-1.00am, Wed-Sat 11:30am-2am and Sun 2pm-1am. **www**.vooruit.be

Het Waterhuis aan de Bierkant

Groentenmarkt 9, 9000 Ghent ***Tel.*** *09-2250680* ***Map*** *1 C2-3.*

Brown café for both Ghent folk and tourists with 165 beers on the menu and three house beers on tap: Gandavum, Kloeke Roeland and Mammelokker. Lovely terrace on the banks of the Leie. Meals made with local produce also served. Opening hours: Mon-Sun 11am-2am. **www**.waterhuisaandebierkant.be

See inside of the back flap for an explanation of the symbols

LEIESTREEK

't Oud Sashuis

Hellestraat 20, 9800 Astene (Deinze) ***Tel.*** *0476-323732* ***Road map*** *B3*

Small, homely café on the Leie docks. While you are having your coffee you can look at the wall poster that will show you how to conjugate verbs. There is a small bar in the corner with the taps serving the Schobiak house beer. Opening hours: Sat-Sun 11am-7pm (in the summer when the weather is nice: 11am-sunset).

Café Oude 3-Leien

Dijkweg 15, 9031 Drongen (Gent) ***Tel.*** *0497-923455* ***Road map*** *C3*

The Oude 3-Leien Inn is strategically place at a three-forked confluence along the Leie.
The tiny terrace has a wonderful view of the pleasure craft that come from all three directions.
Open: various times.

Bobar Lounge

Dorp 10, 9830 St.-Martens-Latem ***Tel.*** *09-3309688* ***Road map*** *B3*

With a sunny terrace complete with bamboo plants, the Bobar feels rather like a seaside resort.
Opening hours: Tue-Sun 3pm-3am.
Closed: Mon. **www**.bobar.be

MEETJESLAND

Koffiehuis Argus

Boelare 38, 9900 Eeklo ***Tel.*** *09-3782875* ***Road map*** *B2*

Koffiehuis Argus is an ideal place for a perfect cup of coffee or tea with homemade cake. They also serve delicious salads and snacks. Opening hours: Wed 11am-7pm, Thu 7am-6pm, Fri-Sat 11am-11pm, Sun 12 midday-9:30pm. Closed: Mon-Tue. **www**.koffiehuisargus.be

Het Biermuseum

Kuipstraat 36, 9940 Ertvelde (Evergem) ***Tel.*** *09-3448147 / 0477-417199* ***Road map*** *C2*

The museum in this rather special tavern has more than 1,200 Belgian and 400 foreign beers. There are lots of beers to sample as well, like La Chouffe on tap, Oerbier, Babar, Dikkenek and various trappist- or monastery beers. Opening hours: Mon, Thu and Fri from 6pm, Sat from 2pm and Sun from 10am. Closed: Tue and Wed.

WAASLAND

De Drij Klakken

Kruibekestraat 2, 9150 Bazel (Kruibeke) ***Tel.*** *03-7741119* ***Road map*** *F2*

An authentic 1900s tavern incorporated into the small botanical museum, to be found in the former rectory in Bazel.
Opening hours: Sun 2pm-6pm. Closed: Mon-Sat.

Theatercafé De Gekke Haan

Hoog Kallostraat 25, 9120 Kallo (Beveren) ***Tel.*** *0474-280743* ***Road map*** *F1*

A former parish hall, now the annexe café next to the theatre, quite an unexpected location in the port village of Kallo. The eye-catching façade with its painted panels simply invites you to look behind the scenes. Opening hours: Fri-Sat from 5pm, Sun from 2pm. Closed: Mon-Thu. **www**.degekkehaan.be

De Boogscheut

Vleeshouwersstraat 28, 9112 Sinaai (St.-Niklaas) ***Tel.*** *03-7724479* ***Road map*** *D2*

De Boogscheut is an old-fashioned local café that has been there time out of mind. Young and old, billiards fans, card players, marksmen, cyclists and walkers love to visit.
Opening hours: various times.

Eetcafé 't Spoor

Schare 12, 9961 Boekhoute (Assenede). ***Tel.*** *09-3735710/0476-887814* ***Road map*** *C1*

't Spoor has an interesting decoration: witches look down upon the guests from all directions. It is the ideal stopping place during a cycle or walking tour. Large terrace.
Opening hours: Wed-Fri noon, Sat-Sun 11am. Closed: Mon-Tue. www.tspoor.be

SCHELDT COUNTRY

't Veerhuis

Waterhoek 25, 9290 Berlare ***Tel.*** *052-426272 / 0478-274696* ***Road map*** *D3*

The best thing about 't Veerhuis is that it lies along the Scheldt just level with the Berlare-Appels ferry. Nothing much has changed in the decades since the café opened. Opening hours: Mon-Tue from 9:30am, Fri-Sat from 12 midday, Sun from 9:30am. Closed: Wed-Thu (July-Aug only Thu). **www**.hetveerhuis.be

Gasthof Affligem

Affligemdreef 324, 9310 Meldert (Aalst) ***Tel.*** *0498-678724* ***Road map*** *E4*

'Gossip and shoot the breeze' while sampling the local beers (Affligem abbey and trappist beers), just across from the abbey of Affligem in the middle of the Aalst hop fields.
Opening hours: Mon, Thu-Sun 2pm- 12 midnight. Closed: Tue-Wed. **www**.gasthofaffligem.be

Posthotel

Stationsplein 11, 9230 Wetteren ***Tel.*** *09-3699161* ***Road map*** *D3*

Authentic café with a flamboyant interior in the Flemish neo-renaissance style. The walls are covered with painted sheets portraying rustic drinking scenes. Selected as one of the loveliest café interiors in Flanders. Opening hours: Fri-Sat 5pm-1am, Sun 11am-1pm. Closed: Mon-Thu.

FLEMISH ARDENNES

In den Hengst

Twaalfbunderstraat 53, 9660 Elst (Brakel) ***Tel.*** *055-428545* ***Road map*** *C5*

In den Hengst is one of the oldest cafés in Vlaanderen. The ambience is Old-Flemish with a touch of Leuven, some old rustic games and an old café counter. The dining room is decorated with three wall paintings. Opening hours: Tue-Fri and Sun from 10am, Sat from 15pm. Closed: Mon.

Kaffee In de Kroon

Mullemstraat 15, 9700 Mullem (Oudenaarde) ***Tel.*** *09-3842820* ***Road map*** *B4*

Typical country café, perfect for a rest after a long walk or cycle ride. Extensive wine- and beer menu. Opening hours: Thu-Sat from 6pm, Sun from 11am.
Closed: Mon-Wed. **www**.indekroon.be

Lounge café Joly

Zuidstraat 5, 9600 Ronse ***Tel.*** *0476-527886* ***Road map*** *B5*

Totally relax in this lounge café in a fully restored castle. The terrace is a quiet and peaceful haven. There is a playground for the children.
Opening hours: 11am-2am (Wed and Sat 9am -2am). **www**.loungecafe-joly.be

Moeder Stiene

Langestraat 31, 9688 Schorisse (Maarkedal) ***Tel.*** *055-455464* ***Road map*** *C5*

Typical local tourist café with a history going back to the end of the 18th-century. Snacks are also served in the café. Try the speciality of the house: Rodenbach soup.
Opening hours: Tue from 4pm, Wed-Fri from 2:30pm, Sat-Sun from 10am. Closed: Mon.

Café De Kartuizer

Kartuizerstraat 1, 9572 St.-Martens-Lierde (Lierde) ***Tel.*** *055-424221 / 0474-510114* ***Road map*** *C5*

Local café in a quiet spot opposite the Kartuizer Priory. Kartuizer beer is served in a unique tankard. Outside terrace. Contemporary interior with a charming, rustic feel.
Opening hours: Thu-Tue from 11am. Closed: Wed.

Den Drijhaard

St.-Ursmarsstraat 33, 9660 Zegelsem (Brakel) ***Tel.*** *0485-134205* ***Road map*** *C5*

An old tavern on the village square dating back to 1771 which was restored and is now a place to meet and chat. There is also a function room. Lovely terrace on the village square.
Opening hours: Tue-Sun from 10am (Fri afternoon closed). Closed: Mon.

Klein Zwitserland

Galerijpad 3, 9630 Zwalm ***Tel.*** *055-497075* ***Road map*** *C4*

'Klein Zwitersland' can be found near the IJzerkotmolen on the Zwalmbeek. This tavern used to be the lock keeper's cottage at the start of the 20th century.
Open: various times.

See inside of the back flap for an explanation of the symbols

SHOPPING

Ghent is a shoppers' paradise, with its lovely shopping streets and alleys, which are mainly pedestrianised. The Veldstraat and Langemunt are busy shopping streets where most of the well-known chain stores are located. In the little alleys surrounding this shopping axis and in the Mageleinstraat-Koestraat-Koortedagsteeg and Vlaanderenstraat-Brabantdam you will find the specialist shops, trendy boutiques, luxury shops and unusual gift shops. Since the advent of custom shops featuring designers from Ghent and other parts of Belgium along with luxury boutiques, Ghent is fast becoming a true fashion city. Ghent delicacies and specialities such as the famous Tierenteyn mustard can be found in the shops selling more nostalgic items. The Gent Zuid shopping centre and the Woodrow Wilsonplein have over forty stores. Thanks to a thriving shopping centre, St.-Niklaas is high on the list of popular shopping towns.

SHOPPING STREETS

The choice for shoppers has increased enormously in Ghent in the last few years. It has an amazing selection of shops, from high-fashion stores for fashionistas to design shops for fun shoppers. The thriving **Veldstraat**, which leads to the Korte- and Langemunt, forms the major shopping axis in Ghent. The Veldstraat can be compared to the famous Meir in Antwerp and the 'Koopgoot' (Beurstraverse) in Rotterdam. Most of the small shops have had to make way for the large chain stores. Patisserie Bloch, cheesemaker Peeters and the cigar merchant Caron were the last independent shops to disappear from the city streets. The Veldstraat is now mostly the domain of clothing stores, shoe shops and mobile phone shops. The Mageleinstraat is the image of the chic shopping street featuring primarily fashion stores. The Koestraat has myriad fashion shops and jewellers. The Kalandeberg square is the perfect place to take a shopping break. In the Kortdagsteeg you will find plenty of stores selling clothing from the major Belgian labels. The Brabantdam and the Vlaanderenstraat are two up-and-coming trendy shopping streets with their exclusive fashion- and design stores. In the Henegouwenstraat that runs parallel to the Brabantdam, you will find mostly shops selling posh designer labels and high quality accessories. You will still find typical smaller Ghent shops, stylish clothing boutiques, unusual gift shops, home accessories, antique shops and second hand stores spread all over the town centre; sometimes you come across them in a busy shopping street or find them clustered along an alley. For a more extensive overview, see Shopping in Ghent *(pages 230-231)*.

The Veldstraat is the major shopping street in Ghent

Confiserie Temmerman, a shop full of goodies

OUTSIDE GHENT

St.-Niklaas can call itself a real shopping town. Station-

Waasland Shopping Centre is one of the largest in Belgium

straat has a generous selection of various stores. On the edge of the town you will find one of the largest shopping centres in the country: **Waasland Shopping Centre**. Almost all of the (pedestrianised) shopping streets in Aalst, (Molenstraat, Nieuwstraat, Kattestraat, and Korte en Lange Zoute straat) lead to the square Grote Markt. A fifth shopping street was added with the arrival of the Pieter van Aelst gallery, a partly-covered shopping area. Other good towns to shop are Dendermonde, Lokeren and Oudenaarde with their wide selection of goods. In the farm shops in the countryside you can buy (organic) produce such as potatoes, eggs, vegetables, fruit, dairy products, and fruit juices direct from the farm.

OPENING TIMES

The shops are usually open from Monday to Saturday from 10am to 6pm. Some shops close for a lunch break. Flanders does not have regular late-night and Sunday shopping, but there are increasing exceptions to the rule of Sunday closing. The shops are closed on May 1st, and November 1st and 11th. The major stores accept credit cards and bank cards.

Junk market round the St.-Jacobskerk

SALES

These aren't your usual sales, but rather the clearance of shoes, clothing and other goods that can be offered at reduced price when the season changes. The winter sales last from January 3rd to January 31st, and the summer sales from July 1st to July 31st.

MARKTEN

On Friday mornings and on Saturdays, Ghents' Vrijdagmarkt turns into one big market. There is a market for both antiques and second hand goods round the St.-Jacobskerk. The Sunday morning flower market on the Kouter is an absolute must-see in Ghent. Music and the oyster and wine bar in de Blauwe Kiosk make the atmosphere just perfect. There is also a free **market walk** on Sunday mornings, round the five Sunday markets, led by the Ghent Town Crier.

ADDRESSES

MARKETS IN GHENT

Flower market, Kouter.
Daily. 7am-1pm.

Antique, bric-a-brac wares market
Next to Sint-Jacobs and Beverhoutplein.
Fri, Sat and Sun 8am-1pm.
www.brocantmarkt-sintjacobsgent.be

Food market
St.-Michielsplein.
Sun 7am-1pm.

Poutry and fish market
Vrijdagmarkt.
Sun 7am-1pm.

Crafts market
Groentenmarkt.
Sat-Sun 10am-6pm.

Second-hand book market
Ajuinlei.
Sun 9am-1pm.

Organic market
Groentenmarkt.
Fri 7:30am-1pm.

Pets market
Oude Beestenmarkt.
Sun 7am-1pm.

General goods market
Vrijdagmarkt.
Fri 7:30am-12 midday and Sat 11 am-6:30pm.

Market walk
Ghent Town Crier.
Start: Kouter, 11am.
May-Aug.

SHOPPING

Ghent
www.gentverwent.be

St.-Niklaas
www.SHOPPINGinsintniklaas.be

Waasland Shopping Center
www.waaslandshoppingcenter.com

SHOPPING IN GHENT

The Fallen Angels

You can wander through small pedestrianised streets, along the Leie, across the bustling Vrijdagmarkt to the St.-Jacobskerk, the centre of the antiques shop quarter. You will pass quirky gift shops, small fashion stores, Ghent speciality and junk shops. The Serpentstraat is a wonderful little street that is full of surprises. You can rest your weary feet on one of the many terraces in the restored Botermarkt, or pop into in a café or bistro for coffee or lunch. The Magaleinstraat and the Kortedagsteeg are a fashionista's paradise. On the way back to the Grasbrug you will walk along the Veldstraat, Ghent's major shopping street.

SYMBOLS

• • • Recommended route

WALKING ROUTE

Jan Breydelstraat ①
Groentenmarkt ②
Kraanlei-Oudburg ③
Vrijdagmarkt ④
Serpentstraat ⑤
Bennesteeg ⑥
Koestraat-Kortedagsteeg ⑦

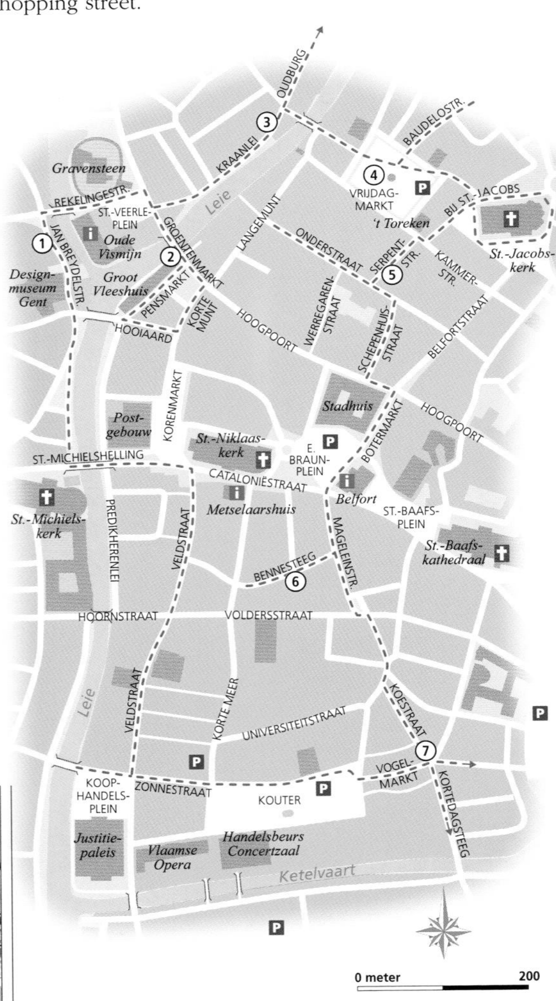

Jan Breydelstraat ①

The Jan Breydelstraat runs between the Grasbrug and the Burgstraat and is a lovely street with some charming shops, galleries and restaurants that hark back to yesteryear. The Appelbrugparkje (park) has a beautiful view over the Leie, the Lieve and the former fish market. Tips: **The Fallen Angels Gallery** (bric-a-brac), **Jeanne en Jules** (bric-a-brac)), **Huiszwaluw** (home accessories).

Groentenmarkt ②

You can't help but notice the Groot Vleeshuis on the Groentenmarkt, where you can enjoy the local produce from East Flanders. Between the Tierenteyn-Verlent Mustard Factory and the Himschoot bakery you will find the Pi (or 3.14) coffee- and tea house so you can try their delicious waffles. Right outside the door is a barrow selling the fabulous cuberdons. Tips: **Tierenteyn-Verlent** (mustard), **Groot Vleeshuis** (East Flanders local produce).

Willi's Wereld for diehard retro fans.

Huiszwaluw sells colourful and eccentric home accessories

Kraanlei-Oudburg ③

The Kraanlei is a nostalgic shopping street along the banks of the Leie. Pop in to the Huis van Alijn for a cup of coffee outside on the terrace or in the museum café (entrance free). Don't miss the Museum's giftshop. Oudburg is a rather cluttered street packed with second hand shops, food shops and exotic eateries.
Tips: **Museum shop** (books, toys) **Confiserie Temmerman** (Ghent specialities) **Craenkindershuys** (gifts and souvenirs) **Willi's Wereld** (gifts and gadgets).

Vrijdagmarkt ④

The Baudelostraat and the Bij St.-Jacobs, the square round St.-Jacobskerk, is the place for lovers of antiques, junk, second-hand goods and everything vintage. There is a flea market every Friday, Saturday and Sunday.
Tips: **Mieke** (latest trends), **Alternatief** (new and second hand), **Antiek Depot** (antiques and junk).

Serpentstraat ⑤

The Serpentstraat and the Hoogpoort are an unusual and refreshing alternative to the Veldstraat and the Langemunt. These shops radiate creativity and charm and – even better – are highly fashionable.
Tips: **Zoot costumiers** (Ghent designers) **Zsa Zsa Rouge** (accessories) **Zsa Zsa Petit** (for children).

Bennesteeg ⑥.

The Bennesteeg is a side street off the Mageleinstraat and is packed with shops selling childrens' articles: shoes, clothes and toys. Galerie Leenknegt sells glass jewellery.
Tips: Fred & Ginger (childrens' designer labels), **Spoonful of sugar** (hand-made childrens' articles), **Achter de maan** (gifts), **Aap.noot.mies** (childrens' shoes).

Antiek Depot

Koestraat-Kortedagsteeg ⑦

The Koestraat is where you will find mostly shops that sell menswear and jewellery, but there is also a fantastic bakery in the neighbourhood. In the Kortedag straat you will come across mostly fashion shops and jewellers.

Zsa Zsa Petit, everything for children

Tips: **Chris Janssens** (designer clothes from this Antwerp designer), **Mer du Nord** (ladies' and men's wear).

Fashion by Antwerp designer Chris Janssens

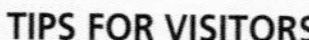

TIPS FOR VISITORS

Opening hours
Most shops are open from *Mon-Sat 10am-6pm.*

Sunday shopping
The shops are open on Sundays only in December (*12 midday-5pm*).

For more addresses of the shops listed see page 232.

ADDRESSES

Addresses for the shopping route Ghent
(pages 230-231)

JAN BREYDELSTRAAT

Van Hoorebeeke
(chocolaterie, pralines)
Jan Breydelstraat 1.
Tel. *09-2242510.*
St.-Baafsplein 15.
Tel. *09-2210381.*
www.chocolatesvan hoorebeke.be

Jeanne & Jules
(bric-a-brac and junk)
Jan Breydelstraat 6.
Tel. *0495-507895.*

The Fallen Angels Gallery
(rummager's paradise)
Jan Breydelstraat 31.
Tel. *09-2251771.*
www.thefallenangels.be

Huiszwaluw
(home accessories)
Jan Breydelstraat 33.
Tel. *09-2332737.*

Phulkari
(crafts and art from India, Nepal and Tibet)
Jan Breydelstraat 40.
Tel. *09-2251895.*
www.phulkari.be

GROENTENMARKT

Groot Vleeshuis
Promotion Centre
East Flanders local produce
Groentenmarkt 7.
Tel. *09-2232324.*
www.grootvleeshuis.be

Tierenteyn-Verlent
(mustard)
Groentenmarkt 3.
Tel. *09-2258336.*
www.tierenteyn-verlent.be

KRAANLEI-OUDBURG

Craenkindershuys
(gifts and souvenirs)
Kraanlei 2.
Tel. *09-2243309.*
www.craenkindershuys.be

Museumshop Huis van Alijn
Kraanlei 67.
Tel. *09-2692350.*
www.huisvanalijn.be

Confiserie Temmerman
(traditional sweet shop)
Kraanlei 79.
Tel. *09-2240041.*
● *zo-di.*

Willi's Wereld
(gifts)
Oudburg 13.
Tel. *09-2332011.*
www.williswereld.be

Les Trésors
(natural wines)
Oudburg 55.
Tel. *0477-933447.*
www.lestresors.be

Sjapoo
(hats for every occasion)
Sluizeken 29.
Tel. *09-2257535.*
www.sjapoo.be

VRIJDAGMARKT AND SURROUNDINGS

Het Oorcussen
(the store for Belgian couture)
Vrijdagmarkt 7.
Tel. *09-2330765.*
www.oorcussen.be

Alternatief
(new and second-hand)
Baudelostraat 15.
Tel. *09-2332311.*

Mieke
(trends, fashion, gifts, accessories)
Baudelostraat 23.
Tel. *09-3307144.*
www.mieke.tv

Antiek-Depot
(furniture, art, collector's items)
Baudelostraat 15.
Tel. *09-2243723.*
www.antiek-depot.com

Pieternel
(vintage)
Bij St.-Jacobs 5.
Tel. *09-2304414.*

Jacob
(colourful children's stuff)
Bij St.-Jacobs 7.
Tel. *0477-589327.*
www.jacobretro.be

SERPENTSTRAAT

Zsa Zsa Petit
(Great ideas for great kids)
Serpentstraat 5.
Tel. *09-2244574.*
www.zsazsarouge.be

Zoot costumiers
(Ghent designer)
Serpentstraat 8.
Tel. *09-2337075.*
www.zootcostumiers.be

Zsa Zsa Rouge
(Great ideas for great living)
Serpentstraat 22.
Tel. *09-2259363.*
www.zsazsarouge.be

BENNESTEEG

Aap.noot.mies
(children's shoes)
Bennesteeg 1A.
Tel. *09-2240600.*
www.aapnootmies.be

Spoonful of sugar
(creative children's clothes)
Bennesteeg 1B.
Tel. *09-2237337.*
www.spoonfulofsugar.be

Fred & Ginger
(children's fashions)
Bennesteeg 6.
Tel. *09-2231788.*

Elisabeth Leenknegt / Glasjuweel
(glass blower, design and jewellery)
Bennesteeg 7.
Tel. *09-3290878.*
www.galerieleenknegt.be
● *Mon-Tue.*

Achter de maan
(gifts)
Bennesteeg 18.
Tel. *09-2332891.*
www.achterdemaan.com

Meridian
(fashion, shoes, accessories)
Bennesteeg 25.
Tel. *09-2233014.*

KOESTRAAT-KORTEDAGSTEEG

Chris Janssens
(designer fashion)
Kortedagsteeg 10.
Tel. *09-2690339.*
www.chrisjanssens.be

Mer Du Nord
(Ladies' wear, mens' wear)
Kortedagsteeg 14-16.
Tel. *09-2238002.*
www.merdunord.com

OTHER SHOPS IN GHENT

A'pril
(original gifts)
Burgstraat 27.
Tel. *09-2230992.*

Patricia Vintage
(luxurious shop packed with vintage)
Henegouwenstraat 75.
Tel. *09-2230301.*

Cream
(urban street-shop)
Hoogpoort 9.
Tel. *09-2240085.*
www.cream.be

Au bon marché
(original gifts)
Hoornstraat 4.
Tel. *09-2690260.*
www.aubonmarchegent.be

Copyright
(trading in art books)
Jakobijnenstraat 8.
Tel. *09-2235794.*
www.copyright bookshop.be

Janssens Stoffen
(unusual materials)
Korenlei 5.
Tel. *09-2339445.*
Atlas & Zanzibar
Kortrijksesteenweg 19.
Tel. *09-2208799.*
www.atlaszanzibar.be

Cargo
(designer lighting)
Kromme Wal 1.
Tel. *09-2241341.*
www.cargo-art.be

ADDRESSES

M.A.R.T.H.A
(Modieus ARTistiek Hedendaagse Accessoires)
Onderbergen 19.
Tel. *09-3306640.*

A.puur.A
(gifts)
Onderbergen 56.
Tel. *09-2230241.*

UBX Gent
(snowboarding, skating, Surfing and freestyle skiing)
St.-Niklaasstraat 27.
Tel. *09-2234250.*

Movies
(clothing, young, hip and cool)
St.-Pietersnieuwstraat 5.
Tel. *09-2235912.*
www.movies.be

Limits
(urban street shop)
St.-Pietersnieuwstraat 38.
Tel. *09-2336693.*

Rewind Store
(Scandinavian-inspired designer labels)
St.-Pietersnieuwstraat 44.
Tel. *09-3248404.*
www.rewindstore.be

De Gentse Kookwinkel
(cooking pots and much, much more)
Steendam 17.
Tel. *09-2250361.*
www.mauricerogge.be

Absolute Design
(new and used design)
Steendam 74.
Tel. *09-2255653.*
www.absoluutdesign.be

Eva Bos
(private label collection, vintage)
Vlaanderenstraat 66.
Tel. *0495-496164.*

Toba Wereld
(quality for body and soul)
Vlaanderenstraat 78.
Tel. *09-2254015.*
www.toba.be

Surround Lifestyle
(kitchen, dining- and living room, garden)
Vlaanderenstraat 90.
Tel. *09-2253203.*
www.surroundlifestyle.be

Music Mania
(vinyl Mecca in Ghent)
Walpoortstraat 3.
Tel. *0477-436213.*
www.musicmania records.com

Yuzu
(chocolaterie)
Walpoortstraat 11a.
Tel. *0473-965733.*

Maaike kleedt
(very lady like store)
Zuivelbrugstraat 8.
Tel. *09-3355840.*
www.maaikekleedt.be

SHOPS OUTSIDE GHENT

LOCAL PRODUCTS

Chocolaterie Royal
(traditional pralines)
Molenstraat 41, Aalst.
Tel. *053-788764.*
www.chocolaterieroyal.be

Grega Vleeswaren
(traditionally prepared hams)
Maalderijstraat 40, Buggenhout.
Tel. *052-334942.*
www.grega.be

Chocolaterie De Zwarte Vos
(pralines, chocolate)
Dorpsstraat 76, Deinze.
Tel. *09-3864205.*
www.dezwartevos.be

Le Larry
(traditional goat's cheese)
Haenhoutstraat 216, Destelbergen.
Tel. *09-3268180.*
www.lelarry.be

Confiserie Geldhof
(cuberdons)
Tieltsesteenweg 107, Eeklo.
Tel. *09-3772159.*
www.conf-geldhof.be

Vierhoekhoeve
(dairy)
Brielstraat 71, Gijzenzele (Oosterzele).
Tel. *09-3627719.*
www.vierhoekhoeve.be

Brouwerij St-Canarus
(Kriegelbeer etc.)
Polderweg 2, Gottem (Deinze).
Tel. *051-636931.*
www.sintcanarus.be

Traditional confectioner Jan van Gent
(Oudenaarden sweets)
Kerselare 98, Kerselare.
Tel. *055-304900.*

Paardenmelkerij Filippus
(horses' milk-liqueur and ice cream)
Vakebuurtstraat 243, Maldegem.
Tel. *050-381610.*
www.filippus.com

't Soete Huys
(local specialities)
Grote Baan 286, Melsele (Beveren).
Tel. *03-7758494.*
www.soetehuys.be

Nougat Vital
(nougat)
Vaart Links 61, Nevele.
Tel. *09-3716313.*
www.vital.be

Den Tseut
(local beers)
Dorp 40, Oosteeklo.
Tel. *0485-372011.*
www.huisbrouwerij dentseut.weebly.com

Callebaut
(cheese shop and local produce)
Markt 16, Oudenaarde.
Tel. *055-300222.*

Hoeve Engelendael
(cherries, jam, quince syrup)
St.-Janspolderdijk 14, St.-Jan-in-Eremo.
Tel. *0479-254460.*
www.engelendael.wordpress.com

Den Ouden Advokaat
(eggnog and spiced biscuits)
Hoogkamerstraat 32-34, St.-Niklaas.
Tel. *03-7765949.*
www.denoudeadvokaat.be

OTHER

Tirlantijn
(original gifts)
Louis D'Haeseleerstraat 8/3, Aalst.
Tel. *053-777910.*
www.tirlantijn.be

Woeste Willem
(original book store)
Pontstraat 4, Aalst.
Tel. *053-703777.*
www.woestewillem.be

Cobana
(coffee, tea and trappings)
Markt 75, 9900 Eeklo.
Tel. *09-3785062.*
www.cobana.be

Galerij en kunstencentrum De Vuyst,
(auction house, gallery)
Kerkstraat 22-54, Lokeren.
Tel. *09-3485440.*
www.de-vuyst.com

Soie Belle
(accessories, beads, jewellery)
Koophandelstraat 36, Lokeren.
Tel. *09-3365361.*
www.soiebelle.be

't Soethuys
(everything for a christening)
Nederstraat 58, Oudenaarde.
Tel. *055-315322.*

Bourlez
(gifts, smokers' requisites and liqueurs)
Peperstraat 7, Ronse.
Tel. *055-213415.*

Pinehouse
(furniture, art deco, textiles)
Charles De Gaullestraat 7, Ronse.
Tel. *055-207784.*
www.pinehouse.be

CULTURE

Ghent is a vibrant cultural city. The historical buildings, the waterways, the shopping streets, Ghent's festivals and its many cultural events attract over one million visitors a year. NTGent, the Vlaamse Opera, the art centre Vooruit, the Ghent Festivals, the International Festival of Flanders Ghent, the Ghent Jazz Festival and many more cultural organizations and events put the city on the cultural map. The new STAM-Stadsmuseum Gent is the icon of Ghent as a city of culture. Music venues, theatres, museums and festivals provide a rich tapestry of performances and exhibitions. The cultural year begins in September every year with Odegand, the opening celebrations for the International Festival of Flanders Ghent, and the culture market on the Kouter.

THEATRE

The grand auditorium at the Flemish Opera

Ghent has many theatres and artistic companies that provide a truly rich cultural dish. **NTGent** is Ghent's municipal theatre and is the theatre company-in-residence at the **Koninklijke Nederlandse Schouwburg (Royal Dutch Theatre)**. Wim Opbrouck has been this internationally acclaimed company's artistic director since 2010. **Toneelgroep Ceremonia** is one of the major modern theatre companies in today's cultural landscape in Flanders. The theatre company **Cie Cecilia** was founded in 2006 by Marijke Pinoy, Arne Sierens and Johan Heldenbergh. The **Europees Figurentheater-centrum (EFTC)** is the focal point of puppet theatre with its puppets and collections. The **Vooruit Centre for Art** has a theatre and concert hall and concentrates on music, literature, media art and current events. **De Centrale** is a global culture house and a meeting place for intercultural exhibitions and workshops. The art centre **Campo** aims for diversity both in its own productions as well as in it (inter)national programmes. Campo has three stages. **De Kopergietery** appeals mostly to young people with its theatre, dance and music. The scheduling for the **Minardschouwburg** is organised by NTGent, Vooruit and Campo. In July and in December you can watch performances by the Gents Volkstheater in this beautifully restored theatre. **Teater Exces** is a street theatre company that performs mostly during the Ghent Festival. **Les Ballets C de la B** was set up in 1984 by Alain Platel. This dance- and theatre group has achieved world-wide renown with its mix of modern dance, cabaret and music.

NTGent is the company-in-residence at the Koninklijke Nederlandse Schouwburg.

MUSIC

The city of Ghent is just full of music from every genre: classical, jazz, pop and rock, performed by both amateur as well as professional musicians who can be found in the countless music venues in the city.

You can find the Lazy River Jazz Club in the cellar underneath the Novotel

The **Vlaamse Opera** doesn't just perform the great works from opera's past but also puts on new works in the Opera House on the Schouwburgstraat. LOD is an atelier for music theatre in Ghent. **Collegium Vocale Gent** is one of the best in the world. The **Bijloke Muziekcentrum Gent** is a modern concert hall fitting perfectly into its historic setting offering an international programme encompassing everything from Flemish to Oriental, along with modern to classical concerts, from world famous stars to up-and-coming talent. **Logos Tetrahedron** is a futuristic pentagonal concert hall where the combination of players, instruments and technology challenge and push forward the boundaries of music. The **Handelsbeurs Concertzaal** organises concerts for both young national bands as well as internationally known names in the genres of jazz, pop, rock, song, blues, flamenco, soul, global music and classical. **Capitole** is a modern theatre in a former cinema for musicals and large events.

MUSIC CAFÉS AND CLUBS

There are lots of clubs around the square Oude Beestenmarkt. **Democrazy** organises pop and rock concerts all around the city, in places like Kunstencentrum Vooruit, de Centrale, Charlatan and the Handelsbeurs. Famous DJs perform at **Decadance**, a well-known underground club where the music goes on into the wee small hours. **Charlatan** is the epicentre of Ghent's night life. It has three rooms, a huge sun terrace and a variety of shows, which make it one of the major entertainment venues in the city. **Kinky Star** puts a concert every Tuesday and there will be DJs on the other evenings. **Culture Club** is one of the trendiest discotheques in Europe setting trends in design as well as music. **The Lazy River Jazz Club**, in the Stadhuissteeg in Ghent, generally organises concerts from September to May and the season traditionally closes during the Pentecost weekend with the international Jazz meeting in Gentbrugge.

FILM

Kinepolis Gent (twelve auditoriums) does show commercial films, but is also the home base for the Ghent Film Festival. **Studio Skoop** (five auditoriums and a film cafe) is a monument in the Ghent cinema world, in its role as an art-house cinema role shows films from all over the world. The **Sphinx Cinema** is Ghent's cultural cinema and offers unusual programmes. The Flemish International Festival is one of the major events in European film. In October every year, they present about one hundred movies and five short films from all over the world. The Belgian police series Flikken, broadcast on Belgian TV from 1999 to 2009, used Ghent as its background.

KINEPOLIS

INFORMATION

The free magazine called **Zone 09** published by the city will give you ideas for an evening out and information about plays, performances and other events. The up-to-date timetables can be found on the website for **Uitbureau** Gent and **Uit in Gent**.

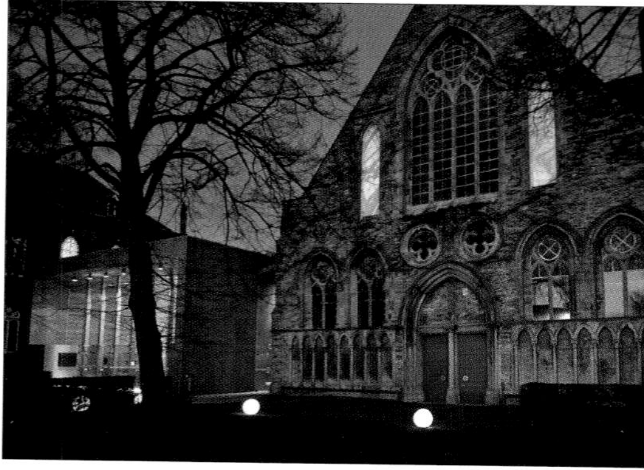

The De Bijloke Centre, combines both contemporary and historical architecture

LITERATURE

Ghent is a thriving liberal arts city with many activities centred around literature. The **Literair Gent** website shows information about literature in Ghent and Ghent in literature, from the Middle Ages to the present day. The website lists all of the authors who were born in Ghent or who have written about Ghent in their work, along with text excerpts. The website also displays five literary walks: Maurice Maeterlinck (winner of the Nobel prize for literature in 1911), Vlaamse Kai, de Karel van de Woestijne, the Poetry walk and Didactische Gevelliteratuur. During the Heritage Week, there is a huge book market in the square between S.M.A.K. and the Museum for Fine Art. Book dealers, antiquarians, museums, galleries and private sellers offer a huge selection of art books and magazines, covering architecture, literature, poetry, film and photography. Writer and poet Peter Verhelst has been the city's poet since 2009.

Young and established artists exhibit in the Tatjana Pieters Gallery

FESTIVALS

The Ghent Festivals (six international festivals: street theatre festival MiramirO, the Puppet Buskers Festival, the dance festival 10 Days Off, the Boomtown Festival, and the Youth Circus Festival), the International Flemish Festival Ghent, The International Film Festival (Flanders-Ghent) and I Love Techno are well-known annual festivals and events held in Ghent. For more information, see the Events calender (*pages 26-31*).

EXHIBITIONS AND GALLERIES

The Ghent museums – the Museum for Fine Arts, S.M.A.K., the Design Museum Ghent, MIAT, Huis van Alijn, Kunsthal St.-Pietersabdij, Provinciaal Cultuurcentrum Caermersklooster, the Dr. Guislan Museum and the Ghent STAM City Museum, all organise various annual, high-profile exhibitions. **Zebrastraat** is a unique complex where promising young artists, unusual themes and new art movements are all given their moment in the spotlight in the huge exhibition hall (750 m²). The **Tatjana Pieters Gallery** is a showcase for young and upcoming artists both local and from abroad. The **S&H De Buck Gallery** shows the works of artists from different disciplines. **Art Track**, found in the former chip shop Helga, shows the work of contemporary artists. The **Fortlaan 17** Gallery is a lively centre for modern art.

GAY GHENT

Ghent has a lively gay scene. **Casa Rosa** is a meeting place for gays in the city centre. You can find a *City Map for Gays* on their website with the addresses of cafes, eateries, and bars. **Hephaestion** is both a café and CD and book shop catering the gay community. **The Out** is a hip straight friendly gay eatery in the centre of Ghent.

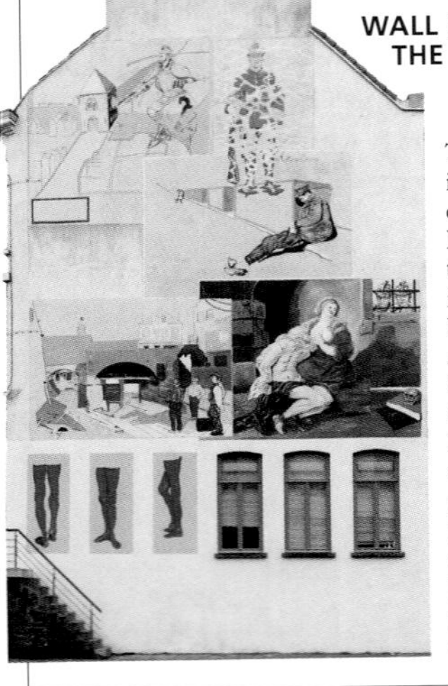

WALL PAINTINGS ON THE BRABANTDAM

The wooden deck with its benches at the top of the Brabantdam looks out over the estuary of the Ketelvaart in the Scheldt. The blank walls on the sides of the small park have been decorated by the artist Jan Van Imschoot, with images of the First World War; prostitution, child labour, Dame Fortune's cornucopia, and a homage to 'waterzooi' the famous Ghent fish or chicken stew.

ADDRESSES

GHENT THEATRES

NTGent Koninklijke Nederlandse Schouwburg
St.-Baafsplein 17.
Tel. *09-2250101.*
booking office: Tue-Fri 10am-8pm, Sat 2pm-6pm.
www.ntgent.be

The Central | Intercultural centre
Kraankindersstraat 2.
Tel. *09-2659828.*
www.decentrale.be

Kunstencentrum Vooruit
St.-Pietersnieuwstraat 23.
Tel. *09-2672820 / 2672828 (reservations).*
Tue-Fri 11am-6pm, Sat 3pm-6pm.
www.vooruit.be

CAMPO nieuwpoort
Nieuwpoort 31-35.
CAMPO boma
Bomastraat 35.
CAMPO Victoria
Fratersplein 7.
Tel. *09-2230000.*
www.campo.nu

Kopergietery
Blekerijstraat 50.
Tel. *09-2661144.*
www.dekopergietery.be

Minardschouwburg
Walpoortstraat 15.
Tel. *09-2658830.*
www.minard.be

Toneelgroep Ceremonia
www.toneelgroepceremonia.be

Cie Cecilia
www.compagnie-cecilia.be

Les Ballets C de la B
www.lesballetscdelab.be

Europees Figuren-theatercentrum EFTC
Trommelstraat 1.
Tel. *09-2231215.*
www.eftc.be

MUSIC

Capitole
Graaf van Vlaanderenplein 5.
Tel. *09-2332999.*
www.capitolegent.be

Logos Tetrahedron
Bomastraat 26.
Tel. *09-2238089.*
www.logosfoundation.org

Muziekcentrum Kinky Star
Vlasmarkt 9.
Tel. *09-2234845.*
www.kinkystar.com

Handelsbeurs Concertzaal
Kouter 29.
Tel. *09-2659165.*
www.handelsbeurs.be

Vlaamse Opera
Schouwburgstraat 9.
Tel. *09-2681011.*
www.vlaamseopera.be

De Bijloke Muziek-centrum Gent
Jozef Kluyskensstraat 2.
Tel. *09-2699292 (reservations).*
www.debijloke.be

LOD
www.lod.be

Collegium Vocale Gent
www.collegiumvocale.com

INFORMATION

Zone 09
www.zone09.be

Uit in Gent
www.uitingent.be

Uitbureau Gent
Kammerstraat 19.
Tel. *09-2337788.*
Mon-Sat 10am-1:30pm and 2:30pm-5:30pm (Sat and Sun until 4:30pm).
www.uitbureau.be

Gratis in Gent
www.gratisingent.be

HERITAGE

Erfgoeddag
www.erfgoeddag.be

Open Monumentendag
www.openmonumentendag.be

MUSIC CAFÉS AND CLUBS

Democrazy
www.democrazy.be

Decadance
Overpoortstraat 76.
www.decadance.be

Charlatan
Vlasmarkt 6.
www.charlatan.be

Kinky Star
Vlasmarkt 9 (club).
www.kinkystar.com

Culture Club
Afrikalaan 174.
www.cultureclub.be

Lazy River Jazz Club
Stadhuissteeg 5.
Tel. *09-2304139.*
www.lazyriverjazzclubgent.be

FILM

Kinepolis Gent
Ter Platen 12.
Tel. *09-2650600.*
www.kinepolis.com

Studio Skoop
Sint-Annaplein 63.
Tel. *09-2250845.*
www.studioskoop.be

Sphinx Cinema
St.-Michielshelling 3.
Tel. *09-2256086.*
www.sphinx-cinema.be

LITERATURE

Literair Gent
www.literair.gent.be

EXHIBITIONS AND GALLERIES

Zebrastraat
Zebrastraat 32.
Tel. *0474-693603.*
www.zebrastraat.be

Galerie Tatjana Pieters
Nieuwevaart 124.
Tel. *09-3244529.*
www.onetwenty.be
Wed-Sun 2pm-6pm.

Galerie S&H De Buck
Zuidstationstraat 25.
Tel. *09-2251081.*
www.siegfrieddebuck.be/galerie
Wed-Sat 3pm-6pm.

Art Track
Zuidstationstraat 8.
Tel. *09-2253949.*
www.arttrack.be
Wed-Sun 2pm-7pm.

Galerie Fortlaan 17
Fortlaan 17.
Tel. *09-2220033.*
www.fortlaan17.com
Wed-Fri 2pm-6pm, Sat 12 midday-6pm.

OUTSIDE GHENT

Belgica
Kerkstraat 24, Dendermonde.
Tel. *052-202626.*
www.ccbelgica.be

De Werf
Molenstraat 51, Aalst.
Tel. *053-732812 / 732849.*
www.ccdewerf.be

Stadsschouwburg
R. Van Britsomstraat 21, St.-Niklaas.
Tel. *03-7663939.*
www.ccsint-niklaas.be

De Woeker
Woeker 3, Oudenaarde.
Tel. *055-335135.*
www.oudenaarde.be

GAY GHENT

Casa Rosa
Kammerstraat 22.
Tel. 09-2692812.
www.casarosa.be

Hephaestion
Kammerstraat 29.
Tel. *09-3353461.*
www.hephaestion.be

The Out
Hoogpoort 53.
Tel. *09-3304590.*
www.the-out.com

OUTDOOR ACTIVITIES

The East-Flemish country side is simply perfect for taking a long or short cycle or walking tours. This doesn't just apply to the hills of the Flemish Ardennes in the south, but also the woods and the polders in the north of the province. Walking or cycling along the banks of the Leie, the Scheldt, the Dender and all the other waterways is just wonderful. Planning a route is simple thanks to the cycle and footpath network. You can cycle or walk from interchange to interchange, following the signposts along the way. The guides have a whole list of suggestions about routes to take along the way.

BICYCLE NETWORK

All over East Flanders you will see green signs, each with a number and an arrow. All the tourist regions, Ghent, Leiestreek, Meetjesland, Waasland, Scheldt Country (Scheldeland) and the Flemish Ardennes have their own cycling network. The networks are all connected and together form a giant provincial network. The interchange numbers are on the green-and-white signs at the relevant meeting points. At the top of the sign is the number and underneath you will see the numbers of the adjacent interchanges. Signposts point you in the direction of the next interchange. Altogether it forms a complete network of the various interchanges. Each section is signposted in both directions. The **Fietsrouteplanner Oost-Vlaanderen** (East Flanders Cycling Planner) is a vital aid when planning a route. Then you simply follow the signs from one interchange to the next which is usually a few kilometres further on. The junctions are also shown on the maps available at the Tourist Office's bookshop.

BICYCLE ROUTES

Each tourist region has a themed trip based on the cycle network. Each route has its own small brochure with both practical and background information. There are also other cycle routes, complied by the tourist services, nature- and other organisations. In East Flanders there are 45 fully signposted 'circuits'. They are all on

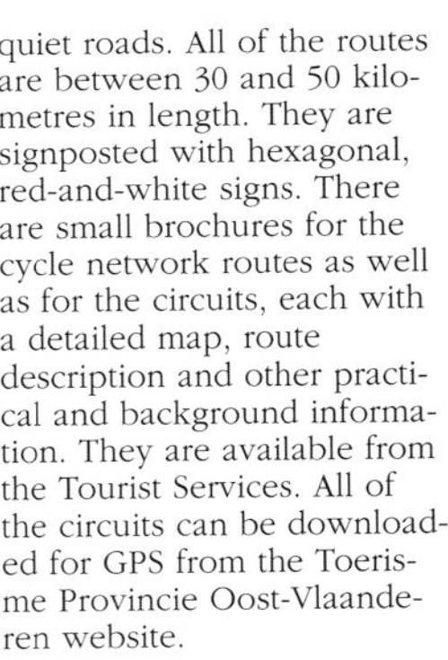

quiet roads. All of the routes are between 30 and 50 kilometres in length. They are signposted with hexagonal, red-and-white signs. There are small brochures for the cycle network routes as well as for the circuits, each with a detailed map, route description and other practical and background information. They are available from the Tourist Services. All of the circuits can be downloaded for GPS from the Toerisme Provincie Oost-Vlaanderen website.

Over the hills and far away in the Flemish Ardennes

CYCLING IN GHENT

Ghent wants to be a cycle-friendly city. There are cycle paths or lanes alongside the major roads. In the city centre, cycling is still allowed in some traffic-free streets. There are main cycle routes leading from the outer areas of the city to the centre. Smaller cycle routes connect with the main routes. All over the city you will find cycle shops, cycle hire, and handy bicycle racks.

There are four pleasant cycle routes: municipal legacy, green in the city, the creation of a water city and a green belt round the city, that take

A guided tour round the monuments of Ghent

the visitors to well-known and less well-known places in the city. The routes vary in length from 10 to 25 km and there are two in each of two brochures. You can buy them at Toerisme Gent or online via **www**.visitgent.be.

WALKING ROUTES

Walking is one of the most pleasant ways to explore the countryside. The footpath network Bulskampveld (near Aalter) the largest area of heathland in Flanders that dates from the Middle Ages, is the first footpath network in East Flanders. This network has more than 120 km of walking paths and 110 interchanges. The footpath network of Getuigenheuvels Vlaamse Ardennen has 300km of footpaths in the rectangle formed by Kluisbergen-Oudenaarde-Brakel-Ronse.A footpath network is being developed in the Krekengebied in Meetjesland. There are also over fifty delightful footpaths, indicated by hexagonal beige-and-green signs placed on wooden posts.

Flemish Ardennes guide book

CITY FOOTPATHS

You can get to know Ghent, Dendermonde, Aalst, Oudenaarde and other towns and villages by talking a walk round the area. Those who want to know more about the history of the area can take a guided tour. Details of the walks are available or can be booked at the Tourist Office in the relevant town. From the **Infokantoor Toerisme Gent** (Ghent Tourist Information Office), a guided walk through the historic centre leaves every day (in November and May, only on Saturday). **Vizit** offers more original ways of discovering Ghent with its many themed walks, culinary exploration tours and bike excursions. **Gandante** also organises city walks along with readings, lectures, bicycle tours and culinary programmes. The **Gidsenbond van Gent en Oost-Vlaanderen** (guides' guild of Ghent and East Flanders) has several classical and themed walks in the city of Ghent. **Ghent-Authentic** also organises city walks.

WALKING TRIPS TAKING SEVERAL DAYS

Those who are interested in taking a few days to explore can choose a fascinating, multi-day walking trip through the rolling hills of the Flemish Ardennes. The Streek-GR Vlaamse Ardennen goes in a circuit of 157km that takes about 7 days through the most beautiful scenery in Flanders. The walk starts in Oudenaarde and goes in a circuit round Kluisbergen, Ronse, Geraardsbergen and Brakel back to the start. The route is marked out with the familiar white-and-red and yellow-with-red stripes (some of the routes follow the 'normal' GR *(Grande Randonnée)* routes). There is a special Dutch guide book, *Topogids Vlaamse Ardennen*, for sale in the bookshops. There are also lots of GPS walking routes that you can download via the internet.

ADDRESSES

CYCLING AND WALKING

Toerisme Oost-Vlaanderen
www.tov.be

GR routes
www.groteroutepaden.be

Fietsrouteplanner Oost-Vlaanderen
www.tov.be/routeplanner.aspx

CITY WALKS

Vizit
www.vizit.be

Gandante
www.gandante.be

Gidsenbond van Gent en Oost-Vlaanderen Stadswandeling Gent
Ghent Tourist Information Office (starting point). *May-Oct. daily. 2pm; Nov-March Sat 2.30pm. Duration: 2hours.*
www.gidsenbond-gent.be

Ghent-Authentic
www.ghent-authentic.com

BOAT TRIPS

Taking a boat trip round the historic city centre is a must for visitors. (*pages 246-247*). You can take trips on the Scheldt, the Dender and the Leie, starting from scores of small towns and villages along the water. You can explore the heart of the Waasland in a round-trip boat in the summer months. There is a boat from Lokeren that sails over the **Durme** and the **Moervaart** to the Provincial Domain of Puyenbroeck.

Round trip by boat on the Leie at St.-Michielsbrug

CANOEING AND KAYAKING

The Moervaart and Zuidlede in Waasland form a 35km kayak circuit. In Mendonk, a village along the Ghent-Terneuzen canal just to the north of Ghent, where the Moervaart separates from the Zuidelede. Both waterways join again near Daknam (Lokeren). There are landing stages all along the water plus signposts and information panels. You can also buy a special map of this area. The section of the Leie between Deinze and Ghent is ideal for kayaking and canoeing.

PROVINCIAL DOMAINS

The province of East Flanders is one of the many provincial 'domains' (recreation parks) which are a happy mix of recreation, nature and education. The domains usually have bathing lakes, beaches, playing fields, foot paths and cycle paths, catering establishments, terraces and visitors' centres. Puyenbroeck is a large domain, offering recreation (canoeing, cycling and walking) nature and the MOLA, the province's windmill centre. De Boerekreek, (St.-Jan-in-Eremo) lies along the largest creek in Meetjesland and has a huge sports centre. The woods on Het Leen (Eeklo) are perfect for brisk walks and don't miss the arboretum. De Gavers (Geraardsbergen) in the Flemish Ardennes lies on the shores of a wide lake. Den Blakken (Wetteren) is the promotion centre for ornamental plant cultivation, rose growing and ornamental trees. Het Gentbos (Merelbeke) is a large wood to the south of Ghent – perfect for walks. In the De Roomakker Provincial Domain (Temse) there are three former clay pits where you will find unusual flora and fauna.

CAMPING

There are eleven camping sites in East Flanders. **Camping Blaarmeersen** is a large, five-star campsite with

Canoeing on the Moervaart near the Kalvebrug

GARDENS

East Flanders has a long tradition of plant cultivation. A thriving plant and flower cultivation industry developed during the 19th and 20th century round Lochristi and Wetteren. At the Gentse Floraliën, cultivators display their azaleas, begonias and other plants to the world. As well as historic gardens, landscaped parks and arboretums, there are also scores of private gardens open to the public on Open Garden Days.
The **B&B Meirlaenhof** garden in St.-Pauwels has a symmetrical layout and comprises a rose garden, a winter garden, terraces, cosy sitting areas, ponds, a garden house, a glasshouse, a vegetable garden and nursery, a field of broad-leafed trees and a an orchard of standard trees. The garden is open to visitors.
Jan and Mieke Bastiaens' garden in Rozebeke (Zwalm) has recently been refurbished and has borders, a sunken garden, ponds, as well as over 800 perennials. During the Garden Days in the spring and autumn at Beervelde (*page 27*), horticulturists from home and abroad display a selection of their loveliest plants and trees.

Somewhere along one of the many mountain bike routes

excellent facilities in a natural setting on the outskirts of Ghent.

You can get to the centre of Ghent easily by public transport. De Gavers in Geraardsbergen and Camping Puyenbroeck in Wachtebeke also have great facilities and are child-friendly.They are both in one of the Provincial Nature Domains.

TOURISM IN THE COUNTRYSIDE

The East-Flemish countryside is attracting an ever-increasing number of visitors. Cyclists and walkers have discovered the peace of the green landscape. More and more farms are selling their produce and offer both long- and short stays on the farm itself. Take a look at the **Plattelandstoerisme** website for a list of guest rooms and holiday homes.

Farm produce includes produce sold directly by the famer to the customer. It covers fresh produce (milk, eggs, vegetable, fruit and potatoes) as well as processed food such as yoghurt, cottage cheese, butter, cheese, fruit juice and jam. There are more than seventy recognised sales outlets for farm produce in the province.

GOLF

The province of East Flanders has seven golf courses. Most courses are rather exclusive, but in the Puyenbroeck Provincial Domain there is an 'open' golf complex with a covered driving range and a putting green, a practice bunker and a 9-hole course.

MOUNTAIN BIKING

All of the mountain bike routes are well signposted and consist of different circuits with varying degrees of difficulty. They attract both beginners and experienced mountain bikers. In some regions, the different routes crisscross each other, which has led the creation of a mountain bike network. You can download the routes from the East Flanders website.

ADDRESSES

BOAT TRIPS

Ghent
(Pages. 246-247).

Rondvaart Durme-Moervaart
Bookings via:
Infopunt Toerisme Lokeren
Markt 2, Lokeren.
Tel. *09-3409474.*

CANOE AND KAYAK HIRE

Kajakverhuur Guido Van Haver
Gaversesteenweg 188, Deinze.
Tel. *0478-971418.*
www.kajakguido.be

Kano- en Kajakcenter
Kalvebrug 1, Wachtebeke.
Tel. *09-3458876.*
www.kajakcenter.be

Kajak Company
Gasstraat zn, Lokeren.
Tel. *0475-454318.*
www.kajakcompany.be

CAMPING SITES

Camping Blaarmeersen
Zuiderlaan 12, Gent.
Tel. *09-2668160.*
◯ *Mar-Nov.*

Camping Provinciaal Domein Puyenbroeck
Puyenbrug 1A, Wachtebeke.
Tel. *09-3424231.*
◯ *Apr-Sept.*

Camping De Gavers
Onkerzelestraat 280, Geraardsbergen
Tel. *054-416324.*
www.degavers.be
◯ *Jan.-Dec.*

COUNTRYSIDE TOURISM

Plattelandstoerisme
www.plattelandstoerisme.be

Hoeveproducten
www.hoeveproducten.be

GOLF

Golf in België
www.golf.be

Golf Puyenbroeck-Open Golf
Craenendam 5, Wachtebeke.
Tel. *09-3424276.*
www.puyenbroeck.be

GARDENS

Mooie Tuinen
www.mooietuinen.be

Jan en Mieke Bastiaens
Kamperstraat 28, Rozebeke
Tel. *055-499387.*
◯ *end May-mid-July by appointment only.*

Meirlaenhof
Wijnstraat 26, St.-Pauwels (St.-Gillis-Waas).
Tel. *03-7769694/ 0474-985586.*
www.meirlaenhof.be

GHENT AND EAST FLANDERS FOR CHILDREN

Ghent is simply overflowing with child-friendy activities including music, theatre, museums, films, dance and fun. Many of these activities are great for the whole family, not just for the kids. Ghent actually has a special natural history museum with two whole sections just for children and young people: De wereld van Kina. A boat trip on the Leie and a visit to the medieval fortress of Gravensteen always go over well, or try a walk through one of the parks in the green belt that surrounds the city. When the weather is good, the kids can really let off steam in the De Blaarmeersen recreation park. During the Ghentse Feesten and other festivals there are special performances and activities for children. When it is raining, you can always find a mueum or indoor swimming pool nearby.

SEEING IS BELIEVING!

In the **Illuseum** *(page 118)*, a fabulous museum all about optical illusions, nothing is quite what it seems. Your eyes will deceive you. Sometimes you will see things that aren't there and sometimes you won't see things that are there. The whole point is that visitors will realise that appearances can be deceptive.

BIJLOKE JONG

In **De Bijloke Muziekcentrum Gent** (page 110) there are Kids Concerts every Sunday, preceded by workshops. Programmes that show the letters KT (Kinderen Toegelaten – children permitted), indicate that kids are especially welcome. There will be a special introduction geared specifically to children before the programme begins.

A voyage of discovery in the Design Museum in Ghent

Kids concerts on Sunday afternoons in the Bijloke Muzic centre in Ghent

BOAT TRIP

What could be nicer than going out on a boat on one of the four waterways – the Leie, the Lieve, the Scheldt and the Ketelvaart – so you can see the historical inner city of Ghent from a completely different perspective.

YOUR OWN DESIGN

Thanks to the Museumgame in the **Ghent Design museum** *(page 61)*, children can find out all about cupboards, chairs, vases and carpets from the 17th to the 20th century in a sort of game. Armed with binoculars, magic slate or map, they can set off, helped by various Playmobil figures. They also get the chance to decorate a giant's house.

PHILIP & MATHILDE

Go back in time, not with the Belgian Crown Prince and his wife but with Philip of Alsace and Mathilde of Portugal. Every stone can tell a story. The movie guide brings the history of the **Gravensteen** *(page 78-79)* to life.

ON THE ROAD WITH ALISON

Alison, a monk from the **St.-Pietersabdij** *(page 98)*, wanders through the centuries-old abbey buildings and takes the young visitors on a journey through time. He leads them along unexpected corridors and rooms and bit by bit, unravels the secrets of the abbey and its former inhabitants.

DE WERELD VAN KINA: HET HUIS EN DE TUIN

This is a unique natural history museum for children and young people in two locations. In the many rooms of **Kina: het huis** (*page 99*) children can find the answers to lots of questions, such as 'how can you eat without using your mouth? **Kina: de tuin** (*page 116-117*) answers natural history questions such as 'do nettles carry out chemical warfare?'

GET THE CREEPS WITH HENDRIK THE HOUSE GHOST

Hendrik the house ghost guides the children on their journey through the **Huis van Alijn** (*page 81*). In every room, there is a text geared towards children. Kids who love excitement can go on a hunt or have an adventure with a fantastic audio tour. In the Huis van Alijn there is a theatre, with performances by puppets. Every Saturday afternoon and during the school holidays there is a performance by Pierke the clown puppet in the theatre.

OORSMEER

This is an exciting music festival for children in the middle of November. The kids, their friends, parents and grandparents can get their fill of every kind of music genre, style and tradition.

SPLASHING ABOUT IN THE BLAARMEERSEN

With its paddling pool with toys, boats for hire, skatepark, minigolf and playground the **Blaarmeersen** (*page 118*) guarantees hours of fun. You can look at the park from the top of the lookout tower.

HIDDEN POETRY

Children get to know the city in a fun and interactive way using this book with ten poems.
Their journey will lead them to the surprisingly poetical corners of the city: Temmerman's sweet shop, the weeping willows on the Lieve quay and the Stropdrager (noose-wearer) statue on the Prinsenhof.

Children amuse themselves with a scavenger hunt at De wereld van Kina

EAST FLANDERS FOR CHILDREN

Many of the museums organise special activities for children in the form of special day and entertaining programmes. In **pam Ename** (*page 197*), parents and grandparents can join the kids for a treasure hunt through the museum. The treasure hunters wander through the woods with rucksacks complete with binoculars, a compass, pens and a plant- and animal guide. The **PAM Velzeke** (*page 203*), **Mola-Provinciaal Molencentrum** (Windmill Centre) (*page 167*), the St.-Niklaas Municipal Museum (*page 167*) and Ronse (*page 200-201*) all offer fabulous activities for children and their parents. The **Maldegen Steam Train Centre** (*page 159*) is a treat for kids and parents alike. **De Hoge Wal** in Evergem is a castle complete with a moat, a fortified edifice standing on a hill, dating from the 12th century. Children can thoroughly enjoy solving the 'Mystery of the Moat' on the archaeological site. In the **Centrum Ronde van Vlaanderen** (*page 194*) kids can really step into the shoes of their cycling heroes or brave the bumps on the cobbled roads. The recreational parks **De Gavers** (*page 191*), **Puyenbroeck** (*page 167*) and **Het Leen** (*page 157*) are the ideal places to go for a day out with the kids, varying from a play village to climbing frames and water playground.

Play village with exciting games in the Puyenbroeck recreational park

PRACTICAL INFORMATION

Softly rolling hills and vast polders. Winding rivers and straight-as-a-die canals. Bustling towns and peaceful countryside. Culture and nature. Historical buildings and modern architecture. That is East-Flanders in a nutshell. The province is divided into six tourist regions: Ghent, Leiestreek, Meetjesland, Waasland, Scheldt Country and the Flemish Ardennes. Each region has its own distinct character, monuments and nature. In East Flanders you never know what is around the next corner: a castle, a church, an area of natural beauty or a small café on the banks of the river.

TOURIST INFORMATION

The East Flanders Tourist Office has an information centre in Ghent where you can buy leaflets and cycle and walking maps of East Flanders. Each region has its own tourist organization and website. Many local authorities have an information bureau which can supply information about the municipality, the region, the province of East Flanders and other Flemish regions and provinces. The Tourist Information Offices ('Dienst voor Toerisme' or 'VVV') are easily recognised by their green signs with a white i and the text *Info Toerisme*. **Toerisme Gent (Ghent Tourist Office)** has an office in the Raadskelder (cellar) in the Belfort on the Botermarkt. In the spring of 2012, Toerisme Gent will be moving into its new office in the Oude Vismijn on the St.-Veerleplein. The office will supply you with everything you need to know about places of interest, exhibitions, events and cycle and footpaths in the city. This is also the place to book a guided tour here. **Use-it** offers tourist information for young people. You can download *The Map of Ghent for young travellers* free from the website, or pick one up at the Ghent Tourist Office.

Always busy at the Tourist Office information desk in Ghent

MEDIA IN GHENT

De Gentenaar is the oldest existing newspaper in Belgium (1879) and since 1959 it has been the Ghent edition of Het Nieuwsblad. **AVS Oost-Vlaamse Televisie** and **TVOost** are two local TV stations in East Flanders. They both broadcast local news, sports and background information for the western and eastern areas of the province. 'Ochtend'-,'Middag' and 'Avondpost' are morning, afternoon and evening regional news programmes on **Radio 2 Oost-Vlaanderen** (FM 89.8,90.7 and 98.6). **Zone 09**, the free city magazine, publishes information about culture, where to eat, drink and shop.

POLICE

The local police station for central Ghent, the **Buurtcommissariaat Gent Centrum**, is located in the Belfortstraat in the city centre. If this office is closed, contact the **Algemeen Politiecentrum** that is open 24 hours a day and 7 days a week.

PEDESTRIAN SIGNPOSTING

You will find highly visible pedestrian signposts at more than one hundred locations in Ghent. Ghent is divided into two districts and each district is divided into several areas (*wijken*). Every signpost shows the stations and the places where you can get on and off the tourists buses. Arrows in a variety of colours point the way from one area to another.

MEDICAL SERVICES

Chemists can be identified easily by the green cross sign and they are open from Monday to Friday from 8.30am-6.30pm. Outside these opening hours several pharmacies have a sign containing information about the nearest chemist on duty. GP surgeries also have an out-of-hours service. The Jan Palfijn General Hospital in Ghent has an **emergency department**.

TRAVEL DOCUMENTS

For British, U.S. and Canadian visitors, a passport is required for a go-day (max) stay. European nationals should be prepared to produce their identity card at any time. On arrival, all visitors should, if asked, be able to produce enough money, or acces to it, on arrival to pay for their entire stay as well as return ticket to their home country.

EXCLUSIEF: KOOKBOEK VAN SERGIO HERMAN
DE GENTENAAR
NOG NOOIT ZOVEEL KLACHTEN OVER NMBS
GEBREK AAN ZITPLAATSEN GROOTSTE BRON VAN ERGERNIS
De Prijsbarometer

Regional News in De Gentenaar

MONEY MATTERS

Most of the banks (ING, BNP Paribas Fortis, Dexia, KBC and Europabank) are open during the week from 9.00am-12 midday and 2pm-4:30pm. In Belgium, credit cards are normally accepted by most of the catering establishments, hotels, shops and petrol stations. Most places will accept a bank card. There are ATM machines at banks and other locations. The logos of the bank cards that are accepted are displayed on those machines.

TELEPHONE

To make a direct call from abroad, dial 00, then the country code (32), followed by the area code without the first zero and finally the number. If you use your mobile you will be connected via the networks Base, Proximus or Mobistar.

ACCESSIBILITY FOR THE DISABLED

The **Infopunt Toegankelijk Reizen** – a service provided by the Flanders Tourist Board – and they will be happy to answer any questions you might have about accessibility for the disabled to museums and other establishments.

ADDRESSES

Toerisme Oost-Vlaanderen (East Flanders Tourism)
Information Office,
St.-Niklaasstraat 2.
Tel. *09-2692600.*
Mon-Fri 9am-12pm and 1:15pm-4:45pm.
www.tov.be

Toerisme Gent (Ghent Tourist Board)
Belfort (Raadskelder)
Botermarkt 17A.
New address (from Spring 2012): Oude Vismijn, St.-Veerleplein 5.
Tel. *09-2665660.*
www.visitgent.be
mid March-mid Oct 9.30am-6.30pm; mid Oct-mid Mar 9.30am-4.30pm.

Use-it, www.use-it.be

REGIONAL INFORMATION CENTRES

Toerisme Leiestreek
www.toerisme-leiestreek.be

Toerisme Meetjesland
www.toerisme meetjesland.be

Toerisme Waasland
www.toerisme waasland.be

Toerisme Scheldeland
www.scheldeland.be

Toerisme Vlaamse Ardennen
www.toerisme vlaamseardennen.be

MEDIA

De Gentenaar
www.gentenaar.be

AVS Oost-Vlaamse Televisie
www.avs.be

TV Oost
www.tvoost.be

Radio 2 Oost-Vlaanderen
www.radio2.be

Zone 09
www.zone09.be

POLICE

Buurtcommissariaat Gent Centrum
Belfortstraat 4.
Tel. *09-2666130.*
daily. 8am-8pm.

Algemeen Politiecentrum
Antonius Triestlaan 12.
Tel. *09-2666111.*
7/7, 24/24.
www.politie.gent.be

MEDICAL SERVICES

Wachtdienst apothekers
Tel. *09-2365000.*
www.apotheek.be

Doctors on call in Ghent
Baudelokaai 7.
Fri 7pm-11pm, Sat-Sun 8am-11pm.
Martelaarslaan 305
Fri from 7pm to Mon 7am.
Tel. *09-2365000.*
Kliniekstraat 27
Fri 7pm-11pm, Sat-Sun 8am-11pm.

Hospital Emergency
AZ Jan Palfijn,
Henri Dunantlaan 5.
Tel. *09-2248967.*
www.janpalfijn.be

MISCELLANEOUS

British Consulate
c/o Meyvaert Glass Engineering NV
Dok Noord 3, Ghent
09-2357221/09-2255427

Bpost
Ghent Main Post Office,
Lange Kruisstraat 55.
www.bpost.be

Infopunt Toegankelijk Reizen (disabled) Flanders Tourist Board
Grasmarkt 61, Brussel.
Tel. *070-233050.*
Mon-Fri 10am-4pm.
www.toegankelijk reizen.be

TRAVEL INFORMATION

Ghent is very easy to get to by car or public transport. The city is a major junction for both train and bus service to various destionations in the province of East Flanders. The main R4 ringroad goes around Ghent, and the smaller ringroad, the R40, goes around the inner city. During the rush hour, traffic is heavy on the approach roads to and around Ghent. Main roads (N-roads) provide an efficient link between Ghent and the other large towns. Out in the East Flanders countryside, the roads are smaller and quieter and public transport is less frequent. In the large towns, there is paid parking or there are blue zones where you need to dispay a parking disc.

Gent-St.-Pieters transports 45,000 passengers every day

ARRIVAL BY CAR

Ghent lies at the junction of two major motorways: the E17 (A14) Antwerp-Kortrijk and the E40 (A10) Brussels-Ostend. From the E40 at the Zwijnaarde junction, follow the signs to Antwerp (E17), then take the exit 'Gent Centrum' to reach the city centre.

PARKING

The centre of Ghent is traffic-free. The Parking Route (P-route) gives directions to free parking in the various parking garages. In the centre there are ten parking garages with nearly 5,000 parking spaces. Ghent is divided into three parking zones. In the centre zone (red) there is paid parking with a maximum of three hours (9am-7pm) or five hours (7pm to midnight), in the non-centre zone (blue) There is short-stay parking (maximum 3 hours) or long-stay parking (9am-7pm). In the non-centre zone with evening parking (green), the same rules apply as in the non-centre zone, but between the hours of 7pm to midnight, it is paid parking. You will find parking garages or parking lots in the other East Flanders cities.

Tram in Gent

ARRIVAL BY TRAIN

Ghent is easy to reach by train from Belgium and the Netherlands. InterCity and Inter-Region trains connect Antwerp, Brussels, and Bruges with the stations of Gent-Dampoort and/or Gent-St.-Pieters. There are frequent connections from Amsterdam to Ghent with one change in Antwerp Central (Thalys and the Brussels InterCity). Travel time is about 3 hours. Tram No.1 connects the Gent-St.-Pieters station and the No. 3 bus the Gent-Dampoort station with the city centre.

BUS AND TRAM IN GHENT

Ghent has the largest trafffic-free city centre in Belgium, making it easy to explore without a car. De Lijn provides a comprehensive tram- and bus network, connecting the centre to the two train stations and the suburbs. You can obtain the 'lijnplan' timetable at the Lijn shops at the Gent-St.-Pieters station, at the Korenmarkt (Cataloniëstraat), in Gent-Zuid and at the information desk in the Tourist Office. You can buy prepaid bus and tram tickets from newsagents, supermarkets, the Lijn shops or from the machines that you will find at most stops. On the bus or tram you would pay up to fifty percent more for a ticket. Free night buses run from Gent-Zuid on Friday and Saturday nights.

SIGHTSEEING IN GHENT BOAT TRIPS

There are boat trips around the city's historical centre from May to October. **De bootjes van Gent** (Rederij Dewaele), **Rederij Gent-Watertoerist** and **Boat in**

Gent all offer a forty-minute guided round-trip tour by boat over the Leie and the Lieve though medieval Ghent. The Bootjes van Gent depart from the Korenlei, the Rederij Gent-Watertoerist boats leave from the Graslei and the Boat in Gent from the Kraanlei. If you take the 'Complete Ghent' round-trip tour (May-Aug, Sat-Sun 2pm) you will enjoy a ninety minute sail over the Leie, the Lieve, the Ketelvaart and the Scheldt. **Rederij De Gentenaer** also does a fifty-minute guided round-trip tour through the centre of Ghent. The boats leave from the Groentenmarkt (near Vleeshuisbrug). **Viadagio** does round trips on the Ghent waterways in authentic wooden boats, pushed along by manpower. They leave from the Zuivelbrug. During the summer, **Benelux Rederij** sails over the Leie to St.-Martens-Latem. The boat sails in the afternoon and returns in the evening, giving you plenty of time to explore the village on foot.

HORSE-DRAWN CARRIAGE

A **horse-drawn carriage** leaves the St.-Baafsplein for a half-hour tour through the historical city centre.

Taking a tour by horse drawn carriage

Self-service ferry Bathio (Bachte) on the Oude Leie

TRAVELLING AROUND EAST FLANDERS

The towns and villages in East Flanders are easily accsessible by train and bus. Ther are regular Inter-City, Inter-Regio or local trains (L-trains) from Gent-St.-Pieters to Eeklo, Bruges-Ostend, Deinze-De Panne, Kortrijk, Ronse, Geraardsbergen, Lokeren-St.-Niklaas-Antwerp Central, Mechelen, Brussels-South and Brussels-North. Ghent, St.-Niklaas, Dendermonde, Aalst and Oudenaarde are the main interchanges for buses.

FERRY BOATS

For the convenience of locals and tourists alike there are ferries over the Scheldt, the Leie and the Dender, forming a vital link in the daily comings and goings across the water and in the cycling and walking networks. Many of the ferries operate all year round on a fixed timetable (Mar-Sept daily from 7am-9pm, Oct-March daily from 7am-6pm, switching over on the hour and the half hour); the other ferries follow a varying timetable. You can find more information, like navigation regulations, on the website of the Belgian Waterways and Maritime Canal. (www.wenz.be).

ADDRESSES

PUBLIC TRANSPORT

De Lijn
www.delijn.be

NMBS
www.b-rail.be

BOAT TRIPS

De bootjes van Gent
Korenlei 4A (small green boathouse).
Tel. *09-2291716/2238853.*
Mar to mid-Nov daily 10am-6pm.
www.debootjesvangent.be

Rederij Gent-Watertoerist
Graslei.
Tel. *09-2690869.*
Mar-Oct daily. 10am-6pm; Nov.-Feb. Sat and Sun 11am-4pm.
www.gent-watertoerist.be

Boat in Gent
Kraanlei near Gravensteen.
Tel. *0478-633630.*
April-early Oct daily 10am-6pm.
www.boatingent.be

Rederij De Gentenaer
Groentenmarkt (Vleeshuisbrug)
Tel. *0473-481036.*
Apr to mid-Oct. Daily 10am-17pm; mid-Oct to Mar. Sat-Sun 10am-4pm.
www.rederijdegentenaer.be

Benelux Rederij
Recollettenlei 32. ***Tel.*** *09-2251505.*
May-Sept. Tue-Sat; June. Tue, Thu and Sat; Jul-Aug. Tue, Sat and Sun, departs 1pm returns to Ghent 5:30pm.
www.benelux-rederij.com

Viadagio vzw
Oudburg 38.
Tel. *09-2250786.*
www.viadagio.be/

CARRIAGES

St.-Baafsplein.
Tel. *0475-821620.*
Sat-Sun 10am-6pm (daily during school holidays).
www.koetsenvangent.be

Index

H

I

J

K

L

N

O

P

R

S

Acknowledgements

The publisher would like to thank the following persons and institutes for their help in compiling this book.

AUTHOR
Bartho Hendriksen

PUBLISHER
Vera Wolf

EDITORIAL STAFF
Marjolijn Braamburg

SPECIAL ASSISTANCE
Mary Kuiper, Culemborg

WITH SPECIAL THANKS TO the employees of the city of Ghent – Tourism Service and Tourism East Flanders and the province of East Flanders

DESIGN AND TECHNIQUE
Teo van Gerwen-Design, Waalre

COVER DESIGN
Teo van Gerwen-Design, Waalre

ILLUSTRATIONS
Jan Egas: 5, 56-57, 78-79, 108-109, 148-149, 198-199, back cover
Gieb van Enckevort: 22-23, 52-53, 74-75, 96-97, 110, 178-179, 192-193, front cover, back cover

CARTOGRAPHY
EMK, Deventer

PHOTOGRAPHIC CREDITS
t = top; tl = top left; tlc = top left centre; tc = top centre; tr = top right; trc = top right centre; c = centre; cl = centre left; clt = centre left top; clb = centre left bottom; ct = centre top; cr = centre right; crt = centre right top; crb = centre right bottom; bc = bottom centre; b = bottom; bl = bottom left; br = bottom right.

Every effort has been made to trace the copyright holder(s). Anyone wishing to claim additional rights can contact the publisher.
The publishers are grateful to the following companies, museums, photographers for their permission to reproduce their images.

All photographs courtesy of Rien van der Helm with the exception of:

Accipio: 206b
Archief CRVV: 25tr, 25br
Archief Provincialaat Broeders van Liefde Gent: 111b
Beeldbank Aalst: 42cl, 43bl
Centrum Ronde van Vlaanderen, CRVV: 24b, 192c
Cleythill: 207b
De Bijloke Muziekcentrum Gent: 110b, 242c
De Wereld van Kina: 243t
Design museum Gent: 242b
Feichtinger Architect: 46-47c
Flanders Classics 2011: 24tl, 24-25c
Foto Goossenaerts: 148tr, 149bl
Foto Mahy: 47tr
Foto's Stad Gent – Dienst Toerisme: 13tr, 30b, 31b, 74b, 97bl, 127tl, 214c, 214b, 222c, 223br, 238r, 244b
Fototheek Toerisme Scheldeland: 29t, 29b, 175cr
Galerie Tatjana Pieters: 236t
Gent Dienst Stadsontwikkeling: 46t, 46b, 47tl, 47cr
Gent Dienst Stadspromotie: 70tl, 70tr, 70cl, 71tl, 71cr, 71bl
Gidsenbond van Gent & Oost-Vlaanderen: 45tl
Havenbedrijf Gent, foto Tom D'Haenens: 44tl
(copyright) Henderyckx: 14b, 15tr, 15b
Bartho Hendriksen: 119tr, 156c
Henry Krul: 28t
Het Godshuis: 207t
Hoeveproducten: 241c
Huis van Alijn: 243c
Daniël de Kievith: 28b
Lazy River Jazz Club: 235t
Liberaal Archief: 43tr
Eric De Mildt: 235b
Museum van Deinze en de Leiestreek (copyright) Lukas –
Art in Flanders non-profit organisation: 146b, 151tr, 151cl, 151cr, 151b
Museum voor Schone Kunsten Gent: 39tr, 104-105
Museum voor Schone Kunsten Gent, photograph Michel Burez: 39c
Museum voor Schone Kunsten Gent (copyright) Lukas – Art in Flanders non-profit organisation: 104tr, 104c, 104b, 105tl, 105tr, 105cr, 105b
Christian Overdeput: 21tl, 21tr, 70b
pam Ename, illustration D. Pietinckx: 37bl
pam Velzeke: 35mr, 35bl
Province of East-Flanders: 33t
(copyright) Wouter Rawoens: 70-71c
H. Roth/CRVV: 24c, 25tl
SABAM: 102br
Sanderus Antiquariaat, Ghent: various images
Sint-Baafskathedraal (copyright) Lukas – Art in Flanders non-profit organisation: 18-19, 18tr, 18cl, 19tl, 19cr, 19bl, 53bl, 56tr, 56cl,
56br, 57t, 57cr, 57br, 57bl
Stad Gent – Gentse Feesten: 20-21, 20tr, 20cl, 20bl, 21cr
Stad Gent, Dienst Monumentenzorg en Architectuur: 45bl
Stad Gent, Dienst Stadsarcheologie: 34t
Stad Gent, Onderwijs, De school van toen – Onderwijs: 37tr
Stad Gent, STAM: 41cr, 109cr
Stad Gent, STAM (copyright) Carl De Keyzer: 109tr
Stad Gent, STAM, photograph Olivier Bekaert: 109b
Stad Gent, STAM, photograph Michel Burez: 35tr, 36c
Stad Gent, STAM, photograph Phile Deprez: 11b, 44-45, 108tr,
108c, 108b, 109tl,
Stadsarchief Gent De Zwarte Doos, photography Storm Calle,
image editing Andre Capiteyn: 33b, 34c, 36b, 37tl, 37cr, 38t, 38c, 38b, 39tl, 39bl, 39bc, 40tl, 40cl, 40bl, 40br, 41tl, 41b, 42-43, 42tl, 42b, 43tl, 43c, 43br, 44br, 45tr, 45br, 52tr, 85br, 87tr, 90tr, 91tl, 91br, 111c, 128c
Stadsarchief Gent De Zwarte Doos, photography Jacobs: 107t
Stadsarchief Gent De Zwarte Doos, photography Edmond
Sacré: 79tr, 112tl
Stefaan Van Hul: 30t
't Gasthuys – Stedelijk Museum Aalst: 177b
(copyright) The British Library Board. All Rights Reserved
061613/2011: 38-39c
Toerisme Geraardsbergen: 26bl
Toerisme Oost-Vlaanderen: 26cr, 27bl, 31t, 146tc, 156b, 156t, 158br, 164t, 164bl, 175tr, 175b, 182t, 182c, 187bl, 187tl, 189b, 197c, 198bl, 201b, 202t, 202b, 223t, 239bl, 241t, 243b
TV Robbrecht-Daem Architecten, Marie-Jose Van Hee, Wirtz International, BAS-Dirk Jaspaert, Dirk Bodens, Marianne France and the Technum nv design studio: 44cl,
46c
Ugent, Archaeology Department: 34bl, 34br, 35tl
Ugent, Archaeology Department, photograph Michel Burez: 34-35
UiTmetVlieg: 26t
Universiteitsbibliotheek Gent: 40-41
Vildaphoto, Ludo Goossens: 16b, 17c

Interesting websites about Ghent and East-Flanders

Tourism
Ghent tourism, **www**.visitgent.be
East Flanders tourism, **www**.tov.be
Leie region tourism, **www**.toerisme-leiestreek.be
Meetjesland tourism, **www**.toerismemeetjesland.be
Waasland tourism, **www**.toerismewaasland.be
Scheldt country tourism, **www**.scheldeland.be
Flemish Ardennes tourism, **www**.toerismevlaamseardennen.be

MOST SIGNIFICANT ATTRACTIONS AND MUSEUMS

General
MovE Musea Oost-Vlaanderen in Evolutie, **www**.museuminzicht.be

Ghent
Design museum Gent, **www**.designmuseumgent.be
Gravensteen – Wapenmuseum, **www**.gent.be/gravensteen
STAM Stadsmuseum Ghent, **www**.stamgent.be
S.M.A.K. Gent, **www**.smak.be
Museum voor Schone Kunsten Ghent, **www**.mskgent.be
MIAT, **www**.miat.gent.be
Het Huis van Alijn, **www**.huisvanalijn.be
Provinciaal Cultuurcentrum Caermersklooster, **www**.caermersklooster.be
St.-Pietersabdij art market, **www**.gent.be

East Flanders
Centrum Ronde van Vlaanderen, Oudenaarde, **www**.crvv.org
Museum van Deinze en de Leiestreek, Deinze, **www**.museumdeinze.be
MDD – Museum Dhondt-Dhaenens, Deurle, **www**.museumdd.be
Provinciaal Archeologisch Museum (pam) Ename, Ename (Oudenaarde), **www**.ename974.org
Mola – Provinciaal Molencentrum, Wachtebeke, **www**.oost-vlaanderen.be
Roger Raveelmuseum, Machelen-aan-de-Leie, **www**.rogerraveelmuseum.be
Bezoekerscentrum Boekhoute, **www**.assenede.be
STeM, Stedelijk Museum Sint-Niklaas, **www**.sint-niklaas.be
Provinciaal Archeologisch Museum, Velzeke, **www**.pam-velzeke.be
't Gasthuys – Stedelijk Museum Aalst, **www**.aalst.be

Heritage and architecture
St.-Baafskathedraal, **www**.sintbaafskathedraal-gent.be
Staats-Spaanse Linies, **www**.staatsspaanselinies.be
Stadsarchief Gent De Zwarte Doos, **www**.gent.be
Beeldbank Gent, **www**.beeldbankgent.be
Kasteel Ooidonk, **www**.ooidonk.be
Kasteel van Poeke, **www**.poeke.net
Groot Begijnhof St.-Elisabeth, Gent, **www**.elisabethbegijnhof.be

Media
De Gentenaar, **www**.gentenaar.be
AVS Oost-Vlaamse Televisie, **www**.avs.be
TV Oost, **www**.tvoost.be

Out and about
Out and about in Ghent, **www**.uitingent.be
Out and about in Flanders, **www**.uitinvlaanderen.be
UiTmetVlieg, **www**.uitmetvlieg.be
Zone 09, **www**.zone09.be
Meetjesland, **www**.uitinhetmeetjesland.be

Province
Province of East Flanders, **www**.oost-vlaanderen.be

Nature
Flemish Ardennes nature reserve, **www**.rlva.be
Meetjesland nature reserve, **www**.rlm.be
Schelde Durme nature reserve, **www**.rlsd.be
Natuurpunt, **www**.natuurpunt.be
Agentschap voor Natuur en Bos, **www**.natuurenbos.be

Walking and cycling routes
East Flanders on foot and by bicycle, **www**.tov.be
Grote Routepaden (Long-distance routes), **www**.groteroutepaden.be
East-Flanders route planner, **www**.tov.be/routeplanner.aspx
Vizit, **www**.vizit.be
Gandante, **www**.gandante.be
Ghent and East-Flanders association of guides, **www**.gidsenbond-gent.be
Ghent-Authentic, **www**.ghent-authentic.com

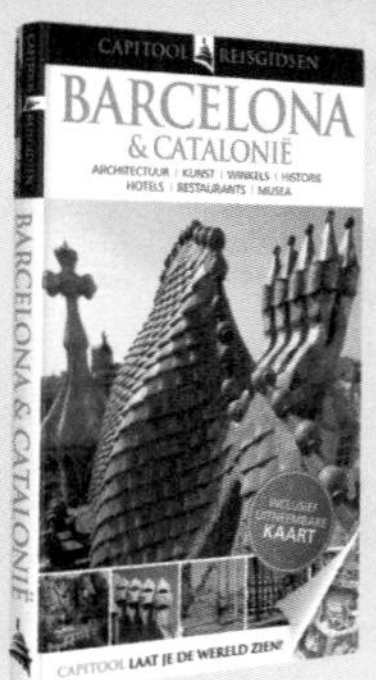

CAPITOOL REISGIDSEN

De Capitool Reisgids is de 3-in-1 reisgids: kleurrijke smaakmaker vóór de reis, gedegen vraagbaak tijdens uw bezoek en fraai naslagwerk bij het ophalen van vakantieherinneringen! Capitool is ongeëvenaard in gebruiksgemak en visuele presentatie.

CAPITOOL NATUURGIDSEN

Alle in Nederland en Europa gangbare bomen, insecten en spinnen, paddestoelen, sterren, vlinders, vogels en wilde bloemen besproken met schitterende foto's en compacte beschrijvingen. Meer dan 400 soorten in elke titel komen tot leven met gedetailleerde close-up foto's.

CAPITOOL COMPACT

Dé gids die zich durft te beperken tot de absolute hoogtepunten van uw bestemming en zo de reiziger helpt om alles uit zijn kostbare vakantietijd te halen. Zelfs het kortste bezoek wordt een complete ervaring.

CAPITOOL AUTOROUTES

Een serie reisgidsen voor autovakanties. Elke gids bevat 24 of 25 toeristische routes door aantrekkelijke gebieden. Iedere autorit is compleet uitgewerkt en bevat een kaart met route, algemene beschrijving van het gebied en nuttige informatie. Inclusief uitneembare kaart.

CAPITOOL MINI

Mini Capitool is weliswaar een kleine en handzame stedengids (past zelfs in je broekzak!), maar ook een reisgids die je de bestemming laat zien zoals alleen Capitool dat kan. Verrassend royaal en extreem duidelijk is ook de uitvouwkaart achterin.

NEDERLANDSE BESTEMMINGEN

Bondige overzichten van geschiedenis, cultuur en bezienswaardigheden zorgen voor de plezierigste kennismaking met Nederland. Honderden foto's, plattegronden en opengewerkte tekeningen brengen Nederland tot leven.

CAPITOOL COMPACT VOOR iPHONE

Van tien populaire bestemmingen zijn er applicaties beschikbaar voor iPhone onder de naam *Het beste van.* Verkrijgbaar in de App Store.

Features:

- Naar eigen voorkeur bladwijzers toevoegen, indelen of verwijderen
- Meer informatie via relevante links
- Praktische informatie, overzichtelijke kaarten en prachtige foto's
- Telefoonnummers ingesteld zodat er vanuit elk land gebeld kan worden
- Eenvoudige navigatie

CAPITOOL OVERIG

Onverwachte ontdekkingen
De 1000 fascinerendste en opwindendste bestemmingen ter wereld

De mooiste vaarroutes in Nederland
Vaarroutes door de prachtigste natuurgebieden en pleisterplaatsen

Capitool Reiskalender
Voor elke dag een reistip van Capitool

Capitool Reisdagboek
Het boek waarin alleen u mag schrijven

Capitool Taalgidsen
Spreken, verstaan, begrijpen

VOOR EEN COMPLEET OVERZICHT ZIE WWW.CAPITOOL.NL

CAPITOOL LAAT JE DE WERELD ZIEN!

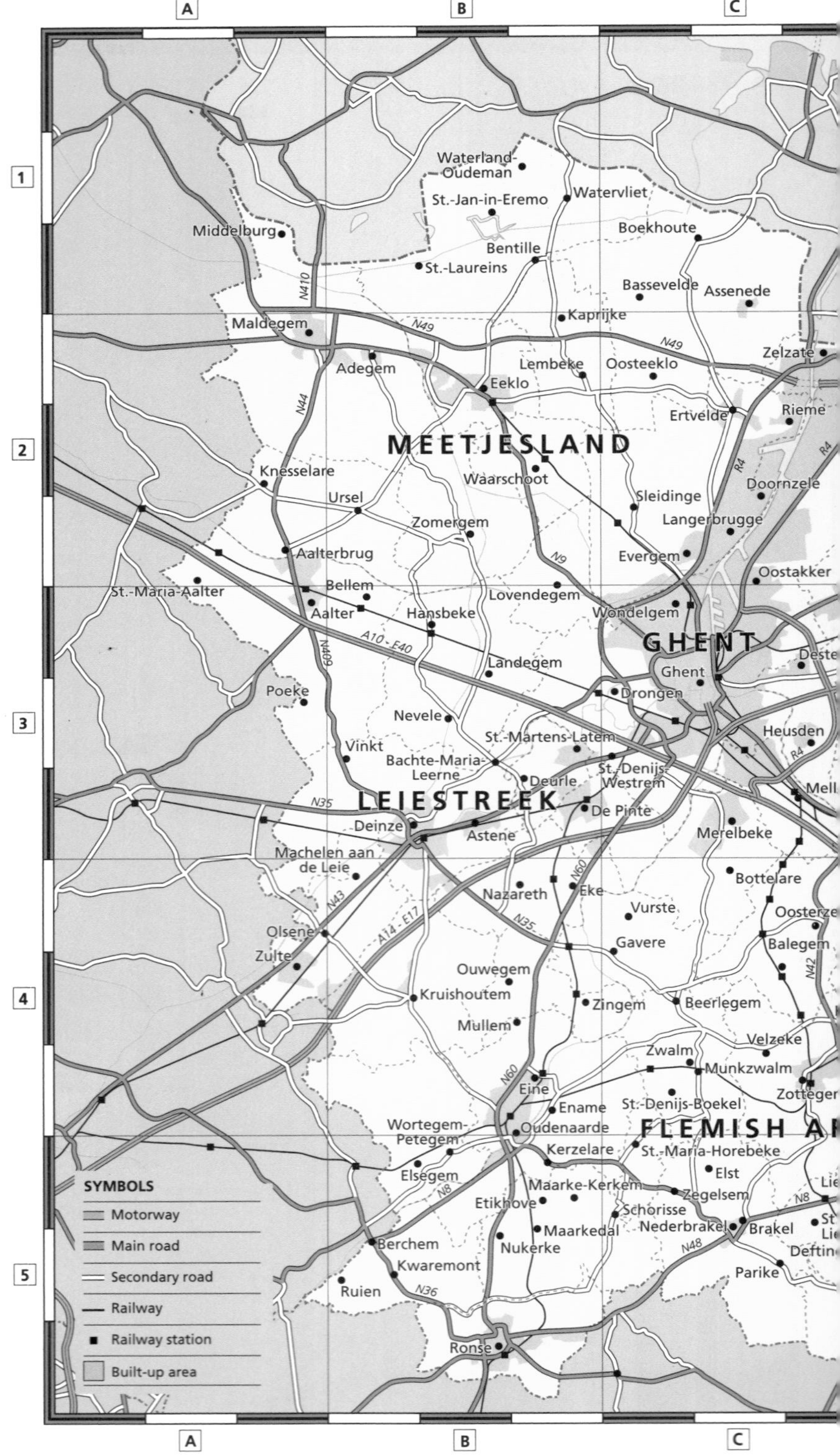
A
B
C
1
2
3
4
5
Waterland-
Oudeman
St.-Jan-in-Eremo
Watervliet
Boekhoute
Middelburg
Bentille
St.-Laureins
Bassevelde
Assenede
N410
Kaprijke
Maldegem
N49
N49
Zelzate
Adegem
Lembeke
Oosteeklo
Eeklo
N44
Ertvelde
Rieme
MEETJESLAND
R4
R4
Knesselare
Waarschoot
Doornzele
Ursel
Sleidinge
Zomergem
Langerbrugge
Aalterbrug
N9
Evergem
Oostakker
St.-Maria-Aalter
Bellem
Aalter
Lovendegem
Hansbeke
Wondelgem
GHENT
A10 - E40
N409
Landegem
Ghent
Poeke
Drongen
Nevele
Heusden
St.-Martens-Latem
Vinkt
Bachte-Maria-
Leerne
St.-Denijs-
Westrem
R4
Deurle
N35
LEIESTREEK
De Pinte
Deinze
Astene
Merelbeke
Machelen aan
de Leie
N60
Bottelare
Nazareth
Eke
N43
Vurste
N35
A14 - E17
Olsene
Gavere
Balegem
Zulte
Ouwegem
N42
Kruishoutem
Zingem
Beerlegem
Mullem
Velzeke
Zwalm
Munkzwalm
N60
Eine
Ename
St.-Denijs-Boekel
Wortegem-
Petegem
Oudenaarde
FLEMISH A
Kerzelare
St.-Maria-Horebeke
Elsegem
Elst
N8
Maarke-Kerkem
Zegelsem
N8
Etikhove
Schorisse
Maarkedal
Nederbrakel
Brakel
Berchem
Nukerke
N48
Kwaremont
Parike
Ruien
N36
Ronse
SYMBOLS
Motorway
Main road
Secondary road
Railway
Railway station
Built-up area